CULTURAL PROCESSES

With the rapid growth of knowledge in the last two decades concerning ethnic and national group differences in human behaviors, researchers are increasingly curious as to why, how, and when such differences surface. The field is ready to leapfrog from the descriptive science of group differences to the science of cultural processes. The goal of this book is to lay down the theoretical foundation for this exciting development by proposing an original process model of culture. This new perspective discusses and extends contemporary social psychological theories of social cognition and social motivation to explain why culture matters in human psychology. We view culture as a loose network of imperfectly shared knowledge representations for coordinating social transactions. As such, culture serves different adaptive functions important for individuals' goal pursuits. Furthermore, with the increasingly globalized and hyperconnected multicultural world, much can be revealed about how different cultural traditions come into contact. The authors discuss the psychological ramifications of these cultural interactions to illuminate the social and practical relevance of the proposed process model of culture.

Angela K.-y. Leung is Assistant Professor of Psychology in the School of Social Sciences at the Singapore Management University (SMU). Her research seeks to understand how people participate actively in dynamic cultural processes in both intra- and intercultural contexts, as well as the psychological implications for multicultural competence (e.g., creativity and intercultural communication). She is also interested in the role of embodiment in the acquisition and endorsement of cultural values. Dr. Leung has won several research awards, including the first honorable mention for the Otto Klineberg Intercultural and International Relations Award from the Society for the Psychological Study of Social Issues (SPSSI) in 2009, the Lee Foundation Research Excellence Award, and the School of Social Sciences Research Excellence Award conferred by SMU.

Chi-yue Chiu is Professor of Management and Marketing at Nanyang Technological University, Singapore. His current research focuses on the social, cognitive, and motivational processes that mediate the construction and evolution of social consensus and on the dynamic interactions of cultural identification and cultural knowledge traditions. Dr. Chiu received the Misumi Award from the Japanese Group Dynamics Association and Asian Association for Social Psychology in 2007, the Best Paper Award in Conflict Resolution from the Academy of Management in 2002, and the Otto Klineberg Intercultural and International Relations Award from the SPSSI in 2001.

Ying-yi Hong is currently Professor at the Business School of Nanyang Technological University, Singapore. Her main research interests include culture and cognition, self, identity, and intergroup relations. She is particularly known for proposing the Dynamic Constructivist Theory to understand how individuals form mental models of multiple cultural knowledge systems and how they switch between cultural frames. Dr. Hong received the Otto Klineberg Intercultural and International Relations Award from the SPSSI in 2001 and the Young Investigator Award (conferred by the International Society of Self and Identity) in 2004 and was elected Fellow of the Association for Psychological Science and Associate of the Center for Advanced Study, University of Illinois, Urbana-Champaign.

CULTURE AND PSYCHOLOGY

Series Editor

David Matsumoto, *San Francisco State University*

As an increasing number of social scientists come to recognize the pervasive influence of culture on individual human behavior, it has become imperative for culture to be included as an important variable in all aspects of psychological research, theory, and practice. Culture and Psychology is an evolving series of works that brings the study of culture and psychology into a single, unified concept.

Ute Schönpflug, *Cultural Transmission: Psychological, Developmental, Social, and Methodological Aspects*

Evert van de Vliert, *Climate, Affluence, and Culture*

David Matsumoto and Fons van de Vijver, *Cross-Cultural Research Methods in Psychology*

Cultural Processes

A SOCIAL PSYCHOLOGICAL PERSPECTIVE

Edited by

Angela K.-y. Leung
Singapore Management University

Chi-yue Chiu
Nanyang Technological University, Singapore

Ying-yi Hong
Nanyang Technological University, Singapore

CAMBRIDGE
UNIVERSITY PRESS

CAMBRIDGE UNIVERSITY PRESS
Cambridge, New York, Melbourne, Madrid, Cape Town, Singapore,
São Paulo, Delhi, Dubai, Tokyo, Mexico City

Cambridge University Press
32 Avenue of the Americas, New York, NY 10013-2473, USA

www.cambridge.org
Information on this title: www.cambridge.org/9780521758413

First published 2011

Printed in the United States of America

A catalog record for this publication is available from the British Library.

Library of Congress Cataloging in Publication data

Cultural processes : a social psychological perspective / edited by Angela K.-y. Leung, Chi-yue
Chiu, Ying-yi Hong.
    p.   cm. – (Culture and psychology)
Includes bibliographical references and index.
ISBN 978-0-521-76523-7 (hbk.) – ISBN 978-0-521-75841-3 (pbk.)
1. Culture – Psychological aspects.   2. Culture – Study and teaching.   I. Leung, Angela K.-y.,
1979–   II. Chiu, Chi-yue, 1963–   III. Hong, Ying-yi, 1964–   IV. Title.   V. Series.
HM621.C853446   2011
306.01–dc22   2010024843

ISBN 978-0-521-76523-7 Hardback
ISBN 978-0-521-75841-3 Paperback

CONTENTS

FIGURES AND TABLES

FIGURES

TABLES

CONTRIBUTORS

EVELYN W. M. AU *Singapore Management University*

MELODY MANCHI CHAO *Hong Kong University of Science and Technology*

JING CHEN *Gettysburg College*

CHI-YUE CHIU *Nanyang Technological University*

KARL DACH-GRUSCHOW *University of Illinois at Urbana-Champaign*

JIAN HAN *China Europe International Business School*

YING-YI HONG *Nanyang Technological University*

PELIN KESEBIR *University of Colorado at Colorado Springs*

YOUNG-HOON KIM *University of Pennsylvania*

ANGELA K.-Y. LEUNG *Singapore Management University*

HSIN-YA LIAO *San Francisco State University*

LEIGH ANNE LIU *Georgia State University*

SUN NO *Macalester College*

SIQING PENG *Peking University*

JING QIU *Samsung Economic Research Institute*

JENNIFER L. ROSNER *University of Illinois at Urbana-Champaign*

WILLIAM TOV *Singapore Management University*

CHING WAN *Nanyang Technological University*

MIN WANG *Beijing Foreign Studies University*

YAN ZHANG *Peking University*

ZHI-XUE ZHANG *Peking University*

PREFACE

This book is a record of the intellectual adventures of a network of researchers who were fortunate enough to have embarked together in their exploration of culture processes.

The journey began in August 2002, when the volume editors left Hong Kong for the University of Illinois at Urbana-Champaign and joined the Social-Personality-Organizational Psychology program at the university at the same time. Angela joined the program as a first-year doctoral student and Ying-yi and C-Y as new faculty members. The University of Illinois is well known for its tradition of cultural research. Although the founder of this tradition, Harry Triandis, had retired by the time we arrived, he nonetheless was available to provide us invaluable direction and guidance.

Jing (Julie) Chan, Hsin-Ya Liao, Sun No, Ching (Catherine) Wan, and Derrick Wirtz were second- or third-year graduate students at Illinois when we arrived and they later joined our efforts to set up the cultural and group processes (CGP) lab there. In 2003, another group of talented graduate students joined the lab. They included Evelyn Au, Manchi (Melody) Chao, Pelin Kesebir, Young-hoon Kim, Letty Kwan, and Will Tov. Avinish Chaturvedi, Yuet-yee (Shirley) Cheng, Karl Dach-Gruschow, Robert Kreuzbauer, Jennifer L. Rosner, Carlos Torelli, and Yung-jui (Daniel) Yang joined later. As a group, we examined cultural processes from different perspectives.

In 2004, the International Congress of Psychology invited us to organize a symposium for its meeting in Beijing. At the Congress, we were delighted to see Zhi-Xue Zhang, a former colleague at the University of Hong Kong, who was then a faculty member at the Guanghua School of Management at Peking University. At his invitation, Ying-yi and C-Y visited Peking University in spring of 2005, where they met Siqing Peng, another former colleague at the University of Hong Kong, and made many new friends, including Jian Han, Hean Tat Keh, Jing Qiu, Min Wang, and Yan Zhang. In the summer of

2006, we (Angela, Julie, Melody, Ying-yi, and C-Y) visited Peking University again. The next year, we were happy to reciprocate the hospitality of Zhi-Xue and Jing Qiu by hosting them at the University of Illinois. With Zhi-Xue's and Jing Qiu's support, we organized the Social and Cultural Organizational Psychology (SCOP) discussion group. Jennifer Klafehn, Silke McCance, Louis Tay, and Sang Eun Woo participated frequently in this group. Many CGP Lab members were also SCOP members. The same year, Leigh Anne Liu also visited, albeit only briefly. The formation of SCOP significantly enhanced the relevance of our cultural process analyses to organizational research, which is evident in this book.

The book represents a subset of ideas and research that resulted from the stimulating discussions among CGP Lab and SCOP members – the contributors are all active members of the Illinois–Beijing research network. All contributors richly deserve authorship of this book.

As of this writing, many former members of the Illinois group have graduated and are teaching in different parts of the world, including at universities in Singapore, Hong Kong, and the United States. Many of the graduate students we met in Beijing have also become faculty members at various universities in China. All continue to conduct rigorous research, providing new insights into the dynamic interactions of society, culture, and the self – the core theme of this book.

The objective of this book is to provide an in-depth analysis of cultural processes and their implications. However, a noteworthy new focus of our research network is on the social psychology of globalization. Daniel, Shirley, Letty, Carlos, Melody, Angela, Zhi-Xue, Hean Tat, and Siqing, as well as many other collaborators in Shanghai, Taiwan, Hong Kong, and the United States, have been working diligently on a project with that focus. The results of that project will have important implications for managing intercultural relations in our increasingly globalized world. Due to space constraints, we will have to present the work on globalization in a different outlet. Nonetheless, in the last section of this book on transcultural processes, the contributors have presented a glimpse of this work.

We are grateful to David Matsumoto for inviting us to contribute this book to the Cambridge University Press Culture and Psychology series. We are also grateful to the following agencies for supporting the publication of this book: Campus Research Board of the University of Illinois; Research Grants Council of the Hong Kong SAR Government (7439/05H); National Science Foundation, USA (NSF BCS 07-43119); and the Ministry of Education, Singapore.

We are thankful to the hundreds of undergraduate research assistants who have helped us at various stages of our research programs. In addition, thousands of research participants kindly shared with us their cultural experiences. We hope that their contributions to our learning through such generous sharing are adequately reflected in the theories and research presented in this book.

We are particularly thankful to the University of Illinois for offering us an incredibly rich and supportive intellectual environment. In addition to the wonderful mentorship that Harry Triandis selflessly offered to us, we are grateful to Dov Cohen, Ed Diener, Sharon Shavitt, Madhu Viswanathan, and many others for being such great colleagues. We are also thankful for the intellectual support that many University of Illinois alumni have offered us. We particularly thank Michele Gelfand, Emi Kashima, and Mark Suh. We also thank Marilynn Brewer, Yoshi Kashima, Kwok Leung, Toshio Yamagishi, Masaki Yuki, and many others who have in the past traveled to Illinois to offer us stimulating talks and conversations.

Finally, we thank the Guanghua School of Management at Peking University for hosting us and providing us with such a rich intellectual environment during our visits. We wish to dedicate this book to our friendship.

Angela K.-y. Leung
Chi-yue Chiu
Ying-yi Hong

PART ONE

INTRODUCTION

1

Cultural Processes: An Overview

CHI-YUE CHIU,[1] ANGELA K.-Y. LEUNG,
AND YING-YI HONG

Bickhard (2004) has made the following comments on the development of science:

> Every science passes through a phase in which it considered its basic subject matter to be some sort of substance or structure. Fire was identified with phlogiston; heat with caloric; and life with vital fluid. Every science has passed beyond that phase, recognizing its subject matter as being some sort of process: combustion in the case of fire; random thermal motion in case of heat; and certain kinds of far from thermodynamic equilibrium in the case of life. (p. 122)

In the case of cross-cultural and cultural psychology, decades of research have revealed many substantive differences among cultures (see Chiu & Hong, 2006, 2007; Lehman, Chiu, & Schaller, 2004). The field is now ready to transition into a new phase "that empirically establishes linkages between the active cultural ingredients hypothesized to cause between-country differences and the observed differences themselves" (Matsumoto & Yoo, 2006, p. 234).

The objective of the present volume is to attempt a systematic inquiry into basic cultural processes. In this chapter, we will provide an overview of the cultural processes presented in this volume. We will begin with defining what culture is, and proceed to discuss its functions, activation principles, and interconnections with society. Next, we will discuss cultural processes in trans-cultural settings as well as future research directions.

[1] Preparation of this chapter was supported by grants awarded to the first author by the National Science Foundation (USA) and the Ministry of Education (Singapore).

3

DEFINITION OF CULTURE

Culture is an elusive concept. Many theorists have offered definitions of culture. In a classic review of the concept in the mid-1950s, Kroeber and Kluckhohn (1952) brought more than 160 definitions to light.

In this volume, we define culture as *a constellation of loosely organized ideas and practices that are shared (albeit imperfectly) among a collection of interdependent individuals and transmitted across generations for the purpose of coordinating individual goal pursuits in collective living.*

This working definition highlights several noteworthy aspects of culture. First, culture refers to a knowledge tradition of ideas or practices, rather than a demarcated population (Barth, 2002; Braumann, 1999; Chiu & Chen, 2004; Hong, Wan, No, & Chiu, 2007; Chapter 7, this volume), although in many empirical investigations of culture, a demarcated population is commonly used as proxy for a certain culture. For example, cross-cultural and cultural psychologists often assess the psychological effects of cultural traditions by comparing national groups (e.g., Japanese vs. Americans) or ethnic groups within a nation (e.g., Asian Americans vs. European Americans). This research practice assumes that the characteristic or mainstream knowledge traditions in the groups being compared are markedly different.

Second, the ideas and practices that characterize a culture are only loosely organized. A common assumption in cross-cultural and cultural psychology is that ideas and practices in a cultural tradition are organized around a dominant theme (e.g., individualism, collectivism, independent self-construal, or interdependent self-construal). This view of culture, which has been referred to as *the system view of culture,* has been seriously criticized in both anthropology (Shore, 2002) and cross-cultural psychology (Kashima, 2009; Tay, Woo, Klafehn, & Chiu, 2010).

As we argue in the second section of this volume, the three major questions that a knowledge tradition tries to answer are:

What is true?
What is important in life?
What is the right thing to do?

As illustrated in Figure 1.1, cultural beliefs (or lay theories; see Chapter 2, this volume) are responses to the first question. Likewise, values (see Chapter 3, this volume) are answers to the second question, and norms (see Chapter 4, this volume) provide answers to the third question. Thus, although the list is not meant to be exhaustive, we contend that every major knowledge tradition in the world includes lay theories, values, and norms.

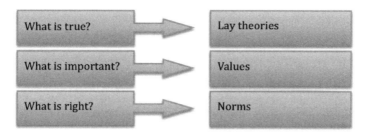

Figure 1.1. Culture provides answers to fundamental questions in life.

People who follow a certain cultural tradition use the lay theories, values, and norms in the tradition as behavioral guides. Thus, these symbolic components of culture are often accompanied by concrete practices and behavioral routines (e.g., rituals).

Oftentimes, the symbolic elements within a cultural tradition are not coherently organized because each tradition may offer several competing answers to the same question (e.g., different solutions to the body–mind problem in Greek philosophy) and competing interpretations of the same answer (e.g., different interpretations of the Gospels in different churches of the Christian tradition). Followers of a knowledge tradition may negotiate the validity of different answers or different interpretations of an answer, but, typically, multiple answers and their interpretations are retained in the knowledge tradition. As Triandis (2004) puts it, "A (cultural) tool that works well may be replaced by a tool that works slightly better, but frequently the culture retains both tools."

The research on collective responsibility attribution described in Chapter 4 provides a good illustration of how seemingly unrelated ideas are retained in a culture. Collective responsibility was first introduced in China by legalist reformers in the state of Qin (which later became the Qin Empire after the state had conquered other feudal powers) in mid-300 B.C. to enforce delegated deterrence – the practice of holding people responsible for monitoring and preventing misdeeds in one's neighborhood. Confucius (551–479 B.C.) also advocated collective responsibility but for a different reason. He held that, for the purpose of maintaining ingroup harmony, ingroup members should share the responsibility to protect individual members from being punished or ostracized. For the purpose of strengthening imperial power, in approximately 100 B.C., the Legalist principle of delegated deterrence was integrated into Confucian thoughts and written into Chinese law. The seemingly unrelated justifications for the practice of collective responsibility had coexisted in the Confucian legal traditions for more than

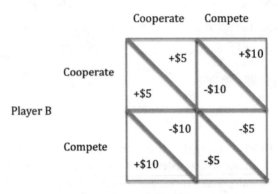

Player A

Figure 1.2. Payoff matrix in a Prisoner's Dilemma game.

two millennia. In fact, the practice continues to influence Chinese people's social judgments. The Chinese increase the extent of collective responsibility attribution both when the goal of delegated deterrence is salient and when the goal of maintaining ingroup harmony is highlighted in the situation (Chao, Zhang, & Chiu, 2008).

Third, culture is an adaptive device for coordinating individual goal pursuits in a society. People in a society simultaneously engage in competitive and cooperative behaviors. People are driven by selfish motives to maximize their personal gains. Meanwhile, the society needs to ensure that competition between individuals does not lead to cutthroat competition that threatens the survival of the society (Chiu & Chao, 2009; Heylighen & Campbell, 1995). As an illustration, consider the following payoff in a Prisoner's Dilemma game. The payoff, as illustrated in Figure 1.2, is symmetrical. If both players choose to cooperate, both parties will win $5. If both players choose to compete, both parties will lose $5. If one player chooses to cooperate and the other chooses to compete, the cooperative player will lose $10 and the competitive player will win $10. This matrix encourages individuals to engage in competition. If Player A assumes that Player B has a 50% chance of choosing to cooperate, the anticipated outcome of cooperation for Player A would be: $(0.5 \times \$5) + (0.5 \times -\$10) = -\$2.5$, and the anticipated outcome of competition for Player A would be: $(0.5 \times -\$5) + (0.5 \times \$10) = \$2.5$. Furthermore, if Player A knows that Player B is aware of the payoff matrix, Player A will expect Player B to compete rather than to cooperate, because Player A knows that Player B knows that he/she will make more money by choosing to compete than cooperate. The same calculation will enter Player B's mind. As a consequence, both players will tend to compete and both players will lose money. Thus, paradoxically, when both players act rationally to maximize their personal gains, the dyad suffers. In summary, unregulated selfish maximization could threaten the survival of the society. A recent example of this is that unregulated selfish maximization of Wall Street bankers has led to the collapse of the financial market.

Accordingly, every society needs social control mechanisms (e.g., the law, culture) to regulate but not to suffocate selfish, maximizing actions of the individual (see Chapter 4, this volume). Culture, as a social control mechanism, evolved to encourage cooperative coordination of individual actions and discourage selfish actions that would threaten the survival of the group. As an analogy, culture, like the conscience (or Superego) of the society, emerged to regulate but not to suffocate selfish maximization (the Id), so that the Society (the Ego) can channel selfish maximization into socially constructive actions and outcomes (Chiu & Chao, 2009; Chiu, Kim, & Chaturvedi, 2009; Chiu, Kim, & Wan, 2008).

Culture also helps direct individual actions to the protection of the society from various kinds of threats. A major threat to the survival of a human group is infectious disease, which, if not contained, could kill many in the group. In societies with high pandemic risk (e.g., societies in warm regions), strict norms were evolved to control the spread of pathogens in the community (e.g., norms that limit interactions with foreigners who could be carriers of exotic pathogens; Schaller & Murray, in press).

Culture also helps mobilize individuals to engage in a collective effort to protect the group from threatening natural disasters and foreign invasions. For example, the emphasis on loyalty in Confucianism gave the ancient rulers of China an inordinate amount of legitimate power to mobilize their people to engage in massive construction projects to protect the country (e.g., fortification of the Yellow River Banks to prevent massive flooding from bank collapses or breaching; the building of the Great Wall to defend against northern invasions). Recent research has shown that strong patriotic belief in Chinese culture contributed to the Chinese government's success in mobilizing the mass to volunteer for the 2008 Summer Olympics in Beijing (Yang et al., 2010).

FUNCTIONS OF CULTURE

Culture serves important social regulatory functions for the society. What does it do for the individual?

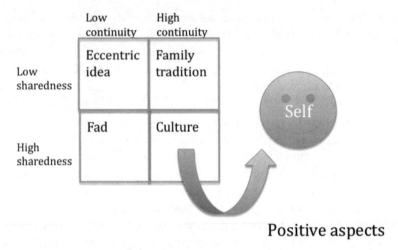

Figure 1.3. Psychological functions of culture.

As mentioned, two defining characteristics of a cultural knowledge tradition are its sharedness and continuity (Chiu & Liu, in press). A unique family tradition is one that has a history but is not widely shared in the community. A fad is a fashion, notion, or manner of conduct followed enthusiastically by a large group, but its popularity is temporary. An individual's eccentric belief is not shared by others and would unlikely be passed down through history. As illustrated in Figure 1.3, unlike a unique family tradition, a fad, or an eccentric belief, a cultural tradition (a) is shared among many people and (b) has a history.

By virtue of its sharedness and consensual validity, culture provides to its followers a sense of epistemic security (Chiu, Morris, Hong, & Menon, 2000; Fu, Morris, Lee, et al., 2007; see Chapter 5, this volume). Widely shared cultural knowledge provides individuals with a consensually validated framework to interpret otherwise ambiguous experiences. It informs individuals in the society what ideas or practices are generally considered to be true, important, and appropriate. Thus, it protects individuals from the epistemic terror of uncertainty and unpredictability.

By virtue of its continuity, culture provides its followers a sense of existential security, protecting the individual from the terror of recognizing one's mortality (Tam, Chiu, & Lau, 2007; see Chapter 6, this volume). Despite the finitude of an individual's life, the cultural tradition to which one belongs, as well as its sacred icons, will be passed down through history. Thus, connecting the self to a seemingly immortal cultural tradition can help assuage existential terror.

Culture also serves a self-definitional need (Hong et al., 2007; see Chapter 7, this volume). Individuals identify with a cultural tradition that enhances the positive distinctiveness of the self. Many components in a cultural tradition represent what most people in the culture agree to be true, valuable, and morally desirable. These components provide individuals with the symbolic materials for constructing a positive self-identity. Individuals can select, internalize, and even connect the self to ideas and practices in a culture with which they identify. Because different individuals may select a different subset of cultural ideas and/or practices for constructing self-identity, the meaning of the cultural self may mean different things to different individuals even within the same culture. Nonetheless, when the individual's cultural self is threatened, he or she will seek to affirm cultural identity and support a broader range of ideas and practices in the culture (Wan, Torelli, & Chiu, in press; Wan et al., 2007).

WHERE DOES CULTURE RESIDE?

Investigators have debated where culture resides. Does it reside in the individuals in the form of a cultural self, or does it reside as public representations carried in various cultural practices and artifacts (Morling & Lamoreaux, 2008)?

In this volume, we take the view that cultural knowledge is a kind of intersubjective knowledge (Chiu, Gelfand, Yamagishi, Shteynberg, & Wan, 2010; Wan & Chiu, 2009; see Chapter 3, this volume). Heylighen (1997) maintains that an intersubjective idea is selected for reproduction in culture based on its publicity (how extensively it is carried in public media), expressivity (how easily it can be expressed in a particular language or medium), formality (how context independent the expression of the idea is), collective utility (how much the idea benefits the collective), conformity (how popular the idea is), and authority (to what extent the idea is backed up by experts or authority).

First, according to this view, an idea is likely to be assimilated into the cultural tradition if its meanings are encoded in tangible, public representations that are accessible to all members of the culture and embodied in the culture's instituted social relations. Thus, important values, beliefs, and norms in a culture usually have many public representations (Morling & Lamoreaux, 2008).

Second, ideas that have high linguistic codability (the ease with which people can describe them in words) tend to prevail in the culture. This idea is consistent with the linguistic relativity hypothesis, which emphasizes

Table 1.1. *Types of cultural elements*

	Lay theories	Values	Norms
Knowledge of	Knowledge of lay theories	Knowledge of values	Knowledge of norms
Cultural self encompasses	Internalized lay theories	Internalized values	Internalized norms

the effects of linguistic encoding of a state of affairs on the development of a shared representation of that state of affairs (Chiu, Leung, & Kwan, 2007; Lau, Chiu, & Lee, 2001; Lau, Lee, & Chiu, 2004). For example, some languages (e.g., Puerto Rican Spanish and Turkish) have formal grammatical markers for false belief states (the state of believing in something that is not true). Children who speak this language, compared to those whose language does not have such markers, are more adept at comprehending false belief states when they use the false belief markers to describe them (Shatz, Diesendruck, Martinez-Beck, & Akar, 2003).

Third, as Sperber (1996) puts it, ideas that are "repeatedly communicated and minimally transformed in the process will end up belonging to the culture" (p. 83). In fact, research has shown that ideas that tend to be distorted in or drop out of a communication chain are unlikely to be assimilated into a cultural tradition (Kashima, 2000).

Furthermore, according to the collective utility principle, an idea is likely to be assimilated into a cultural tradition if it serves the social regulatory functions described in the previous section. According to the authority principle, ideas circulated among cultural elites are more likely to become a part of a culture. Finally, well-known ideas, practices, and people tend to maintain their cultural prominence in the presence of equally good or better alternatives, because people tend to use shared knowledge to establish common ground with their conversation partners. Consistent with this principle of conformity, research has shown that, regardless of performance, familiar baseball players are discussed more often than lesser-known players in natural discussions on the Internet. More important, regardless of performance, baseball players who are discussed more often on the Internet receive more All-Star votes, an institutionalized measure of cultural prominence (Fast, Heath, & Wu, 2009).

As mentioned, individuals may internalize a subset of ideas and practices in their culture. These ideas and practices form the contents of the individual's cultural self. As emphasized in Chapter 7 and illustrated in Table 1.1, for each idea and/or practice in a cultural tradition, only a portion of individuals will internalize it. For each individual, the cultural self consists of only a subset of the ideas and practices that are circulated in the culture. The separation of cultural knowledge from cultural mind creates the pretext for exploring the active identity negotiation processes presented in Chapters 7 and 12 (see Tadmor, Hong, Chiu, & No, in press).

Thus, culture exists both as tangible, public representations as well as in communication practices. Indeed, Sperber (1996) suggests that the best way to study how culture spreads and evolves is by examining how shared representations "are cognized by individuals and how they are communicated within a group" (p. 97). Likewise, Bruner (1990) submits: "our culturally adapted way of life depends upon shared meanings and shared concepts and depends as well upon shared modes of discourse for negotiating differences in meaning and interpretation" (pp. 12–13).

This distinction between cultural mind and cultural self has an important implication. Because all culturally competent individuals possess knowledge of their culture and may use this knowledge as a behavioral guide irrespective of whether they personally identify with it, knowledge of cultural expectations may have a more consistent effect on behaviors than do personal endorsement of these expectations. Indeed, recent research shows that cultural differences in judgments and behaviors are better predicted by knowledge of the shared lay theories and values in a particular culture than by personal endorsement of these lay theories or values (Shteynberg, Gelfand, & Kim, 2009; Zou et al., 2009).

Crossing the three kinds of knowledge representations (lay theories, values, and norms) with whether these representations are simply cultural knowledge or parts of the cultural self gives rise to the six types of cultural elements illustrated in Table 1.1. Chapter 2 illustrates how personal endorsement of shared lay theories about the world, race, and fate affect decisions and behaviors. Similarly, Chapter 9 illustrates how cultural differences in personal endorsement of lay theories of the self give rise to cultural differences in subjective well-being (Wirtz, Chiu, Diener, & Oishi, 2009). Chapters 3 and 7 discuss how knowledge of cultural values and personal endorsement of these values jointly determine overall level of cultural identification. Chapter 5 describes how knowledge of shared conflict resolution norms affects conflict resolution behaviors when people manage conflicts in their own culture and in a foreign culture (Chao, Zhang, & Chiu, 2010).

Intersubjective knowledge is different from objective knowledge. People may believe that a certain value is popular in the society, although few people in the society actually endorse it (Chiu, Gelfand, Yamagishi, et al.,

2010). In Chapter 3, Wan and Chiu relate this to the phenomenon of pluralistic ignorance, which refers to the situation in which a majority of group members privately reject a norm but assume (incorrectly) that most others accept it (Katz & Allport, 1931). In Chapter 11, Zhang illustrates this argument with the example of the social harmony norm in Chinese conflict situations. Chinese typically assume that others value interpersonal harmony and avoid direct confrontation, despite the fact that most Chinese actually prefer using direct confrontation to resolve a conflict. Because of pluralistic ignorance, the Chinese tend to avoid direct confrontation in conflict situations. Paradoxically, because of the motivation to maintain harmony through confrontation avoidance, the conflicts are not resolved and their negative interpersonal effects linger on, creating tensions in subsequent interactions between the disputants.

PRINCIPLES OF CULTURAL KNOWLEDGE ACTIVATION

Through cultural immersion, individuals acquire knowledge about the various lay theories, values, and norms as well as about their distributions in their culture. These lay theories, values, and norms are stored in the individual's memory as knowledge items. In response to the cultural demands of the situation, individuals will retrieve from memory the pertinent knowledge items as behavioral guides (Chiu & Hong, 2007; Hong & Chiu, 2001).

Application of cultural knowledge follows three basic principles: (1) availability, (2) accessibility, and (3) applicability. A knowledge item must be cognitively available to the individual before it can be applied. Among the cognitively available cultural knowledge items, those that are frequently or recently used are more cognitively accessible; they can be more readily retrieved from memory. Among the cognitively accessible cultural knowledge items, those that can be used to guide behaviors or solve problems in an immediate situation are more likely to be applied (Hong, Benet-Martinez, Chiu, & Morris, 2003; Hong, Morris, Chiu, & Benet-Martinez, 2000; Wong & Hong, 2005). These principles are illustrated in Chapter 4 using the example of collective responsibility attribution.

Finally, when the psychological functions of culture are highlighted in the situation, cultural knowledge (vs. personal or other types of knowledge) is more likely to be used. Evidence for this principle abounds. The research evidence cited in Chapters 5–7 illustrates that the tendency to apply cultural knowledge is heightened when the need for epistemic security is salient (Chao et al., 2010; Chiu et al., 2000; Fu, Morris, Chiu, et al., 2007; Chapter 5), when mortality is primed (Tam et al., 2007; Chapter 6), or when the situation presents a threat to one's cultural self (Chapter 7; Wan et al., 2007, in press).

SOCIETY, CULTURE, AND THE INDIVIDUAL

A major emphasis in our analysis is that cultural processes do not emerge in a social vacuum. Instead, individuals pursue their goals and construct their identities in a social context and are subject to the constraints that society imposes on individual behaviors. As a consequence, individuals need to negotiate personal control under such constraints. Shared lay theories – a part of the cultural tradition in the society – emerge in response to these constraints. Recent studies have shown that people living in a society with limited job mobility tend to endorse the lay theory that the world is fixed (Chen, Chiu, & Chan, 2009; see Chapter 2, this volume) and to display role conformance in job situations. In Chapter 2, Dach-Gruschow, Au, and Liao describe how pursuing goals under severe societal constraints could lead to the development of a fate belief that simultaneously recognizes the power of fate and personal agency. This lay theory is referred to as negotiable fate – the idea that fate determines one's outcomes but that one can negotiate with fate for better treatment (Chaturvedi, Chiu, & Viswanathan, 2009).

The social environment also constrains the way people express their basic needs (Chiu & Kim, in press). In Chapter 8 of this volume, Kim concludes from a review of the extant empirical evidence that, like Americans, Asians also desire positive self-regard and public acknowledgment of their strengths. Nonetheless, blatant expressions of one's strengths go against the culturally prescribed norms of self-presentation (modesty, dialectical self-presentation) and self-regulatory values (prevention focus, self-improvement) in Asian societies. As a result, individuals from Asian backgrounds often need to find indirect ways to express their positive selves (Kim, Chiu, Peng, Cai, & Tov, 2010; Kim, Peng, & Chiu, 2008).

Such negotiation processes also take place in identity construction processes and are particularly intense in bicultural identity negotiation (Hong et al., 2007; Tadmor et al., in press). As discussed in Chapter 12, cultural identity negotiations invariably take place in a social context in which different ethnic and/or cultural groups are associated with different statuses and stereotypes. On the one hand, strong between-group status differences and group stereotypes may lead to the development of essentialist beliefs about ethnic and/or cultural groups (Chapter 2). On the other hand, believing that each group is a fixed entity with a certain essence reinforces the perceived impermeability of intergroup boundaries, rendering cognitive crossing of cultural boundaries difficult (Chao, Chen, Roisman, & Hong, 2007; Hong, Chao, & No, 2009; No et al., 2008; see Chapter 12, this volume). Thus, the intergroup reality and its attendant cultural lay theories can have tremendous impact on the outcome of bicultural identity negotiation.

Even positively evaluated minority groups often experience subtle forms of discrimination. Take the model minority stereotype in the United States as an example. Asian Americans are considered a model minority with such positive traits as being quiet and hardworking. This stereotype obscures huge within-group variations among the Asians in the United States, particularly in their need for public assistance. Not all Asian groups in the United States perform well, and those who do not are denied public assistance simply because Asians are believed to know how to overcome obstacles through hard work. Also, the achievements of the model minority are sometimes cited as evidence for withdrawing public assistance to other minority groups – if Asians can manage without help, so can other minorities. Such cultural comparisons can create further tensions between Asians and other minority groups (Chao, Chiu, & Lee, 2010).

Finally, unequal status in multicultural contexts may create silent, marginalized cultural minorities. Members of these minorities often hesitate to voice their opinions in multicultural groups. Such a self-sanctioning process reduces opportunities for intercultural learning and limits the creative potential of a multicultural group (see Chapter 15, this volume). Thus, an analysis of cultural processes cannot be complete without considering the broader societal context in which they are embedded.

THE BENEFITS OF MULTICULTURAL EXPERIENCES

Although culture confers many benefits to the individual, it also limits the individual's intellectual horizons. People who are deep in a cultural tradition see the world primarily through the lens of that tradition (Leung, Maddux, Galinsky, & Chiu, 2008). In contrast, individuals who have extensive exposure to multiple cultures can view the world from different cultural lenses. Multicultural experiences have at least four cognitive benefits. First, they allow acquisition of knowledge about the dominant lay theories, values, norms, and behavioral scripts in other cultures (Chiu & Hong, 2005). Second, they enable flexible switching of cultural frames in response to the changing cultural demand in the situation (Fu, Chiu, Morris, & Young, 2007; Hong et al., 2000; Sui, Zhu, & Chiu, 2007). For example, Chinese Americans with rich bicultural knowledge can switch to a Chinese communication style when interacting with a Chinese and to an American communication style when interacting with an American. Such flexible switching will in turn improve intercultural communication (see Chapter 13, this volume). Third, in a multicultural work team, knowing what people in other cultures know, believe in, and value also facilitates coordination of team activities, leading to a higher level of team performance (see Chapter 10, this volume). Finally, with knowledge from different cultures at one's disposal, individuals can use knowledge from different cultures as resources to create new knowledge (Leung & Chiu, in press; Chapters 14 and 15, this volume).

Nonetheless, as pointed out in Chapters 13–15, the presence of some situational factors can curtail the cognitive benefits of multicultural experiences. For example, when the epistemic, existential, and self-definitional functions of culture are emphasized in a situation, individuals tend to follow the knowledge tradition of their own culture rather than learn from other cultures (Leung & Chiu, 2008, in press; Chapters 13 and 14, this volume). Also, the presence of unequal statuses in a multicultural group may lead to marginalization of low status groups and self-sanctioning (see Chapter 15, this volume).

SUMMARY AND FUTURE DIRECTIONS

In this volume, we describe a collection of works that were carried out to systematically examine cultural processes. We believe that this analysis has deepened our understanding of the active transactions of the society, the culture, and the individual.

Our analysis emphasizes the social coordination functions of culture. Indeed, only humans have the ability and motivation to (a) form shared goals and intentions with others in collaborative activities and (b) share experiences with others via joint attention, cooperative communication, and teaching. These abilities are believed to be the cognitive foundation of the evolution of culture (Tomasello, 2009).

As individual actors negotiate meanings and coordinate their goal pursuits through communication, culture as a collectively constructed knowledge tradition emerges. The symbolic contents of a cultural tradition address the fundamental questions of what is true, what is important, and what is right. By virtue of their sharedness, continuity, and positive values, a cultural tradition helps individuals meet their epistemic security, existential security, and self-definition needs.

A cultural tradition consists of intersubjective knowledge. The main body of it is externalized in various public representations, and a subset of it is internalized and forms the individual's cultural self.

Contents of cultural knowledge are organized in memory into knowledge structures, which are applied when they are cognitively available, accessible, and applicable. When the psychological functions of culture are made salient, the tendency to access and apply cultural knowledge (vs. other forms of knowledge) increases.

Cultural processes do not occur in a social vacuum. Existing social structures can shape the lay theories and norms in a culture, which in turn can affect the ways in which individuals express and try to meet their basic needs. Existing status structures and group stereotypes can also affect cultural identity choices and intercultural interactions.

Multicultural experiences can create many cognitive and social benefits. Specifically, multicultural experiences can improve cultural sensitivity, behavioral flexibility in intercultural interaction, and coordination in multicultural teamwork and creative performance. Nonetheless, these benefits will be curtailed if the needs for epistemic security, existential security, and cultural identity are salient or when there are unequal statuses among different cultural groups in intercultural interactions.

Several questions remain to be answered in future research. First, our analysis focuses on the social coordination function of culture. Sometimes, however, culture not only fails to perform this function, it actually promotes social disorganization. An example is the evolution of the culture of corruption in many societies.

Another example is the evolution of a materialist culture in some industrialized societies. A dominant lay theory in materialist culture is "wealth = worth"; wealth is used as the primary criterion for evaluating a person's worth and contribution to the society. A recent study carried out by the New Economics Foundation challenges the objective validity of this lay theory. The Foundation calculated the total contribution that six jobs make to society, including the impact on communities and the environment. These six jobs are waste recycler, hospital cleaner, childcare worker, elite banker, advertising executive, and tax accountant.

As shown in Table 1.2, elite bankers, advertising executives, and tax accountants make a lot more money than do waste recyclers, hospital cleaners, and childcare workers. Waste recyclers, hospital cleaners, and childcare workers, however, all make a positive contribution (from £9.5 to £12) to the society for every pound they are paid, whereas elite bankers, advertising executives, and tax accountants all make a negative contribution

Table 1.2. *Contributions of six job categories to society*

Job category	Value created for every £1 paid
Hospital cleaner	£10
Childcare worker	£9.50
Waste recycler	£12
Elite banker	−£7
Advertising executive	−£11
Tax accountant	−£47

Note: Based on New Economics Foundation study results reported in Shankleman (2009).

(from −£7 to −£47) to the society for every pound they are paid. Nonetheless, the materialist culture rewards elite bankers, advertising executives, and tax accountants with higher income and social status.

As Eilís Lawlor, spokeswoman for the New Economics Foundation, put it: "Pay levels often don't reflect the true value that is being created. As a society, we need a pay structure which rewards those jobs that create most societal benefit rather than those that generate profits at the expense of society and the environment" (Shankleman, 2009). Research is needed to understand when culture would fail its social coordination function and what can be done to fix the problem.

A second important future research topic concerns the cultural effects of globalization. As globalization proceeds at an increasingly rapid rate, research is needed to understand how globalization affects people's perceptions of their culture as their national economy globalizes (Cheng et al., 2010), as well as how individuals react to foreign cultures (Chen & Chiu, 2010; Chiu, Mallorie, Keh, & Law, 2009; Fu & Chiu, 2007). Will globalization weaken parochial, provincial identities and foster the development of cosmopolitan identities, or will globalization lead to fear of cultural contamination and erosion, which may in turn spur intercultural animosity (Chiu & Cheng, 2007)?

A major contribution of the process analysis advocated in this volume is that it sheds light on cultural differences but is not restricted to explaining cultural differences. This process analysis also connects cultural analysis to basic principles of social cognition, social motivation, and group processes. Its focus on the dynamic interplay of society, culture, and the individual invites integration of insights from psychology and other social science disciplines (e.g., anthropology, political science, sociology). As such, a process view of culture could lay the foundation for an integrated cultural science.

At the beginning of this chapter, we quoted Matsumoto and Yoo (2006) to argue for the timeliness of process analysis of culture. We wish to end by concluding that process research of culture, as exemplified in the present volume, is also highly theoretical as well as practical.

REFERENCES

Barth, F. (2002). An anthropology of knowledge. *Current Anthropology, 43,* 1–18.

Bickhard, M. H. (2004). Part II: Applications of process-based theories: Process and emergence: Normative function and representation. *Axiomathes, 14,* 121–155.

Braumann, C. (1999). Writing for culture: Why a successful concept should not be discarded. *Current Anthropology, 40,* S1–S27.

Bruner, J. (1990). *Act of meaning.* Cambridge, MA: Harvard University Press.

Chao, M. M., Chen, J., Roisman, G., & Hong, Y. (2007). Essentializing race: Implications for bicultural individuals' cognition and affect. *Psychological Science, 18,* 341–348.

Chao, M. M., Chiu, C., & Lee, J. S. (2010). Asians as the model minority: Implications for U.S. government's policies. *Asian Journal of Social Psychology, 13,* 44–52.

Chao, M. M., Zhang, Z., & Chiu, C-y. (2008). Personal and collective culpability judgment: A functional analysis of East Asian-North American differences. *Journal of Cross-Cultural Psychology, 39,* 730–744.

Chao, M. M., Zhang, Z-X., & Chiu, C-y. (2010). Adherence to perceived norms across cultural boundaries: The role of need for cognitive closure and ingroup identification. *Group Processes and Intergroup Relations, 13,* 69–89.

Chaturvedi, A., Chiu, C-y., & Viswanathan, M. (2009). Literacy, negotiable fate, and thinking style among low income women in India. *Journal of Cross-Cultural Psychology, 40,* 880–893.

Chen, J., Chiu, C-y., & Chan, F. S-F. (2009). The cultural effects of job mobility and the belief in a fixed world: Evidence from performance forecast. *Journal of Personality and Social Psychology, 97,* 851–865.

Chen, X., & Chiu, C-y. (2010). Rural-urban differences in generation of Chinese and Western exemplary persons: The case of China. *Asian Journal of Social Psychology, 13,* 9–18.

Cheng, Y-y., Chao, M. M., Kwong, J., Peng, S., Chen, X., Kashima, Y., et al. (2010). The good old days and a better tomorrow: Historical representations and future imaginations of China during the 2008 Olympic Games. *Asian Journal of Social Psychology, 13,* 118–127.

Chiu, C-y., & Chao, M. M. (2009). Society, culture, and the person: Ways to personalize and socialize cultural psychology. In R. Wyer, C-y. Chiu, & Y. Hong (Eds.), *Understanding culture: Theory, research and application* (pp. 457–466). New York: Psychology Press.

Chiu, C-y., & Chen, J. (2004). Symbols and interactions: Application of the CCC model to culture, language, and social identity. In S-h. Ng, C. Candlin, & C-y. Chiu (Eds.), *Language matters: Communication, culture, and social identity.* Hong Kong: City University of Hong Kong Press.

Chiu, C-y., & Cheng, S. Y-y. (2007). Toward a social psychology of culture and globalization: Some social cognitive consequences of activating two cultures simultaneously. *Social and Personality Psychology Compass, 1*, 84–100.

Chiu, C-y., Gelfand, M., Yamagishi, T., Shteynberg, G., & Wan, C. (2010). Intersubjective culture: The role of intersubjective perceptions in cross-cultural research. *Perspectives on Psychological Science, 5*, 482–493.

Chiu, C-y., & Hong, Y. (2005). Cultural competence: Dynamic processes. In A. Elliot & C. S. Dweck (Eds.), *Handbook of motivation and competence* (pp. 489–505). New York: Guilford.

Chiu, C-y., & Hong, Y. (2006). *Social psychology of culture.* New York: Psychology Press.

Chiu, C-y., & Hong, Y. (2007). Cultural processes: Basic principles. In E. T. Higgins & A. E. Kruglanski (Eds.), *Social psychology: Handbook of basic principles* (pp. 785–809). New York: Guilford.

Chiu, C-y., & Kim, Y-H. (in press). Rethinking culture and the self: Some basic principles and their implications. In S. Breugelmans, A. Chasiotis, & F. J. R. van de Vijver (Eds.), *Fundamental questions in cross-cultural psychology.* New York: Cambridge University Press.

Chiu, C-y., Kim, Y-H., & Chaturvedi, A. (2009). The case for collective evolution: Revisiting the Donald Campbell legacy. In M. Schaller, A. Norenzayan, S. J. Heine, T. Yamagishi, & T. Kameda (Eds.), *Evolution, culture, and the human mind* (pp. 39–47). New York: Psychology Press.

Chiu, C-y., Kim, Y-H., & Wan, W. N. (2008). Personality: Cross-cultural perspectives. In G. J. Boyle, G. Matthews, & D. H. Salofske (Eds.), *Sage handbook of personality theory and assessment, Vol. 1. Personality theory and testing.* London: Sage.

Chiu, C-y., Leung, A. K-y., & Kwan, L. (2007). Language, cognition, and culture: Beyond the Whorfian hypothesis. In S. Kitayama & D. Cohen (Eds.), *Handbook of cultural psychology* (pp. 668–688). New York: Guilford.

Chiu, C-y., & Liu, Z. (in press). Culture. In C. D. Mclwain & S. M. Caliendo (Eds.), *Routledge companion to race & ethnicity.* New York: Routledge.

Chiu, C-y., Mallorie, L., Keh, H-T., & Law, W. (2009). Perceptions of culture in multicultural space: Joint presentation of images from two cultures increases ingroup attribution of culture-typical characteristics. *Journal of Cross-Cultural Psychology, 40*, 282–300.

Chiu, C-y., Morris, M., Hong, Y., & Menon, T. (2000). Motivated cultural cognition: The impact of implicit cultural theories on dispositional attribution varies as a function of need for closure. *Journal of Personality and Social Psychology, 78*, 247–259.

Fast, N. I., Heath, C., & Wu, G. (2009). Common ground and cultural prominence: How conversation strengthens culture. *Psychological Science, 20*, 904–911.

Fu, H-y., & Chiu, C-y. (2007). Local culture's responses to globalization: Exemplary persons and their attendant values. *Journal of Cross-Cultural Psychology, 38*, 636–653.

Fu, H-y., Chiu, C-y., Morris, M. W., & Young, M. (2007). Spontaneous inferences from cultural cues: Varying responses of cultural insiders and outsiders. *Journal of Cross-Cultural Psychology, 38*, 58–75.

Fu, H-y., Morris, M. W., Lee, S-l., Chao, M-c., Chiu, C-y., & Hong, Y-y. (2007). Epis-temic motives and cultural conformity: Need for closure, culture, and context as determinants of conflict judgments. *Journal of Personality and Social Psychology, 92*, 191–207.

Heylighen F. (1997). Objective, subjective and intersubjective selectors of knowl-edge. *Evolution and Cognition, 3*, 63–67.

Heylighen, F., & Campbell, D. T. (1995). Selection of organization at the social level: Obstacles and facilitators of metasystem transitions. *World Futures: The Journal of General Evolution, 45*, 181–212.

Hong, Y., Benet-Martinez, V., Chiu, C-y., & Morris, M. W. (2003). Boundaries of cultural influence: Construct activation as a mechanism for cultural dif-ferences in social perception. *Journal of Cross-Cultural Psychology, 34*, 453–464.

Hong, Y., Chao, M. M., & No, S. (2009). Dynamic interracial/intercultural pro-cesses – The role of lay theories of race. *Journal of Personality (Special issue: Personality and racial/ethnic relations), 77*, 1283–1310.

Hong, Y., Morris, M., Chiu, C-y., & Benet-Martinez, V. (2000). Multicultural minds: A dynamic constructivist approach to culture and cognition. *American Psychol-ogist, 55*, 709–720.

Hong, Y-y., & Chiu, C-y. (2001). Toward a paradigm shift: From cross-cultural dif-ferences in social cognition to social-cognitive mediation of cultural differences. *Social Cognition, 19*, 181–196.

Hong, Y-y., Wan, C., No, S., & Chiu, C-y. (2007). Multicultural identities. In S. Kitayama & D. Cohen (Eds.), *Handbook of cultural psychology*. New York: Guilford.

Kashima, Y. (2000). Maintaining cultural stereotypes in the serial reproduction of narratives. *Personality and Social Psychology Bulletin, 26*, 594–604.

Kashima, Y. (2009). Culture comparison and culture priming: A critical analysis. In R. Wyer, C-y. Chiu, & Y. Hong (Eds.), *Understanding culture: Theory, research and application* (pp. 53–78). New York: Psychology Press.

Katz, D., & Allport, F. H. (1931). *Student attitudes*. Syracuse, NY: Craftsman.

Kim, Y-h., Chiu, C-y., Peng, S., Cai, H., & Tov, W. (2010). Explaining East-West differences in the likelihood of making favorable self-evaluations. *Journal of Cross-Cultural Psychology, 41*, 62–75.

Kim, Y-h., Peng, S., & Chiu, C-y. (2008). Explaining self-esteem differences between Chinese and North Americans: Dialectical self (vs. self-consistency) or lack of positive self-regards. *Self and Identity, 7*, 113–128.

Kroeber, A. L., & Kluckhohn, C. (1952). *Culture: A critical review of concepts and definitions*. Cambridge, MA: Harvard University Press.

Lau, I., Lee, S-L., & Chiu, C-y. (2004). Language, cognition and reality: Construct-ing shared meanings through communication. In M. Schaller & C. Crandall (Eds.), *Psychological foundations of culture* (pp. 77–100). Mahwah, NJ: Lawrence Erlbaum.

Lau, I. Y-M., Chiu, C-y., & Lee, S-L. (2001). Communication and shared reality: Implications for the psychological foundations of culture. *Social Cognition, 19*, 350–371.

Lehman, D., Chiu, C-y., & Schaller, M. (2004). Culture and psychology. *Annual Review of Psychology, 55*, 689–714.

Leung, A. K-y., & Chiu, C-y. (2008). Interactive effects of multicultural experiences and openness to experience on creativity. *Creativity Research Journal, 20*, 376–382.

Leung, A. K-y., & Chiu, C-y. (in press). Multicultural experiences, idea receptiveness, and creativity. *Journal of Cross-Cultural Psychology.*

Leung, A. K-y., Maddux, W. W., Galinsky, A. D., & Chiu, C-y. (2008). Multicultural experience enhances creativity: The when and how? *American Psychologist, 63*, 169–181.

Matsumoto, D., & Yoo, S. H. (2006). Toward a new generation of cross-cultural research. *Perspectives on Psychological Science, 1*, 234–250.

Morling, B., & Lamoreaux, M. (2008). Measuring culture outside the head: A meta-analysis of cultural products. *Personality and Social Psychology Review, 12*, 199–221.

No, S., Hong, Y., Liao, H., Lee, K., Wood, D., & Chao, M. M. (2008). Lay theory of race affects and moderates Asian Americans' responses toward American culture. *Journal of Personality and Social Psychology, 95*, 991–1004.

Schaller, M., & Murray, D. R. (in press). Infectious disease and the creation of culture. In M. Gelfand, C-y. Chiu, & Y-y. Hong (Eds.), *Advances in culture and psychology, Vol. 1.* New York: Oxford University Press.

Shankleman, M. (2009). Cleaners 'worth more to society' than bankers – study. BBC News, December 14, 2009. Retrieved December 29, 2009, from http://news .bbc.co.uk/2/hi/business/8410489.stm

Shatz, M., Diesendruck, G., Martinez-Beck, I., & Akar, D. (2003). The influence of language and socioeconomic status on children's understanding of false belief. *Developmental Psychology, 39*, 717–729.

Shore, B. (2002). Taking culture seriously. *Human Development, 45*, 226–228.

Shteynberg, G., Gelfand, M. J., & Kim, K. (2009). Peering into the "magnum mysterium" of culture: The explanatory power of descriptive norms. *Journal of Cross-Cultural Psychology, 40*, 46–69.

Sperber, D. (1996). *Explaining culture: A naturalistic approach.* Oxford, England: Blackwell.

Sui, J., Zhu, Y., & Chiu, C-y. (2007). Bicultural mind, self-construal, and recognition memory: Cultural priming effects on self- and mother-reference effect. *Journal of Experimental Social Psychology, 43*, 818–824.

Tadmor, C. T., Hong, Y-y., Chiu, C-y., & No, S. (in press). What I know in my mind and where my heart belongs: Multicultural identity negotiation and its cognitive consequences. In R. Crisp (Ed.), *The psychology of social and cultural diversity.* Oxford: Blackwell.

Tam, K-p., Chiu, C-y., & Lau, I. Y-m. (2007). Terror management among Chinese: Worldview defense and intergroup bias in resource allocation. *Asian Journal of Social Psychology, 10*, 93–102.

Tay, L., Woo, S. E., Klafehn, J., & Chiu, C-y. (2010). Conceptualizing and measuring culture: Problems and solutions. In E. Tucker, M. Viswanathan, & G. Walford (Eds.), *The handbook of measurement: How social scientists generate, modify, and validate indicators and scales* (pp. 179–201). London: Sage.

Tomasello, M. (in press). Human culture in evolutionary perspective. In M. Gelfand, C-y. Chiu, & Y-y. Hong (Eds.), *Advances in culture and psychology, Vol. 1.* New York: Oxford University Press.

Triandis, H. C. (2004). Dimensions of culture beyond Hofstede. In H. Vinken, J. Soeters, & P. Ester (Eds.), *Comparing cultures: Dimensions of culture in a comparative perspective.* Leiden, The Netherlands: Brill Publishers.

Wan, C., & Chiu, C-y. (2009). Intersubjective consensus approach to culture. In R. Wyer, C-y. Chiu, & Y. Hong (Eds.), *Understanding culture: Theory, research and application* (pp. 79-91). New York: Psychology Press.

Wan, C., Chiu, C-y., Tam, K-p., Lee, S-l., Lau, I. Y-m., & Peng, S-q. (2007). Perceived cultural importance and actual self-importance of values in cultural identification. *Journal of Personality and Social Psychology, 92,* 337–354.

Wan, C., Torelli, C., & Chiu, C-y. (in press). Intersubjective consensus and the maintenance of normative shared reality. *Social Cognition.*

Wirtz, D., Chiu, C-y., Diener, E., & Oishi, S. (2009). What constitutes a good life? Cultural differences in the role of positive and negative affect in subjective well-being. *Journal of Personality, 77,* 1167–1196.

Wong, R. Y-M., & Hong, Y-y. (2005). Dynamic influences of culture on cooperation in the Prisoner's Dilemma. *Psychological Science, 16,* 429–434.

Yang, Y., Chen, M., Chen, W., Ying, X., Wang, B., Wang, J., et al. (2010). The effects of boundary-permeated self and patriotism on social participation in Beijing Olympic Games. *Asian Journal of Social Psychology, 13,* 109–117.

Zou, X., Tam, K. P., Morris, M. W., Lee, S-l., Lau, I. Y-m., & Chiu, C-y. (2009). Culture as common sense: Perceived consensus versus personal beliefs as mechanisms of cultural influence. *Journal of Personality and Social Psychology, 97,* 579–597.

PART TWO

REPRESENTATIONAL THEORIES

OF CULTURE

2

Culture as Lay Personal Beliefs

KARL DACH-GRUSCHOW, EVELYN W. M. AU,
AND HSIN-YA LIAO

Our perception of the world is unavoidably influenced by our beliefs about the world (Feyerabend, 1965; Nisbett & Wilson, 1977). These beliefs serve as an organizational structure through which new experiences and observations are understood. Consequently, people's perceptions of the world color their interpretations of events and behaviors, and shape the goals they wish to attain. The effect of our beliefs becomes most apparent when we encounter situations in which the majority do not share our beliefs, such as when we immerse ourselves in a foreign cultural setting. In these situations, questions arise as to what is, in fact, universal.

For example, death is widely perceived as a time of loss, mourning, and sadness. At certain American funerals, however, in particular for devoted Christian families, it is not uncommon for the close friends and family of the deceased to be genuinely happy and to express that feeling. This is not to say that they are not sad as well, but that this sadness is not as visible as it is in other cultures. The reason for this muted sadness and at times overt happiness is rooted in a strong Christian belief that the deceased is still alive and has moved to someplace better than Earth, and moreover that the living will join the deceased there someday. In this context, it is not unheard of for people to feel somewhat selfish or guilty if they are sad, as it means that they wish that the deceased were still with them instead of with God.

The same setting of a funeral may be quite different even within the United States, if the attendees do not believe in an afterlife. Participants may instead perceive the death as a pure loss and focus on consoling each other over that loss. Expressing joy in this setting may strike other attendees as quite bizarre, and perhaps be seen as an insult. The contrast between the two different reactions to death illustrates the overwhelming power of belief and its integral nature in forming not only individual experiences, but also our social world.

In this example, whether death is to be celebrated in joy or mourned in sadness is determined by the funeral attendees' beliefs. In this way, the example demonstrates how these *lay beliefs* shape our interpretation of and reaction to events. An example directly from psychological research is that students' beliefs about intelligence determine whether students respond to failure by abandoning a subject or trying harder: Students may respond helplessly to an achievement failure if they believe that the failure reflects on their low ability or constructively if they believe that the failure signals a need for remedial effort.

The purpose of this chapter is to illustrate the utility of lay theories in understanding the structure of culture, the differences between cultures, and an individual's conception of self within that culture. We will begin by first defining lay theories and discussing their history in social psychology, then how they have been applied to examining issues between cultures, within cultures, and in defining the cultural self. Throughout this discussion, we will emphasize new directions in lay theory research and how lay theories can be seen in a broader perspective.

DEFINING LAY THEORIES

We began with an example of how beliefs shape cultural experience, and it is belief that is ultimately the focus of this chapter. It is nonetheless necessary to limit our discussion to only certain beliefs. Although the belief that $1 + 1 = 2$ and the belief that smoking is immoral can certainly be seen as cultural knowledge or the contents of culture, these are not the sorts of beliefs that are considered lay theories. Lay theories are the sorts of beliefs that provide some manner of explanation, definition, or assumption that allows navigation of the social world. In other words, they are the theories that form each individual's own commonsense psychology (cf., Heider, 1958).

Lay theories have been given several different names within social psychology. We choose to call them lay theories, because they are basic and unscientific theories about how the world is or works. Other names that have been used include *folk theories*, emphasizing that such theories often come from old traditions or sayings (Stich & Nichols, 1992); *common sense psychology* (Heider, 1958); and *implicit theories* (Dweck, Chiu, & Hong, 1995), emphasizing that we often apply these theories without thinking about them (Chiu, Morris, Hong, & Menon, 2000).

INITIAL LAY THEORIES RESEARCH

Although lay theories were already discussed within social psychology as early as in Gordon Allport's (1954) classic, *On the Nature of Prejudice*, lay theories gained particular prominence in psychological research with the works of Carol Dweck in social and developmental psychology (e.g., children's theories of intelligence; Dweck & Bempechat, 1983) and Adrian Furnham in organizational and clinical psychology (e.g., lay theories of delinquency; Furnham & Henderson, 1983).

The current face of lay theory research in culture has been heavily influenced by Carol Dweck's work on intelligence. Dweck and her students began by examining learned helplessness and learning motivation in children. This examination eventually led to the development of the lay theory of intelligence as an explanatory construct. This lay theory has two forms: *entity theory*, which hypothesizes that intelligence is a trait, essentially fixed from birth, and *incremental theory*, which hypothesizes that intelligence is something slowly gained through experiences and effort (for thorough review, see Dweck, 1999; see also Molden & Dweck, 2006). This basic distinction of fixed/entity versus incremental/malleable theories is identifiable in much of the subsequent work on lay theories.

In the intelligence domain, Dweck and her colleagues (Dweck et al., 1995) have demonstrated how the belief that intelligence is fixed (versus malleable) is associated with different responses when confronted with failure. Entity theorists (who view intelligence as fixed) are more likely to see failure as reflecting a fixed amount of ability and tend to attribute performance setbacks to low intelligence. In contrast, incremental theorists (who consider intelligence to be malleable) do not see failure as indicative of an ability to succeed and tend to attribute setbacks to controllable personal qualities (such as effort). Furthermore, the need to exert effort has different connotations for entity and incremental theorists. Specifically, entity theorists subscribe to the inverse rule – the idea that the need to exert effort suggests lack of ability, whereas incremental theorists believe that effort increases the likelihood of success.

Lay theories of intelligence and their attendant inferences regarding effort expenditure have important implications for individuals' adjustment in challenging achievement contexts. In the face of achievement setbacks, entity theorists may infer that low ability limits future success. Although additional effort expenditure may improve future performance, the need to exert such effort is taken as further evidence for lack of ability. As a result, entity theorists tend to display an aversion to effort and respond helplessly to achievement setbacks.

Conversely, in the face of the same setback, incremental theorists, believing that effort improves ability and increases the chance of success, often remain optimistic about future success and are willing to take remedial actions (Hong, Chiu, Lin, Wan, & Dweck, 1999). Analogous results have been obtained in studies linking (a) entity and incremental theories of personality to social trait inferences and responses to social rejection (Chiu, Hong, & Dweck, 1997; Dweck et al., 1995; Erdley & Dweck, 1993) and (b) entity and incremental theories of morality to moral trait inferences and responses to injustices (Chiu, Dweck, Tong, & Fu, 1997; Gervey, Chiu, Hong, & Dweck, 1999). Taken together, the results suggest that the differentiation between entity theorists and incremental theorists in different domains has important implications, such as enabling the prediction of systematic differences in people's reactions to observed behaviors and experienced events.

THE TRANSITION OF LAY THEORIES TO CULTURAL PSYCHOLOGY

The lay theory of intelligence is described in terms of entity versus incremental. In some sense, this dichotomy could also be seen as trait versus state, personality versus behavior, or person versus situation. It is perhaps no surprise then that one of the first connections between lay theories research and cultural psychology occurred in the context of person perception and the fundamental attribution error.

Miller (1984) examined social explanations in America and India, and found that as Americans grew older they became more likely to make dispositional attributions, whereas this was not the case for Indians. More importantly, this cross-culture difference was linked to cultural conceptions of the person. This finding was both one of the first pieces of evidence that the fundamental attribution error was neither fundamental nor universal, as well as one of the first studies to link psychology, culture, and lay conceptions of the person.

Lay beliefs about personal attributes had been found to affect people's social judgment, actions, and outcomes (Dweck et al., 1995). Moreover, research had shown that holding an entity theory of personality draws one's attention to people's stable traits, whereas holding an incremental theory of personality draws one's attention to people's dynamic social situations (see Levy, Plaks, & Dweck, 1999). This theoretical framework has been applied in an attempt to examine dispositional biases and culture.

Chiu, Hong, and colleagues (1997) found that persons holding an entity theory of others' personality were more likely to display lay dispositionism, overemphasizing the role of individuals' personality traits and underemphasizing the role of varying social environments in interpreting the choices and actions of others. Research in this area has found that East Asians tend to adopt incremental theory, which emphasizes embeddedness of the individuals in social contexts, whereas Western Europeans tend to hold entity theory, which emphasizes the individual as a bounded unit with stable internal attributes (see review from Markus & Kitayama, 1991; see also Heine, 2001). This is of course also consistent with Miller's (1984) prior research on cultural differences in attribution.

One advantage of adopting a lay theory approach, in comparison to traditional cross-cultural psychology, is that it allows us to use the same theoretical constructs (e.g., lay theory of personality and lay theory of the world) and to examine their roles in two different cultures. Adopting a theory approach also allows culture-specific systems of thought to be described in terms of differing levels of chronic endorsement of various lay theories. The end result is that the lay theory approach can integrate both within- and between-culture research traditions into one conceptual framework.

Su and colleagues (1999), for example, provide an analysis of Chinese and American views of the self based on lay theories. They conclude that differences in the view of the self cannot be explained simply on the basis of differing levels of endorsement of a single belief or dimension, but must be attributed to differences in the system of belief. Whereas American and Chinese beliefs about individuals' ability to change are similar, Chinese people believe that the world or social structure is much more rigid. Consequently, the belief about individuals and subsequent expectations about individuals' adaptation are different in Chinese culture, because the relative flexibility of the individual is greater than the social system.

Applying this theoretical framework, researchers have examined the cultural implications of the lay belief about the malleability of personality and the world. For instance, Chiu, Dweck, and colleagues (1997) argued that individuals' moral beliefs are associated with their perception of the fixedness of reality. More specifically, it was proposed that individuals who see reality as fixed (*entity theory*) are more likely to hold moral beliefs that center around duties, whereas those who perceive reality as malleable (*incremental theory*) tend to hold moral beliefs that value individual rights. To determine participants' view of the fluidity of reality, Chiu, Dweck, and colleagues (1997) assessed respondents' implicit theory of morality (i.e., their beliefs about the changeability of a person's basic moral qualities) and implicit theory of the world (i.e., their beliefs about the nature of basic social institutions). Individuals who believe in the entity theory see both individuals' basic moral qualities *and* basic social institutions as unchangeable, whereas incremental theorists view both of these as dynamic.

In one study, participants were given two statements that reflect the violation of certain moral principles (either duty-based or rights-based), and were asked to choose which violation was more unacceptable. Findings revealed that, when duty-based violations were pitted against rights-based violations, entity theorists were far more likely than were the incremental theorists to choose the duty-based ones (which also means that incremental theorists were more likely than were entity theorists to choose the rights-based violations).

To explore the implications of this finding, another study examined people's responses to rule violations. The investigators hypothesized that, within a duty-based moral framework, misbehavior should be met with punishment and desirable behavior is not entitled to reward because it is one's duty to act appropriately. In contrast, when morality is considered from a rights-based point of view, rule violations may not be seen as innately serious; therefore, good behavior would be more likely to be appreciated, whereas rule violations may be met with less harsh punishment. Results from the study supported these predictions.

Finally, to establish cross-cultural generality of the findings, a study was conducted in a Chinese society, which is relatively more duty-based when compared to America. Findings revealed that, consistent with the investigators' hypotheses, there were more entity theorists in Hong Kong than in America. Further, entity theorists among the Chinese sample were more likely to reason in ways consistent with duty-based moral beliefs than were those who subscribed to incremental theory.

Chiu and Hong (1999) also explored how different implicit theories of the world may shape individuals' social identification. They carried out an experimental study situated in the context of the 1997 return of Hong Kong to China. This political transition challenged the social identity of the citizens of Hong Kong: Should they identify with the larger inclusive Chinese group or affirm their distinctive Hong Konger identity? In this study, participants were first primed with 1997-related or 1997-unrelated pictures under the pretext of a study about graphic designs. Then, under the cover of a different study, participants were asked to read an article about a supervisor of an assembly plant (who was depicted as being from Hong Kong in one condition and from China in another condition). In this fictitious newspaper article, the supervisor had neglected to put on a safety cover properly, resulting in accidents that severed the fingers of other employees of the plant. After reading the article, participants were asked to judge how unfair it would be if the supervisor went unpunished.

It was predicted that when the 1997 issue was made salient, entity theorists would see the return of Hong Kong to China and China's dominance over Hong Kong as inevitable and align themselves with the anticipated unalterable power structure after 1997. Therefore, it was hypothesized that entity theorists would display less ingroup favoritism toward the Hong Kong supervisor and less outgroup bias toward the Mainland supervisor in the 1997-related condition compared to the 1997-unrelated condition. In contrast, malleable theorists, who did not perceive China's dominance over Hong Kong to be unassailable, were predicted to exhibit the opposite pattern – displaying the need for a distinctive Hong Konger identity when the 1997 issue was made salient. Consequently, they would be more likely to show ingroup favoritism toward the Hong Kong supervisor and discriminate against the outgroup Mainland supervisor in the 1997-related condition compared to the 1997-unrelated condition.

Results from the study generally supported these hypotheses. In such a case, the data suggest that persons who believe in a fixed world were more likely to align themselves with an unchangeable reality by assimilating attitudes to the attitudes expected from the status quo. By contrast, persons who perceive the world as changeable may have a relatively more agentic view of the self and are driven to defy political changes that may overpower their personal identity.

CURRENT RESEARCH ON LAY THEORIES AND CULTURE

Lay Theories of Race

Recently lay theories have been applied within cultural psychology to examine individuals' theories of race in relation to individuals' views of the self and groups. Instead of focusing on rigidity of social structure, work on lay theory of race focuses on whether individuals think that racial groups have an essential, unalienable core. On the societal level, this belief may be related to whether one sees race as a meaningful way of partitioning groups (Chao, Hong, & Chiu, 2008). On the individual level, lay theory of race may influence the extent to which individuals are expected to attribute similar traits to racial ingroup members (e.g., stereotypes).

If one believes that an individual has a fixed moral character from birth, then one might also believe that certain groups of people have a fixed moral character from birth. This is a starting point for the work on the lay theory of race (No et al., 2008). The lay theory of race is not, however, simply a measure of whether individuals are prone to committing the ultimate attribution error by attributing behavior to group dispositions (Pettigrew, 1979). Rather, the lay theory of race sees race as something that is an inherent trait of a given individual or group of individuals (entity theory) or an arbitrary, malleable, social construct (No et al., 2008).

Theoretically, lay theory of race has strong implications for both self and other perceptions. Specifically, viewing race as a fixed and essential trait of one's self is likely to cause one to view one's racial identity as immutable and to perceive greater distance between one's self and other racial groups. In contrast, lay theory of race also has implications for other perceptions, in that individuals who believe that race is fixed are more likely to see traits as "racial" than as "personal."

Research to date has focused more on the effects of the fixed belief about race on the perceived difference of the self and other racial groups . No and colleagues (2008) examined the effect of endorsing a fixed theory of race for Asian Americans, finding that the extent to which Asian Americans saw their personality as different from that of a typical European American was positively correlated with their endorsement of a biological/fixed lay theory of race. Likewise, No and colleagues (2008) found that Korean Americans who endorsed a fixed theory of race were less likely to identify with American culture when thinking about American culture, and more likely to exhibit contrast effects (i.e., responding in a more typical Korean way when shown an American cultural prime).

Similarly, subsequent research by Chao, Chen, Roisman, and Hong (2007) has found that Chinese Americans endorsing a biological theory of race exhibited heightened emotional reactivity when being questioned about their cultural experiences in the United States and experienced resistance to cultural frame switching similar to that of participants of the study by No and colleagues (2008).

Taken together, these studies provide evidence that an essentialist, fixed view of race is associated with perceiving other cultural groups as more distal (and the self as more separate) from the majority culture, at least for racial minority group members (see Chapter 12, this volume).

An important point to note in the research by No and colleagues (2008) and Chao and colleagues (2007) is that the lay theories of race refer only to race in the abstract, without any reference to any specific race, ethnicity, or cultural group. Nonetheless, these researchers found their expected results on culture. Thus, it is evident that, for their participants, race had an inherent linkage to culture; moreover, the results of these two studies depend on a "racial group = cultural group" assumption both theoretically and methodologically.

Consequently, these findings reflect the widespread tendency for individuals to psychologically confound racial, cultural, and national groups (Sidanius & Petrocik, 2001). This tendency is particularly well documented in the United States, where there is an assumption widely shared by both majority Whites and minority groups that the term *American* refers to Whites (Devos & Banaji, 2005). To be explicit about this point, psychologically when one discusses a Chinese, this likely means more than just that an individual holds Chinese citizenship, but also refers to a person of a specific culture and race.

The implication is that social identities, such as national, ethnic, racial, and cultural identities, are psychologically confounded. Although these terms are semantically differentiated in academia, in lay psychological belief they refer to the same thing. All of these categories may or may not be essentialized, and tend to be confounded with each other.

A possible explanation of this occurrence is that, for the most part, these groups are typically defined by a common origin and development over time. Moreover, to the extent that one sees the groups as essential, they may also share a common developmental trajectory and fate. Thus, on an individual level, although White (a *racial* category) and Hispanic (an *ethnic* category) may exist within different taxonomies, such that one may be both White and Hispanic, psychologically they are seen as either/or categories, as both imply membership in a group determined by shared fate. This explanation seems compatible with both recent work on lay theories of race, as well as recent work on groups (cf., Yzerbyt, Corneille, & Estrada, 2001; Spencer-Rodgers, Hamilton, & Sherman, 2007).

Although lay theories about individuals and groups may be structured around giving a sense of meaning and agency to a given individual or group, they also can be extended to cover a wide variety of ways to conceive the construct of fate. This new area of lay theory research is particularly exciting in that it extends lay theory outside the realm of simple fixed versus malleable dimension.

Lay Conceptions of Fate and Agency

Definition of Negotiable Fate

Past research on perceived control often pits the ideas of fate and personal agency against each other; one either has control over the outcome or relinquishes it (e.g., Lefcourt, Miller, Ware, & Sherk, 1981; Seligman, 1975).

Au and colleagues (2008) argue, however, that the acknowledgement of uncontrollability is not necessarily accompanied by a sense of helplessness; individuals can still negotiate control with fate by exercising agency within the limits determined by fate or by initiating actions to lobby for fate's favor. Therefore, a different conceptualization of the relationship between fate and agency is embodied by the new construct of negotiable fate (Au et al., 2008).

Negotiable fate captures the idea of acknowledging fate's authority over one's outcomes, while believing in some degree of personal control; an idea succinctly summarized by the popular idiom, "If fate hands you lemons, make lemonade." Negotiable fate is different from insurmountable fate and conquerable fate, the other two fate beliefs that have received extensive research attention. Unlike insurmountable fate, which holds that all events are predetermined by fate and are therefore unalterable, negotiable fate entertains the possibility of bringing about desired outcomes through agentic actions. Unlike conquerable fate, which boasts the ability to allow one to self-determine one's course of action and considers outcomes to be unconstrained by external agents and circumstances, negotiable fate recognizes fate as a powerful causal agent. In sum, negotiable fate is a fusion of both insurmountable fate and conquerable fate beliefs.

To better understand the societal environment that is conducive to the development of negotiable fate, Au and colleagues developed a theoretical framework that examines the impact of two societal level factors: action–outcome contingency and constraint malleability. Action–outcome contingency refers to the extent to which personal outcomes are contingent on one's actions, whereas constraint malleability refers to the degree to which societal constraints are perceived to be changeable. It was proposed that negotiable fate is most likely to develop when people are rewarded for their efforts but face immutable societal constraints that affect their ability to attain these goals.

Past findings on perceived control have consistently demonstrated that the lack of action–outcome contingency contributes to fatalism (e.g., Lefcourt et al., 1981; Seligman, 1975). Although Au and colleagues (2008) agree with this point of view, they maintain that even when action–outcome contingency is high, if people experience immutable constraints in their lives, they would also believe in fate. When faced with immutable constraints, the types of goals people can pursue (as well as the means and opportunities available to attain these goals) are limited. Consequently, even though people believe that they will be rewarded for their efforts, fate will still be used as an explanation for the outcomes because their outcomes are not completely within their control. Au and colleagues (2008) predicted that it is under these circumstances that the belief in negotiable fate will propagate. A belief in conquerable fate, in contrast, is expected to be prevalent when action–outcome contingency is high but experienced constraints are low.

To test this model, two studies were conducted to explore fate beliefs across samples that believed strongly in reward application (the belief that efforts will be rewarded by society; Leung & Bond, 2004) but varied in the degree of experienced constraints (Au et al., 2008). The investigators found both between-culture and within-culture variations in the belief in negotiable fate. In the first study, the belief in negotiable fate was compared between samples from the United States (high on reward application, and low on experienced constraints) and China (high on reward application, but also high on experienced constraints). In the second study, the investigators examined belief in negotiable fate of individuals who differed in years of formal education. In both studies, the results suggested that individuals who faced greater experienced constraints (i.e., the Chinese sample, and individuals with few years of formal education) were more likely to subscribe to negotiable fate than were their less-constrained counterparts (i.e., the American sample, and individuals with many years of formal education). Furthermore, the construal of negotiable fate differed across individuals who experienced different degrees of constraints: Individuals who experienced greater constraints considered negotiable fate to be similar to conquerable fate, whereas those who are faced with fewer constraints saw these two constructs as being unrelated.

Taken together, these findings suggest that both between- and within-culture variations in beliefs about fate are associated with different degrees of experienced constraints, given high levels of perceived action–outcome contingency. It seems that fate beliefs serve important adaptive goals in the environments in which they are observed; negotiable fate encourages perseverance in the face of difficulty, whereas conquerable fate enables the motivation to excel by emphasizing personal control over outcomes when constraints are few. Do experiences with constraints and action–outcome contingency truly shape fate beliefs or do they simply coexist?

The Role of Institutions on Negotiable Fate

"Institutions are the rules of the game in society, or more formally . . . the human devised constraints that shape human interaction" (North, 1990). Therefore, to study the impact of constraint experiences on fate beliefs, Au and her colleagues simulated different political, social, and economic institutions through an experimental economics game. In each study, participants were assigned to different conditions that varied in the experience of constraints. Although overall mean differences in negotiable fate did not emerge, across three studies that simulated different types of institutions, the experience of constraints (while perceived action–outcome contingency was high) led to the acquisition of a more agentic construal of negotiable fate (Au et al., 2008). That is, rather than considering negotiable fate and conquerable fate as being unrelated (as participants in low-constraint environments did in the studies described previously), participants who experienced constraints began to see negotiable fate as being akin to conquerable fate. In contrast, the conceptualization of negotiable fate for persons who experienced fewer constraints was similar to the that of the Americans and highly educated individuals mentioned earlier: Conquerable fate and negotiable fate were considered to be unrelated. These findings suggest that the experience of constraints, even after a short 45-minute game, could lead to adaptive changes in the conceptualization of negotiable fate.

THE FUTURE OF LAY THEORIES IN CULTURAL PSYCHOLOGY

This chapter began with an example of cultural practice that was based on specific cultural explanatory theory, specifically that of a happy funeral. This example was picked because it shows how lay theories need not simply fit into the dichotomy of entity/incremental versus fixed/malleable theories. As mentioned at the beginning of this chapter, another name for lay theories is *folk theories*. Folk theories touch on the concept of folk psychology or even folk psychologies. To conclude this discussion of the role of lay theories in cultural psychology, we return to this concept.

The strength of the lay theories approach in cultural psychology is most evident in its ability to look at the effects of pre-existing and sometimes indigenous explanations of human psychology. These culture-bound explanations, taken from idioms or even myths, can often be boiled down to somewhat more abstract theories. These abstract lay theories can often prove to be surprisingly universal. For example, one can consider that Lerner's (1980) *belief in a just world* is a simplification of a great many culture-specific belief systems, such as the Hindu karma concept, but also "the law of cause and effect" found in esoteric Christian traditions, and even arguably within the protestant work ethic (Levy, West, Ramirez, & Karafantis, 2006).

Through this manner of operation, the lay theories perspective is deemed particularly useful and meaningful to cultural psychologists. Specifically, lay theories allow cultural psychologists to simultaneously refine a sort of universal, cross-culturally valid vocabulary of folk theories to describe lay beliefs of human behavior, while at the same time using this vocabulary to explain the at times vast differences in human behaviors and interpretations across cultures. Thus lay theories are able to describe differences in the day-to-day psychological underpinnings of different cultures while emphasizing underlying similarities.

REFERENCES

Au, E. W. M., Chiu, C-y., Zhang, Z-x., Mallorie, L., Chaturvedi, A., Viswanathan, M., et al. (2008). *Negotiating with fate: How its meaning changes as function of experienced constraints.* Unpublished manuscript.

Allport, G. W. (1954). *The nature of prejudice.* Cambridge, MA: Addison-Wesley.

Chao, M. M., Chen, J., Roisman, G., & Hong, Y. (2007). Essentializing race: Implications for bicultural individuals' cognition and physiological reactivity. *Psychological Science, 18*, 341–348.

Chao, M. M., Hong, Y., & Chiu, C-y. (2008, May). *Essentialist belief of race: Its implication to social categorization and intercultural processes.* Poster session presented at the RiSE-UP Research Award symposium of the 20th Annual Convention of Association for Psychological Science. Chicago, IL.

Chiu, C-y., Dweck, C., Tong, J., & Fu, J. (1997). Implicit theories and conceptions of morality. *Journal of Personality and Social Psychology, 73*, 923–940.

Chiu, C-y., & Hong, Y. (1999). Social identification in a political transition: The role of implicit beliefs. *International Journal of Intercultural Relations, 23*, 297–318.

Chiu, C-y., Hong, Y., & Dweck, C. (1997). Lay dispositionism and implicit theories of personality. *Journal of Personality and Social Psychology, 73*, 19–30.

Chiu, C.-y., Morris, M., Hong, Y., & Menon, T. (2000). Motivated cultural cognition: The impact of implicit cultural theories on dispositional attribution varies as a function of need for closure. *Journal of Personality and Social Psychology, 78*, 247–259.

Devos, T., & Banaji, M. (2005). American = White? *Journal of Personality and Social Psychology, 88*, 447–466.

Dweck, C. (1999). *Self-theories: Their role in motivation, personality, and development.* Philadelphia, PA: Psychological Press.

Dweck, C., & Bempechat, J. (1983). Children's theories of intelligence. In S. Paris, G. Olsen, & H. Stevenson (Eds.), *Learning and motivation in the classroom* (pp. 239–256). Hillsdale, NJ: Lawrence Erlbaum.

Dweck, C., Chiu, C-y., & Hong, Y. (1995). Implicit theories and their role in judgments and reactions: A word from two perspectives. *Psychological Inquiry, 6*, 267–285.

Erdley, C., & Dweck, C. (1993). Children's implicit personality theories as predictors of their social judgments. *Child Development, 64*, 863–878.

Feyerabend, F. (1965). Problems of empiricism. In R. G. Colodny (Ed.), *Beyond the edge of certainty: Essays in contemporary science and philosophy* (pp. 145–260). Englewood Cliffs, NJ: Prentice-Hall.

Furnham, A., & Henderson, M. (1983). Lay theories of delinquency. *European Journal of Social Psychology, 13*, 107–120.

Gervey, B., Chiu, C.-y., Hong, Y., & Dweck, C. (1999). Differential use of person information in decisions about guilt versus innocence: The role of implicit theories. *Personality and Social Psychology Bulletin, 25*, 17.

Heider, F. (1958). *The psychology of interpersonal relations.* New York: John Wiley & Sons.

Heine, S. (2001). Self as cultural product: An examination of East Asian and North American selves. *Journal of Personality, 69*, 881–906.

Hong, Y., Chiu, C-y., Lin, D., Wan, W., & Dweck, C. (1999). Implicit theories, attributions, and coping: A meaning system approach. *Journal of Personality and Social Psychology, 77*, 588–599.

Lefcourt, H., Miller, R., Ware, E., & Sherk, D. (1981). Locus of control as a modifier of the relationship between stressors and moods. *Journal of Personality and Social Psychology, 41*, 357–369.

Lerner, M. (1980). *The belief in a just world: A fundamental delusion.* New York: Plenum Press.

Leung, K., & Bond, M. (2004). Social axioms: A model for social beliefs in multicultural perspective. In M. Zanna (Ed.), *Advances in experimental social psychology, Vol. 36* (pp. 119). San Diego, CA: Academic Press.

Levy, S., Plaks, J., & Dweck, C. (1999). Modes of social thought. In S. Chaikin & Y. Trope (Eds.), *Dual-process theories in social psychology* (pp. 179–202). New York: Guilford Press.

Levy, S., West, T., Ramirez, L., & Karafantis, D. (2006). The Protestant work ethic: A lay theory with dual intergroup implications. *Group Processes & Intergroup Relations, 9*, 95–115.

Markus, H., & Kitayama, S. (1991). Culture and the self: Implications for cognition, emotion, and motivation. *Psychological Review, 98*, 224–253.

Miller, J. (1984). Culture and development of everyday social explanation. *Journal of Personality and Social Psychology, 46*, 961–978.

Molden, D., & Dweck, C. (2006). Finding "meaning" in psychology: A lay theories approach to self-regulation, social perception, and social development. *American Psychologist, 61*, 192–203.

Nisbett, R., & Wilson, T. (1977). Telling more than we can know: Verbal reports on mental processes. *Psychological Review, 84*, 231–259.

No, S., Hong, Y., Liao, H., Lee, K., Wood, D., & Chao, M. M. (2008). Lay theory of race affects and moderates Asian Americans' responses toward American culture. *Journal of Personality and Social Psychology, 95*, 991–1004.

North, D. C. (1990). *Institutions, institutional change and economic performance (Political economy of institutions and decisions).* Cambridge, UK: Cambridge University Press.

Pettigrew, T. (1979). The ultimate attribution error: Extending Allport's cognitive analysis of prejudice. *Personality and Social Psychology Bulletin, 5*, 461–476.

Seligman, M. (1975). *Helplessness.* San Francisco, CA: Freeman.

Sidanius, J., & Petrocik, J. (2001). Communal and national identity in a multiethnic state: A comparison of three perspectives. In R. D. Ashmore, L. Jussim, & D. Wilder (Eds.), *Social identity, intergroup conflict and conflict resolution.* Oxford, UK: Oxford University Press.

Spencer-Rodgers, J., Hamilton, D., & Sherman, S. (2007). The central role of enti-tativity in stereotypes of social categories and task groups. *Journal of Personality and Social Psychology, 92*, 369–388.

Stich, S., & Nichols, S. (1992). Folk psychology: Simulation or tacit theory? *Mind & Language, 7*, 35–71.

Su, S., Chiu, C-y., Hong, Y., Leung, K., Peng, K., & Morris, M. (1999). Self-organization and social organization: US and Chinese constructions. In T. R. Tyler, R. M. Kramer, & O. P. John (Eds.), *The psychology of the social self* (pp. 193–222). Mahwah, NJ: Lawrence Erlbaum.

Yzerbyt, V., Corneille, O., & Estrada, C. (2001). The interplay of subjective essen-tialism and entitativity in the formation of stereotypes. *Personality and Social Psychology Review, 5*, 141–155.

3

Culture as Intersubjective Representations of Values

CHING WAN AND CHI-YUE CHIU

To many Americans, the Charters of Freedom of the United States symbolize the striving of a young nation to create a society where human rights, freedom, and independence prevail. To his compatriots, Nelson Mandela's long-time involvement in South Africa's antiapartheid struggle and his eventual leadership in postapartheid South Africa made him a symbol of peace, equality, and freedom. Cultures are often built on a set of values, and these values are often symbolized by important artifacts such as the Charters of Freedom, social figures such as Nelson Mandela, historical events, and traditions of the cultures. The values of a culture and their symbolic embodiments, however, could be representative of the culture only if members of the culture recognize them to be so. Nelson Mandela would not symbolize the ideals of peace, equality, and freedom in South Africa if most South Africans did not recognize him to be symbolic. Human rights, freedom, and independence as embodied by the Charters of Freedom are important in American culture because most Americans know of their historical and cultural significance. To a large extent, the cultural importance of values comes from cultural members' consensual representations of the importance of the values. To understand the values of a culture, it is necessary to understand the consensual representations that members of the culture hold concerning those values.

This chapter is about cultural members' shared knowledge of their culture's value priorities. Values are conceptions of what is desired, preferable, and important in a person's life. They serve as guiding principles for people's behaviors and judgments in various situations and for their evaluation of life experiences (Feather, 1996; Kluckhohn, 1951; Rokeach, 1973; Schwartz & Bilsky, 1987). A culture's values constitute an important part of the culture. They guide the desired and appropriate behaviors of members of the culture.

Research on cultural values in cultural and cross-cultural psychology has identified the values mostly in the form of cultural members' self-endorsement of what is important in their own lives. Cultural values are more than what members of the culture personally endorse, however. Early value researchers presented perceived social importance of values as another meaningful measure of cultural values (Feather, 1975; Rokeach, 1973). This socially shared aspect of cultural values, however, has somehow escaped the spotlight in more recent research on values. Drawing from early value theorists' discussion of cultural values and other research on the sharedness of culture, we present an intersubjective consensus approach to cultural values, which identifies cultural values from collective representations of culture and its values. We contend that this approach is complementary to the common way of identifying cultural values through cultural members' self-endorsed values, and has unique contributions to understanding the connection between cultural values and psychological processes. In the following text, we first discuss the sharedness of a culture's characteristic elements. We then elaborate on the theoretical and methodological importance of the intersubjective consensus approach to cultural values. Finally, we examine the implications of the intersubjective consensus approach in the study of the dynamic interaction between culture and individual psychological processes.

CULTURE'S SHAREDNESS

Culture has always been shared. A majority of American families celebrate Thanksgiving with a family dinner featuring a turkey. Most Americans also know that the American Thanksgiving turkey dinner is a common practice of American families. The Thanksgiving turkey dinner is a part of American culture because most Americans either engage in the practice or know that it is a practice shared in the culture. Similarly, the Christian cross is a symbol of Christianity and Jesus' sacrifice for mankind because most Christians recognize the symbolic meaning of the cross in Christianity. Artifacts, rituals, practices, attitudes, values, and beliefs can all be a part of a culture. They constitute a culture's building blocks, however, only when they are socially shared in some way instead of being held by only a few persons within a large collective.

The sharedness of cultural elements has been discussed extensively among culture theorists across disciplines (e.g., Brumann, 1999; Keesing, 1981; Sperber, 1996; Triandis, 1995), yet, despite the common conceptualization of culture as shared, there are multiple meanings of culture's

sharedness as different theorists focus on different aspects of this sharedness. To some theorists, culture is shared among a collective of people as
they engage in common behaviors and practices and hold similar personal
values and beliefs (Brumann, 1999; Triandis, 1996). To some others, culture
is shared as the collective of people share similar symbolic representations of
reality (D'Andrade, 1987; Geertz, 1973; Pelto & Pelto, 1975; Romney, Boyd,
Moore, Batchelder, & Brazill, 1996). Put succinctly by Keesing (1981), culture is a shared system of competence among a group of people. This shared
system of competence involves a person's "theory of what his fellows know,
believe and mean, of the code being followed, the game being played"
(Keesing, 1981, p. 58). Thus, for any single behavior, attitude, belief, or
value, one meaning of cultural sharedness is the extent to which members
of the culture engage in the same behavior, hold the same attitude and belief,
or endorse the same value. Another meaning of cultural sharedness is the
extent to which members of the culture commonly represent something
as defining the culture. Whichever meaning of sharedness one adheres to,
cultural elements are not distributed perfectly and evenly among the collective (Barth, 2002; Brumann, 1999). Few, if any, elements of a culture
are completely shared among members of that culture. Different cultural
elements differ in the extent to which they are shared, as some are more
widely shared than others. The most widely shared elements of a culture are
often the most central characteristics of the culture.

As part of culture, cultural values are often central to the definition and
practice of a culture because they are widely shared in the culture. Culturally
important values are ubiquitous, as they manifest themselves in a multitude
of social situations and are linked to a lot of practices in which people and
the society engage. American culture's valuing of effort and optimism can
be observed by people working hard and having fun, and by the dominance
of icons, in the form of cultural sayings, entertainment, advertisement,
and the education system, which stand for the importance of striving for
a better future (du Bois, 1955). As with other cultural elements, cultural
values can be shared as members of the culture hold similar values or similar
representations of what is important in the culture. It is to these meanings
of value sharedness that we now turn.

OBJECTIVE SHAREDNESS OF VALUES

Values can be shared in a culture as members of the culture hold similar
personal values. Every individual has a personal value system that consists
of the individual's personal evaluations of the relative importance of a set of

interrelated values (Rohan, 2000; Rohan & Zanna, 2001). Although no two individuals have identical personal value systems, there is a certain level of overlap between the personal value systems of members of the same culture. Importantly, this within-culture overlap is not just a random occurrence. Instead, the similarity of personal value systems of members of the same culture is a result of both the common basic human concerns and the common eco-cultural environment that the cultural members are exposed to, which provides a socialization milieu that fosters the development and internalization of certain culture-specific values. Thus, the overlap in cultural members' personal value systems can be used as a meaningful indication of the culture's value system. With a representative sample of members of the culture, one can identify the most important values of the culture through the consensus in members' self-endorsed values. The values that most members of the culture endorse can be considered to be the most important values of the culture. This approach of basing cultural value importance on the actual self-importance (Wan, Chiu, Tam, et al., 2007) of value provides an indicator of what values are objectively shared among members of a culture.

Identifying cultural values based on cultural members' personal value endorsement represents one of the most typical ways of studying cultural values in the literature. By aggregating the value priorities of a sample of people from a culture, researchers are able to estimate the values that represent that culture. The methodology involves asking participants to indicate their self-endorsement of various values by selecting the values that are most important to the self; by rating the importance, desirability, or their agreement to the values on a Likert-type scale; or by ranking the relative importance of the values. Then, the percentage of participants who endorsed the values or the mean endorsement of the values by the sample of participants is used as an indicator of the cultural importance of the values (e.g., Schwartz & Sagie, 2000; Triandis & Gelfand, 1998; see Conway & Schaller, 1998). With this method, researchers have been successful in mapping the similarities and differences in the value systems of cultures around the world using matched cultural samples (Hofstede, 1980) and representative or near-representative national samples (Inglehart, 1997; Schwartz & Bardi, 2001).

Despite its usefulness in past research on cultural values, several issues challenge the use of objectively shared values as the sole indicator of a culture's important values. First, the characterization of cultures based on cultural members' personal values does not necessarily fit the expectations of cultural experts (Oyserman, Coon, & Kemmelmeier, 2002; Peng, Nisbett,

& Wong, 1997). Either cultural experts have a much biased (and thus, inaccurate) view of the cultures studied, or the measure of cultural values based on personal value importance does not capture all there is to the culture's values.

Second, to accurately reflect the values of a culture, one would need a representative sample of members of the culture. This sample can be found if one is interested in a culture that is clearly bounded by a delineated population and has access to a large enough random sample from the population. Not all cultures as shared knowledge traditions (Barth, 2002) are bounded by a clearly delineated population, however. Christianity, for instance, does not have a well-defined physical population boundary. With the increasingly dynamic definition of culture in the field beyond shared nationality, ethnicity, and language, it becomes hard, if not impossible, to identify the population for a culture.

Third, with increasing globalization, more and more people are becoming bicultural or even multicultural. As these individuals are exposed to more than one culture, they are often considered to have been "contaminated" in the study of a culture. Their self-endorsed value responses are likely a combination of the values of the multiple cultures that they are exposed to instead of being predominantly of a single culture. Also, research has shown that multicultural individuals' responses in a particular context depend on the cultural frame that is salient to them (Hong, Morris, Chiu, & Benet-Martínez, 2000) and the perceived compatibility of the multiple cultures (Benet-Martínez, Leu, Lee, & Morris, 2002). The objective sharedness approach to cultural values would have to exclude these individuals because their responses cannot be representative of one culture.

Finally, as discussed earlier, culture involves both the shared practices and values held by members of the culture and the symbolic representations of reality that are distributed among members of the culture. Identifying values through objective sharedness taps the first part of culture as shared personal characteristics and experiences but not the second part of culture as shared symbolic representations. Although the two definitions of culture should have some overlap as they are, after all, descriptions of the same culture, evidence also suggests that cultural members' self-characteristics are not necessarily the same as their perceptions of the culture (e.g., Prentice & Miller, 1993; Terracciano et al., 2005). All in all, to more fully capture a culture's value system, one needs to consider an additional way of measuring cultural value importance that can complement the current common practice.

INTERSUBJECTIVE CULTURAL VALUES

Focusing on culture as shared knowledge representations, cultural values can be identified through people's perceptions of the importance of values to the culture. This approach, with a focus on the perceived cultural importance (Wan, Chiu, Tam, et al., 2007) of values is called the *intersubjective consensus approach* (Wan, Chiu, Peng, & Tam, 2007). Intersubjective consensus examines cultural members' common representations of what is considered to be important and desirable in the culture. When members collectively believe that a value is important to a culture, the value has high intersubjective importance and can be considered to be a core value that defines the culture. Different from the conventional approach to cultural values, which is based on objective sharedness, the intersubjective consensus approach does not concern cultural members' self-concept or personal values. Rather, the main question is what cultural members commonly know about the culture's values. Therefore, instead of asking cultural members to report their self-endorsed values, the intersubjective consensus approach asks cultural members to report their estimates of the endorsement of values by the culture or a typical member of the culture.

The intersubjective consensus approach to cultural values is based on the existence of intersubjectivity among members of a culture. In using cultural members' knowledge about the culture as an indicator of the culturally important values, the assumption is that cultural members share meaningful common representations of the values that are important to specific social others (Feather, 1975; Rokeach, 1973), to the generalized other (Mead, 1956; Terry & Hogg, 1996), and to the culture. As such, cultural members not only share cultural representations, they also hold the belief that these representations are mutually shared by other members of the culture (D'Andrade, 1987). Early value research asserted that both people's personal beliefs about what is desirable to themselves and the values that people attribute to reference others and social groups are meaningful, valid measures of values (Feather, 1975; Rokeach, 1973). People's representations of the value importance in a social group that they belong to are indications of the social group's value system (Rohan, 2000). Similarly, collective representations of value importance to a culture can be used to identify the core values of a culture.

Within a culture, the cultural value representations that individual cultural members hold have a certain level of consensus as members of a cultural collective share common cultural experience and participate in collective meaning construction, negotiation, and maintenance. Individuals engage in social interactions with others who share the same culture, both at the individual and the collective levels. These interactions range from direct communication between two or a small group of individuals, to dialogues between groups of individuals, to social discourse engaged within social institutions and in the mass media. During these interactions, common grounds of reference are negotiated (Clark & Brennan, 1991) and meanings are socially shared (Resnick, Levine, & Teasley, 1991; Thompson & Fine, 1999). Individuals not only receive information about what the culture is about, they also participate directly and indirectly in the creation and propagation of what is important in the culture. Through these communication and discourse processes, collective representations of the culture evolve (Blumer, 1969; Harton & Bourgeois, 2004; Mead, 1934; Moscovici, 1984) and are repeatedly transmitted (McIntyre, Lyons, Clark, & Kashima, 2004; Sperber, 1996). These collective representations then serve as the basis of common ground for further social interactions and meaning negotiations within the culture (Krauss & Chiu, 1998; Lau, Lee, & Chiu, 2004). The outcome of this iterative process is a set of common representations of the culture held by most members of the culture.

In several ways, the intersubjective consensus approach complements the conventional approach in identifying the values that are central to a culture. First, it looks at culture from a shared representations perspective. It draws attention to the part of a culture that is created and maintained through the dynamic interactions among individuals who share some common cultural experiences and participate in the coconstruction of cultural meanings. Second, by focusing on representations of culture, it provides a tool for studying the role of cultural values on psychological processes such as cultural identification and normative behaviors beyond representative samples of a culture. As with the measure of a representative cultural sample's personal values, that sample's intersubjective representations of the values of the culture would provide a valid measure of the values important to the culture. At the same time, a nonrepresentative sample's perceived cultural ratings would provide meaningful information for cultural research. With a nonrepresentative sample, researchers can understand how a particular culture is perceived by a particular social group within the culture. Such understanding is especially useful when the goal of research is to study different groups in the same culture, the interrelations among the groups, and the interactions between the groups and the culture. For example, African Americans and European Americans might have different views on the values that define American culture. When asked about the importance of values to American culture, their answers would reflect these differences. These differences would then be useful in studying inter-group dynamics within a culture. Third, people's psychological processes are often driven by their representations of the culture instead of by the actual characteristics of the culture (Wan, Chiu, Tam, et al., 2007). The core cultural values identified through the intersubjective consensus approach should theoretically be more closely related to these psychological processes than should the values identified through cultural members' personal value priorities.

CONGRUENCE BETWEEN OBJECTIVE AND INTERSUBJECTIVE VALUES

Both of the approaches that we mentioned earlier in this chapter are valid approaches for identifying a culture's core values. As both are indicators of the same culture, there should be a certain level of overlap between the core cultural values identified through the two approaches. Individuals carry their personal values to social situations, and these personal values might affect their behaviors, perceptions, and their interactions with others. As individuals interact with other members of the culture, they would have insights on the personal values that others in the culture hold. These insights would then contribute to the collective representations of the culture's value system. Thus, it is reasonable to expect that the values that most members of the culture strongly endorse would also be the values that most members of the culture believe to be important in the culture.

Evidence from empirical research suggests, however, that the self-characteristics of a collective do not necessarily match the characteristics that members of the collective perceive of that collective. In social psy-chology, the phenomenon of pluralistic ignorance is a good example of the discrepancy between collectively shared conceptions of behaviors and individuals' actual attitudes toward the behaviors (Miller & Prentice, 1994). In one study, college students were asked about their personal attitudes toward drinking and their perceptions of the average student's attitude toward drinking (Prentice & Miller, 1993). The results showed that the students' perceptions of other students' attitudes on drinking was much more positive than their reported self-attitudes, indicating a discrepancy between perceived and actual norms. In personality research, a recent study has found much discrepancy between self-report personality ratings and perceived cultural ratings (Terracciano et al., 2005). In the study, partici-pants from 49 cultures were asked to rate the typical member of their own culture on the Big Five personality dimensions. These perceived personality ratings were then aggregated across participants within each culture and compared to the aggregated self-report personality ratings of members in the culture. Both within and across cultures, the perceived personality ratings and the actual self-report personality ratings either did not correlate at all or correlated only weakly. Finally, in a study on cultural values, we asked college students to rate the importance of the 56 Schwartz values (Schwartz, 1992) to themselves and to an average member of their culture. We found a positive but far from perfect correlation between the importance of values based on participants' self-ratings and the perceived cultural importance of the values (Wan, Chiu, Tam, et al., 2007).

The degree of congruence between a collective's self-characteristics and its perceived collective characteristics also varies, sometimes showing a close match, other times showing a much stronger mismatch. For example, in our own research, we have examined the congruence between the self-endorsed personal attributes of men and women and their perceptions of the importance of these attributes to their own and the opposite gender (Wan & Chiu, 2005). The correlation between self-endorsement and perceived own-gender endorsement of the attributes was much stronger for women than for men. Interestingly, there was a higher congruence between men's perception of women's attribute endorsement and women's actual self-endorsement than between women's perception of men's attribute endorsement and men's actual self-endorsement. In a recent study, Fischer (2006) examined the level of congruence between self-report and perceived cultural values and found varying degrees of congruence across the 10 Schwartz value types. The results showed that among the value types, values associated with embeddedness and affective autonomy had the highest degree of self-cultural perception congruence.

Cultural values identified through cultural members' self-endorsement and perceived cultural endorsement may or may not be the same. For researchers to appropriately use the two approaches to identify the core values of a culture, it is pertinent to understand when cultural characteristics identified from the two approaches might have a higher congruence. Unfortunately, not much research has directly addressed this issue. Based on the limited relevant research and the conceptual distinctions between the two approaches, we offer some possible factors in the following text for further examination in future research.

Representativeness of Sample

Assume that there exists a certain level of congruence between cultural members' self-endorsed values and their collective representations of the culture's values. This congruency would most likely be detected empirically when representative samples of members of the culture are used.

A measure of a collective's values based on aggregating the personal value systems of individuals of the collective provides a description of the values actually endorsed by the individuals who have responded to the value measure. When a representative sample of the cultural members is used, the measure would be an accurate reflection of the culture's value priorities as objectively shared. The representative sample can come from a large enough random sample from the population or arguably from prototypic members of the culture who are supposed to embody the widely shared values of the culture (cf. the use of grade school teachers in Schwartz, 1992). When a nonrepresentative sample of the cultural group is used, the values identified would represent the value priorities of only the subgroup being sampled. For example, because of limitations of resources and sample accessibility, one common practice in cultural and cross-cultural psychology research is to recruit college students from the most developed parts of a country or region to respond to questions about their personality and personal values. These responses are then used to give researchers insights about the national or regional culture. Such a practice provides a biased representation of the culture because it confounds the national or regional culture of interest with the cultures of the social groups to which the college students belong, such as the college culture and the culture of middle-class, highly educated young adults.

Intersubjective consensus, in contrast, does not confound the target culture being studied with other cultures as participants are asked specifically to indicate their representations of the target culture. People do not need to internalize a culture to be members of that culture and to possess knowledge about that culture. Thus, even nonrepresentative members of a culture would be able to tap their knowledge of the culture and provide value-importance ratings concerning the target culture. Although different subgroups in a culture might have different representations of the culture's values, the representations would also have similar elements because of joint participation in cultural processes common to the subgroups. These similar elements are likely to be those most central to the culture as a result of repeated transmission (Sperber, 1996). No prior study has directly compared nonrepresentative and representative samples' representations of the same culture. Based on the process through which culture is transmitted, however, we would expect both samples to have similar representations of at least the most central elements of the culture.

With a representative sample, both cultural values identified from personal value endorsement and perceived cultural endorsement would be indicative of the culture's values, and thus would show higher correspondence empirically. With a nonrepresentative sample, however, the sample's perceived cultural endorsement would likely provide a less biased measure of the target culture's values than of its personal value endorsement, resulting in a lower correspondence between the two types of value measure.

Salience of Culture

An individual's self consists of multiple parts (see Chapter 7, this volume). The collective self (Brewer & Gardner, 1996; Sedikides & Brewer, 2001) or the social self (Turner, Oakes, Haslam, & McGarty, 1994) refers to the part that is related to the individual's membership in a social group. From the perspective of social identity theories (Hogg, 2003; Tajfel & Turner, 1986; Turner, Hogg, Oakes, Reicher, & Wetherell, 1987), the prototypic characteristics of the collective provide the collective self with its content (Hogg, 2003), which becomes salient and influential in an individual's psychological processes when membership in the collective becomes salient. According to the self-categorization theory (Turner et al., 1987), situational contrast makes certain group boundary and thus social identity salient. The salience of one's group membership then triggers the process of depersonalization, in which the social self instead of the personal self comes to the fore and the individual sees the self as an interchangeable member of the group. An outcome of depersonalization is self-stereotyping, in which the individual sees the self as endorsing the prototypic characteristics of the group (Hogg & Turner, 1987).

Cultural identity is not exactly the same as social identity as culture is defined in terms of shared knowledge traditions (Hong, Wan, No, & Chiu, 2007) and not all social groups have a shared knowledge tradition. Cultural identity, however, does involve membership in a cultural group. As such, certain principles presented by social identity theories would also be applicable to the cultural self. It is possible that when cultural membership is salient, the same process of self-stereotyping would occur, so that cultural members would endorse the core values perceived to be defining of the culture more than they would when the cultural membership is not salient. This self-stereotyping process would then result in the values that individuals personally endorse to shift toward the values that are collectively perceived to be the most important to the culture. The outcome of such a process is a higher congruence between the personally endorsed values and the perceived culturally endorsed values.

Internalization of Culture

Measuring cultural value importance through the objective sharedness of the values presents the values that are personally endorsed by members of the culture. Cultural value importance based on intersubjective consensus presents what people know about the culture. These two measures of value importance would have high congruence if representations of the culture are turned into self-representations. In other words, when most members of the culture have strongly internalized the culture, knowledge about the culture's value system would become the members' personal value systems. As a result, the cultural value system identified from aggregates of cultural members' personal value systems would be virtually the same as the cultural value system identified from aggregates of cultural members' intersubjective representations of the culture (see Chapter 7, this volume).

An implicit assumption in research on culture and self (Markus & Kitayama, 1991; Triandis, 1989) is that culture is internalized as part of cultural members' self-concepts, so that by understanding the self-concepts of members of a culture, one can understand the important characteristics of the culture. Individuals differ, however, in the extent to which they identify with a culture and internalize elements of the culture as part of the self. Culture does not mill out clones of the prototypical cultural member. Rather, the cultural self is the product of a negotiated process of cultural identification, in which the individual plays an active role in choosing his or her self-position in relation to the widely shared knowledge tradition of the culture (Herman, 2001; Nussbaum, 2000; also see Chapter 7, this volume). Thus, in any culture, there coexist individuals who strongly identify with the culture and endorse the defining elements of the culture and individuals who do not include the culture's knowledge tradition in their self-representations, placing the self at the margin of the culture.

Recent application of the self-determination theory in cultural psychology research has dealt directly with the issue of differential internalization of culture. According to the theory (Ryan & Deci, 2003), people have knowledge about the shared norms in the culture; however, these norms regulate people's behavior at different levels of internalization, going from external regulation, introjection, and identification to integration. At a low level of internalization, people's behaviors conform to cultural norms because of external rewards and pressure. At a high level of internalization, people behave autonomously according to their self-endorsed values and beliefs, which are the internalized cultural norms. Recent empirical research (Chirkov, Ryan, Kim, & Kaplan, 2003; Chirkov, Ryan, & Willness, 2005) based on predictions of self-determination theory has shown that cultural members across and within cultures differ in the extent to which they actually internalize elements of the culture as a part of the self. Also, when the need for autonomy is supported, there is a higher level of internalization. The implication of this line of research for the current discussion is that people can hold the same intersubjective representations of a culture's values, but they do not necessarily need to endorse them. Whereas a high level of congruence between objectively and intersubjectively shared values indicates a high level of internalization of the culture, a low level of congruence indicates the dissociation between the culture and cultural members' personal values.

Type of Values

Research has also suggested that not all intersubjectively represented cultural values are equally easy to be internalized. Some values are more difficult to be internalized than others because of potential conflict with basic human needs or a lack of emphasis of the values in the socialization process. As level of internalization affects the congruence observed for cultural members' personal values and the collectively represented cultural values, we would expect a higher level of congruence when the cultural values are in line with basic human needs and are emphasized in the socialization process.

Self-determination theory predicts that certain cultural elements are easier to internalize than others. Specifically, those cultural elements that support the three basic human needs – relatedness, competence, and autonomy – should be more easily internalized than those that are in conflict or incompatible with the fulfillment of these basic needs. For example, a focus of verticality, which requires individuals to submit to authority and status difference, might restrict the fulfillment of the autonomy need (Chirkov et al., 2003, 2005). Thus, values focusing on verticality would have a lower level of internalization. As a result, in a culture that is vertical, people might believe that the culture sees verticality values such as competition and power as important, but they might not strongly endorse the values personally. Thus, when the actual endorsement and perceived cultural endorsement of these values are compared, there would be a large discrepancy between the two (see Chapter 7, this volume).

In another study, Fischer (2006) examined the degree of overlap between self value ratings and ratings of perceived cultural values on Schwartz value dimensions. It was predicted that values that are the foci of socialization would be more easily internalized and thus show a higher level of congruence between objectively and intersubjectively shared value importance.

For example, parents as socialization agents would be very concerned about their children's ability to fit into the sociocultural environment and maintain appropriate relationships with other individuals and social groups. This concern for social relationships should lead to the socialization and internalization of embeddedness values. Also, parents would be concerned about the socialization of appropriate emotional display rules of their culture, which would result in a high level of internalization of affective autonomy values. For values that are less socialized within the family, such as intellectual autonomy values, there would be a lower level of internalization. To test these predictions, Fischer (2006) correlated the self-referent value ratings and the culture-referent value ratings of 10 cultural samples. As expected, the correlations were strongest for embeddedness and affective autonomy values and weakest for intellectual autonomy and egalitarian values.

All in all, there is some evidence suggesting that not all values are equally internalized. The above-mentioned research has provided some possible reasons for it. Some values are more easily internalized then others, possibly because they fulfill some basic human needs or they are the foci of socialization and are important to an individual's survival as a competent member of the culture. More rigorous tests involving the predicted process variables are needed for more reliable evidence of these possibilities.

UTILITY OF INTERSUBJECTIVE VALUES

A redirection of research from values that cultural members personally endorse to values that are collectively represented as culturally important is a theoretically fruitful effort. As the intersubjective consensus approach to cultural values identifies cultural values from a source distinctly different from that of the conventional approach based on objective value sharedness, it also has utility distinct from the conventional approach. Thus, the intersubjective consensus approach adds to and would be useful in extending extant research on the dynamics between culture and individual psychological processes. In this section, we discuss several such utilities.

Characterizing Culture

Cross-cultural and cultural psychology has produced much well-conducted research by examining the personal characteristics of members of different cultures. In recent years, however, researchers have questioned the validity of this approach in characterizing cultures. In a meta-analysis on individualism and collectivism (Oyserman et al., 2002), it was found that existing evidence on cross-cultural differences in individualism and collectivism is not as consistent as researchers would like to believe. For example, although it is commonly believed that Japanese persons are collectivistic whereas Americans are individualistic, the results of the meta-analysis suggest that Japanese persons are not more collectivistic than Americans whereas Americans are not more individualistic than Hispanics and African Americans. Also, the magnitude of cultural differences in individualism and collectivism is larger in some domains than in others. As most measures of individualism and collectivism that have been used are based on respondents' reports of their personal agreement to statements and values and, more generally, their personal characteristics, the meta-analysis results suggest that using self-endorsement measures of individualism–collectivism in cross-cultural comparisons may not generate results that are consistent with the field's long-held beliefs of cultural differences. On a similar note, results with a Schwartz value survey have also shown low agreement between conventional self value ratings and expert's ratings of the importance of the values to the cultures (Peng et al., 1997).

The validity of using aggregates of cultural members' self value ratings as measures of the culture's values has been challenged because of difficulties in getting a pure measure of self values. Heine and others (Heine, Lehman, Peng, & Greenholtz, 2002; Peng et al., 1997) have argued that measures of self-endorsed values are confounded with social comparison processes. Specifically, when asked about their personal values, people often compare themselves with others in their social group in making judgments. This reference group effect would lead to respondents in individualistic and collectivistic cultures underreporting their levels of individualism and collectivism, respectively. According to these researchers, to accurately measure a culture's true characteristics, one would need to minimize the reference group effect. Thus, cultural members' representations about the culture and other members of the culture are considered as *noise* that needs to be minimized in measuring culture.

With the intersubjective consensus approach to culture, cultural members' representations of the culture are turned from noise to be minimized to the focus of research and, in doing so, offer an alternative but valid way of measuring culture. Responses concerning knowledge about the culture should be less affected by the process of comparing the self to a reference group. Instead, tapping people's representations of the culture might generate cultural characteristics that are more consistent with expectations from cultural experts. In one of our studies (Wan, Chiu, Tam, et al., 2007), we compared American college students' intersubjective representations of the values endorsed by Americans and Hong Kong Chinese and the actual self-endorsement of these values by American and Hong Kong Chinese college students. The common expectation in the field is that Americans are more individualistic and Hong Kong Chinese are more collectivistic. We found that the distinction between American and Hong Kong Chinese was more consistent with the common expectation when it was examined through intersubjective ratings rather than personal value ratings.

As mentioned before, culture consists of more than just cultural members' shared personal characteristics. It also consists of the shared symbolic representations that members of the culture hold. Culture as characterized by the two definitions may or may not be the same. In either case, for a more complete picture, it is important for researchers to examine both when trying to characterize a culture.

Unique Association with Psychological Processes

If cultural values as objectively shared and those as intersubjectively shared completely overlap, then both approaches would offer the same accounts of a culture's value priorities and be similarly associated with psychological processes. As mentioned before, however, the overlap between objectively shared values and intersubjectively shared values is often imperfect and sometimes almost nonexistent. Unless every important cultural element is completely internalized, the two approaches would each tap a distinct aspect of a culture. Thus, intersubjectivity as a definition of cultural values should have unique associations with psychological processes beyond those of the objectively shared values.

Predicting Behavior

One major interest in cultural psychology is to understand the behaviors that people in a culture might engage in as a result of the influence of the culture. Much effort has been dedicated to documenting cultural differences in various behaviors, such as choice (e.g., Kim & Drolet, 2003), resource allocation (e.g., Leung & Iwawaki, 1988), parenting (e.g., Keller, Borke, Yovsi, Lohaus, & Jensen, 2005), conformity (e.g., Bond & Smith, 1996), and interpersonal communication (e.g., Holtgraves & Yang, 1992). These cultural differences in behavior are often linked to the value orientations that characterize the different cultures, most notably individualism and collectivism (Triandis, 1995).

Whether these cultural orientations are objectively or intersubjectively shared has important implications in understanding the role of culture in behavior. If the cultural value orientations are objectively shared, then most members of the culture actually endorse the orientations themselves. Thus, the cultural behaviors that they are demonstrating would be a result of them following their own personal values. In contrast, if the cultural value orientations are intersubjectively shared, then they are the collectively represented norm that exists in cultural members as knowledge about the culture's values instead of self values. In this case, the display of cultural behavior would be a result of people conforming to the perceived cultural norms. These two sources of influence are likely to have unique predictive effects on behaviors with the strength of independent predictive power varying according to the situation.

In a line of research based on the theory of reasoned action (Fishbein & Ajzen, 1975) and the theory of planned behavior (Ajzen, 1991), researchers have found that although personal attitudes predict behavioral intention and behaviors, the perceived norms of the salient social group with which people strongly identify also play a role in affecting intention and behavior (Smith & Terry, 2003; Terry & Hogg, 1996). In one study on women's sun-protective behaviors (Terry & Hogg, 1996), it was found that personal attitudes and perceived group norms of sun-protective behaviors have distinct predictive effects on intentions to engage in sun-protective behaviors. Interestingly, the effect of personal attitudes on behavioral intentions was more pronounced for people who weakly identify with the reference group of friends and peers at the university, whereas the effect of perceived group norms was more pronounced for people who strongly identify with the reference group. Thus, people's behaviors are not always driven by their personal characteristics. Their perceptions of what is accepted and desirable in the social group salient to them and their identification with the social group also play a part in influencing their behavior.

Regarding the relationship between values and behavior, Bardi and Schwartz (2003) examined the correlation between personal endorsement of the 10 Schwartz (1992) value types and behavior. Values with the strongest correlation between personal value endorsement and behavior were tradition and stimulation; values with the weakest correlation were benevolence, security, conformity, and achievement. Although there was no direct test, the researchers suggested that values important to a culture would have stronger normative pressure for the display of behavior consistent with the value, which would result in a weaker correlation between personal values and behavior. In a more direct comparison of the relation between self and perceived cultural values and behaviors, Fischer (2006) correlated the self-reference and group-reference ratings of the 10 Schwartz (1992) value types with participants' engagement in value-related behaviors. The results showed that the values differ in the extent to which their self-referenced and group-referenced ratings are related to their corresponding behaviors. The results of the study also showed that self-referenced value ratings are more closely related to universalism-related behaviors, whereas culture-referenced ratings are more closely related to conservation-related behaviors. Such a relationship between values and behavior was again explained by the strength of norms, in that universalism-related behaviors are possibly less strongly related to social norms than are conservation-related behaviors.

The studies just mentioned point to the possibility that some behaviors in some situations are more influenced by representations of the culture than by self characteristics. No known research, however, has directly examined the factors that lead to representations of culture being better predictors of behavior than self characteristics, and vice versa. One possibility is the situational goal that people have to differentiate the self and be unique from others versus the desire to experience belongingness in the cultural group. When people have the need to differentiate, they might refrain from conforming to collectively represented cultural values, and instead behave according to their personal values. In contrast, when they have the need to belong, they might behave according to collectively represented cultural values. Further research on this issue would benefit the field's understanding of the relationship between culture and behavior.

Explaining Cultural Identification

Theory and research on social identity have presented the argument that social identification and endorsement of the widely shared prototypic characteristics of the social group are closely related, as people self-stereotype as a result of identifying with a social group (Hogg & Turner, 1987) and construct their social identity based on the widely shared characteristics of the social group (Duveen, 2001). Extending this argument, identification with a cultural group is related to the endorsement of the culture's core values (e.g., Feather, 1994; Gouveia, de Albuquerque, Clemente, & Espinosa, 2002; Heaven, 1999; Jetten, Postmes, & McAuliffe, 2002). To the extent that both value importance by objective sharedness and value importance by intersubjective cultural representations are valid indicators of the core values of a culture, people's endorsement of both sets of values should be related to their identification with the culture. As with the prediction of behavior, however, the question remains as to whether the intersubjective consensus

approach has additional utility in identifying core cultural values that are
related to cultural identification.

To address this question, in a set of studies (Wan, Chiu, Tam, et al.,
2007), we examined the relationship between people's endorsement of the
core cultural values identified by both approaches and their identification
with the culture. We identified a set of core cultural values based on the
actual self-importance of the values in the sample and another set of core
cultural values based on the perceived cultural importance of the values.
We then correlated participants' own endorsement of each of the two sets
of values with their cultural identification. The results showed that participants' personal endorsement of values identified from perceived cultural
importance predicted identification with the culture above and beyond
the effect of their personal endorsement of values identified from actual
self-importance. Also, in a longitudinal study, we found that university
freshmen's identification with the university student culture at the end of
their first semester was predicted by their endorsement of values with high
intersubjective importance but not values with high objective importance
at the beginning of that semester. Thus, values identified through intersubjective consensus have a unique contribution to the process of cultural
identification above and beyond the effect of values identified through the
conventional approach.

Study of Multiple Cultures

Intersubjective representations of cultural values are useful not only for
examining monocultural individuals' representations of their own culture,
but also for understanding multicultural individuals' representations of the
cultures to which they belong. When two or more cultures are studied at the
same time, the conventional approach to cultural values based on cultural
members' personal value endorsement requires representative samples of
monocultural individuals from all the cultures studied to provide information on the cultural value systems of the multiple cultures. This approach
would not work when multicultural individuals are the target of study,
as it is not feasible to ask the multicultural individuals to report on their
personal values as monocultural members of one of the multiple cultures.
In contrast, the intersubjective consensus approach allows researchers to
understand how the values of the multiple cultures are represented within
the same group of people who have experience in and thus possess knowledge of the multiple cultures.

More importantly, the multiple cultures might interact to influence
the psychological processes of multicultural individuals. The intercultural

dynamics in the society would result in unique representations of the similarities and differences in the value systems of the multiple cultures. The psychological processes of multicultural individuals are often affected by their representations of the interaction outcomes of the multiple cultures instead of a single culture (e.g., bicultural identity integration, Benet-Martínez et al., 2002). Such processes can be captured by the intersubjective consensus approach. Identifying values of the multiple cultures by the value endorsement of monocultural persons belonging to one of the multiple cultures would not be able to capture this product of interaction between the cultures. As an example, we conducted research on the cultural identities of members of nested cultural groups (Wan, Chiu, Peng, et al., 2007). Participants provided their representations of the value priorities of the two cultures. Based on these intersubjective value ratings, we identified values with highly different perceived cultural importance. We found that participants' endorsement of these values that differentiate the two cultures was related to their differentiation of the two cultural identities.

Such a link between intersubjective representations of multiple cultures and multiple cultural identities has implications for the acculturation process. It is possible that identification with host versus heritage culture in acculturation is a function of how different the two cultures' value systems are intersubjectively represented to be, and how closely aligned the acculturating individual's personal values are with the intersubjectively represented values of the cultures. Integration of heritage and host cultures may be more difficult when the two cultures are represented to have different values and when the self holds values that are closely aligned with one of the two cultures' intersubjectively represented values (see Chapter 12, this volume).

CONCLUDING REMARKS

In this chapter, we have introduced the intersubjective consensus approach as an alternative, complementary approach to the conventional approach in the field of the study of cultural values. Intersubjective consensus focuses on the common representations that members of a culture have concerning the culture. Part of this shared representation is based on the actual values being endorsed by members of the culture; however, a significant part of it is based on the product of a dynamic, iterative process of meaning negotiation that occurs among cultural members at different levels of discourse. Due to the influence of the meaning-negotiation process in the generation of intersubjective representations, it is often the case that there is imperfect correspondence between cultural value importance based on intersubjective consensus and that based on cultural members' personal value endorsement. This imperfect correspondence provides a window for a fuller understanding of cultural values and their role in psychological processes. We do not argue that the intersubjective consensus approach is superior to the conventional approach in the study of cultural values, as both approaches have their merits and limitations. Although the intersubjective consensus approach to cultural values does not undermine the value of the conventional approach, it fills a gap in the extant research by addressing a part of culture that has not received its due attention in the field.

REFERENCES

Ajzen, I. (1991). The theory of planned behavior. *Organizational Behavior and Human Decision Processes, 50,* 179–211.

Bardi, A., & Schwartz, S. H. (2003). Values and behavior: Strength and structure of relations. *Personality and Social Psychology Bulletin, 29,* 1207–1220.

Barth, F. (2002). An anthropology of knowledge. *Current Anthropology, 43,* 1–18.

Benet-Martínez, V., Leu, J., Lee, F., & Morris, M. (2002). Negotiating biculturalism: Cultural frame-switching in biculturals with 'oppositional' vs. 'compatible' cultural identities. *Journal of Cross-Cultural Psychology, 33,* 492–516.

Blumer, H. (1969). *Symbolic interactionism: Perspective and method.* Berkeley, CA: University of California Press.

Bond, R., & Smith, P. B. (1996). Culture and conformity: A meta-analysis of studies using Asch's (1952b, 1956) line judgment task. *Psychological Bulletin, 119,* 111–137.

Brewer, M. B., & Gardner, W. (1996). Who is this "we"? Levels of collective identity and self representations. *Journal of Personality and Social Psychology, 71,* 83–93.

Brumann, C. (1999). Writing for culture: Why a successful concept should not be discarded. *Current Anthropologist, 40,* S1–S13.

Chirkov, V., Ryan, R. M., Kim, Y., & Kaplan, U. (2003). Differentiating autonomy from individualism and independence: A self-determination theory perspective on internalization of cultural orientations and well-being. *Journal of Personality and Social Psychology, 84,* 97–110.

Chirkov, V. I., Ryan, R. M., & Willness, C. (2005). Cultural context and psychological needs in Canada and Brazil: Testing a self-determination approach to the internalization of cultural practices, identity, and well-being. *Journal of Cross-Cultural Psychology, 36,* 423–443.

Clark, H. H., & Brennan, S. E. (1991). Grounding in communication. In L. B. Resnick, J. M. Levine, & S. D. Teasley (Eds.), *Perspectives on socially shared cognition* (pp. 127–149). Washington, DC: American Psychological Association.

Conway, L. G., III, & Schaller, M. (1998). Methods for the measurement of consensual beliefs within groups. *Group Dynamics: Theory, Research, & Practice, 2,* 241–252.

D'Andrade, R. (1987). A folk model of the mind. In D. Holland & N. Quinn (Eds.), *Cultural models in language and thought* (pp. 112–148). New York: Cambridge University Press.

du Bois, C. (1955). The dominant value profile of American culture. *American Anthropologist, 57,* 1232–1239.

Duveen, G. (2001). Representations, identities, resistance. In K. Deaux & G. Philogène (Eds.), *Representations of the social* (pp. 257–270). Malden, MA: Blackwell.

Feather, N. T. (1975). *Values in education and society.* New York: Free Press.

Feather, N. T. (1994). Values and national identification: Australian evidence. *Australian Journal of Psychology, 46,* 35–40.

Feather, N. T. (1996). Values, deservingness, and attitudes toward high achievers: Research on tall poppies. In C. Seligman, J. M. Olson, & M. P. Zanna (Eds.), *The Ontario symposium: The psychology of values, Vol. 8* (pp. 215–251). Mahwah, NJ: Lawrence Erlbaum Associates.

Fischer, R. (2006). Congruence and functions of personal and cultural values: Do my values reflect my culture's values? *Personality and Social Psychology Bulletin, 32,* 1419–1431.

Fishbein, M., & Ajzen, I. (1975). *Belief, attitudes, intention, and behavior: An introduction to theory and research.* Reading, MA: Addison-Wesley.

Geertz, C. (1973). *The interpretation of cultures.* New York: Free Press.

Gouveia, V. V., de Albuquerque, F. J. B., Clemente, M., & Espinosa, P. (2002). Human values and social identities: A study in two collectivist cultures. *International Journal of Psychology, 37,* 333–342.

Harton, H. C., & Bourgeois, M. J. (2004). Cultural elements emerge from dynamic social impact. In M. Schaller & C. S. Crandall (Eds.), *The psychological foundations of culture* (pp. 41–75). Mahwah, NJ: Lawrence Erlbaum Associates.

Heaven, P. C. L. (1999). Group identities and human values. *Journal of Social Psychology, 139,* 590–595.

Heine, S. J., Lehman, D. R., Peng, K., & Greenholtz, J. (2002). What's wrong with cross-cultural comparisons of subjective Likert scales? The reference-group effect. *Journal of Personality and Social Psychology, 82,* 903–918.

Herman, H. J. M. (2001). The dialogical self: Toward a theory of personal and cultural positioning. *Culture & Psychology, 7,* 243–281.

Hofstede, G. (1980). *Culture's consequences: International differences in work-related values.* Beverly Hills, CA: Sage.

Hogg, M. A. (2003). Social identity. In M. R. Leary & L. P. Tangney (Eds.), *Handbook of self and identity* (pp. 462–479). New York: Guilford Press.

Hogg, M. A., & Turner, J. C. (1987). Intergroup behaviour, self-stereotyping and the salience of social categories. *British Journal of Social Psychology, 26,* 325–340.

Holtgraves, T., & Yang, J. (1992). Interpersonal underpinnings of request strategies: General principles and differences due to culture and gender. *Journal of Personality and Social Psychology, 62,* 246–256.

Hong, Y., Morris, M. W., Chiu, C-y., & Benet-Martínez, V. (2000). Multicultural minds: A dynamic constructivist approach to culture and cognition. *American Psychologist, 55,* 709–720.

Hong, Y., Wan, C., No, S., & Chiu, C-y. (2007). Multicultural identities. In S. Kitayama & D. Cohen (Eds.), *Handbook of cultural psychology* (pp. 323–345). New York: Guilford.

Inglehart, R. (1997). *Modernization and postmodernization: Cultural, economic and political change in 43 societies.* Princeton, NJ: Princeton University Press.

Jetten, J., Postmes, T., & McAuliffe, B. J. (2002). 'We're all individuals': Group norms of individualism and collectivism, levels of identification and identity threat. *European Journal of Social Psychology, 32*, 189–207.

Keesing, R. M. (1981). Theories of culture. In R. W. Casson (Ed.), *Language, culture and cognition: Anthropological perspectives* (pp. 42–66). New York: Macmillan.

Keller, H., Borke, J., Yovsi, R., Lohaus, A., & Jensen, H. (2005). Cultural orientations and historical changes as predictors of parenting behaviour. *International Journal of Behavioral Development, 29*, 229–237.

Kim, H., & Drolet, A. (2003). Choice and self-expression: A cultural analysis of variety-seeking. *Journal of Personality and Social Psychology, 85*, 373–382.

Kluckhohn, C. K. M. (1951). Values and value orientations in the theory of action. In T. Parsons & E. Sils (Eds.), *Toward a general theory of action* (pp. 388–433). Cambridge, MA: Harvard University Press.

Krauss, R. M., & Chiu, C. (1998). Language and social behavior. In D. T. Gilbert & S. Fiske (Eds.), *The handbook of social psychology, Vol. 2* (4th ed., pp. 41–88). New York: McGraw-Hill.

Lau, I. Y.-M., Lee, S-l., & Chiu, C-y. (2004). Language, cognition, and reality: Constructing shared meanings through communication. In M. Schaller & C. S. Crandall (Eds.), *The psychological foundations of culture* (pp. 77–100). Mahwah, NJ: Lawrence Erlbaum Associates.

Leung, K., & Iwawaki, S. (1988). Cultural collectivism and distributive behavior. *Journal of Cross-Cultural Psychology, 19*, 35–49.

Markus, H. R., & Kitayama, S. (1991). Culture and the self: Implications for cognition, emotion, and motivation. *Psychological Review, 98*, 224–253.

McIntyre, A., Lyons, A., Clark, A., & Kashima, Y. (2004). The microgenesis of culture: Serial reproduction as an experimental simulation of cultural dynamics. In M. Schaller & C. S. Crandall (Eds.), *The psychological foundations of culture* (pp. 227–258). Mahwah, NJ: Lawrence Erlbaum Associates.

Mead, G. H. (1934). *Mind, self and society.* Chicago: University of Chicago Press.

Mead, G. H. (1956). *On social psychology.* Chicago, IL: University of Chicago Press.

Miller, D. T., & Prentice, D. A. (1994). Collective errors and errors about the collective. *Personality and Social Psychology Bulletin, 20*, 541–550.

Moscovici, S. (1984). The phenomenon of social representations. In M. Farr & S. Moscovici (Eds.), *Social representations* (pp. 3–69). Cambridge, UK: Cambridge University Press.

Nussbaum, M. C. (2000). Emotions and social norms. In L. P. Nucci, G. B. Saxe, & E. Turiel (Eds.), *Culture, thought, and development. The Jean Piaget symposium series* (pp. 41–63). Mahwah, NJ: Lawrence Erlbaum Associates.

Oyserman, D., Coon, H. M., & Kemmelmeier, M. (2002). Rethinking individualism and collectivism: Evaluation of theoretical assumptions and meta-analyses. *Psychological Bulletin, 128*, 3–72.

Pelto, P. J., & Pelto, G. H. (1975). Intra-cultural diversity: Some theoretical issues. *American Ethnologist, 2*, 1–18.

Peng, K., Nisbett, R. E., & Wong, N. Y. C. (1997). Validity problems comparing values across cultures and possible solutions. *Psychological Methods, 2*, 329–344.

Prentice, D. A., & Miller, D. T. (1993). Pluralistic ignorance and alcohol use on campus: Some consequences of misperceiving the social norm. *Journal of Personality and Social Psychology, 64,* 243–256.

Resnick, L., Levine, J., & Teasley, S. D. (1991). *Perspective on socially shared cognition.* Washington, DC: American Psychological Association.

Rohan, M. J. (2000). A rose by any name? The values construct. *Personality and Social Psychology Review, 4,* 255–277.

Rohan, M. J., & Zanna, M. P. (2001). Values and ideologies. In A. Tesser & N. Schwarz (Eds.), *Blackwell handbook of social psychology: Intraindividual processes* (pp. 458–478). Oxford, UK: Blackwell.

Rokeach, M. (1973). *The nature of human values.* New York: Free Press.

Romney, A. K., Boyd, J. P., Moore, C. C., Batchelder, W. H., & Brazill, T. J. (1996). Culture as shared cognitive representations. *Proceedings of the National Academy of Sciences USA, 93,* 4699–4705.

Ryan, R. M., & Deci, E. L. (2003). On assimilating identities to the self: A self-determination theory perspective on internalization and integrity within cultures. In M. R. Leary & L. P. Tangney (Eds.), *Handbook of self and identity* (pp. 253–272). New York: Guilford Press.

Schwartz, S. H. (1992). Universals in the content and structure of values: Theoretical advances and empirical tests in 20 countries. In M. P. Zanna (Ed.), *Advances in experimental social psychology, Vol. 25* (pp. 1–65). New York: Academic Press.

Schwartz, S. H., & Bardi, A. (2001). Value hierarchies across cultures: Taking a similarities perspective. *Journal of Cross-Cultural Psychology, 32,* 268–290.

Schwartz, S. H., & Bilsky, W. (1987). Toward a universal psychological structure of human values. *Journal of Personality and Social Psychology, 53,* 550–562.

Schwartz, S. H., & Sagie, G. (2000). Value consensus and importance: A cross-national study. *Journal of Cross-Cultural Psychology, 31,* 465–497.

Sedikides, C., & Brewer, M. B. (Eds.). (2001). *Individual self, relational self, collective self.* Philadelphia, PA: Psychology Press.

Smith, J. R., & Terry, D. (2003). Attitude-behaviour consistency: The role of group norms, attitude accessibility, and mode of behavioural decision-making. *European Journal of Social Psychology, 33,* 591–608.

Sperber, D. (1996). *Explaining culture: A naturalistic approach.* Oxford, UK: Blackwell.

Tajfel, H., & Turner, J. (1986). The social identity theory of intergroup relations. In W. Austin & S. Worchel (Eds.), *The social psychology of intergroup relations* (pp. 7–24). Chicago, IL: Nelson-Hall Publishers.

Terracciano, A., Abbel-Khalek, A. M., Ádám, N., Adamovová, L., Ahn, C.-k., Ahn, H.-n., et al. (2005, October 7). National character does not reflect mean personality trait levels in 49 cultures. *Science, 310,* 96–100.

Terry, D. J., & Hogg, M. A. (1996). Group norms and the attitude-behavior relationship: A role for group identification. *Personality and Social Psychology Bulletin, 22,* 776–793.

Thompson, L., & Fine, G. A. (1999). Socially shared cognition, affect, and behavior: A review and integration. *Personality and Social Psychology Review, 3,* 278–302.

Triandis, H. C. (1989). The self and social behavior in differing cultural contexts. *Psychological Review, 96,* 506–520.

Triandis, H. C. (1995). *Individualism and collectivism.* Boulder, CO: Westview Press.

Triandis, H. C. (1996). The psychological measurement of cultural syndromes. *American Psychologist, 51,* 407–415.

Triandis, H. C., & Gelfand, M. J. (1998). Converging measurement of horizontal and vertical individualism and collectivism. *Journal of Personality and Social Psychology, 74,* 118–128.

Turner, J. C., Hogg, M., Oakes, P., Reicher, S., & Wetherell, M. (1987). *Rediscovering the social group: A self-categorization theory.* Oxford, UK: Blackwell.

Turner, J. C., Oakes, P. J., Haslam, S. A., & McGarty, C. (1994). Self and collective: Cognition and social context. *Personality and Social Psychology Bulletin, 20,* 454–463.

Wan, C., & Chiu, C-y. (2005, January). *They think men and women are different, and I agree! The role of intersubjective consensus in gender identification.* Poster presented at the 6th Annual Meeting of the Society of Personality and Social Psychology, New Orleans, LA.

Wan, C., Chiu, C-y., Peng, S., & Tam, K. (2007). Measuring cultures through intersubjective cultural norms: Implications for predicting relative identification with two or more cultures. *Journal of Cross-Cultural Psychology, 38,* 213–226.

Wan, C., Chiu, C-y., Tam, K., Lee, V. S., Lau, I. Y., & Peng, S. (2007). Perceived cultural importance and actual self-importance of values in cultural identification. *Journal of Personality and Social Psychology, 92,* 337–354.

4

Culture as Norm Representations: The Case of Collective Responsibility Attribution

MELODY MANCHI CHAO AND CHI-YUE CHIU[1]

Norms, spoken or implicit, regulate much of our social life. They are social control devices evolved to coordinate human activities in collective living (Fiske, 2000; Heylighen & Campbell, 1995). In this chapter, focusing on the social regulatory functions of cultural norms and using collective responsibility attribution as an example, we will discuss the role of norms, which are major components of knowledge tradition, in cultural processes.

CULTURE AS SHARED REPRESENTATIONS

Similar to other forms of knowledge representations (such as lay theories, see Chapter 2, this volume; and intersubjective values, see Chapter 3, this volume), social norms are knowledge representations that are shared among individuals within a collective. They provide premises in normative social inferences (e.g., inferences about whether a certain action should be carried out) and define the normative standards of behavior (e.g., determine whether a certain behavior is punishable or forgivable in the eyes of the public).

Social norms, together with their antecedent and consequent conditions, produce a normative representation (Chiu & Hong, 2006). An antecedent condition refers to the circumstances under which the norm can be activated and applied (e.g., the causes of a car accident, say, speeding). A consequent condition refers to the behavioral implications of the norm (e.g., punishing the speeding driver will deter reoccurrence of the same behavior). Normative representations are knowledge structures; and, like other knowledge

[1] Preparation of this chapter was supported by a grant awarded to the second author by the Campus Research Board, the University of Illinois.

structures, their use is governed by three basic principles of knowledge activation (Higgins, 1996): The principles of availability, accessibility, and applicability.

Availability

Certain cultural knowledge is available to an individual if that individual has acquired the knowledge and has a representation of it in memory. People acquire knowledge of cultural norms through learning, and individuals who have extensive experiences in several cultures might have acquired the knowledge in all of these cultures (Hong, Morris, Chiu, & Benet-Martinez, 2000; LaFromboise, Coleman, & Gerton, 1993; see Chapter 2, this volume).

Norms are external to the individual. They are products of collective negotiations over what constitute acceptable and unacceptable behaviors in the society, and they are externalized in institutions (e.g., the law), organizational rules and regulations, idioms, and other cultural artifacts. Norm representations are not only available in an individual's memory as private cognitions, they are also shared among others in the society. For a given norm representation, an individual would be aware of the extent to which the norm is shared in the society (e.g., the extent to which members in the collective agree that drivers should be punished for speeding; Lau, Chiu, & Hong, 2001; also see Chapter 3, this volume). In fact, the regulatory power of norms over individual behaviors is derived from the shared knowledge that the norm is available to the others in the society as well. Thus, when norms regarding a certain behavior are activated, the anticipated collective responses to the behavior are also activated. Therefore, rather than experiencing a behavioral choice as a personal choice, the individuals would feel that they are making a choice in the limelight and are answerable to the society for their action.

Accessibility

According to the principle of knowledge activation, accessibility refers to the activation potential of available knowledge. A norm can influence behaviors when it becomes cognitively accessible. Situational cues that increase the accessibility of a norm include direct reminders of the contents and the social regulatory functions of the norm, as well as situational primes that reinforce one's accountability to an external audience, which could be a real or an imagined one.

Applicability

Although the activation of norm representations by situational cues appears to be spontaneous, it is not a knee-jerk reaction. Application of norm representations also follows the applicability principle of knowledge activation (Higgins, 1996). Applicability refers to the appropriateness of applying the activated norm representation to a given situation. Whether an activated norm would influence individuals' behaviors and judgments depends on its applicability to the immediate context. For example, in a Prisoner's Dilemma game, individuals can choose to compete or cooperate with their partners. The cooperation norm in Chinese culture encourages the adoption of a cooperation script. In one study (Wong & Hong, 2005), prior to playing the Prisoner's Dilemma game, Hong Kong Chinese players were reminded of their Chinese cultural tradition through subtle situational cueing (i.e., through incidental exposure to symbolic icons of Chinese culture). This culture-priming procedure rendered the Chinese norm of cooperation cognitively accessible to the players. The players did not apply the cognitively accessible norm indiscriminately in the game, however. Rather, they applied it only when it was appropriate to the situation, such as when they were playing the game with a friend (vs. a stranger).

In short, norm representations are a kind of knowledge representation. Their activation follows the principles of availability, accessibility, and applicability, just like other forms of knowledge. Because a norm representation encodes the acceptable standards of behavior that are widely shared in one's community, it is also a powerful social control tool for regulating individual behaviors in the society (Fiske, 2000; Heylighen & Campbell, 1995).

SOCIAL REGULATORY FUNCTIONS OF CULTURAL NORMS: THE CASE OF RESPONSIBILITY ATTRIBUTION

Norms are evolved social control mechanisms for coordinating individual activities in collective living. They prescribe socially desirable behaviors and proscribe behaviors that would disrupt smooth coordination of behaviors in the society. Norms are often reflected in the dominant practices that are intended for sanctioning disruptive behaviors. Because of differences in physical and social ecologies and variations in adaptive responses to these ecological factors, different cultural groups have developed different knowledge traditions, which consist of amalgamations of lay theories and intersubjective values (see Chapters 2 and 3, this volume). The dominant social control practices in a society typically cohere with its prevailing beliefs and values. For instance, some societies tend to practice personal responsibility as a way of social regulation, whereas others tend to rely on collective responsibility.

Personal Responsibility

A common social control practice in many contemporary Western societies holds the wrongdoer and the wrongdoer alone responsible for a transgression. In establishing personal responsibility, the relative contribution of personal causality and environmental influence are typically taken into consideration. The social reasoning behind personal responsibility judgment is articulated in Heider's (1958) attribution model. According to Heider (1958), lay people use five criteria to determine an actor's personal responsibility for a negative event: association, causality, foreseeability, justification, and intentionality. Association is the connection of the individual with a negative event (e.g., whether the driver is associated with the car accident). Causality refers to whether the individual, regardless of intention, was causally responsible for the event (e.g., whether the car accident resulted from the driver's speeding). Foreseeability refers to whether the individual could foresee the act's negative consequences (e.g., whether the driver foresaw that speeding could cause the accident). Justification refers to whether the individual could justify the act (e.g., whether the driver had a legitimate reason for speeding). Finally, intentionality refers to whether an individual intended to cause the harm (e.g., whether the driver deliberately sped, causing the car accident).

The amount of personal responsibility assigned to the wrongdoer increases from mere association with a negative outcome to intentional wrongdoing. It also increases with the subjective evaluation of the person's contributions and decreases with the perceived amount of environmental contributions to the harm. There is ample evidence that these social reasoning processes underlie personal responsibility attribution (Fincham & Shultz, 1981; Shultz, Schleifer, & Altman, 1981), which aims to deter future wrongdoings and serves as a means of social control.

Collective Responsibility

In addition to the wrongdoer, individuals who are not causally responsible for the wrongdoing but are associated with the wrongdoer may also be held accountable. This practice is known as collective responsibility attribution (Chao, Zhang, & Chiu, 2008; Chiu & Hong, 1992; Zemba, Young, & Morris,

2006). In societies marked by interlocking obligations (e.g., some East Asian societies), the collective as a whole has the duties and opportunities to monitor each individual's behavior (Nishida, 1985; Zhang, 1984). Thus, when a member performs a malevolent act, it reflects not only the moral failure of the member but also the failure of the collective in meeting its social obligation. Hence, collective responsibility attribution is relatively prevalent in Eastern cultural contexts (Chiu, Morris, Hong, & Menon, 2000; Menon, Morris, Chiu, & Hong, 1999). For example, in American organizations, an individual "bad apple" is often identified as the target of blame, whereas in clanlike Japanese organizations, blame is often handled by "cleansing" the organization. The head of the organization often becomes the sacrificial lamb in the company blunder (Bell & Tetlock, 1989).

There is consistent evidence for the greater prevalence of collective responsibility attribution in East Asia. In one study (Chiu & Hong, 1992), 87 Hong Kong Chinese junior business executives read a scenario that depicted an industrial accident in a toy-manufacturing company. In the story, the action of a foreman in the factory caused the accident, in which a machine operator lost his fingers when the machine's emergency brake failed. That accident happened either because the foreman tampered with the emergency brake to improve productivity (high intentionality) or because he failed to check the condition of the brake (low intentionality). The investigators measured personal and collective responsibility attributions by having the participants rate the extent to which the foreman and his boss should be held responsible for the accident. When assigning personal responsibility, the participants considered personal causality and assigned greater responsibility to the foreman when intentionality was high than when it was low. They also assigned a substantial amount of responsibility to the foreman's boss, who was causally unconnected to the accident. Consistent findings were obtained in a second study (Chiu & Hong, 1992, Study 2), in which Hong Kong Chinese participants assigned responsibility to a child and his parents for the child's misbehavior. Again, although participants considered personal causality when attributing personal responsibility, they also assigned a considerable amount of responsibility to the child's parents, who were not causally connected to the negative incident.

In another study (Zemba, Young, & Morris, 2006; Study 2), 56 American students and 60 Japanese students studied a food-poisoning case in a school, in which a student got sick after eating contaminated eggs prepared by the school cook. Compared with their American counterparts, the Japanese participants were more likely to blame the school principal, who was not causally connected to the food-poisoning incident. In addition, the more they perceived the school as responsible, the more responsibility they attributed to the principal.

In sum, social norms evolved to coordinate activities among individuals within the collective and to discourage disruptive behaviors. Although both Easterners and Westerners consider personal causality when attributing responsibility to the wrongdoer, Easterners are more likely than Westerners to attribute collective responsibility and generalize responsibility to causally unconnected others in the collective. Moving beyond mean-level comparisons (Bond, 2007), recent studies have explored why people assign collective responsibility to causally unconnected individuals (Chao et al., 2008).

Functions of Collective Responsibility

Despite the higher prevalence of collective responsibility attribution in Eastern than Western cultures, collective responsibility is also practiced in Western societies, albeit much less extensively (Denson, Lickel, Curtis, Stenstrom, & Ames, 2006). For example, perceivers may blame the national leader for the national problems created by his/her predecessor, or attribute the responsibility of the damages in a riot to a mob. In these instances, responsibility is attributed to individuals who are not causally responsible for the action or outcome. Why do people in Eastern and Western cultures practice collective responsibility? Legal and social philosophers (e.g., Levinson, 2003; Nishida, 1985; Zhang, 1984) have identified two major reasons for practicing collective responsibility: delegated deterrence and group harmony.

Delegated Deterrence

In societies marked by interlocking interpersonal relations, responsibility is delegated to the collective to monitor each other's behavior and prevent or deter individuals in the collective from committing malevolent acts. In legal philosophy, this practice is referred to as delegated deterrence and is expected to increase the group's vigilance in monitoring and controlling potential troublemakers' behaviors. The delegated deterrence function of collective responsibility was heavily emphasized in the traditional Chinese legal system. Starting from 746 B.C., the system of *yuan zuo* was widely practiced in China (Nishida, 1985; Zhang, 1984). Under this system, when a crime was committed, besides the wrongdoer, the wrongdoer's superiors, kinsmen, neighbors, and other associates could be held responsible for the wrongdoer's behavior. The rationale underlying this practice is the belief that one's superiors, neighbors, and kinsmen have the obligation and opportunity to monitor the offender's behavior, and therefore should be able to prevent the offender from doing harm. In other words, in Chinese societies, collective responsibility assignment serves to delegate responsibility to the group to deter individual members from committing malevolent acts.

Although collective sanction is also used as delegated deterrence in Western societies, the idea of punishing group members simply because they could have monitored and controlled the responsible individuals is at odds with the basic principle of legal liability in Western legal philosophy. This principle of legal liability holds that individuals should be responsible for their own actions. From this perspective, generalizing blame to others who have no direct causal connection to an offense is inappropriate. Indeed, extant research findings show that collective responsibility as a delegated deterrence mechanism is more widely practiced in Asian countries than in Western countries. For example, compared to European Americans, Asians are found to have a higher likelihood of blaming a group for the wrongdoing of a group member because the wrongdoing of a member is seen as a reflection of the group's inability to regulate that member's actions (Chiu et al., 2000; Menon et al., 1999). Zemba and her associates (Zemba, 2006; Zemba et al., 2006) also found that, in Japan, the collective's leader, who is causally unconnected to the wrongdoing, could be punished when the perceivers feel that the organization should be punished and that the leader is a representative of the organization.

To directly examine the delegated deterrence function of collective responsibility in Asian cultural contexts, in one study (Chao et al., 2008, Study 2), Asian-American and European-American participants were presented with a scenario depicting a team of students taking part in a design contest. The team had come up with two proposals, and the project coordinator submitted one of them to the contest. The team lost in the contest. Worse still, the proposal that the project coordinator did not submit was similar to the winning proposal. In one experimental condition, the goal of delegated deterrence was made salient: The participants were told that there was a concern that similar events might happen again in other student organizations in school. Thus, the school felt that there was a need to find out how this incident happened and to identify the parties who could have prevented this incident from happening. In another condition (the control condition), this description was omitted in the scenario.

After reading the scenario, participants were asked to indicate how much responsibility and blame they would attribute to the project coordinator, other members of the project team, the teacher, and the headmaster of the school. Although the teacher and the headmaster were members of the school, they were not causally associated with the decision. Assignment of responsibility and blame to the teacher and the headmaster constituted a measure of collective responsibility attribution.

Consistent with previous findings, Asian-American participants assigned higher levels of collective responsibility than did European Americans. Furthermore, compared to the control condition, in the condition under which the goal of delegated deterrence was made salient, Asian-American participants attributed more collective responsibility. In comparison, European-American participants did not show an increase in collective responsibility attribution when the goal of delegated deterrence was made salient. These results indicate that, in Asian cultural contexts, where there are many interlocking social relations, collective responsibility serves the function of delegated deterrence and motivates individuals within a collective to increase their vigilance in monitoring the actions of one another. Therefore, situations that call for collective actions to deter future wrongdoing increase collective responsibility attribution.

Group Harmony

Another function that collective responsibility serves is maintenance of group harmony. Sharing of collective responsibility may protect an individual wrongdoer from potentially becoming the target of public denouncement and social isolation. The collective's willingness to share the blame also increases a wrongdoer's emotional bonding to the group (Tetlock, 2002). Given that maintaining group harmony is an important interpersonal goal in Asian cultures (Kwan, Bond, & Singelis, 1997), activating the goal of group harmony can increase collective responsibility attribution among individuals with an Asian background. Similarly, in Western societies, group punishment may also be justified when groups show signs of group solidarity (e.g., shared interests, positive interdependency). Denson and colleagues (2006), for instance, reported that American undergraduates found collective responsibility to be most acceptable when the group is an intimacy group, which has a high level of positive interdependency. Consistent with the empirical observations made by Denson and colleagues, in contemporary Western social philosophy, group solidarity is often cited as a justification for collective responsibility (Feinberg, 1968; Friedman & May, 1985; May, 1987; McGray, 1987).

To examine the group harmony maintenance function of collective responsibility, in the design contest study mentioned earlier in this chapter (Chao et al., 2008, Study 2), besides the delegated deterrence and control conditions, an interpersonal harmony condition was included. In the interpersonal harmony situation, the participants were told that, after that incident, there was a concern that students' morale and trust among them might deteriorate. Thus, the school authority felt that there was a need to minimize the negative impact of this incident on students' morale and on their social relationships in the school. The results showed that both Asian- and European-American participants increased responsibility attribution to the collective when the goal of maintaining interpersonal harmony was made salient (compared to the baseline level in the control condition). In other words, when the situation called for harmony maintenance, the practice of collective responsibility became more acceptable to both Asian Americans and European Americans, because collective responsibility could protect the wrongdoer from social isolation and promote group solidarity.

In short, collective responsibility is practiced in both Asian and American contexts. It is practiced for different social regulatory purposes, however. In Western cultures, collective responsibility is practiced occasionally to promote ingroup harmony. In Asian cultures, collective responsibility is practiced relatively frequently. Aside from promoting ingroup harmony, the practice of collective responsibility also serves to deter disruptive behaviors in the collective.

Context-Specificity of Collective Responsibility Attribution

Thus far, we have illustrated that situational goals can increase the normative practice of collective responsibility in both Asian and American contexts. People do not indiscriminately attribute responsibility to causally unconnected members of the collective when the goal of delegated deterrence or group harmony is activated, however. As mentioned, the principle of applicability states that an activated norm and its associated practice will be adopted only when they are applicable to the immediate situation (Higgins, 1996). In the Asian context, when the goal of delegated deterrence is activated, perceivers will assign responsibility to the wrongdoer's associates only when the associates are perceived to have the responsibility to monitor the wrongdoer's behaviors and prevent the wrongdoing. For example, collective responsibility for a work-related wrongdoing will be assigned only when the wrongdoing took place when the wrongdoer was on duty.

To test these predictions, Chao and colleagues (2008, Study 1) presented American and Chinese participants with a traffic accident scenario modified from the one used in the study by Zemba and colleagues (2006, Study 1). In the scenario, while speeding in his own car, an employee of a transportation company hit a person. Two variables were manipulated: situational goal and the context of the wrongdoing. As in the design contest scenario discussed earlier in this chapter (Chao et al., 2008, Study 2), participants were assigned to one of the three situational goal conditions: delegated deterrence, group harmony, or control. The context of the wrongdoing was manipulated by telling the participants that the accident happened when the driver was (a) on duty, (b) off duty helping his supervisor, or (c) off duty helping a friend to move. Next, the participants assigned responsibility and blame to five targets: (a) the employee who caused the accident, (b) other drivers in the company, (c) the employee's supervisor at the time of the accident, (d) the employee's new supervisor who took up the position after the accident, and (e) the company. Assignment of responsibility and blame to targets other than the driver constituted a measure of collective responsibility attribution, because these targets were not causally involved with the accident.

When the wrongdoing occurred while the driver was on duty, as in the design contest study (Chao et al., 2008, Study 2), Chinese participants assigned higher levels of responsibility to members of the collective who were not causally connected to the accident, compared to European-American participants. Furthermore, when the goal of delegated deterrence was made salient, only Chinese participants were more likely to hold the collective accountable in the on-duty condition (compared to the baseline level in the control condition). These effects were not observed when the wrongdoing occurred while the driver was off duty (as in the other conditions). These results underscore the context specificity of collective responsibility attribution. Activating the goal of delegated deterrence increases Asians' collective responsibility only when they perceive the collective as having the responsibility to monitor the wrongdoer's behaviors and prevent the occurrence of the wrongdoing, as in the on-duty condition. Finally, when the goal of group harmony was emphasized, both Chinese and European-American participants made more collective responsibility attribution if the driver was on duty (compared to the baseline level in the control condition).

In summary, similar to other knowledge representations, the activation and application of norm representations and their attendant normative practices follow the basic principles of knowledge activation (Higgins, 1996). The practice of collective responsibility as delegated deterrence is available to people in Asian contexts but not in American contexts, thus making the goal of delegated deterrence salient increases collective responsibility attribution among Asians, but not among Americans. The practice of collective responsibility as a harmony maintenance mechanism is available in both Asian and American cultural contexts; hence, making salient the goal of harmony maintenance increases collective responsibility attribution among individuals in both cultural groups. After an available norm representation is activated, its level of cognitive accessibility increases. A cognitively accessible norm representation would not be used, however, unless it is applicable to the normative expectations in the immediate situation. For instance, coworkers and superiors are responsible for monitoring and deterring disruptive behaviors of employees only when the employees are on duty. Therefore, as demonstrated in the car accident experiment reviewed earlier in this chapter, the practice of collective responsibility was applicable only when the driver was on duty, when members of the collective were expected to monitor and deter disruptive behaviors.

IMPLICATIONS FOR STUDYING CULTURE

In this chapter, using collective responsibility as an example, we examined the nature and function of norms in cultural processes. Culture is a global, elusive concept. To understand cultural processes, it is necessary to unpack culture. One way to unpack culture is to focus on the effects of its constituent symbolic elements. From this perspective, we have examined the normative influence of culture through the activation of specific shared norms and their attendant social regulatory practices. Through this analysis, we are able to understand cross-cultural variations in the social regulatory functions of collective responsibility attribution. We are also able to move beyond mean-level comparison between cultures and to specify more concretely the psychological processes leading to the observed cultural differences. Specifically, this analysis enables us to understand not only *whether* there are cultural differences, but also *when* and *why* cultural differences would emerge (or disappear).

Our analysis connects cultural processes to basic processes of knowledge activation. As the research program on collective responsibility attribution illustrates, applying the basic knowledge activation principles to understanding cultural processes does not preclude investigators from taking a macroscopic perspective to culture. On the contrary, our analysis highlights the dynamic interplay of social control mechanisms in the society, normative expectations in the immediate situation, and the individual processes of sense making. Precise predictions of when people in Eastern and Western cultures would make collective responsibility attribution are rendered possible by considering simultaneously (a) the social regulatory functions of collective responsibility attribution (e.g., harmony maintenance, delegated deterrence) that have evolved through the cultural group's history of creative responses to basic problems of social coordination in its particular physical and social ecology, (b) the normative expectations and social regulatory goals in the immediate situation, and (c) the basic cognitive processes whereby individuals learn, retrieve from memory, and apply knowledge of cultural norms and their attendant practices. In short, a process analysis of culture and its constituent elements has helped highlight the dynamic unfolding of normative judgments in concrete situations. It illustrates how individuals actively participate, both as individual agents and as their culture's representatives, in addressing major concerns regarding the coordination of human activities within the collective by recruiting symbolic cultural resources (in the forms of normatively sanctioned ideas and practices).

REFERENCES

Bell, N. E., & Tetlock, P. E. (1989). The intuitive politician and the assignment of blame in organizations. In R. A. Ciacalone & P. Rosenfeld (Eds.), *Impression management in the organization* (pp. 105–123). Hillsdale, NJ: Lawrence Erlbaum.

Bond, M. H. (2007). Fashioning a new psychology of the Chinese people: Insights from developments in cross-cultural psychology. In S. J. Kulich & M. H. Prosser (Eds.), *Interpersonal perspectives on Chinese communication. Intercultural research, Vol. 1* (pp. 233–251). Shanghai, China: Shanghai Foreign Language Education Press.

Chao, M. M., Zhang, Z., & Chiu, C-y. (2008). Personal and collective culpability judgment: A functional analysis of East Asian-North American differences. *Journal of Cross-Cultural Psychology, 39*, 730–744.

Chiu, C-y., & Hong, Y. (1992). The effects of intentionality and validation on individual and collective responsibility attribution among Hong Kong Chinese. *The Journal of Psychology, 126*, 291–300.

Chiu, C-y., & Hong, Y. (2006). *The social psychology of culture.* Oxford: Taylor & Francis, Inc.

Chiu, C-y., Morris, M. W., Hong, Y., & Menon, T. (2000). Motivated cultural cognition: The impact of implicit cultural theories on dispositional attribution varies as a function of need for closure. *Journal of Personality and Social Psychology, 78*, 247–259.

Denson, T. F., Lickel, B., Curtis, M., Stenstrom, D. M., & Ames, D. (2006). The roles of entitativity and essentiality in judgments of collective responsibility. *Group Processes and Intergroup Relations, 9*, 43–61.

Feinberg, J. (1968). Collective responsibility. *Journal of Philosophy, 65*, 674–688.

Fincham, F. D., & Shultz, T. R. (1981). Intervening causation and the mitigation of responsibility for harm. *British Journal of Social Psychology, 20*, 113–120.

Fiske, A. P. (2000). Complementarity theory: Why human social capacities evolved to require cultural complements. *Personality and Social Psychology Review, 4*, 76–94.

Friedman, M., & May, L. (1985). Harming women as a group. *Social Theory and Practice, 11*, 218–221.

Heider, F. (1958). *The psychology of interpersonal relations.* New York: Wiley.

Heylighen, F., & Campbell, D. T. (1995). Selection of organization at the societal level: Obstacles and facilitators of metasystem transitions. *World Futures: The Journal of General Evolution, 45,* 181–212.

Higgins, E. T. (1996). Knowledge activation: Accessibility, applicability, and salience. In E. T. Higgins & R. W. Kruglanski (Eds.), *Social psychology: Handbook of basic principles* (pp. 195–211). New York: The Guilford Press.

Hong, Y., Morris, M. W., Chiu, C-y., & Benet-Martinez, V. (2000). Multicultural minds: A dynamic constructivist approach to culture and cognition. *American Psychologist, 55,* 709–720.

Kwan, V. S. Y., Bond, M. H., & Singelis, T. (1997). Pancultural explanations for life satisfaction: Adding relationship harmony to self-esteem. *Journal of Personality and Social Psychology, 73,* 1038–1051.

LaFromboise, T., Coleman, H. L., & Gerton, J. (1993). Psychological impact of biculturalism: Evidence and theory. *Psychological Bulletin, 114,* 395–412.

Lau, I. Y., Chiu, C-y., & Hong, Y. (2001). I know what you know: Assumptions about others' knowledge and their effects on message construction. *Social Cognition, 19,* 587–600.

Levinson, D. J. (2003). *Collective sanctions.* NYU Law School, Public Law Research Paper No. 57.

May, L. (1987). *The morality of groups.* Notre Dame: University of Notre Dame Press.

McGray, H. (1987). Morality and collective liability. *Journal of Value Inquiry, 20,* 157–165.

Menon, T., Morris, M. W., Chiu, C-y., & Hong, Y. (1999). Culture and the construal of agency: Attribution to individual versus group dispositions. *Journal of Personality and Social Psychology, 76,* 701–717.

Nishida, T. (1985). *A study of the history of Chinese criminal laws.* Peking: Peking University Press.

Shultz, T. R., Schleifer, M., & Altman, I. (1981). Judgments of causation, responsibility, and punishment in case of harm-doing. *Canadian Journal of Behavioral Science, 13,* 238–253.

Tetlock, P. E. (2002). Social functionalist frameworks for judgment and choice: Intuitive politicians, theologians, and prosecutors. *Psychological Review, 109,* 451–471.

Wong, R. Y., & Hong, Y. (2005). Dynamic influences of culture on cooperation in the Prisoner's Dilemma. *Psychological Science, 16,* 429–434.

Zemba, Y. (2006). Responses to organizational harm: Mechanism of blaming managers as proxies for a culpable organization. *Asian Journal of Social Psychology, 9,* 184–194.

Zemba, Y., Young, M. J., & Morris, M. W. (2006). Blaming leaders for organizational accidents: Proxy logic in collective- versus individual-agency cultures. *Organizational Behavior and Human Decision Processes, 101,* 36–51.

Zhang, J. (1984). Preliminary research on the characteristics of the feudal judicial system of China. *Theses of Law of China, 1,* 245–266.

PART THREE

PSYCHOLOGICAL FUNCTIONS

OF CULTURE

5

Epistemic Functions of Culture

MELODY MANCHI CHAO AND CHI-YUE CHIU[1]

Norms prescribe culturally appropriate behaviors and proscribe inappropriate ones (see Chapter 4, this volume), but why do individuals follow cultural norms? One answer to this question, informed by the theory of lay epistemic (Kruglanski, 2004), holds that people adhere to cultural norms because norms are closure providers; they are widely accepted behavior standards within a given culture (Chao, Zhang, & Chiu, 2009; Chiu, Morris, Hong, & Menon, 2000; Fu, Morris, Lee, et al., 2007). According to the lay epistemic theory (Kruglanski, 2004), the need for cognitive closure (NFCC) is a basic epistemic motive. Individuals who have high NFCC have the need to reduce uncertainty and to hold on to firm answers for questions. Because cultural norms are consensually validated social knowledge, they help reduce uncertainty and provide firm answers to otherwise ambiguous issues. In the present chapter, we will discuss the epistemic functions of culture, focusing on how cultural knowledge can serve as closure providers that confer epistemic security.

EPISTEMIC NEED: NFCC

The lay epistemic theory (Kruglanski, 2004) posits that individuals have a basic desire for cognitive closure (the need for order, predictability, and certainty). People differ in how much they desire cognitive closure. Thus, NFCC can be measured as a chronic individual difference (Webster & Kruglanski, 1994). Individuals with high NFCC are characterized by a felt urgency to seize a firm answer in the face of uncertainty and freeze on the answer once they have found it (Kruglanski & Webster, 1996).

---

[1] Preparation of this chapter was supported by a grant awarded to the second author by the Campus Research Board, University of Illinois.

NFCC has strong effects on information processing, judgment, and behaviors in interpersonal contexts. It has been shown that individuals who have high NFCC are more likely to rely on stereotypical information (a kind of conventional knowledge) in person perception (Dijksterhius, Van Knippenberg, Kruglanski, & Schaper, 1996). In interpersonal communication, individuals with high NFCC also tend to adhere to their dominant communication strategies and tend not to accommodate their communication style to the unique attributes of their interaction partners (Richter & Kruglanski, 1999). Furthermore, in negotiation, high NFCC individuals also tend to rely on stereotypes when rendering judgments of and interacting with their negotiation partner, and tend not to make concessions (De Dreu, Koole, & Oldersma, 1999). In short, individuals with high NFCC tend to rely on established knowledge to structure their experiences. In the face of ambiguity, they have an urgency to seize information that can help them reach a decision. After a judgment is formed, they would close their mind to novel information (e.g., Kruglanski, 2004; Kruglanski & Webster, 1996; Webster & Kruglanski, 1998; also see Chapters 13 and 14, this volume).

Because group norms – particularly norms in a homogeneous group – are established behavioral guides with high consensual validity (Kruglanski, Pierro, Mannetti, & de Grada, 2006), high NFCC individuals are attracted to homogeneous groups and group consensus (Kruglanski, Shah, Pierro, & Mannetti, 2002), and these individuals would readily conform to group consensus. They also tend to resist changes and to exclude deviates (Kruglanski & Webster, 1991).

EPISTEMIC NEED AND CULTURE

Like group norms, cultural norms are also closure providers. They are evolved tools to guide individuals' actions and enable individuals to grasp experiences (Chiu et al., 2000). Certain norms are prevalent in a culture because members of the culture generally agree that they are appropriate for solving problems. Given their consensual validity, conventional ideas and norms constitute a shared reality for the individual (Sechrist & Stangor, 2001). Hence, responses that follow these ideas or norms will be readily accepted in the culture as legitimate and appropriate. In this sense, conventional ideas and cultural norms confer epistemic security and have a strong appeal to high NFCC individuals who desire certain and definite answers (e.g., Chiu et al., 2000).

Supportive evidence for this idea abounds. In the domain of person perception, it has been shown that, compared to each other, Americans are more likely to make dispositional attributions to the individual, and

Chinese are more likely to make dispositional attributions to the group (Menon, Morris, Chiu, & Hong, 1999). In one study, Chiu and colleagues (2000, Study 1) presented Hong Kong Chinese and American participants with two accidents that occurred in pharmacies. In a fever medicine mix-up scenario, children were given mouthwash to drink instead of their prescribed syrup by a pharmacist, and many children became sick. In the second scenario, a pharmacy worker failed to dilute cough medicine, resulting in patients' sickness. After reading the scenarios, participants responded to the attribution items, which depicted dispositions of an individual agent (e.g., the pharmacist) or dispositions of a collective agent (e.g., the hospital). They also completed the Need for Cognitive Closure Scale that assessed their level of cognitive closure (Webster & Kruglanski, 1994). As expected, the Chinese participants were more likely to make dispositional attribution to the group than to the individual, whereas the American participants were more likely to make dispositional attribution to the individual than to the group. More importantly, these cultural differences were more pronounced among participants with high NFCC.

This effect of NFCC on cultural conformity was replicated in another study (Chiu et al., 2000, Study 2) in which NFCC was experimentally manipulated. In this study, Hong Kong Chinese and American participants were asked to respond to a "rouge cattle" scenario (Menon et al., 1999) in which an agitated bull on a cattle farm charged directly at the farmer. The vignette was constructed to assess the tendency to make dispositional attribution of the incident to an individual bull and dispositional attribution to the herd. Participants' NFCC was manipulated by inducing time pressure, because people tend to prefer a firm answer when they work under time pressure (De Dreu, 2003). In the high-time-pressure condition, participants were led to believe that they needed to finish the questionnaire quickly to complete the study on time and were reminded of the time every three minutes. In the low-time-pressure condition, participants were told that they had more than enough time to complete the questionnaire and could take their time. As predicted, only the participants in the high-time-pressure condition followed the prevalent norms in their culture when making attributions. That is, when put under high time pressure, Chinese participants made more dispositional attributions to the group than to the individual, and American participants made more dispositional attributions to the individual than to the group. These cultural differences were not observed when the participants were not under time pressure.

Convergent results have been reported in the domain of justice behaviors. There are marked differences between justice norms in Eastern and Western cultures. For example, compared to individuals in Western cultures, those in

Eastern cultures have stronger preferences for conflict resolution strategies that maintain social harmony and reduce animosity between the disputants (Leung, 1987). Relative to Westerners, Easterners are also more likely to make compromises (Gelfand et al., 2001; Sullivan, Peterson, Kameda, & Shimada, 1981) and are more concerned about "blending in" when making justice judgment (Gelfand et al., 2001; also see Chapter 11, this volume). These divergent conflict resolution goals in Eastern and Western cultures are also reflected in the preferred procedures to manage conflicts (Leung & Morris, 2001): Easterners tend to look for relational information regarding the anticipated effects of taking various managerial actions on the involved parties for the purpose of finding a settlement that is acceptable to the disputants. In contrast, Westerners tend to look for diagnostic information that would reveal the truth for the purpose of identifying the wrongdoers and meting out punishment (Fu, Morris, Lee, et al., 2007). In addition, in reward allocation situations, compared to each other, Westerners prefer the contribution rule that fosters productivity more, whereas Easterners favor the equality principle that promotes social harmony more (e.g., Chiu & Hong, 1997; Leung & Bond, 1984). These established justice norms in Eastern and Western cultures possess high consensual validity in the respective culture; hence, they offer epistemic security to their followers. As such, individuals with high NFCC are particularly likely to follow the prevalent justice norms in their culture (Chao et al., 2009; Fu, Morris, Lee, et al., 2007).

In a study that examined NFCC and preference of conflict resolution style (Fu, Morris, Lee, et al., 2007), 175 Chinese students in Hong Kong and 160 American students in the United States completed a survey that assessed their need for closure (Webster & Kruglanski, 1994) and preferences for five conflict management styles (Rahim, 1983): competing, avoiding, accommodating, compromising, and collaborating. Previous cross-cultural studies have found that compared with Chinese, Americans prefer the competing style more (Morris et al., 1998). Results from the study by Fu, Morris, Lee, and colleagues (2007) showed that this cultural difference was particularly pronounced among high NFCC participants, suggesting that high NFCC Americans and Chinese are particularly motivated to follow the conflict resolution norms in their own culture.

In another study (Fu, Morris, Lee, et al., 2007), 58 Hong Kong Chinese students and 57 American students responded to a conflict scenario after completing the Need For Cognitive Closure Scale (Webster & Kruglanski, 1994). The vignette depicted a dispute between two associate managers in the marketing division of a firm. They had a dispute over who deserved credit for an idea and agreed to find a third party to help settle the dispute.

Participants took the role of one of the disputants in the situation and were asked to indicate their preference for one of four managers who could be approached as a conflict mediator. Two candidates were common friends of the disputants and two were not. Previous studies have found that Chinese preferred a mediator who had an existing relationship with the disputants, believing that a mediator who knows both parties well can reduce animosity between the disputants (Leung, 1987). Consistent with this finding, Fu, Morris, Lee, and colleagues found that Chinese participants preferred mediators who knew both disputants well more than did American participants. More importantly, this cultural difference was more pronounced among high (vs. low) NFCC participants. Follow-up mediation analysis results revealed that consensus expectancy mediated the interaction of culture and NFCC on mediator selection, suggesting that high (vs. low) NFCC individuals are particularly motivated to follow cultural norms, which are consensually validated cultural knowledge.

The same result came from a third study (Fu, Morris, Lee, et al., 2007) that examined cultural differences in information seeking in conflict management settings. In this study, Asian- and European-American participants completed the need for closure measures (Webster & Kruglanski, 1994) and responded to two conflict scenarios. They were assigned to take the role of midlevel managers in two conflict situations. One scenario depicted a conflict between a pharmacist at a drugstore and a client who felt sick after taking the medicine he bought from the store. The other scenario described an authorship dispute between two university professors. In the drugstore scenario, Sue, a manager of a drug chain store, was assigned to handle a dispute between a pharmacist and a customer who felt sick after taking the medicine bought from the store. After reading the scenario, participants were shown seven pieces of diagnostic information and six pieces of relational information. Diagnostic information was useful for deciding the disputants' causal responsibility in the incident (e.g., whether the pharmacist had a record of making similar mistakes), and relational information was useful for assessing the potential interpersonal impact of a certain way of handling the conflict (e.g., how the pharmacist's coworkers would feel if the pharmacist was fired). The participants were instructed to take the perspective of Sue. For each information item, they rated on a 6-point scale how important it was to have that information to resolve the conflict.

In the second scenario, Johnson, a university professor, was assigned to settle an authorship dispute between two university professors, Yang and Jones. After reading the scenario, participants took the role of Johnson and rated the perceived importance of five pieces of diagnostic information (e.g.,

Was there evidence that could help determine who was telling the truth?) and six pieces of relational information (e.g., How much concession was Yang/Jones willing to make?) for resolving the conflict. Consistent with previous research findings, compared to each other, European Americans considered diagnostic information to be more important, whereas Asian Americans found relational information to be more important. Again, this cultural effect was more pronounced among high (vs. low) NFCC participants.

Consistent results were also obtained in a study conducted in a reward allocation setting (Fu, Morris, Lee, et al., 2007). In this study, culture was experimentally manipulated among Hong Kong Chinese participants. Previous research has shown that because of Hong Kong's cosmopolitan environment, both Chinese and Western norms are prevalent in this city (Fu, Chiu, Morris, & Young, 2007). Consequently, it is possible to increase the salience of Chinese or Western norms to Hong Kong Chinese by priming them with Chinese or Western culture (presenting to them iconic symbols of Chinese or Western cultures; Hong, Morris, Chiu, & Benet-Martinez, 2000). As mentioned, the norms governing reward allocation are different in American and Chinese cultures, with American norms emphasizing contribution more and Chinese norms emphasizing equality more (Leung & Bond, 1984). Consistent with this cultural difference, Hong Kong Chinese adhered to the equality rule more when primed with Chinese culture and the contribution rule more when primed with American culture. Again, this culture-priming effect was particularly pronounced among individuals with high NFCC.

In sum, there is consistent evidence that individuals with high NFCC are more likely to adhere to the prevailing norms in their own culture, possibly because cultural norms, being established behavior guides in the culture, confer epistemic security. A question remains: Would norms in a foreign culture also provide closure to high NFCC individuals when these individuals interact with others in a foreign culture? We now turn to this question.

EPISTEMIC NEED IN TRANSCULTURAL CONTEXTS

NFCC and Cultural Assimilation

As mentioned, cultural norms offer epistemic protection against unpredictability, ambiguity, and uncertainty (Chiu et al., 2000; Fu, Morris, Lee, et al., 2007; Kruglanski, 2004). The norms in one's native culture, however, would have questionable epistemic utility in transcultural contexts, where individuals interact with people from other cultures. This is the case because norms in one's native culture may not be widely accepted in foreign cultures, particularly in cultures whose cultural traditions are markedly different from those in the native culture. Given the low consensual validity of native cultural norms in foreign cultures, high NFCC individuals should be particularly motivated to follow the norms in foreign cultures instead of adhering to the norms in their own culture when interacting with people from foreign cultures.

Results from several acculturation studies (Kashima & Loh, 2006; Kosic, Kruglanski, Pierro, & Mannetti, 2004) are consistent with this idea. In a series of studies, Kosic and colleagues (2004) surveyed 157 Croatian immigrants (Study 1) and 162 Polish immigrants (Study 2) residing in Rome, Italy. When immigrants move to a new country, they face a lot of uncertainty and rely on the norms in their reference group to provide behavior guides. Thus, to the new immigrants, norms in their reference group are closure providers. In the immigration studies, participants were asked to respond to a questionnaire that assessed what their initial reference group was when they first immigrated to Rome from their own country. Their acculturation strategies and NFCC were also assessed.

Because high NFCC individuals desire closure, they should be motivated to adhere to the behavioral norms in their reference group. Indeed, when the immigrants' initial reference group was made up of mainly host nationals (i.e., Italians), high (vs. low) NFCC immigrants were more motivated to assimilate to the Italian culture. When the immigrants' initial reference group was made up of their coethnics, however, high (vs. low) NFCC immigrants were more motivated to adhere to the norms in their native culture and were relatively slow in assimilating into the Italian culture.

In another study (Kashima & Loh, 2006), when Polish immigrants were asked to express their attitude toward different acculturation strategies, those with high (vs. low) NFCC rated assimilation more favorably and separation more negatively if they had many social connections with host nationals. Contrarily, high NFCC immigrants rated separation favorably and assimilation unfavorably if they had many social ties with their coethnics. For immigrants, norms in their social networks are closure providers. Thus, Polish immigrants who desire epistemic security would feel inclined to follow the norms in their social network.

The same results were obtained among Asian students studying in Australia. In one study (Kashima & Loh, 2006), 100 Asian international students responded to a questionnaire that assessed their social ties in Australia, their psychological and sociocultural adjustment in the host culture, and individual differences in NFCC. Among students with high NFCC, the more social ties they had with host nationals (i.e., Australians), the better they adjusted to Australian culture, presumably because these students were motivated to assimilate into the host culture.

In short, individuals who desire firm answers are motivated to follow cultural norms that confer epistemic security. When new immigrants' reference group and social network are composed mostly of host nationals, the norms in the host culture confer epistemic security, and high NFCC individuals would tend to follow norms in the host culture instead of those in their native culture. Conversely, when the reference group and social network are composed mostly of coethnics, the norms in the native culture confer epistemic security, and high NFCC individuals would tend to follow norms in the native culture instead of those in their host culture.

Effects of Cultural Identification

Culture also serves self-definition needs (see Chapter 7, this volume). Individuals who define the self vis-à-vis their cultural tradition (i.e., those with strong cultural identification) are likely to follow the norms in their culture. This may apply, however, to interactions in the local cultural contexts only.

According to social identity theory, individuals with strong ingroup identification tend to attribute to the self and other ingroup members the ingroup's defining characteristics and expect ingroup members to adhere to the ingroup norms (Tajfel, 1978; Tajfel & Turner, 1986; Turner, Hogg, Oakes, Reicher, & Wetherell, 1987). At the same time, high identifiers also seek to distinguish outgroups from the ingroup. Thus, they would attribute characteristics that are markedly different from the prototypic ingroup features to the outgroups and expect outgroup members to follow outgroup norms (Jetten, Spears, & Manstead, 1996). Accordingly, ingroup identification should increase the perceived homogeneity of both the ingroup and the outgroup and enhance the salience of between-group differences (Denson, Lickel, Curtis, Stenstrom, & Ames, 2006; Lickel, Miller, Stenstrom, Denson, & Schmader, 2006; Turner & Oakes, 1989). That is, compared with low identifiers, individuals who highly identify with their own culture are more likely to perceive intercultural boundaries as discrete (see Chapters 12 and 13, this volume). Consequently, relative to low identifiers, high identifiers would perceive (a) norms in their own culture to be better closure providers in local cultural contexts and (b) norms in foreign cultures to be better closure providers in foreign cultural contexts. This analysis implies that ingroup cultural identification should enhance high NFCC individuals' conformity to the local norms in the culture where the interaction takes place (Chao et al., 2009).

Recent evidence supports these predictions. In one study, Chao and colleagues (2009, Study 1) examined the effects of NFCC and cultural identification on the way European-American students manage conflicts in the United States and China. They assessed participants' NFCC (Webster & Kruglanski, 1994) and identification with American culture (Kosterman & Feshbach, 1989). Next, the participants responded to modified versions of the two conflict situations – the drugstore scenario and the authorship dispute scenario – used in the study by Fu, Morris, Lee and colleagues (2007, Study 2). In the drugstore scenario, Sue was depicted as a New Jersey–born European-American manager of a drug store. She was assigned to handle a dispute between a pharmacist and a customer who felt sick after taking medicine bought from the store. In the U.S. condition, the participants were told that, because the chain store expanded, Sue was relocated to a branch in Pittsburgh, Pennsylvania, and was now the manager there. The conflict involved the pharmacist Donna and the customer Chris and took place in the Pittsburgh branch. In the China condition, the participants were told that Sue was relocated to a branch in China because the chain store expanded and that the conflict involved the pharmacist Xue-lin and the customer Dong. After reading the scenario, the participants were told to take the role of Sue and handle the situation. As in the study by Fu, Morris, Lee and colleagues (2007), the participants were presented with diagnostic information and relational information and were asked to rate how important it was to have each kind of information to resolve the conflict.

In the authorship dispute scenario, Johnson, a university professor, was assigned to settle an authorship dispute between two university professors. In the U.S. condition, the participants learned that Johnson accepted a job offer from a big research university in California and was now the head of the Department of Alternative Medicine in the university. The conflict took place in this university between Professor Jones of Golden Gate University and Professor Tony Smith in Johnson's department. In the China condition, participants learned that Johnson accepted a job offer from a big research university in China and that the conflict took place between Professor Yang of Zhongyuen University and Professor Huei Chen in Johnson's department. Participants were told to take the role of Johnson and rate the perceived importance of diagnostic information and relational information for resolving the conflict.

Results of a pretest showed that American students were aware of the different normative expectations in American and Chinese contexts. When asked to indicate how American or Chinese managers would handle the drugstore conflict if the conflict occurred in the United States or China, the 52 American participants who took the pretest expected that American managers would seek out diagnostic information when handling conflict situations in the United States and that Chinese managers would seek out relational information when the conflict took place in China.

The results from the main study revealed that, as expected, high (vs. low) NFCC American students were more inclined to follow the American norm of seeking diagnostic information when handling the conflict in the United States and to follow the Chinese norm of seeking relational information when handling the conflict in China. More importantly, the NFCC effects on conformity to American norms in American contexts and Chinese norms in Chinese contexts were more pronounced among individuals who strongly identify with American culture.

Results from another study conducted in China provided convergent evidence for the effects of NFCC and cultural identification on cultural norm adherence. In this study (Chao et al., 2009, Study 2), the participants were 241 Chinese master of business administration (MBA) students in Beijing who responded to a reward allocation situation that took place in China or the United States. All the participants had at least five years of work experience. In the China condition, participants were told that Chen Dong was a manager of the sales department of a company. Because the company expanded, he was relocated to Nan Zhou, China. One day, he asked his accountants Li Jian and He Bo Li to figure out the department's performance, and promised to reward them for their overtime work. The participants were told that Li Jian worked hard and was able to finish twice as much work as He Bo Li. In the U.S. condition, Chen Dong was relocated to Chicago, Illinois, as the company expanded, and the reward was to be allocated between Jim Smith and Peter Hudson.

After reading the scenario, participants were asked to estimate how the two employees in the scenario would allocate the reward if they were given the money to allocate among themselves. Results confirmed that participants were aware of a well-documented cultural difference in normative expectations (Chiu & Hong, 1997; Leung & Bond, 1984; see Chapter 11, this volume): They expected the two American employees to follow the contribution rule to motivate job performance and Chinese employees to follow the equality rule to maintain a good coworker relationship. Furthermore, consistent with the social identity theory – which predicts that ingroup cultural identification would increase the salience of perceived cultural differences (Turner & Oakes, 1989) – participants who more strongly identified with Chinese culture tended to perceive greater cultural differences between the allocation norms in American and Chinese cultures: They believed that most Americans valued productivity and that most Chinese valued harmony.

Next, half of the participants in the China condition and half in the U.S. condition were assigned to one of the two allocation goal conditions. In the productivity condition, participants were told that, when distributing the reward, the manager sought to promote productivity. In the harmony condition they learned that the manager's allocation goal was to promote interpersonal harmony. For example, participants in the China-productivity condition were told that Chen Dong wanted to improve productivity, and they believed that his allocation decision would motivate Li Jian and He Bo Li to work harder and increase productivity in the future. Participants in the China-harmony condition were told that Chen Dong wanted to promote coworker relationships in the company, and they believed that his allocation decision would make Li Jian and He Bo Li enjoy working together more in the future.

After reading the allocation method of Chen Dong, participants evaluated his allocation decision in terms of its perceived fairness, desirability, and appropriateness. As expected, participants with high (vs. low) NFCC evaluated the allocation more favorably when the manager followed the American norm of promoting productivity in the American context and when the manager followed the Chinese norm of promoting harmony in the Chinese context. Furthermore, these effects of NFCC on norm adherence were more pronounced among individuals who more strongly identified with Chinese culture.

In sum, cultural norms confer epistemic security through their consensual validity. Factors that increase the perceived consensual validity of cultural norms should also enhance the utility of cultural norms as a closure provider. Ingroup cultural identification may increase the perceived consensual validity of local cultural norms in local cultural contexts and foreign cultural norms in foreign cultural contexts. Individuals with high NFCC desire closure. Thus, they are motivated to follow local cultural norms in local cultural contexts, as well as foreign cultural norms in foreign cultural contexts, particularly if they have high levels of ingroup cultural identification.

CONCLUSIONS

In this chapter, using individual differences in the need for firm answer as an example, we sought to illustrate the epistemic function of culture. Specifically, by virtue of its high level of consensual validity, cultural norms offer members of a culture firm answers and widely accepted behavioral guides. They reduce ambiguity and uncertainty in social interactions and confer epistemic security. Thus, individuals who have high NFCC are particularly likely to follow cultural norms.

This analysis also indicates that people do not always adhere to the cultural norms in their own culture. Indeed, in situations in which norms in their own culture can no longer confer epistemic security, individuals, particularly those with high NFCC, tend not to follow these norms. This is the case for new immigrants whose social network and reference group consist primarily of host nationals. This is also the case in transcultural interactions. Indeed, under these circumstances, individuals who desire firm answers are the first to follow norms in a foreign culture because foreign norms are better able to confer epistemic security.

Our analysis challenges the idea that cultural conformity is always an indication of passivity and submission. Rather, cultural conformity can be an expression of personal NFCC. This analysis also accounts for individual and situational variations in cultural norm conformance within a culture. Individuals vary in NFCC, and situations vary in the salience of NFCC. Thus, within a culture, some people (e.g., high NFCC individuals) are more likely than others to follow cultural norms, and some situations (e.g., high time pressure) are more likely than others to elicit cultural conformity.

We show that high NFCC individuals are relatively likely to follow cultural norms. It should be emphasized, however, that cultural conformity does not always lead to cultural competence. This is particularly the case in transcultural interactions. When interacting with foreign nationals, high NFCC individuals may be inclined to follow the cultural norms in the foreigners' culture. If these individuals do not possess a nuanced understanding of the relevant cultural differences, however, they are likely to act on their stereotypes rather than accurate representations of foreign cultures. As a result, quality of the transcultural interactions will suffer (see Chapter 13, this volume). Furthermore, situation-specific behavioral expectations in a concrete interaction may deviate from global cultural norms. In this kind of situations, individuals who indiscriminately follow cultural norms will not function effectively.

REFERENCES

Chao, M. M., Zhang, Z.-X., & Chiu, C-y. (2009). Adherence to perceived norms across cultural boundaries: The role of need for cognitive closure and ingroup identification. *Group Processes and Intergroup Relations, 13*, 69–89.

Chiu, C-y., & Hong, Y. (1997). Justice in Chinese societies: A Chinese perspective. In H. S. R. Kao and D. Sinha (Eds.), *Asian perspectives on psychology* (pp. 164–184). Thousand Oaks, CA: Sage Publications, Inc.

Chiu, C-y., Morris, M. W., Hong, Y., & Menon, T. (2000). Motivated cultural cognition: The impact of implicit cultural theories on dispositional attribution varies as a function of need for closure. *Journal of Personality and Social Psychology, 78,* 247–259.

De Dreu, C. K. W. (2003). Time pressure and closing of the mind in negotiation. *Organization Behavior and Human Decision Processes, 91,* 280–295.

De Dreu, C. K. W., Koole, S. L., & Oldersma, F. L. (1999). On the seizing and freezing of negotiator inferences: Need for cognitive closure moderates the use of heuristics in negotiation. *Personality and Social Psychology Bulletin, 25,* 348–362.

Denson, T. F., Lickel, B., Curtis, M., Stenstrom, D. M., & Ames, D. R. (2006). The roles of entitativity and essentiality in judgments of collective responsibility. *Group Processes and Intergroup Relations, 9,* 43–61.

Dijksterhius, A., Van Knippenberg, A., Kruglanski, A., & Schaper, C. (1996). Motivated social cognition: Need for closure effects on memory and judgment. *Journal of Experimental Social Psychology, 32,* 254–270.

Fu, H., Morris, M. W., Lee, S., Chao, M., Chiu, C-y., & Hong, Y. (2007). Epistemic motives and cultural conformity: Need for closure, culture, and context as determinants of conflict judgments. *Journal of Personality and Social Psychology, 9,* 191–207.

Fu, J. H., Chiu, C-y., Morris, M. W., & Young, M. (2007). Spontaneous inferences from cultural cues: Varying responses of cultural insiders and outsiders. *Journal of Cross-Cultural Psychology, 38,* 58–75.

Gelfand, M. J., Nishii, L. H., Holcombe, K. M., Dyer, N., Ohbuchi, K., & Fukuno, M. (2001). Cultural influences on cognitive representations of conflict: Interpretations of conflict episodes in the United States and Japan. *Journal of Applied Psychology, 86,* 1059–1074.

Hong, Y., Morris, M. W., Chiu, C-y., & Benet-Martinez, V. (2000). Multicultural minds: A dynamic constructivist approach to culture and cognition. *American Psychologist, 55,* 709–720.

Jetten, J., Spears, R., & Manstead, A. S. R. (1996). Intergroup norms and intergroup discrimination: Distinctive self-categorization and social identity effects. *Journal of Personality and Social Psychology, 71,* 1222–1233.

Kashima, E. S., & Loh, E. (2006). International students' acculturation: Effects of international, conational, and local ties and need for closure. *International Journal of Intercultural Relations, 30,* 471–485.

Kosic, A., Kruglanski, A. W., Pierro, A., & Mannetti, L. (2004). Social cognition of immigrants acculturation: Effects of the need for closure and the reference group at entry. *Journal of Personality and Social Psychology, 86,* 1–18.

Kosterman, R., & Feshbach, S. (1989). Toward a measure of patriotic and nationalistic attitudes. *Political Psychology, 10,* 257–274.

Kruglanski, A. W. (2004). *The psychology of closed-mindedness.* New York: Psychology Press.

Kruglanski, A. W., Shah, J. Y., Pierro, A., & Mannetti, L. (2002). When similarity breeds content: Need for closure and the allure of homogeneous and self-resembling groups. *Journal of Personality and Social Psychology, 83,* 648–662.

Kruglanski, A. W., & Webster, D. M. (1991). Group members' reactions to opinion deviates and conformists at varying degrees of proximity to decision deadline and of environmental noise. *Journal of Personality and Social Psychology, 61,* 212–225.

Kruglanski, A. W., & Webster, D. M. (1996). Motivated closing of the mind: "Seizing" and "freezing." *Psychological Review,* 103, 263–283.

Leung, K. (1987). Some determinants of reactions to procedural models for conflict resolution: A cross-national study. *Journal of Personality and Social Psychology, 53,* 898–908.

Leung, K., & Bond, M. H. (1984). The impact of cultural collectivism on reward allocation. *Journal of Personality and Social Psychology, 47,* 793–804.

Leung, K., & Morris, M. W. (2001). Justice through the lens of culture and ethnicity. In J. Sanders and V. L. Hamilton (Eds.), *Handbook of justice research in law* (pp. 343–378). Dordrecht, The Netherlands: Kluwer Academic Publishers.

Lickel, B., Miller, N., Stenstrom, D. M., Denson, T. F., & Schmader, T. (2006). Vicarious retribution: The role of collective blame in intergroup aggression. *Personality and Social Psychology Review, 10,* 372–390.

Menon, T., Morris, M. W., Chiu, C-y., & Hong, Y. (1999). Culture and the construal of agency: Attribution to individual versus group dispositions. *Journal of Personality and Social Psychology, 76,* 701–717.

Morris, M. W., Williams, K. Y., Leung, K., Larrick, R., Mendoza, M. T., Bhatnagar, D., et al. (1998). Conflict management style: Accounting for cross national differences. *Journal of International Business Studies, 29,* 729–747.

Rahim, M. A. (1983). A measure of styles of handling interpersonal conflict. *Academy of Management Journal, 26,* 368–376.

Richter, L., & Kruglanski, A. W. (1999). Motivated search for common ground: Need for closure effects on audience design in interpersonal communication. *Personality and Social Psychology Bulletin, 25,* 1101–1114.

Sechrist, G. B., & Stangor, C. (2001). Perceived consensus influences intergroup behavior and stereotype accessibility. *Journal of Personality and Social Psychology, 80,* 645–654.

Sullivan, J., Peterson, R. B., Kameda, N., & Shimada, J. (1981). The relationship between conflict resolution approaches and trust: A cross cultural study. *Academy of Management Journal, 24,* 803–815.

Tajfel, H. (Ed.). (1978). *Differentiation between social groups: Studies in the social psychology of intergroup relations.* London, UK: Academic Press.

Tajfel, H., & Turner, J. C. (1986). The social identity theory of intergroup behavior. In S. Worchel & W. G. Austin (Eds.), *Psychology of intergroup relations* (pp. 7–24). Chicago: Nelson.

Turner, J. C., Hogg, M., Oakes, P., Reicher, S., & Wetherell, M. (1987). *Rediscovering the social group: A self-categorization theory.* Oxford: Blackwell.

Turner, J. C., & Oakes, P. J. (1989). Self-categorization theory and social influence. In P. B. Paulus (Ed.), *Psychology of group influence* (2nd ed., pp. 233–275). Hillsdale, NJ: Lawrence Erlbaum Associates.

Webster, D. M., & Kruglanski, A. W. (1994). Individual differences in need for cognitive closure. *Journal of Personality and Social Psychology, 67,* 1049–1062.

Webster, D. M., & Kruglanski, A. W. (1998). Cognitive and social consequences of the need for cognitive closure. In S. Wolfgang (Ed.), *European review of social psychology,* Vol. 8 (pp. 133–161). Hoboken, NJ: John Wiley & Sons, Inc.

6

Existential Functions of Culture: The Monumental Immortality Project

PELIN KESEBIR

It is difficult to imagine a culture that serves no adaptive functions. Indeed, scholars agree that, for a culture to endure, it must contribute to the survival of the species, the optimal functioning of the society in which it exists, as well as to the optimal psychological functioning of the individuals comprising that culture (Chiu & Hong, 2006; Lehman, Chiu, & Schaller, 2004; Schaller & Crandall, 2004). Although there are various adaptive roles that cultures play, my focus in this chapter will be on the existential functions of culture; more specifically, on how cultures help their constituents deal with the ultimate questions of existence, such as how to live a meaningful life in the face of inevitable death. I will argue that individuals are strongly motivated to deny their basic creatureliness and to try to outshine death and decay; and it is through participating in and contributing to culture that they attempt to become eligible for immortality – be it literal or symbolic. I will start with a discussion of why the human craving to transcend death is so potent, and then move on to the various ways in which culture permits us to satisfy this craving.

THE DREAD OF MORTALITY

Evolution has imbued humans with the capacity to mentally travel through time and to represent the self's extended existence through time by reminiscing about the past, being aware of the present, and anticipating the future (Wheeler, Stuss, & Tulving, 1997). This unique ability has allowed our ancestors to learn from the past and to plan for the future; freed human kind from becoming slaves to the immediate environment; and, combined with the development of symbolic thought, rendered the accumulation of cultural knowledge possible. The exact same developments that set the stage for the emergence of culture and bestowed humans with an unsurpassed position of dominance in nature, however, concomitantly led them to the agonizing awareness of mortality. Novelist David Lodge vividly portrays the tragic consequences of self-consciousness for humans: "Imagine what a terrible shock it was to Neanderthal Man, or Cro-Magnon Man, or whoever it was that first clocked the dreadful truth: that one day he would be meat. Lions and tigers don't know that. Apes don't know it. We do" (2002, p. 102).

An eternal life would be, in all probability, more a curse than a blessing. Many philosophers agree that what gives life its depth and intensity is its limited duration. In a tongue-in-cheek manner, an observer communicates the same insight when she says that millions long for immortality who do not know what to do with themselves on a rainy Sunday afternoon. Rational thought experiments about the aggravations of a never-ending life, however, are far from sufficient to reconcile ourselves to the dark, unsettling idea of death. The knowledge of ultimate annihilation is at complete odds with the biologically rooted desire for self-preservation, and the dread accompanying the idea that "our existence is but a brief crack of light between two eternities of darkness" (Nabokov, 1951/1999, p. 9) is simply lodged in our deepest psyche; the inescapable dread is felt almost in our marrow. In Ernest Becker's words, "This is the terror: to have emerged from nothing, to have a name, consciousness of self, deep inner feelings, an excruciating inner yearning for life and self-expression – and with all this yet to die" (Becker, 1973, p. 87). This tension between the instinctual urge to continue being and the certainty of death constitutes a fundamental quandary for humankind, which is apt to generate tremendous anxiety. William James dubbed this kind of anxiety "the worm at the core" (1912, p. 158), emphasizing how the awareness of death is continually on the edge of our consciousness, affecting us as nothing else does.

Knowledge of ineludible death, a fate shared with the basest of creatures, brings with itself also the awareness of one's basic creatureliness. Humans have a dual nature: They are both Gods and food for worms; half animal and half symbolic, "up in the stars and yet housed in a heart-pumping, breath-gasping body that once belonged to a fish" (Becker, 1973, p. 26). Awareness of infinite superiority over the animal kingdom, juxtaposed against the real-ization of ultimate sameness with the rest of nature in death and decay, has the potential to induce extreme existential anxiety. This anxiety can offer an explanation for why humans are often ill at ease with their own corporeality, with being "fornicating, defecating, urinating, vomiting, flatulent, exfoli-ating pieces of meat" (Solomon, Greenberg, & Pyszczynski, 2004, p. 16). Evidence for the interrelation between fear of creatureliness and death anx-iety is provided by studies showing that reminders of mortality induce an intensified need to distance oneself from one's body, whereas reminders of one's physicality lead to increased accessibility of death-related thoughts (Goldenberg, 2005; Landau et al., 2006).

The dread of mortality and creatureliness, a dread born of consciousness, constitutes a potent problem for the human psyche, which needs to be dealt with on both an individual and a societal level. Cultural anthropologist Ernest Becker, in his Pulitzer winning book, *The Denial of Death* (1973), wrote that "of all things that move man, one of the principal ones is his terror of death" (p. 11), and went on to argue that a wide array of human actions could be explained by the terror-inducing awareness of death. Furthermore, to survive, cultures were forced to offer means of managing this terror too. Accordingly, humans, trying to perceive themselves (and to be perceived) as anything but animals, used the symbols of culture to assure triumph over nature, to rise above creatureliness, to have lives that somehow counted more than the existence of merely physical things (1975, p. 4). Culture, in its essence, was "a heroic denial of creatureliness" (1973, p. 159).

In the mid 1980s, largely inspired by Ernest Becker's writings, a group of social psychologists proposed Terror Management Theory (Pyszczyn-ski, Greenberg, & Koole, 2004). The theory posited that the potential for terror emanating from the knowledge of mortality is kept under control by an anxiety buffering system that consists of self-esteem and faith in one's worldview. In subsequent years, close personal relationships have also been proposed as an important component of this anxiety-buffering sys-tem. Applying experimental methods to existential psychological questions, Terror Management Theorists attempted to show how humans strive to live up to the standards of their cultural worldviews as a shield against being "merely transient animals groping to survive in a meaningless universe, des-tined only to die and decay" (Pyszczynski, Greenberg, Solomon, Arndt, & Schimel, 2004, p. 436). In the rest of this chapter, I will elaborate on the various ways culture provides a solution to the deep rooted fear of death and creatureliness.

CULTURE AS A FOUNTAIN OF IMMORTALITY

As British writer Samuel Butler once remarked, to himself everyone is immortal; the person may know he is going to die, but he can never know that he is dead. Freud expressed the same idea when he said, "We cannot, indeed, imagine our own death; whenever we try to do so we find that we survive ourselves as spectators... At bottom no one believes in his own death, which amounts to saying: in the unconscious every one of us is convinced of his immortality" (Freud, 1918, p. 41). As much as we may subconsciously subscribe to the irrational belief of invulnerability and imperishability, however, the fact of death remains. The instinctive craving to continue to exist is still all-encompassing, rendering immortality the ultimate Holy Grail. What cultures do, at this juncture, is to set the stage on which humans pursue this vision in various and even conflicting ways. Cultures, functioning as shared symbolic conceptions of reality, not only give meaning and order to existence, but also provide a venue for expanding and perpetuating oneself in a larger beyond. In other words, cultures carry within themselves the prospect that death can be transcended, either literally or symbolically.

Literal Immortality

Literal immortality is promised by religions to their believers, in the form of heaven, reincarnation, or some other type of afterlife. Experimental findings that subtle intimations of mortality produce increased belief in an afterlife and that artificially increasing beliefs in an afterlife decrease death-related anxiety (Dechesne et al., 2003) testify to how religions can mollify existential anxiety by granting the prospect of eternal life. It would be a mistake, however, to confine the existential value of religion to its promise of an afterlife. Religions, apart from everything else, effectively address the distinctive human need "to spiritualize human life, to lift it onto a special immortal plane, beyond the cycles of life and death that characterize all other organisms" (Becker, 1973, p. 231). There is little doubt that religions offer systematic answers to the profound existential questions provoked by our awareness of mortality. "Here is the real core of the religious problem: Help! Help!" observed William James (1912, p. 162); "Religion saves man from a surrender to death and destruction" maintained anthropologist Bronislaw Malinoswki (1954, p. 51), and Leo Tolstoy claimed that the essence of all religions is composed of the answer to a single question: "What is the purpose of such momentary, uncertain and vacillating existence in this eternal, well-defined and never-ending world?" (1987, p. 134).

In addition to anecdotal evidence, empirical data also lend support to the notion that devout, intrinsic religious beliefs are associated with lessened death anxiety and heightened existential well-being (Batson, Schoenrade, & Ventis, 1993). It is worth pointing out, however, that it is only an intrinsic orientation to religion that leads to such outcomes, and not an extrinsic one. Intrinsic religion, according to the original conceptualization by Allport, refers to genuine, heartfelt religion that is lived as an end in itself. Extrinsic religion, in contrast, is "religion as a means," religion that serves utilitarian purposes such as gaining security, sociability, and status (Allport & Ross, 1967). It stands to reason that only an honestly held and deeply internalized belief system – an intrinsic orientation toward religion – can furnish the individual with the means necessary to manage existential terror. In line with this theory, recent research has shown that, compared to people low in intrinsic religiousness, people high in intrinsic religiousness do not engage in worldview defense after a reminder of their mortality, and also experience lessened death-thought accessibility following mortality salience if they are given a chance to affirm their religious belief (Jonas & Fischer, 2006).

The enchantment that religion adds to life, which is "not rationally or logically deducible from anything else" (James, 1912, p. 47), can also be partly attributed to the innumerable experiences with the "sacred" provided by religion. Indeed, all religions have their own sacred times (e.g., Sabbath and other holidays, or "holy days"), sacred texts (e.g., Bible, Talmud), sacred places (e.g., churches, mosques, Mecca, Jerusalem), sacred personalities (e.g., prophets, saints), and sacred experiences (e.g., pilgrimages, ritual meals). "Sacred" refers to something that is timeless and supremely meaningful, something of an entirely different order than ordinary life, and as such is capable of taking the person outside of self, matter, and mortality (Belk, Wallendorf, & Sherry, 1989). The opportunities presented by religion to interact with the sacred; to transcend one's mundane, creaturely existence; and to get in touch with something from the realm of immortality might thus engender jolts of meaning for the individual, thereby helping to ease death anxiety.

Religions, through a variety of mechanisms, address the need to combat death anxiety and seek immortality, born of humankind's desperation when dealing with the ultimate problems of existence. For a comprehensive terror management analysis of the functions of religion, please see Vail et al. (2010). Evidently, the same mission of rendering death more palatable can be accomplished by certain aspects of culture other than religion, and this is where I turn next.

Symbolic Immortality: The Next Best Thing

For those who do not subscribe to beliefs in any form of the hereafter, the only remaining way to transcend death is through achieving "symbolic immortality." Symbolic immortality can be defined as the sense that one is a valuable part of something larger, more significant, and longer lasting than one's individual existence. Robert Jay Lifton (1979) has elaborated on the different ways in which humans strive to obtain symbolic immortality, the most common of which seem to be living on through one's progeny and living on through one's works. Studies showing that the aftermath of major disasters (e.g., earthquakes, floods) witness significant increases in the number of newborn children (Cohan & Cole, 2002) provide indirect support for the claim that children, in a way, embody "symbolic immortality projects" for their parents.

Identification with Culture
One mode in which humans strive for symbolic immortality that is most intimately linked to the death-defying role of culture is identifying oneself with entities larger and longer-lasting than the self, such as one's nation, ethnicity, or religion. In their article aptly titled "I Belong, Therefore, I Exist," Castano, Yzerbyt, Paladino, and Sacchi argue that "through identification with social groups, the individuals can project themselves in space and time, beyond their personal death. They participate in an entity that is not subject to the mortal fate that characterizes them as human beings" (2002, p. 137). Similarly, Becker notes that being part of something bigger puts the individual at peace and at oneness, "gives him a sense of self-expansion in a larger beyond, and so heightens his being, giving him truly a feeling of transcendent value" (1973, p. 152).

Research provides evidence for the notion that the need to immerse oneself in a larger entity and the desire to ward off existential terror are closely related. Castano and colleagues (2002) have revealed, for example, that reminders of mortality increase participants' identification with their ethnic identities as Italians, compared to a control condition. After a mortality salience prime, the participants also rated Italians as a significantly more stable and coherent group, possibly reflecting a desire to see their bulwark against death as highly durable and imperishable. It is important to point out, however, that only a social identity with positive connotations for the individual is capable of offering a balm for existential insecurity. As a case in point, Hispanic participants evaluated paintings by Hispanic painters more positively after a mortality salience prime, but only when they had not been exposed to a negative example of their ingroup by reading about a "Mexican drug cartel chief" (Arndt, Greenberg, Schimel, Pyszczynski, & Solomon, 2002). In a similar vein, Dechesne, Greenberg, Arndt, and Schimel (2000) have demonstrated that participants who were reminded of their own mortality exhibited reduced affiliation with their college football team after a loss. Apparently, being part of an imperishable, yet despised, social entity does not constitute a desirable means of attaining symbolic immortality.

Endorsement of Cultural Values

If cultural entities do indeed serve as buffers against death anxiety, then one would expect that the norms and values that define these cultures would be fervently endorsed by individuals after reminders of mortality. Hundreds of studies conducted in a variety of countries in the last two decades substantiate this hypothesis. Persons who follow cultural norms are rewarded more generously, and those who violate them are punished more severely after mortality is made salient. Rosenblatt, Greenberg, Solomon, Pyszczynski, and Lyon (1989) found, for instance, that reminding people of their mortality led to harsher treatments of a prostitute and more favorable treatments of a hero (a woman who helped police apprehend a criminal). In a similar vein, Greenberg, Pyszczynski, Solomon, Simon, and Breus (1994) showed that mortality salience inductions increased the preference for an author with pro-American views over an author with anti-American views among American students (also see Chapter 14, this volume). In addition, a study by Strachman and Schimel (2006) revealed that, after they wrote about their own deaths, undergraduates in a romantic relationship reported reduced commitment to partners with different cultural worldviews.

Outgroup Hostility

Unfortunately, existential dread not only propels ingroup bias and preference for similar others, but heightens outgroup hostility and intolerance for dissimilar others as well. Given that cultural worldviews are ultimately fragile human constructions, social consensus is imperative for sustaining individual and collective belief in them (Solomon, Greenberg, & Pyszczynski, 2004). It is through consensual validation that "one's beliefs and perceptions of the world are bolstered and rendered subjectively certain" (Dechesne & Kruglanski, 2004, p. 252), which is what makes the existence of people with differing conceptions of reality so threatening. Conflicts between cultural worldviews are, in their essence, conflicts between immortality projects. This explains why nationalism, religious fanaticism, outgroup derogation, prejudice, and discrimination are prone to escalate whenever existential anxieties are heightened.

A study by Greenberg and colleagues (1990) demonstrated, for instance, that participants with a Christian religious background evaluated a Christian target more positively and a Jewish target more negatively after a mortality salience treatment. Greenberg, Schimel, Martens, Solomon, and Pyszczynski (2001) found that White Americans exhibited increased sympathy toward a White racist following a death prime. Others have shown that, compared to a control condition, participants in the mortality salience condition administered a particularly large amount of hot sauce to a target who disparaged their political views (McGregor et al., 1998). These and other similar studies support the bleak observation that "prejudice, scapegoating, ideological fervor, and ongoing ethnic strife may be the psychological price to be paid for psychological equanimity via death-denying cultural worldviews" (Solomon, Greenberg, Schimel, Arndt, & Pyszczynski, 2004, p. 36).

Cultural Icons as Carriers of Symbolic Immortality

Cherished symbols of groups with which an individual identifies also serve a terror management function, as a creative study by Greenberg, Porteus, Simon, Pyszczynski, and Solomon (1995) illustrated. The authors found that, when participants were reminded of death before an alleged creativity task requiring them to use a flag as a sieve and a crucifix as a hammer, they had a more difficult time solving the problem, expressed more reluctance to use the icons in culturally inappropriate ways, and also experienced greater tension when doing so. This finding indicates that cultural icons, serving as enduring symbols of a culture, are an integral part of individuals' death-denying repertoire. These icons are quasi-sacred props in the human drama of overcoming one's basic animal condition and achieving symbolic immortality.

The inexhaustible need for heroes and the universal fascination with fame can also be seen as reflections of the same need for symbolic self-perpetuation. Psychoanalyst Otto Rank is echoing this idea when he notes that "every group, however small or great, has . . . an impulse for eternalization, which manifests itself in the creation of and care for national, religious, and artistic heroes" (1968, p. 415). These heroes – particularly those who represent the culture's core values and achieve iconic status – serve as a buffer against existential anxiety. Their perceived imperishability is a source of existential stamina for the masses, allowing them to experience immortality by proxy. In Ernest Becker's words, "the urge to deification, the constant placing of certain select persons on pedestals, the reading into them of extra powers: the more they have, the more rubs off on us. We participate in their immortality" (1973, p. 148). The hysterical crowds at the funerals of such cultural icons as Princess Diana or Pope John Paul II, weeping hysterically and tearing their clothes, in that sense, were displaying the shock they felt at the annihilation of their bulwark against death – something they subconsciously deemed to be indestructible.

Research conducted by Kesebir and Chiu (2008) provides empirical support for how reminders of death motivate participants to regard famous people, who embody core cultural values as "less mortal" than ordinary humans, both symbolically and literally. The researchers demonstrated, for example, that American undergraduates, when reminded of their own mortality, expect famous Americans (e.g., Abraham Lincoln, John F. Kennedy, Oprah Winfrey) who exemplify American values to live longer. Similarly, they expect that famous Americans (already dead or still alive), and especially those who represent the values of the American culture, will be remembered for a longer time in the future when they are primed with mortality. In another study, Turkish participants estimated the likelihood of a plane crash when there was a famous Turkish person on board. The results revealed that the more the participant perceived the famous person to represent core Turkish values, the lower was the estimated probability of the plane crash. In another study, in which participants read a scenario about running into Oprah Winfrey in a Chicago coffee shop, they found this encounter more pleasant to the extent that they believed Oprah represents American values. More importantly, for those who had been reminded of their mortality, this effect was even stronger. Taken together, these studies attest to the semi–god status that famous people occupy in people's hearts and minds, and shed some light on how existential concerns, at least partly, drive this phenomenon.

OTHER ROADS FROM HERE TO ETERNITY

Leaving a Legacy

If one way to achieve symbolic immortality is to passively immerse oneself in culture and partake in its eternality, another way is to be an active contributor to culture and leave a legacy that will defy ultimate insignificance. "Creating visible testaments to one's existence in the form of great works of art or science, impressive buildings or monuments, amassing great fortunes or vast properties" (Solomon, Greenberg, & Pyszczynski, 2004, pp. 16–17) can all aid individuals in their efforts to overcome the excruciating sense of transience by "leaving their footprints . . . on the sands of time" (Schmitt, & Leonard, 1986, p. 1089). It is this kind of immortality that Goethe had in mind when he remarked that "life is the childhood of our immortality" and that led Don Carlos in Friedrich Schiller's eponymous play to lament "[T]wenty-three years old, and I've done nothing for my immortality!" In Irvin Yalom's words, "To the extent that one attains power, one's death fear is further assuaged and belief in one's specialness further reinforced. Getting ahead, achieving, accumulating material wealth, leaving works behind as imperishable monuments becomes a way of life which effectively conceals the mortal questions churning below" (1980, p. 121).

The act of contributing to culture through creativity and accomplishment is perceived as a triumph over one's basic animal nature, a leap toward immortality, and, as such, a cure for existential angst. Interestingly, the hunger for such symbolic immortality may even trump the desire for life. As reported in *The Economist*, more than half of 198 Olympic-level American athletes gave an affirmative response when asked whether they would take a banned drug if they knew that by taking it they would win every competition for the next five years but then die from the substance's side effects ("Superhuman Heroes," 1998).

Materialism

One mode of symbolic immortality that is particularly valued in modern societies is the acquisition of money and material goods. Materialism, or "the importance a person attaches to worldly possessions" (Arnould, Price, & Zinkhan, 2002, p. 165), has been recognized by many thinkers as a means to attain existential assurance. Tennessee Williams makes the Big Daddy character in his Pulitzer-winning play, *Cat on a Hot Tin Roof*, observe that, "The human animal is a beast that dies and if he's got money he buys and buys and buys and I think the reason he buys everything he can buy is that in the back of his mind he has the crazy hope that one of his purchases will be life ever-lasting" (Williams, 1955, p. 73). Similarly, Elizabeth Hirschman contends that underlying the American ideology of affluence is the pursuit of secular personal immortality through material means (1990). The ideas linking materialism to existential concerns have also been subjected to empirical inquiry by scholars inspired by Terror Management Theory. Mandel and Heine (1999) have demonstrated, for instance, that subtle reminders of mortality increase preferences for high-status products such as Lexus automobiles or Rolex watches. This increased preference for high-status brands can also be partly explained by the idea that such well-established, upscale brands are associated with notions like excellence, permanence, and timelessness – the desire for which may be intensified by reminders of mortality. Another study by Kasser and Sheldon (2000) revealed that participants who were primed with mortality not only reported higher financial expectations for themselves 15 years in the future, they also became greedier in a forest-management simulation game.

Overall, these studies suggest that avaricious, materialistic behavior mitigates existential terror, among other things, by securing the acquisition of commodities that are exempt, as inanimate objects, from the mortal fate awaiting human beings.

As Rank emphasizes, "it is more than mere economic need or social ambition which spurs the individual to rise above the mass and become distinguished through wealth, power or creativity"; rather, it is the "need for fulfillment in terms of his personal immortality" (1941, p. 233). From this perspective, one may expect that children who had to confront the harsh realities of life and their defenselessness against those realities at an early age would be more highly motivated to strive for greatness and to attain symbolic immortality, compared to their peers who had not been treated so unkindly in their early years. Indeed, the number of eminent personalities who had physical or sensory disabilities, who suffered from chronic illnesses in childhood or adolescence, or who experienced economic reversals or changes of fortune during their formative years, seems to be disproportionately high. Likewise, studies indicate a propensity for geniuses of all kinds to have lost one or both parents at an early age. In one inquiry, 55% of creative writers were found to have lost a parent before age 15, a percentage that is noticeably higher than the comparable ratio for the general population. Even more dramatically, incidence rates of early parental death were found to be 63% among British prime ministers (Simonton, 1999).

Artistic Creations

One realm in which the urge to extend one's being into eternity can find immense fulfillment is the uniquely human institution of art. The artist escapes death and oblivion by creating a timeless work. In Rank's words, "in creation the artist tries to immortalize his mortal life" (1968, p. 39). After all, *ars longa, vita brevis* – art is long and life is short. Notably, the same works of art that propel their creators to immortality penetrate the culture and become candidates for immortalization themselves. Mickey Mouse, for example, not only bequeathed Walt Disney's name to eternity, but also came to be an imperishable icon of the American culture. It is in this way that the personal immortality projects of individual artists give birth to the collective immortality project that is culture. Furthermore, encounters with great works of art, oftentimes described as sublime and awe-inspiring, engender opportunities for individuals to transcend their smallness in the grand scheme of things, to step up to a plane beyond creaturely existence, and to touch the eternal. Such "divine" experiences, be they with music, literature, architecture, or any other form of art, may serve as jolts of existential vigor and make the individual feel that life is worth living.

CONCLUSION

Thrown out into a universe where everything but death is uncertain, vulnerable individuals look for a sense of purpose and meaning, for something to distinguish themselves from all other creatures and to overcome their basic animal nature. In this chapter, I have argued that one function that cultures across the world serve is to offer viable solutions to this set of problems. One way in which individuals attempt to deal with the horror of their basic animal condition and their mortality is by clinging to cultural worldviews or identifying with cultural symbols because these worldviews and symbols are believed, consciously or subconsciously, to afford opportunities for living forever, either literally or symbolically. In that sense, we are like children of culture. Just as well-loved children cultivate a sense of indestructibility and magical omnipotence, we feel ourselves fortified against the terror of death as long as we devotedly uphold the values of our individualized cultural worldviews. Another mode of defying death is to actively contribute to culture and thus leave behind a legacy that transcends the bounds of time and corporeality. This kind of hunger for symbolic self-perpetuation must be at least partially responsible for motivating people to write novels, amass fortunes, or run for president. It is precisely this idea that Woody Allen was poking fun at when he observed, "I don't want to achieve immortality through my work. I want to achieve it through not dying."

In his poem entitled *A Bag of Tools*, R. Lee Sharpe asks whether it isn't strange that "common people, like you and me, are builders of eternity," and then goes on to say: "Each is given a list of rules; / A shapeless mass; a bag of tools. / And each must fashion, ere life is flown, / A stumbling block, or a stepping-stone" (Alexander, 1984, pp. 31–32). My conviction is that culture, with its list of rules and its bag of tools, resembles the shapeless mass to which Sharpe is referring. One of the indispensable functions fulfilled by culture is an existential one – the one that allows mortals to be "builders of eternity."

REFERENCES

Alexander, A. L. (1984). *Poems that touch the heart*. New York: Doubleday.
Allport, G. W., & Ross, J. M. (1967). Personal religious orientation and prejudice. *Journal of Personality and Social Psychology, 5*, 432–443.

Arndt, J., Greenberg, J., Schimel, J., Pyszczynski, T., & Solomon, S. (2002). To belong or not to belong, that is the question: Terror management and identification with gender and ethnicity. *Journal of Personality and Social Psychology, 83*, 26–43.

Arnould, E. J., Price, L. L., & Zinkhan, G. M. (2002). *Consumers.* New York: McGraw-Hill.

Batson, C. D., Schoenrade, P., & Ventis, W. L. (1993). *Religion and the individual: A social-psychological perspective.* New York: Oxford University Press.

Becker, E. (1973). *The denial of death.* New York: Free Press.

Becker, E. (1975). *Escape from evil.* New York: Free Press.

Belk, R. W., Wallendorf, M., & Sherry, J. F., Jr. (1989). The sacred and the profane in consumer behavior: Theodicy on the Odyssey. *Journal of Consumer Research, 16*, 1–37.

Castano, E., Yzerbyt, V., Paladino, M.-P., & Sacchi, S. (2002). I belong, therefore, I exist: Ingroup identification, ingroup entitativity, and ingroup bias. *Personality and Social Psychology Bulletin, 28*, 135–143.

Chiu, C.-y., & Hong, Y.-Y. (2006). *The social psychology of culture.* New York: Psychology Press.

Cohan, C. L., & Cole, S. W. (2002). Life course transitions and natural disaster: Marriage, birth, and divorce following Hurricane Hugo. *Journal of Family Psychology, 16*, 14–25.

Dechesne, M., Greenberg, J., Arndt, J., & Schimel, J. (2000). Terror management and the vicissitudes of sports fan affiliation: The effects of mortality salience on optimism and fan identification. *European Journal of Social Psychology, 30*, 813–835.

Dechesne, M., & Kruglanski, A. W. (2004). Terror's epistemic consequences: Existential threats and the quest for certainty and closure. In J. Greenberg, S. Koole, & T. Pyszczynski (Eds.), *Handbook of experimental existential psychology* (pp. 247–262). New York: Guilford.

Dechesne, M., Pyszczynski, T., Arndt, J., Ransom, S., Sheldon, K. M., van Knippenberg, A., et al. (2003). Literal and symbolic immortality: The effect of evidence of literal immortality on self-esteem striving in response to mortality salience. *Journal of Personality and Social Psychology, 84*, 722–737.

Freud, S. (1918). *Reflections on war and death* (A. A. Brill, & A. B. Kuttner, Trans.). New York: Moffat Yard.

Goldenberg, J. L. (2005). The body stripped down: An existential account of ambivalence toward the physical body. *Current Directions in Psychological Science, 14*, 224–228.

Greenberg, J., Porteus, J., Simon, L., Pyszczynski, T., & Solomon, S. (1995). Evidence of a terror management function of cultural icons: The effects of mortality salience on the inappropriate use of cherished cultural symbols. *Personality and Social Psychology Bulletin, 21*, 1221–1228.

Greenberg, J., Pyszczynski, T., Solomon, S., Rosenblatt, A., Veeder, M., Kirkland, S., et al. (1990). Evidence for terror management theory II: The effects of mortality salience on reactions to those who threaten or bolster the cultural worldview. *Journal of Personality and Social Psychology, 58*, 308–318.

Greenberg, J., Pyszczynski, T, Solomon, S., Simon, L., & Breus, M. (1994). The role of consciousness and accessibility of death-related thoughts in mortality salience effects. *Journal of Personality and Social Psychology, 67*, 627–637.

Greenberg, J., Schimel, J., Martens, A., Solomon, S., & Pyszczynski, T. (2001). Sympathy for the devil: Evidence that reminding Whites of their mortality promotes more favorable reactions to White racists. *Motivation and Emotion, 25,* 113–133.

Hirschman, E. C. (1990). Secular immortality and American ideology of affluence. *Journal of Consumer Research, 17,* 31–42.

James, W. (1912). *The varieties of religious experience; a study in human nature.* New York: Longmans, Green.

Jonas, E., & Fischer, P. (2006). Terror management and religion: Evidence that intrinsic religiousness mitigates worldview defense following mortality salience. *Journal of Personality and Social Psychology, 91,* 553–567.

Kasser, T., & Sheldon, K. M. (2000). Of wealth and death: Materialism, mortality salience, and consumption behavior. *Psychological Science, 11,* 348–351.

Kesebir, P., & Chiu, C.-Y. (2008). [The stuff that immortality is made of: Existential functions of fame]. Unpublished raw data.

Landau, M. J., Goldenberg, J., Greenberg, J., Gillath, O., Solomon, S., Cox, C., et al. (2006). The siren's call: Terror management and the threat of men's sexual attraction to women. *Journal of Personality and Social Psychology, 90,* 129–146.

Lehman, D. R., Chiu, C.-y., & Schaller, M. (2004). Psychology and culture. *Annual Review of Psychology, 55,* 689–714.

Lifton, R. J. (1979). *The broken connection.* New York: Simon & Schuster.

Lodge, D. (2002). *Thinks.* London: Penguin Books.

Malinowski, B. (1954). *Magic, science and religion: And other essays.* Garden City, NY: Doubleday Anchor Books.

Mandel, N., & Heine, S. J. (1999). Terror management and marketing: He who dies with the most toys wins. *Advances in Consumer Research, 26,* 527–532.

McGregor, H., Lieberman, J. D., Solomon, S., Greenberg, J., Arndt, J., Simon, L., et al. (1998). Terror management and aggression: Evidence that mortality salience motivates aggression against worldview threatening others. *Journal of Personality and Social Psychology, 74,* 590–605.

Nabokov, V. (1999). *Speak, memory.* New York: Everyman's Library. (Original work published 1951)

Pyszczynski, T., Greenberg, J., & Koole, S. L. (2004). Experimental existential psychology: Exploring the human confrontation with reality. In J. Greenberg, S. L. Koole, & T. Pyszczynski (Eds.), *Handbook of experimental existential psychology* (pp. 3–12). New York: Guilford Press.

Pyszczynski, T., Greenberg, J., Solomon, S., Arndt, J., & Schimel, J. (2004). Why do people need self-esteem? A theoretical and empirical review. *Psychological Bulletin, 130,* 435–468.

Rank, O. (1941). *Beyond psychology.* Camden, NJ: Haddon Craftsmen. Published privately by friends and students of the author.

Rank, O. (1968). *Art and artist: Creative urge and personality development.* New York: W. W. Norton.

Rosenblatt, A., Greenberg, J., Solomon, S., Pyszczynski, T, & Lyon, D. (1989). Evidence for terror management theory. I: The effects of mortality salience on reactions to those who violate or uphold cultural values. *Journal of Personality and Social Psychology, 57,* 681–690.

Schaller, M., & Crandall, C. S. (2004). *The psychological foundations of culture.* Mahwah, NJ: Lawrence Erlbaum Associates.

Schmitt, R. L., & Leonard, W. M. (1986). Immortalizing the self through sport. *American Journal of Sociology, 91,* 1008–1111.

Simonton, D. K. (1999). *Origins of genius: Darwinian perspectives on creativity.* New York: Oxford University Press.

Solomon, S., Greenberg, J., & Pyszczynski, T. (2004). The cultural animal: Twenty years of terror management theory and research. In J. Greenberg, S. L. Koole, & T. Pyszczynski (Eds.), *Handbook of experimental existential psychology* (pp. 13–34). New York: Guilford.

Solomon, S., Greenberg, J., Schimel, J., Arndt, J., & Pyszczynski, T. (2004). Human awareness of mortality and the evolution of culture. In M. Schaller & C. S. Crandal (Eds.), *The psychological foundations of culture* (pp. 15–40). Mahwah, NJ: Lawrence Erlbaum Associates.

Strachman, A., & Schimel, J. (2006). Terror management and close relationships: Evidence that mortality salience reduces commitment among partners with different worldviews. *Journal of Social and Personal Relationships, 23,* 965–978.

Superhuman heroes. (1998, June 6). *The Economist, 347,* 10–12.

Tolstoy, L. N. (1987). *A confession and other religious writings* (J. Kentish, Trans.). New York: Penguin.

Vail, K., III, Rothchild, Z., Weise, D., Solomon, S., Pyszczynski, T., & Greenberg, J. (2010). A terror management analysis of the psychological functions of religion. *Personality and Social Psychology Review, 14,* 84–94.

Wheeler, M. A., Stuss, D. T., & Tulving, E. (1997). Toward a theory of episodic memory: The frontal lobes and autonoetic consciousness. *Psychological Bulletin, 121,* 331–354.

Williams, T. (1955). *Cat on a hot tin roof.* New York: New Directions Books.

Yalom, I. D. (1980). *Existential psychotherapy.* New York: Basic Books.

7

Self-Definitional Functions of Culture

CHING WAN, KARL DACH-GRUSCHOW, SUN NO,
AND YING-YI HONG

In families strongly influenced by Chinese culture, it is not uncommon to find an adult man and his wife living with his parents under the same roof. This behavior can be due to the man's perceived cultural obligation that he needs to take care of his parents while not particularly endorsing the value of filial piety, or the man's genuine endorsement of filial piety as his personal value. Culture has always had a strong influence on human life. It affects the behaviors and attitudes that people display by prescribing culturally approved and proscribing culturally inappropriate ways of conducting the self in specific social settings. This is not the only way that culture affects a person's behavior, however. Culture can exert indirect influence on a person's behavior through the person's self-representations. When a person internalizes a culture's values and beliefs, those values and beliefs become the person's own. People acting out of internalized values and beliefs would display behaviors that are consistent with the cultural norms. Thus, in addition to setting guides for people's life, culture also features in people's definitions of the self.

In this chapter, we examine the role that culture plays in people's self-representations. We present a distinction between cultural knowledge (mind) and cultural self, and discuss the implications of disentangling cultural knowledge and cultural self in furthering work in the area of culture and self, particularly with respect to research on cultural identity. We contend that being experienced with and having knowledge of a culture does not necessarily entail passive internalization of the culture as part of the self. Instead, cultural identity is a product of the dynamic interactions between the individual and the culture as knowledge represented by the individual and by the society. Specifically, we will examine how cultural knowledge provides meaning to the self, the process by which individuals use cultural knowledge to create their own identity, and how cultural knowledge can be used in the affirmation of one's identity.

THE STUDY OF CULTURE AND SELF

Scholarly examination of the relation between culture and self flourished in the early part of the 20th century when "culture and personality" studies emerged as a rapidly expanding and exciting research frontier (Honigmann, 1954; LeVine, 2001). The motivation behind this early interdisciplinary work among psychologists, anthropologists, sociologists, and psychiatrists was in finding systematic relationships between personality and culture to support the idea that individual differences in self characteristics are a function of differences in culturally patterned ways of being and doing (Mead, 1956). In this endeavor, researchers have relied on a variety of data collection techniques, ranging from participant observation, to interviews, to responses generated by the Thematic Apperception Test and Rorschach inkblots. For example, Caudill and de Vos (1956) used the culture and personality framework in their attempt to understand the rapid rise of second-generation Japanese Americans to white-collar and managerial positions upon release from relocation camps shortly after World War II. Their work displays a thorough and sophisticated understanding of the dangers of broad generalizations as well as a desire to present a holistic view of personality systems that are in dynamic interactions within a specific cultural context. Despite some of the interesting work that came out of this tradition, however, the field suffered substantial decline during the 1950s and 1960s, as criticisms mounted against a variety of unresolved theoretical issues (Bock, 2000; Shweder, 1979a, 1979b) and problematic practices, such as the use of sweeping statements in describing national character or modal personalities (Wallace & Fogelson, 1961).

The past 20 years saw a resurgence of interest within psychology in examining the relationship between culture and self (Sedikides & Brewer, 2001; Triandis & Suh, 2002). With this resurgence, researchers have devised new models and coined new terms to represent differences in content, structure, and process of the self across cultures, with Triandis (1989) and Markus and Kitayama (1991) authoring two seminal articles that have presented two major models on culture and self. Triandis (1989) identified the private self, the public self, and the collective self as three parts of a person's self-concept, the distribution and sampling of which differ across cultures. Markus and Kitayama (1991) identified independent self-construal and interdependent self-construal as the two self-constructs that differ in prevalence in different cultures of different degrees of focus on individuality and sociality. These discussions have revitalized interest in research on culture and self, providing rich descriptions of cultural processes and testable hypotheses. The two articles have since generated extensive research on differences in the prevalence of particular types of selves across geographical regions. Similar to that of the early culture and personality researchers, the motivation underlying this renewed interest is to find systematic relationships between culture-level variables (e.g., individualism–collectivism, looseness–tightness) and individual-level variables (e.g., self-concept, self-construal).

Although this renewed interest has provided much needed insights into how selves are culturally patterned, certain key issues require clarification. Specifically, the heavy reliance on self-reports to characterize cultural differences presents multiple concerns. For one, inconsistent results across studies (Oyserman, Coon, & Kemmelmeier, 2002) call into question the validity of using self-reports as objective indicators of the participants' true self (Heine, Lehman, Peng, & Greenholtz, 2002; Peng, Nisbett, & Wong, 1997). Also, the characterization of culture has relied mainly on aggregating personal characteristics of individuals from a particular culture to produce a cultural index. Such methods have unwittingly promoted the assumption that all individuals characterized as belonging to a particular culture have internalized the cultural characteristics to the same extent and thus possess the same level of cultural identification. Having knowledge about a culture, however, does not necessarily entail internalization of the culture as members of a cultural group may differ in the extent to which they endorse the normative characteristics of and identify with the culture (Hong, Wan, No, & Chiu, 2007; Spiro, 1992). In short, current models of culture and self have overlooked the distinction between "cultural self," acquired through identification with and internalization of a knowledge tradition, and "cultural mind," acquired through knowing the contents of a knowledge tradition.

A DISTINCTION BETWEEN CULTURAL KNOWLEDGE (MIND) AND CULTURAL SELF

Most experienced members of a culture have some knowledge about the culture's beliefs, values, life practices, norms, and other characteristics. Possessing extensive knowledge about a culture does not, however, entail strong identification with the culture. The American anthropologist conducting field research in Samoa and the Chinese ambassador to the United States are likely to have gained much knowledge of the cultures in which they work through extensive exposure to the cultures. Despite their expertise in the cultures, however, they may not strongly identify with the respective cultures and construct an important part of their self-definitions based on the cultures. Even for individuals who are normally categorized as members of certain cultures, such as European Americans born and raised in the United States and Chinese persons born and raised in China, there are individual differences in how much an individual sees the culture as part of the self. The possession of cultural knowledge and the identification with a culture are two separate, albeit related, processes. In this section, we elaborate on the distinction between cultural knowledge and cultural self, which we contend to be essential in the study of culture and self. In a later section, we will discuss the dynamic relationships between cultural knowledge and cultural self.

Cultural Knowledge

Culture encompasses the practices, behaviors, attitudes, values, and beliefs that are shared among a collective of people (Brumann, 1999; Triandis, 1996; also see Chapters 2 and 4, this volume). It also involves the symbolic representations of reality shared among the collective (Geertz, 1973; Pelto & Pelto, 1975; Romney, Boyd, Moore, Batchelder, & Brazill, 1986; also see Chapter 3, this volume). These elements constitute a culture's tradition of knowledge (Barth, 2002). To varying extents, experienced members of a culture know about the shared knowledge traditions that define the culture. They know about the practices and behaviors appropriate in various social encounters in the culture, the common attitudes and beliefs that members of the culture hold on various issues, and the values considered to be important in the culture. The possession of such cultural knowledge allows experienced members appropriate representations of and competent navigation in various situations in the cultural milieu.

People acquire shared knowledge through a dynamic and active process of meaning negotiation and sharing. The knowledge traditions of a culture are represented, distributed, and negotiated via multiple channels: language, symbols, social institutions, and individual actions, to name a few (Barth, 2002). Most people acquire such knowledge traditions through their daily social encounters. Meanings are socially shared as people engage in direct and indirect interactions with other individuals, social groups, and institutions (Resnick, Levine, & Teasley, 1991; Thompson & Fine, 1999). In interpersonal communication, people engage in the process of grounding as they search for and eventually establish a common ground of reference and understanding to successfully communicate with each other (Clark & Brennan, 1991). The presence of a shared reality (Hardin & Higgins, 1996) then allows for efficient coordination, tuning, and mutual influence among communicating individuals. At a more collective level, knowledge gets distributed among a collective. In the process, social representations are created, negotiated, and crystallized, as the specific ways in which certain knowledge is interpreted are repeatedly communicated in social discourse (Moscovici, 1984). Through participation in these one-on-one interactions and collective meaning negotiations, people take the perspective of their interaction partners and the generalized collective others in the culture, and develop common representations of the culture (Blumer, 1969; Mead, 1934).

Members of a culture have different social experiences. Therefore, they would not hold exact replicas of cultural knowledge. We would expect a certain level of consensus of knowledge, however, among experienced members of a culture on the most central aspects of the culture (see Chapters 2–4, this volume, for more detailed discussion). Pieces of knowledge differ in their shareabilty (Freyd, 1983) and sharedness. Shareability refers to whether a piece of knowledge is easy to be shared, whereas sharedness refers to the extent to which a piece of knowledge is widely shared. Some pieces of knowledge are more easily (higher shareability) and widely (higher sharedness) shared than others. The pieces of knowledge that are most likely to be central to the culture and relate to cultural processes would be those that are highly shareable and actually shared. Individuals who have spent some time in a particular culture would have picked up the consensual knowledge on these central defining characteristics of the culture.

As long as individuals possess knowledge about the most central aspects of a culture, they should be able to respond in culturally appropriate ways in situations that demand such responses. The influence of cultural knowledge follows the principles of knowledge activation (Higgins, 1996; Wyer & Srull, 1986), as cultural knowledge drives psychological processes when the knowledge is available, accessible, and applicable (Hong, Benet-Martínez, Chiu, & Morris, 2003; Hong, Morris, Chiu, & Benet-Martínez, 2000). The cultural self might be a moderator in the process (Jetten, Postmes, & McAuliffe, 2002; Terry & Hogg, 1996). Even people who do not internalize the cultural knowledge into their self-definitions, however, would still rely on their cultural knowledge to guide their decisions and behaviors when the situation calls for its use.

Cultural Self

The self-concept involves multiple self-representations in relation to different aspects of a person's life. Triandis (1989) discussed the differential sampling of three aspects of the self in different cultures: the private self as a person's personal attributes, the public self as a person's cognition of how generalized others view him or her, and the collective self as membership in some collectives. On a similar note, Brewer and colleagues (Brewer & Gardner, 1996; Sedikides & Brewer, 2001) divided the self-concept into the individual self, which is similar to the private self; the relational self, which refers to the aspect of the self defined by interpersonal relationships; and the collective self, which is similar to Triandis's (1989) collective self. In these conceptualizations of multiple selves, the partitioning is mainly based on the relationships of the person with other people – the absence of social others in private and individual selves; the imagined presence of a nonspecific other in public self; the presence of one or a small group of specific social others in relational self; and the presence of a larger collective of people in a group in collective self. This type of partitioning has provided a useful framework for research on relationships between individuals and different kinds of social others. Its usefulness, however, is somewhat limited for the study of the relationship between individuals and culture, for the reason that culture is defined by knowledge traditions instead of the presence or absence of specific social others and groups of people.

In light of the difficulty of applying the just-mentioned tripartite distinctions of the self in studying culture and self, Hong and colleagues (2007) have added the notion of cultural self, which refers to that part of a person's self-concept that is related to the shared knowledge tradition of a culture. As discussed before, culture is defined by a knowledge tradition instead of by a group of people. Although a specific knowledge tradition might be shared by a group of individuals, culture refers to the values, beliefs, practices, and symbolic meanings that together constitute a knowledge tradition – not the people holding the knowledge tradition. Thus, the cultural self is defined by a person's internalization of the knowledge tradition of a culture and his or her choice of defining the self with reference to that knowledge tradition instead of with reference to a collective of people.

It is important to note that the cultural self goes beyond the mere possession of the shared knowledge about a culture. It also goes beyond the mere application of cultural knowledge according to situational demands. Americans who know about the shared knowledge in American culture and use such shared knowledge in navigating their everyday lives do not necessarily identify with American culture. On the one hand, it is possible for people to observe the self behaving in culturally appropriate ways and interpreting such behaviors as indications of their cultural self. In this scenario, successful applications of shared cultural knowledge contribute to the development of a cultural self. On the other hand, a cultural self could develop from an active choice on the part of the individual to use a shared cultural knowledge tradition to define the self. This active choice does not necessarily depend on the experience of using the cultural knowledge tradition.

Relation with the Collective Self

The cultural self is most closely related to the collective self. The distinction between the cultural self and the collective self, however, is a theoretically important one as they provide different bases for people's self-definition. The collective self provides the basis for collective identity as people define themselves through categorical membership in a group of other individuals. These social categories would typically be those that divide people into different social groups, such as racial, ethnic, or gender groups. Individuals with strong collective identification with respect to a social group would see their membership in the group as a defining aspect of the self. They might experience strong emotional attachment to the group as a category and also to other individuals who are members of that group. In contrast, the cultural self provides the basis for cultural identity as people define themselves through a set of ideas and practices – that is, a knowledge tradition. A person with strong cultural identification would see the knowledge tradition of that culture as a defining characteristic of the self. Thus, the distinction between collective identity and cultural identity separates categorical membership from the shared ideas that might exist within the category.

The distinction between collective identity and cultural identity can best be illustrated in cases in which (a) ascribed members of a group do not identify with the knowledge tradition shared within that group and/or (b) nonmembers of a group come to endorse the knowledge tradition that is shared within that group. The former scenario is sometimes the case for racial minority group members. Such individuals may identify with their racial group because of the reality that others will categorize them as such but, at the same time, not identify with the culture typically associated with their racial group. This could be the case either because the individual has not been exposed to that culture (e.g., because of transracial adoption) or because that individual has simply rejected that culture.

For the latter scenario, although a knowledge tradition exists by virtue of knowledge being shared within a group of people, it is often the case that this knowledge becomes accessible to nonmembers either through direct intergroup contact (see Chapter 13 on intercultural communication) or through cultural artifacts such as written texts or music. The transmission of a knowledge tradition outside of the culture of origin may lead a wide variety of people to identify the self with the culture, even though they do not consider themselves a member of the people in the culture. This situation could arise in such cases as expatriation, when an individual may enter a new cultural environment and come to identify with many aspects of it, while at the same time not being accepted or not seeing the self as a member of the host cultural group. There are also other interesting possibilities. For example, via globalization a growing number of people may have regular exposure to a culture through the media while not having contact with the group that produces it. Thus a European-American youth may develop an affinity, admiration, and indeed identification with Japanese culture through video games, *manga*, and sushi without being ethnically Japanese or having a Japanese friend.

That being said, cultural identity and collective identity often go hand in hand in real life. In a lot of cases, members of a collective also share a knowledge tradition. People born and raised in the United States often consider themselves as belonging to the group of the American people, and they are also likely to endorse a common set of ideas and practices that can be labeled as the American culture. Thus, the American identity can include a categorical membership of being an American and the internalization of widely shared American cultural ideas. It is highly likely that people who strongly identify with a collective would also strongly identify with the knowledge tradition that is most widely shared by the collective, thus using the shared knowledge tradition to define the group membership. As previously discussed, however, it should not be expected that each member of the group equally endorses aspects of the knowledge tradition.

The addition of the cultural self as a distinct construct allows for a more nuanced understanding of identity processes. Collective identity can be ascribed or achieved, whereas cultural identity is mostly achieved through internalization of a knowledge tradition. Collective identity can exist without a knowledge tradition, which makes research using the minimal group paradigm (Tajfel, Billig, Bundy, & Flament, 1971) feasible, whereas cultural identity exists only when people have at least some knowledge about a culture's knowledge tradition. Culture is not limited to knowledge traditions shared by clearly delineated populations. There are knowledge traditions that go beyond physical, geographical boundaries, as people are linked by the same set of ideas and practices instead of common history, geographical location, or physical characteristics. For example, the knowledge tradition of Christianity cannot be localized in any one physically bounded group. Examining the cultural self as a distinct construct would direct cultural identity research to focus on the appropriate definition of culture as shared knowledge traditions. This is a more appropriate practice than making indirect inferences of cultural identity from collective membership.

In short, the cultural self is based not on collective membership but on a person defining the self with reference to the knowledge tradition shared in a culture. People need certain knowledge of a culture to identify with that culture; however, acquisition of extensive knowledge of a culture does not entail identification with the culture.

CONNECTING CULTURAL KNOWLEDGE (MIND) AND THE SELF

The possession of cultural knowledge does not necessitate the use of that knowledge in the definition of the self. Also, membership in a social group is not always accompanied by endorsement of the cultural knowledge tradition that is shared within the group. The American anthropologist in Samoa has extensive knowledge of the Samoan culture, in many regards more than the Samoans. The anthropologist would not necessarily endorse the values of Samoan culture, however. As a result of being in a culture that is largely different from his or her heritage culture, the anthropologist might find him- or herself holding onto the American cultural knowledge tradition even more so in the presence of Samoans. He or she might engage in American cultural practices and endorse the values of American culture more than he or she would have if it were not for the intergroup contrast experienced on the Samoan island. In contrast, it is also possible that the anthropologist eventually finds Samoan culture appealing, and as a result, although he or she still belongs to the collective of the American people, he or she comes to strongly identify with the knowledge tradition of Samoan culture. These two outcomes in the anthropologist's cultural identity are certainly different, but they both involve using the shared knowledge tradition of a culture in an individual's self-definition.

In this section, we explicate the possible processes in which cultural knowledge is involved in people's self-definition. One of the main questions from social identity research has been whether individuals seek out membership in groups that espouse values that they personally endorse, or adopt the prevailing norms and values within the group to which they already belong. Empirical evidence seems to support both directions. Although people with similar values cluster together and eventually form a collective identity based on their shared values (Kitayama, Ishii, Imada, Takemura, & Ramaswamy, 2006), they also endorse the prototypic characteristics of their group when the group identity is made salient (Hogg & Turner, 1987). As suggested by past research, we would expect a bidirectional relationship between cultural knowledge and cultural self. On the one hand, cultural knowledge provides the meaning for existing identities so that people who identify with a cultural group also endorse the cultural knowledge tradition distributed in the group. On the other hand, the formation of a cultural identity depends on the negotiated and personalized internalization of cultural knowledge.

Cultural Knowledge Provides Meaning for Collective Identity

People who claim a particular social identity often possess the basic qualities that give the identity its social meanings (Deaux, 1996). This phenomenon is most discussed as self-stereotyping under the rubric of social identity theories. Social identity theories (Hogg, 2003; Tajfel & Turner, 1979; Turner, Hogg, Oakes, Reicher, & Wetherell, 1987) have provided one of the most widely used frameworks in research on collective identity. Social identity is "the part of the individual's self-concept which derives from his [*sic*] knowledge of his membership of a social group (or groups) together with the value and emotional significance attached to that membership" (Tajfel, 1981, p. 255). Membership in a social group carries as its content the prototypic characteristics that define the group (Hogg, 2003; Turner, Oakes, Haslam, & McGarty, 1994). When a person's social identity is salient, the person views the self as an interchangeable member of the social group and attributes to the self the prototypic characteristics that define the group (Turner et al., 1987). In the classic study of self-stereotyping, men and women were found to endorse the attributes perceived to be prototypic of their gender when their membership in their own gender group was made salient (Hogg & Turner, 1987).

Self-stereotyping happens not only as a cognitive consequence of collective identity salience: It can also be a result of need fulfillment. Optimal distinctiveness theory (Brewer, 1991) posits that an individual's social identity is simultaneously regulated by the need for assimilation and the need for differentiation. These two opposing needs for individuality and belonging can be fulfilled simultaneously when the person identifies with an optimally distinctive social group (Brewer, 1991). Recent research has found self-stereotyping as a strategy that people who strongly identify with a group use to fulfill the two needs (Pickett, Bonner, & Coleman, 2002). By becoming a prototypic member of the social ingroup, the individual who strongly identifies with the ingroup is able to fulfill the need for (a) assimilation by increasing the perceived inclusiveness of the ingroup and (b) differentiation by increasing the perceived contrast of the ingroup with other outgroups.

In collectives that have a culture, the knowledge tradition of the culture provides the content of the collective identity for members of the collective. What it means to be a member of a collective is in part determined by the culture within the collective and the larger cultural context in which the collective exists. In a collective with a shared knowledge tradition, members of the collective hold common representations of the knowledge tradition. In the language of social identity theory, the shared knowledge tradition represents the prototypic characteristics that define the cultural group. Extending the arguments of social identity theories to the identification with a cultural group, when membership in this cultural group is salient, or when a person is strongly identified with the cultural group, it is logical to expect this person to see the self as embodying the defining shared knowledge tradition of the cultural group. Based on this social identity perspective, past research has shown that, in groups with a shared culture, people who identify strongly with the group often display the behavioral intentions prototypic of the group (e.g., Jetten et al., 2002; Terry & Hogg, 1996; Terry, Hogg, & White, 1999) and the espousal of identity-related values (Feather, 1994; Gouveia, de Albuquerque, Clemente, & Espinosa, 2002; Heaven, Stones, Simbayi, & Le Roux, 2000).

Knowledge traditions exist as knowledge is passed and shared and meanings are negotiated between individuals directly or indirectly. It is important to note that the prototypic beliefs and social meanings of a group also exist as part of these knowledge traditions. Thus, to the American anthropologist, being an American entails knowing what the widely shared knowledge tradition in American culture is. When one self-stereotypes as a member of a particular cultural group, although one does not necessarily adopt the actual beliefs and traits of the group, one must have learned which beliefs and traits characterize the group. These representations are personal, in the sense that each individual acquires personal knowledge of what the cultural tradition is. At the same time, social identity and culture researchers would both argue that the representations are also socially shared. What it means to be an African American, a female, or a Texan is defined from within the group and outside of the group in the larger society. The widely shared representations are outcomes of the intersubjectivity created through cultural meaning negotiation. The resulting consensus among a collective on the representations of the knowledge tradition that defines the culture can be called *intersubjective consensus* (Wan, Chiu, Peng, & Tam, 2007; Chapter 3, this volume). As individuals achieve shared reality (Hardin & Higgins, 1996) with close others in social interactions, the content of their self-stereotyping is affected by what these close others view as the defining content of the collective (Sinclair, Hardin, & Lowery, 2006). In addition, as individuals participate in collective meaning negotiations, the content of their self-stereotyping depends on the representations of the defining characteristics of the collective that are widely shared both within the collective and in the larger society.

The Negotiation of Cultural Identity

Shared cultural knowledge provides social meanings to existing membership in cultural groups. At the same time, people also look for identities that have personal meanings for them (Deaux, 1993; Rosenberg & Gara, 1985). In other words, identification with a cultural group would be strong when individuals find the defining qualities of the group personally meaningful. Cultural identification is a matter of person–culture match. Strong identification with a culture comes when there is a good match between an individual's personal characteristics and the culture's widely shared knowledge tradition. For example, in a longitudinal study (Wan, Chiu, Tam, et al., 2007), college freshmen estimated the value endorsement of an average student at their university and rated their own personal endorsement of the values at the beginning and end of their first semester at the university. They also reported their identification with the student culture of the university. Results of the study showed that the students' endorsement of the values that were collectively believed to be important to an average student of the university at the beginning of the semester predicted their change in identification over the course of the semester. The more the students endorsed the values at the beginning of the semester, the more they identified with the student culture of the university at the end of the semester. In contrast, identification with the student culture at the beginning of the semester did not predict change in endorsement of values collectively believed to be important to an average student at the university. Thus, alignment between personal values and the widely shared cultural values resulted in identification with the culture.

Cultural identity is not chosen solely by the individual or dictated by the people around the individual. Rather, achieving positive attachment to a culture and maintaining one's individuality is a negotiated process among the person, the shared representations in that person's culture, and the representations held by that person's social others. In other words, cultural identity is a product of negotiation. It is a person's personal choice, yet it is limited by the culture and social contexts to which one is exposed. Marginalized members of a culture might find it hard to identify with the culture, despite their personal desire to do so, because of exclusion from or limited participation in mainstream society and culture (e.g., Dalits in India, African Americans in the United States). Also, when the culture's values contradict a person's personal values, or when what is valued in the culture is in conflict with a person's basic needs (Chirkov, Ryan, & Willness, 2005), it is much harder for the person to identify with the culture. For example, the American anthropologist would likely find that, even after several years of living in Samoa, he or she still feels uncomfortable wearing the more revealing traditional Samoan clothing because of highly internalized American sensibilities. Thus there would remain a part of the self that was attached to the American knowledge tradition despite joining the Samoan culture. This effect of potential value conflict on cultural identity would be especially true for aspects of culture that are essentially automatic (Cohen, 1997). Nevertheless, it is also possible that the anthropologist's prolonged immersion and identification with the Samoan knowledge tradition would bring him or her to develop a Samoan cultural identity on top of his or her American cultural identity so that, even if he or she returned to the United States, his or her connection to Samoa would remain part of his or her cultural self.

Two possibilities in the negotiation process could result in a person–culture match. The first one is the internalization of the important elements of the culture, which would result in the individual moving to become more like the culture. Internalization would lead to a stronger identification with the culture as what is in the culture gets assimilated into the person (Ryan & Deci, 2003). The second possibility is a person choosing a definition of the identity that fits his or her personal characteristics. As the meaning of an identity is often complex, it is possible for a person to actively choose the part of the culture to identify with and remain strongly identified with the culture in general.

Internalization of Culture

G. H. Mead (1934) argued that the self is constructed through taking the perspective of first specific then generalized others, and that through social interactions the individual adopts the view of others and the society in the individual's self-concept. In the construction of cultural identity, individuals take the perspective of social others and the society on the knowledge tradition of the culture. Individuals gain cultural competence as they go through enculturation. They also internalize the culture to different extents. Internalization of the important elements of a culture's knowledge tradition allows an eventual match between the individuals' personal characteristics and the corresponding characteristics in the culture. When the cultural elements are internalized, they guide an individual's behaviors not because the individual desires social approval or external reward, but because the individual is acting on his or her personal characteristics, which happen to correspond to the culture's characteristics (Ryan & Deci, 2003).

Internalization of culture has received attention in research on culture and child development. From infancy to adulthood, children are socialized to become competent members of the society in various settings. Parents and other immediate caretakers are usually the first socialization agents, followed by the school, the peers, and other social contacts as the child grows older. Within the family, values that are important to the culture are transmitted from parents to the child through such processes as personal narrative construction (Wiley, Rose, Burger, & Miller, 1998), play (Bornstein, Haynes, Pascual, Painter, & Galperín, 1999), and children's participation in adult activities as active observers (Childs & Greenfield, 1980). Through the socialization process, children not only learn the appropriate behaviors for various social settings, but also, to a certain extent, personally adopt the knowledge tradition of the culture. It is often assumed that, when a cultural characteristic is the focus of socialization efforts, it is easier for the characteristic to come out as a highly internalized characteristic personally endorsed by a lot of people who share the culture (e.g., Fischer, 2006).

Outcomes of socialization are affected by various factors. For example, in a study on the family transmission of values (Rohan & Zanna, 1996), parent–child value similarities were predicted by parents' right-wing authoritarianism so that the higher the parents' right-wing authoritarianism, the lower the similarity between parents' and children's value priorities. This relationship was mediated by children's perception of parents' parenting style – parents high on authoritarianism were perceived as less responsive and more demanding than those low on authoritarianism, which led to a lower level of parent–child value similarity. Also, research based on self-determination theory has suggested that values that are in conflict with the three basic human needs – autonomy, relatedness, and competence – would be more difficult to be internalized (Chirkov, Ryan, Kim, & Kaplan, 2003; Chirkov et al., 2005). For example, the emphasis of verticality in some cultures might make it hard for members of the culture to personally endorse this aspect of the culture because the demand of verticality on submissiveness to authority and conformity is in conflict with the human need of autonomy (Chirkov et al., 2005).

Internalization not only concerns members of a collective going through enculturation and socialization from an early age. Cultural identification often happens as individuals encounter a new culture and participate in this culture for some time. This is the case for sojourners and immigrants who move from one culture to another for an extended period of time. It is also the case for people who come into contact with individuals or artifacts that carry a knowledge tradition different from their own. In these cases, the individuals already possess certain personal values and beliefs that are a result of their cultural experience prior to the contact with the new culture. These preexisting personal values and beliefs might hinder the internalization of the knowledge tradition of the new culture if the individual finds difference and incompatibility between the preexisting values and beliefs and those of the new culture. This situation can be illustrated by the difficulties in adjustment and adaptation that sojourners and immigrants often face when there is a large cultural distance between their heritage culture and the host culture (Searle & Ward, 1990; Ward & Searle, 1991). There are several possible identity consequences of this perceived mismatch. The individual may choose not to identify with the new culture at all, try to resolve the coexistence of the new culture with the preexisting values and beliefs by endorsing part of the new culture, or completely shed the preexisting values and beliefs and embrace the new culture (cf. bicultural identity negotiation in Chapter 12 of this volume).

Personalized Cultural Identity

In the process of cultural identification, individuals are not passive, blank slates that meekly receive whatever is painted on them. Instead, they are active in the identity negotiation process. They have the option of making a personal decision on what the culture is about, and on the selective identification with that part of the culture that suits their own personal preferences and needs. After all, identification is a personal business, albeit only in part.

Although representations of a culture are constructed as socially shared knowledge (Moscovici, 1984), the way these representations are shared is not uniform. Moscovici (1988) has identified three types of social representations. Hegemonic representations are uniformly shared but are not generated by the collective. Emancipated representations are formed when subgroups with close contact communicate their own slightly different versions of symbolic interpretations with each other. Polemical representations are generated through social conflict and controversy and are not shared by the society. Emancipated and polemical representations are most relevant in the current discussion as they imply the possibility of individuals and groups in a society having different representations. In addition, individuals also have their own versions of cultural representations based on their social representations concerning the culture. For example, whereas some Hispanics associate being Hispanic with mainly positive characteristics, other Hispanics might have more ambivalent associations (Ethier & Deaux, 1990). Individuals differ in the extent to which they are aware of, understand, and accept the social representations of a culture and the degree to which the social representations are merged with their existing personal representations of reality (Breakwell, 2001). Thus, although there is general consensus in the meaning of cultural identity, individuals do differ in their interpretation and use of social representations in constructing their own cultural identity. Such differences in personal meaning would result in a cultural identity that is partly personalized.

The multiplicity of an identity allows an individual to try and construct an identity by emphasizing the aspects of the self and the culture's knowledge tradition that are most compatible. By focusing on part of the complex meaning, an individual who does not endorse all of a culture's important knowledge tradition can still identify strongly with the culture in general. The meaning of a culture is shared alike among members and nonmembers of the cultural collective. Although individuals are often socialized to adopt an identity based on this shared knowledge, they have the freedom to choose where to position the self in the social representations of the identity and whether to adopt or resist the shared representations in the society about the culture (Duveen, 2001). In collectives where there are both positive and negative associations, people may selectively adopt the characteristics that are positively associated with the group but not the characteristics that are negatively associated with the group so as to maintain a positive self-evaluation (e.g., Biernat, Vescio, & Green, 1996). This may especially be the case in stigmatized groups in which the general representations of the group by the society is negative. For a member of a stigmatized group, the experience of membership in that group and its cultural traditions may be a joyous experience within the group and among group members but a source of shame when among outgroup members who devalue the group (c.f. Major & O'Brien, 2005). Members of the stigmatized group often possess the same knowledge about the negative representations of the group as do others in the society (Crocker, Major, & Steele, 1998). For these individuals, apart from the option of disidentification, they can also refocus their representations of the group so as to cast the group in a positive light (Crocker et al., 1998). Identification then is a business of distancing the self from the negative aspects of the representation and focusing on the positive.

In short, a person's cultural identification is the product of both his or her personal ideals and the extent to which those ideals are considered to be characteristics of the culture's knowledge tradition. Whereas socialization processes influence the internalization of a culture's knowledge traditions, people also construct their own cultural identities by personalizing the defining characteristics of the culture. Cultural identity is a product of negotiation among the person, social others, and the culture.

Cultural Knowledge in Identity Affirmation

As cultural knowledge provides meaning for identification in a cultural collective, it can be used strategically in identity affirmation. People can defend their collective identity by showing preference for the ingroup in attributions (e.g., Islam & Hewstone, 1993), outcome allocation (e.g., Otten, Mummendey, & Blanz, 1996), and trait evaluations (Bettencourt, Charlton, & Kernahan, 1997). They can also defend the widely shared knowledge traditions that define the cultural collective when their identity as a member of a cultural collective is threatened. By adhering more closely to the knowledge tradition shared within one's cultural collective, one would be able to restore the positive value of the self.

This phenomenon of identity affirmation has been demonstrated in research on linguistic and nonlinguistic aspects of shared culture. In an early study on speech divergence (Bourhis & Giles, 1977), Welsh participants were made to overhear a British English speaker make derogatory comments about the Welsh language. Participants who had strong Welsh identity subsequently used more heavily Welsh-accented English. This speech divergence effect was also found with Flemish participants in Belgium. When the participants' Flemish identity was threatened by an outgroup member's negative attitude, they displayed more affirmation of their Flemish identity by speaking in Flemish instead of English (Bourhis, Giles, Leyens, & Tajfel, 1979). More recent studies have focused on nonlinguistic aspects of shared knowledge tradition. For example, Jetten and colleagues (2002) experimentally manipulated the norm of a group to be either individualist or collectivist. They demonstrated that, when the group identity was threatened, high identifiers in the group endorsed collectivism more when the group norm was collectivist than when the norm was individualist.

As cultural knowledge defines a cultural collective, a threat to the importance of the most important part of the knowledge tradition of a culture would result in identity affirmation. This result was demonstrated in two studies with different identity affirmation measures. In both studies, European-American participants were asked to either promote or denounce the importance of the values widely considered to be the most or least important to American culture. In one study (Wan, Torelli, & Chiu, in press), compared to participants in the other three conditions, participants who denounced core American values displayed the most positive estimate of American achievement in international awards and competitions relative to the achievement of other countries. In another study (Wan, Chiu, Tam, et al., 2007), participants in the core value denouncement condition showed the most positive evaluation of American-English relative to British-English user.

In summary, the internalized cultural knowledge tradition is an integral part of a person's cultural self. By providing the content for identification with a cultural collective, cultural knowledge tradition offers a route for people to maintain a positive evaluation of the self through affirming the importance of the knowledge tradition. Also, identity affirmation as a consequence of threats to knowledge tradition demonstrates the close connection between cultural knowledge tradition and the self.

CHOICE AND CONSTRAINTS IN THE CONSTRUCTION
OF THE CULTURAL SELF

In discussing the connections between cultural knowledge (mind) and cultural self, we have focused mostly on an individual's choice of using cultural knowledge in various ways in the construction of a cultural self. We have stressed that identification with a culture's widely shared knowledge tradition is not a default outcome of possessing knowledge about the knowledge tradition. Instead, the individual can use the knowledge tradition creatively in the definition, negotiation, and maintenance of a positive evaluation of the self.

At the same time, it is important to acknowledge the possibility of situational and societal constraints on cultural self construction even when the individual tries to exert his or her agency in the process. One such constraint is the marginalization of one's social subgroup in the mainstream cultural milieu. Migrant workers from rural China working in urban cities are of much lower socioeconomic status than residents of the cities, experiencing poor working and living conditions, and are not considered registered residents of the cities where they work, which seriously limits their education and housing opportunities (Wong, Li, & Song, 2007). Dalits are members of the lowest caste in India and have historically been considered the "untouchables" and subjected to stigma and suppression (Mahalingam, 2003). African Americans often experience prejudice and discrimination in majority White environments, with African-American men in particular being stereotypically associated with crime and violence (Smith, Allen, & Danley, 2007). Members of these marginalized groups may have knowledge about the mainstream culture, but the experience of marginalization might pose difficulties for these members to actually identify with it.

The extant research in the field does not provide enough empirical evidence for detailed formulation of the relative contribution of personal choice and external constraints in the construction and negotiation of the cultural self. It should be emphasized, however, that, within the constraints in the immediate social situations and the larger cultural milieu, an individual can play an active role in using cultural knowledge for a negotiated cultural self-definition.

CONCLUDING REMARKS

Culture's dynamic relationships with a person range from the culture presenting an external force guiding the person's appropriate behaviors and responses in various situations to the culture being an inherent part of the person's self-representations and influencing the person's psychological processes as deeply internalized personal characteristics. In the former relationship, culture's role lies in the knowledge that people hold about the culture. People differ in the knowledge that they have about a culture. Experienced members of a culture, however, would at least hold similar representations of the most central aspects of that culture. Such consensual representations can then be used in competent participations in the culture. In the latter relationship, culture's role lies in the cultural self that people have constructed based on their representations of the culture's knowledge tradition. These two relationships can be separated only when the conceptual distinction between cultural knowledge (mind) and cultural self is made. The conceptual distinction represents one step further in the field's understanding of culture and self, beyond the implicit assumption in past research that often blurred the boundary between what people know about the culture and what they personally endorse.

Culture's knowledge tradition provides a basis for people to define who they are. The process is not uniform across individuals. How a person uses his or her cultural knowledge in the construction of cultural self is a matter of personal choice in the midst of constraints presented by the sociocultural milieu. We have focused our effort in discussing this utility of cultural knowledge in cultural self. The process in no way stops after the construction of a cultural self, however. Cultural knowledge and cultural self both have a certain level of stability, but they are also fluid constructs subject to change. The cultural identity constructed from a certain cultural knowledge representation provides a lens through which a person adjusts his or her existing views about the culture as the person engages in further collective meaning negotiations concerning the culture's knowledge tradition. The revised representations could then be used in further cultural identity construction, maintenance, and change. At a collective level, the revised representations of individual members of a culture might trigger a change in the culture at large. This changed culture can subsequently become the subject of further meaning negotiation, perpetuation, and use in cultural members' self-definitions, and so the cycle continues.

REFERENCES

Barth, F. (2002). An anthropology of knowledge. *Current Anthropology, 43*, 1–18.
Bettencourt, B. A., Charlton, K., & Kernahan, C. (1997). Numerical representation of groups in cooperative settings: Social orientation effects on ingroup bias. *Journal of Experimental Social Psychology, 33*, 630–659.
Biernat, M., Vescio, T. K., & Green, M. L. (1996). Selective self-stereotyping. *Journal of Personality and Social Psychology, 71*, 1194–1209.
Blumer, H. (1969). *Symbolic interactionism: Perspective and method.* Berkeley, CA: University of California Press.
Bock, P. K. (2000). Culture and personality revisited. *American Behavioral Scientist, 44*, 32–40.
Bornstein, M. H., Haynes, O. M., Pascual, L., Painter, K. M., & Galperín, C. (1999). Play in two societies: Pervasiveness of process, specificity of structure. *Child Development, 70*, 317–331.
Bourhis, R. Y., & Giles, H. (1977). The language of intergroup distinctiveness. In H. Giles (Ed.), *Language, ethnicity and intergroup relations* (pp. 119–135). New York: Academic Press.

Bourhis, R. Y., Giles, H., Leyens, J. P., & Tajfel, H. (1979). Psycholinguistic distinctiveness: Language divergence in Belgium. In H. Giles & R. S. Clair (Eds.), *Language and social psychology* (pp. 158–185). Oxford, UK: Blackwell.

Breakwell, G. M. (2001). Social representational constraints upon identity processes. In K. Deaux & G. Philogène (Eds.), *Representations of the social* (pp. 271–284). Malden, MA: Blackwell.

Brewer, M. B. (1991). The social self: On being the same and different at the same time. *Personality and Social Psychology Bulletin, 17*, 475–482.

Brewer, M. B., & Gardner, W. (1996). Who is this "we"? Levels of collective identity and self representations. *Journal of Personality and Social Psychology, 71*, 83–93.

Brumann, C. (1999). Writing for culture: Why a successful concept should not be discarded. *Current Anthropology, 40*, S1–S27.

Caudill, W., & de Vos, G. (1956). Achievement, culture and personality: The case of the Japanese Americans. *American Anthropologist, 58*, 1102–1126.

Childs, C. P., & Greenfield, P. M. (1980). Informal modes of learning and teaching: The case of Zinacanteco weaving. In N. Warren (Ed.), *Studies in cross-cultural psychology, Vol. 2* (pp. 269–316). New York: Academic Press.

Chirkov, V. I., Ryan, R. M., Kim, Y., & Kaplan, U. (2003). Differentiating autonomy from individualism and independence: A self-determination theory perspective on internalization of cultural orientations and well-being. *Journal of Personality and Social Psychology, 84*, 97–110.

Chirkov, V. I., Ryan, R. M., & Willness, C. (2005). Cultural context and psychological needs in Canada and Brazil: Testing a self-determination approach to the internalization of cultural practices, identity, and well-being. *Journal of Cross-Cultural Psychology, 36*, 423–443.

Clark, H. H., & Brennan, S. E. (1991). Grounding in communication. In L. B. Resnick, J. M. Levine, & S. D. Teasley (Eds.), *Perspectives on socially shared cognition* (pp. 127–149). Washington, DC: American Psychological Association.

Cohen, D. (1997). Ifs and thens in cultural psychology. In R. S. Wyer (Ed.), *The automaticity of everyday life: Advances in social cognition, Vol. 10* (pp. 121–131). Mahwah, NJ: Lawrence Erlbaum Associates.

Crocker, J., Major, B., & Steele, C. (1998). Social stigma. In S. Fiske, D. Gilbert, & G. Lindzey (Eds.), *Handbook of social psychology, Vol. 2* (pp. 504–553). Boston, MA: McGraw Hill.

Deaux, K. (1993). Reconstructing social identity. *Personality and Social Psychology Bulletin, 19*, 4–12.

Deaux, K. (1996). Social identification. In E. T. Higgins & A. W. Kruglanski (Eds.), *Social psychology: Handbook of basic principles* (pp. 777–798). New York: Guilford.

Duveen, G. (2001). Representations, identities, resistance. In K. Deaux & G. Philogène (Eds.), *Representations of the social* (pp. 257–270). Malden, MA: Blackwell.

Ethier, K., & Deaux, K. (1990). Hispanics in ivy: Assessing identity and perceived threat. *Sex Roles, 22*, 427–440.

Feather, N. T. (1994). Values and national identification: Australian evidence. *Australian Journal of Psychology, 46*, 35–40.

Fischer, R. (2006). Congruence and functions of personal and cultural values: Do my values reflect my culture's values? *Personality and Social Psychology Bulletin, 32*, 1419–1431.

Freyd, J. J. (1983). Shareability: The social psychology of epistemology. *Cognitive Science, 7*, 191–210.

Geertz, C. (1973). *The interpretation of cultures.* New York: Basic Books.

Gouveia, V. V., de Albuquerque, F. J. B., Clemente, M., & Espinosa, P. (2002). Human values and social identities: A study in two collectivist cultures. *International Journal of Psychology, 37*, 333–342.

Hardin, C. D., & Higgins, E. T. (1996). Shared reality: How social verification makes the subjective objective. In R. M. Sorrentino & E. T. Higgins (Eds.), *Handbook of motivation and cognition, Vol. 3. The interpersonal context* (pp. 28–84). New York: Guilford Press.

Heaven, P. C. L., Stones, C., Simbayi, L., & Le Roux, A. (2000). Human values and social identities among samples of white and black South Africans. *International Journal of Psychology, 35*, 67–72.

Heine, S. J., Lehman, D. R., Peng, K., & Greenholtz, J. (2002). What's wrong with cross-cultural comparisons of subjective Likert scales? The reference-group effect. *Journal of Personality & Social Psychology, 82*, 903–918.

Higgins, E. T. (1996). Knowledge activation: Accessibility, applicability and salience. In E. T. Higgins & A. E. Kruglanski (Eds.), *Social psychology: Handbook of basic principles* (pp.133–168). New York: Guilford.

Hogg, M. A. (2003). Social identity. In M. R. Leary, & L. P. Tangney (Eds.), *Handbook of self and identity* (pp. 462–479). New York: Guilford Press.

Hogg, M. A., & Turner, J. C. (1987). Intergroup behaviour, self-stereotyping and the salience of social categories. *British Journal of Social Psychology, 26*, 325–340.

Hong, Y., Benet-Martínez, V., Chiu, C., & Morris, M. W. (2003). Construct activation as a mechanism for cultural differences in social perception. *Journal of Cross-Cultural Psychology, 34*, 453–464.

Hong, Y., Morris, M. W., Chiu, C., & Benet-Martínez, V. (2000). Multicultural minds: A dynamic constructivist approach to culture and cognition. *American Psychologist, 55*, 709–720.

Hong, Y., Wan, C., No, S., & Chiu, C. (2007). Multicultural identities. In S. Kitayama & D. Cohen (Eds.), *Handbook of cultural psychology* (pp. 323–345). New York: Guilford.

Honigmann, J. J. (1954). *Culture and personality.* New York: Harper and Brothers.

Islam, M. R., & Hewstone, M. (1993). Intergroup attributions and affective consequences in majority and minority groups. *Journal of Personality and Social Psychology, 64*, 936–950.

Jetten, J., Postmes, T., & McAuliffe, B. (2002). "We're all individuals": Group norms of individualism and collectivism, levels of identification and identity threat. *European Journal of Social Psychology, 32*, 189–207.

Kitayama, S., Ishii, K., Imada, T., Takemura, K., & Ramaswamy, J. (2006). Voluntary settlement and the spirit of independence: Evidence from Japan's "Northern Frontier." *Journal of Personality and Social Psychology, 91*, 369–384.

LeVine, R. A. (2001). Culture and personality studies, 1918–1960: Myth and history. *Journal of Personality, 69*, 803–818.

Mahalingam, R. (2003). Essentialism, culture, and power: Representations of social class. *Journal of Social Issues, 59*, 733–749.

Major, B., & O'Brien, L. (2005). The social psychology of stigma. *Annual Review of Psychology, 56*, 393–421.

Markus, H. R., & Kitayama, S. (1991). Culture and the self: Implications for cognition, emotion, and motivation. *Psychological Review, 98*, 224–253.

Mead, G. H. (1934). *Mind, self and society.* Chicago: University of Chicago Press.

Mead, M. (1956). The cross-cultural approach to the study of personality. In J. L. McCary (Ed.), *Psychology of personality: Six modern approaches* (pp. 203–252). New York: Logos Press.

Moscovici, S. (1984). The phenomenon of social representations. In M. Farr & S. Moscovici (Eds.), *Social representations* (pp. 3–69). Cambridge, UK: Cambridge University Press.

Moscovici, S. (1988). Notes towards a description of social representations. *European Journal of Social Psychology, 18*, 211–250.

Otten, S., Mummendey, A., & Blanz, M. (1996). Intergroup discrimination in positive and negative outcome allocations: Impact of stimulus valence, relative group status, and relative group size. *Personality and Social Psychology Bulletin, 22*, 568–581.

Oyserman, D., Coon, H. M., & Kemmelmeier, M. (2002). Rethinking individualism and collectivism: Evaluation of theoretical assumptions and meta-analyses. *Psychological Bulletin, 128*, 3–72.

Pelto, P. J., & Pelto, G. H. (1975). Intra-cultural diversity: Some theoretical issues. *American Ethnologist, 2*, 1–18.

Peng, K., Nisbett, R. E., & Wong, N. Y. C. (1997). Validity problems comparing values across cultures and possible solutions. *Psychological Methods, 2*, 329–344.

Pickett, C. L., Bonner, B. L., & Coleman, J. M. (2002). Motivated self-stereotyping: Heightened assimilation and differentiation needs result in increased levels of positive and negative self-stereotyping. *Journal of Personality and Social Psychology, 82*, 543–562.

Resnick, L., Levine, J., & Teasley, S. D. (1991). *Perspective on socially shared cognition.* Washington, DC: American Psychological Association.

Rohan, M. J., & Zanna, M. P. (1996). Value transmission in families. In C. Seligman, J. M. Olson, & M. P. Zanna (Eds.), *The psychology of value: The Ontario symposium, Vol. 8* (pp. 253–276). Hillsdale, NJ: Lawrence Erlbaum Associates.

Romney, A. K., Boyd, J. P., Moore, C. C., Batchelder, W. H., & Brazill, T. J. (1996). Culture as shared cognitive representations. *Proceedings of the National Academy of Sciences USA, 93*, 4699–4705.

Rosenberg, S., & Gara, M. A. (1985). The multiplicity of personal identity. In P. Shaver (Ed.), *Self, situations, and social behavior: Review of personality and social psychology, Vol. 6* (pp. 87–113). Beverly Hills, CA: Sage.

Ryan, R. M., & Deci, E. L. (2003). On assimilating identities to the self: A self-determination theory perspective on internalization and integrity within cultures. In M. R. Leary & L. P. Tangney (Eds.), *Handbook of self and identity* (pp. 253–272). New York: Guilford.

Schweder, R. A. (1979a). Re-thinking culture and personality, part I: A critical examination of two classical postulates. *Ethos, 7*, 255–278.

Schweder, R. A. (1979b). Re-thinking culture and personality, part II: A critical examination of two classical postulates. *Ethos, 7,* 279–312.

Searle, W., & Ward, C. (1990). The prediction of psychological and sociocultural adjustment during cross-cultural transitions. *International Journal of Intercultural Relations, 14,* 449–464.

Sedikides, C., & Brewer, M. B. (2001). Individual self, relational self, and collective self: Partner, opponents, or strangers? In C. Sedikides & M. B. Brewer (Eds.), *Individual self, relational self, collective self* (pp. 1–4). Ann Arbor, MI: Psychology Press.

Sinclair, S., Hardin, C. D., & Lowery, B. S. (2006). Self-stereotyping in the context of multiple social identities. *Journal of Personality and Social Psychology, 90,* 529–542.

Smith, W. A., Allen, W. R., & Danley, L. L. (2007). "Assume the position . . . You fit the description": Campus racial climate and the psychoeducational experiences and racial battle fatigue among African American male college students. *American Behavioral Scientist, 51,* 551–578.

Spiro, M. E. (1992). *Anthropological other or Burmese brother? Studies in cultural analysis.* New Brunswick, NJ: Transaction Publishers.

Tajfel, H. (1981). *Human groups and social categories: Studies in social psychology.* Cambridge, UK: Cambridge University Press.

Tajfel, H., Billig, M. G., Bundy, R. P., & Flament, C. (1971). Social categorization and intergroup behaviour. *European Journal of Social Psychology, 1,* 149–178.

Tajfel, H., & Turner, J. C. (1979). An integrative theory of intergroup conflict. In W. G. Austin & S. Worchel (Eds.), *The social psychology of intergroup relations* (pp. 33–47). Monterey, CA: Brooks-Cole.

Terry, D. J., Hogg, M. A., & White, K. M. (1999). The theory of planned behaviour: Self-identity, social identity and group norms. *British Journal of Social Psychology, 38,* 225–244.

Terry, D. J., & Hogg, M. J. (1996). Group norms and the attitude-behavior relationship: A role for group identification. *Personality and Social Psychology Bulletin, 22,* 776–793.

Thompson, L., & Fine, G. A. (1999). Socially shared cognition, affect, and behavior: A review and integration. *Personality and Social Psychology Review, 3,* 278–302.

Triandis, H. C. (1989). The self and social behavior in differing cultural contexts. *Psychological Review, 96,* 506–520.

Triandis, H. C. (1996). The psychological measurement of cultural syndromes. *American Psychologist, 51,* 407–415.

Triandis, H. C., & Suh, E. M. (2002). Cultural influences on personality. *Annual Review of Psychology, 53,* 133–160.

Turner, J. C., Hogg, M. A., Oakes, P. J., Reicher, S. D., & Wetherell, M. S. (1987). *Rediscovering the social group: A self-categorization theory.* Hillsdale, NJ: Lawrence Erlbaum Associates.

Turner, J. C., Oakes, P. J., Haslam, S. A., & McGarty, C. (1994). Self and collective: Cognition and social context. *Personality and Social Psychology Bulletin, 20,* 454–463.

Wallace, A. F. C., & Fogelson, R. D. (1961). Culture and personality. *Biennial Review of Anthropology, 2,* 42–78.

Wan, C., Chiu, C.-y., Peng, S., & Tam, K. (2007). Measuring cultures through intersubjective cultural norms: Implications for predicting relative identification with two or more cultures. *Journal of Cross-Cultural Psychology, 38,* 213–226.

Wan, C., Chiu, C-y., Tam, K., Lee, V. S., Lau, I. Y., & Peng, S. (2007). Perceived cultural importance and actual self-importance of values in cultural identification. *Journal of Personality and Social Psychology, 92,* 337–354.

Wan, C., Torelli, C., & Chiu, C-y. (in press). Intersubjective consensus and the maintenance of normative shared reality. *Social Cognition.*

Ward, C., & Searle, W. (1991). The impact of value discrepancies and cultural identity on psychological and sociocultural adjustment of sojourners. *International Journal of Intercultural Relations, 15,* 209–225.

Wiley, A. R., Rose, A. J., Burger, L. K., & Miller, P. J. (1998). Constructing autonomous selves through narrative practices: A comparative study of working-class and middle-class families. *Child Development, 69,* 833–847.

Wong, D. F. K., Li, C. Y., & Song, H. X. (2007). Rural migrant workers in urban China: Living a marginalised life. *International Journal of Social Welfare, 16,* 32–40.

Wyer, R. S., & Srull, T. K. (1986). Human cognition in its social context. *Psychological Review, 93,* 322–359.

PART FOUR

MANIFESTATIONS OF CULTURAL

PROCESSES

8

Culture and Self-Enhancement

YOUNG-HOON KIM

People desire positive self-perceptions. A College Board (1976–1977) survey of nearly one million high school seniors found that only 2% of them perceived themselves to be worse than average on leadership ability, and no respondents believed that they were worse than average on the ability to get along with others. High school seniors are not alone in displaying this bias. In other surveys, more than 94% of university professors thought that they had better-than-average teaching ability (Cross, 1977); college students rated themselves as better than average on 38 of 40 positive personality traits (e.g., dependable, intelligent; Alicke, Klotz, Breitenbecher, Yurak, & Vredenburg, 1995); and a randomly selected sample of 296 New Jersey residents perceived that they were less susceptible than others to a diverse set of hazards (Weinstein, 1987).

Other psychological processes attend to this persistent Pollyanna view of the self. For instance, individuals who construct unrealistically positive self-perceptions are motivated to maintain positive regards of the self (see Taylor & Brown, 1988; Heine, Lehman, Markus, & Kitayama, 1999). Holding a Pollyanna self-view dovetails such biases as displaying unrealistic optimism (e.g., Weinstein, 1980; Kuiper & MacDonald, 1982), making internal attributions for successes and external attributions for failures (e.g., Zuckerman, 1979; Heine, Kitayama, & Lehman, 2001), and exhibiting the false uniqueness effect (e.g., Markus & Kitayama, 1991). For the purpose of maintaining a positive self-view in the face of self-esteem threats, individuals may also engage in compensatory self-deceptive behaviors, including adopting self-handicapping strategies (e.g., Tice & Baumeister, 1990), undergoing defensive attitude change (e.g., Steele, 1988), displaying aggressive behaviors (e.g., Bushman & Baumeister, 1998), engaging in downward social comparison (e.g., Gibbons & McCoy, 1991), and discounting negative feedback (Heine, Kitayama, & Lehman, 2001).

Holding a positive self-view predicts many important outcomes, including better psychological well-being (as reflected in fewer anxious responses to mortality threats; Greenberg et al., 1992) and better psychological health (as reflected in higher levels of happiness, optimism, and positive mood; see Taylor & Brown, 1988). Positive self-perceptions also facilitate intellectual functioning (efficiency in problem-solving and optimal utilization of cognitive resources) through the mediating effect of positive affect (e.g., Taylor & Brown, 1988). Positive self-perceptions are also associated with increased motivation (e.g., Bandura, 1977), persistence (e.g., Baumeister & Tice, 1985), and performance (e.g., Baumeister, Hamilton, & Tice, 1985).

Nonetheless, despite the prevalence and psychological benefits of self-enhancive perceptions, the universality of the self-enhancement motivation has been questioned. For example, Heine and his colleagues (1999) stated, "The empirical literature provides scant evidence for a need for positive self-regard among Japanese . . . The need for positive self-regard, as it is currently conceptualized, is not universal, but rather is rooted in significant aspects of North American culture" (p. 766). In support of this claim, evidence from cross-cultural studies has been cited to show that the psychological benefits of positive self-regard are absent among East Asians (Heine et al., 1999).

In response to the claim regarding the cultural relativity of self-enhancive motivation, some researchers have recently found evidence for self-enhancement and its psychological benefits among East Asians. Reviewing the recent evidence, Brown (2003) concluded, "the self-enhancement motive is alive and well in collectivistic cultures, but cultural norms limit its expression" (p. 604).

The primary objective of this chapter is to provide a theoretical framework for understanding the universal need for self-enhancive perceptions and their culture-specific expressions. To achieve this objective, I will expand on the differences in the expression of self-enhancement motivation between European Americans and East Asians. Although both European Americans and East Asians are motivated to self-enhance, the two cultural groups differ in how they express this motivation. Furthermore, I posit that the prevailing self-presentation norms (e.g., modesty norms) in East Asian cultures proscribe blatant expressions of self-enhancement. Consequently, East Asians experience more contextual constraints on self-expression and feel a need to express positive self-views more subtly. Finally, I argue that self-enhancement is associated with higher subjective well-being among both European Americans and East Asians.

THE SELF-ENHANCEMENT MOTIVE

The Seeming Absence of the Self-Enhancement Motive in East Asian Contexts

Heine and his colleagues (1999; 2007) questioned the presence of self-enhancement motivation in East Asia for the following reasons. First, East Asians do not self-enhance as much as European Americans do on conventional measures of self-enhancement. For example, in a meta-analytic study of 91 cross-cultural comparisons, Heine and Hamamura (2007) found that European Americans self-enhanced more than did East Asians in 88 of the 91 comparisons. The weighted average effect size of this cross-cultural difference was large ($d = .84$). In addition, European Americans showed self-enhancement in 44 of 48 studies. The weighted average effect size of the self-enhancement bias among European Americans was large ($d = .87$). In contrast, East Asians showed self-effacement in 24 of 46 studies and self-enhancement in 19 studies. The weighted average effect size of the self-enhancement bias among East Asians was not significant ($d = -.01$).

Second, self-enhancement–related behaviors seem to be infrequent among East Asians. For example, compared to European Americans, East Asians (a) have lower levels of unrealistic optimism (e.g., Chang & Asakawa, 2003; Chang, Asakawa, & Sanna, 2001; Heine & Lehman, 1995), (b) make fewer internal attributions for successes and external attributions for failure (e.g., Heine et al., 1999), and (c) are less likely to display the false uniqueness effect (e.g., Markus & Kitayama, 1991). In addition, East Asians do not protect their positive self-perception through engaging in the following compensatory self-deceptive processes: discounting negative feedback (e.g., Heine, Kitayama, Lehman, et al., 2001), devaluation of a failed task (Heine, Kitayama, Lehman, et al., 2001), and lowering the perceived self-relevance of a failure situation (Kitayama, Markus, Matsumoto, & Norasakkunkit, 1997).

Finally, East Asians are found to be self-critical. For example, Markus and Kitayama (1991) and Heine and colleagues (1999) found that East Asians tend to be self-critical and sensitive to the emotion of shame; in addition, they constantly opt for opportunities to self-improve.

Understanding Cultural Differences in Self-Enhancive Expressions

East Asians' inconsistent, weak tendencies to self-enhance on conventional measures of self-enhancement should not be taken as evidence for the absence of self-enhancement in East Asian cultures (Brown, 2003; Kim, Chiu, Peng, Cai, & Tov, 2010; Kurman, 2003) because although the self-enhancement motive might be present in East Asian cultures, it is expressed in subtle forms. These expressions could therefore have escaped researchers' attention. Furthermore, the argument for the absence of self-enhancement motivation in East Asian contexts is largely based on null findings, which are by nature not interpretable.

Some investigators (Kim et al., 2010; Kurman, 2001, 2003; Sedikides, Gaertner, & Toguchi, 2003; Sedikides, Gaertner, & Vevea, 2005) have offered an alternative explanation for the findings summarized in the previous sub-section. According to this explanation, self-presentation and self-regulation norms and values in East Asian cultures proscribe arrogance and sanction blatant expressions of self-enhancement. That is, East Asians also desire positive self-regard as do Americans, but in light of the dominant cultural norms and values that govern self-presentation and self-regulation, East Asians need to express their positive self-views in culturally acceptable ways. Thus, expressions of self-enhancement in East Asian contexts could be rather subtle and indirect.

Normative Influence on Expressions of Positive Self-Regard in East Asian Cultures

As mentioned, some prevalent self-presentation and self-regulation norms and values in East Asian cultures sanction blatant expressions of self-enhancement and necessitate expression of self-enhancement in subtle and indirect fashions. These norms and values include dialectical self-presentation, the modesty norm, self-improvement, prevention focus, and relational harmony.

Dialectical Self
The dialectical self, a prevalent conception of the self in East Asia, encourages individuals to acknowledge their strengths as well as their weaknesses and shortcomings (Spencer-Rodgers, Peng, Wang, & Hou, 2004). From the perspective of the dialectical self, acknowledging one's weaknesses (or shortcomings) does not entail denial of one's strengths (Chiu & Hong, 2006). Thus, endorsement of the dialectical self renders externalization of failures and compensatory self-protection strategies unimportant for self-protection – because one can admit failures while holding positive perceptions of the self.

In contrast, European American culture values self-consistency, which requires individuals who recognize their strengths to also deny their shortcomings. North Americans' emphasis on consistent self-expressions is evident in finding that European Americans who rate themselves as extraverted do not rate themselves as introverted, and vice versa. By comparison, the demand for self-consistency is weaker in East Asian cultures, as evident in the finding that Koreans would rate themselves as either extraverted or introverted depending on the contexts of the questions (Choi & Choi, 2002).

Evidence from several cross-cultural studies (e.g., Kim, Peng, & Chiu, 2008; Spencer-Rodgers et al., 2004) shows that having a dialectical view of the self is partly responsible for East Asians' lesser tendency to express positive views of the self. Because the dialectical self insulates positive self-perceptions from the acknowledgment of personal weaknesses, the dialectical self encourages its East Asian subscribers to acknowledge their shortcomings, which would lower overall positivity of East Asians' self-ratings.

This argument has two implications. First, the primary driver of East Asians' lower level of overall positivity in self-perception is their greater willingness to admit having negative self-attributes, and not their greater reluctance to affirm their positive traits. Second, in East Asian contexts, acknowledging one's weaknesses may reflect adherence to a dialectical self-presentation style rather than a lack of self-enhancement motivation. Consistent with these ideas, Kim and colleagues (2008) found that the Chinese-American difference in self-esteem was driven primarily by Chinese participants' greater tendency to agree with negatively worded self-esteem items (e.g., "I think I am not good at all"). In fact, Chinese persons and Americans do not differ in their agreement with positively worded self-esteem items (e.g., "I feel that I have a number of good qualities").

Modesty

The cultural norm of modesty in East Asian cultures also affects the way East Asians express their positive self-view. The modesty norm proscribes blatant expressions of positive self-views. Research has shown that, in East Asia, children start to internalize the modesty norm in Grades 2–5 (Yoshida, Kojo, & Kaku, 1982). Furthermore, in East Asian contexts, individuals who make self-effacing attributions are perceived more favorably than are those who make self-enhancing attributions. In addition, from an early age, East Asians begin to criticize others who show a self-enhancing tendency (Bond, Leung, & Wan, 1982; Yoshida et al., 1982). Taken together, these findings suggest that individuals in East Asian cultures are socialized to avoid public and direct expressions of a public self-view.

The prevalence of the modesty norm in East Asian cultures explains why East Asians tend to rate themselves less positively than do European Americans. Kurman and Sriram (2002) found that endorsement of the modesty norm is negatively related to the extent of self-enhancement (vs. self-criticism). In general, modest individuals consider it inappropriate to (a) express unrealistically positive self-perceptions directly or (b) display the self-serving bias (Kurman, 2001).

If East Asians also desire to express their positive self-views, but hesitate to do so because of modest self-presentation concerns, they would show self-enhancive behaviors in situations where modesty concerns are not salient. There is ample evidence for this prediction. First, in collectivist cultures, there is a negative correlation between modesty and the extent of self-enhancement on agentic traits and a nonsignificant correlation between modesty and the extent of self-enhancement on communal traits (Kurman, 2001). This result suggests that, although the modesty norm proscribes self-enhancement on agentic traits, it does not proscribe self-enhancement on collectivist traits. Indeed, a recent meta-analysis shows that East Asians show self-enhancement on collectivist traits/behaviors (Sedikides et al., 2005). Second, the modesty norm also does not proscribe self-enhancement in competitive relationships, and research shows that East Asians engage in compensatory self-protection strategies when they lose in a competition (Takata, 2003). Third, although the modesty norm discourages bragging about one's positive qualities, it does not prohibit expressions of self-liking. A recent study shows that, although East Asians do not brag about their personal qualities as much as Americans do, East Asians express equally strong self-liking as Americans do (Cai, Brown, Deng, & Oakes, 2007). Finally, consistent with the idea that East Asians would self-enhance when modest self-presentation concerns are weak, when guaranteed complete anonymity of responses, East Asians make internal attributions for their success and external attributions for their failure (Kudo & Numazaki, 2003).

Self-Improvement

Self-improvement is another cultural norm that discourages overt self-enhancement in East Asia. Self-improvement is a motif that runs through the parenting styles (Miller, Wiley, Fung, & Chung-Hui, 1997), the widely circulated incremental theory of self (Chiu, Hong, & Dweck, 1997), and the emphasis on self-discipline (Azuma, Kashiwagi, & Hess, 1981) in Asian contexts. Given their strong self-improvement motivation, East Asians would avoid using defensive strategies (e.g., self-serving biases and compensatory self-deceptive processes) for the purpose of protecting self-esteem. For example, making external attributions for failure or discounting negative feedback prevents individuals from recognizing their weaknesses and learning from failures, which are both important for self-improvement to take place. Instead, the self-improvement motivation often invites self-criticism. Thus, the strong self-improvement motivation in East Asian culture may account for the greater prevalence of self-criticism among East Asians.

Prevention Focus

Compared to each other, East Asians are more motivated by avoidance of negative outcomes (more prevention focused) and European Americans are more motivated by attainment of positive outcomes (more promotion focused) (Lee, Aaker, & Gardner, 2000). Given these cultural differences in motivational predilections, East Asians should be less motivated than European Americans to attain positive self-evaluations and to engage in defensive strategies to avoid loss of positive self-esteem.

Consistent with this idea, recent studies show that East Asians are more likely than Americans to adopt a prevention-focused strategy in self-presentation. For example, Kim and colleagues (2010)showed that Chinese participants were less likely than American participants to agree with positively framed statements (e.g., "I am smart"), although they disagreed with negatively framed statements (e.g., "I am not intelligent") as much as American participants did. Also, although East Asians show less unrealistic optimism for positive events than do European Americans, East Asians show unrealistic optimism for negative events as much as European Americans do (Chang et al., 2001). Similarly, Japanese do not expect positive life events to occur to them more often than to others, but they believe that negative life events would not occur more often to them than to others (Heine & Lehman, 1995).

Harmony

Finally, maintaining relational harmony is an important cultural value in East Asia (see Markus & Kitayama, 1991). Perceived relational harmony predicts East Asians' life satisfaction level more than it does that of Americans (Kwan, Bond, & Singelis, 1997). The harmony norm also discourages direct expressions of positive self-evaluations in public because such expressions highlight the positive distinctiveness of the self and undermine group cohesion.

Nonetheless, the harmony norm also encourages self-enhancive behaviors if such behaviors would enhance group harmony. For example, although the harmony norm discourages exhibition of the self-serving bias, it permits and even encourages exhibition of ingroup-favoring perceptions and attributions (e.g., making internal attribution for the ingroup's high performance and external attribution for the ingroup's low performance). Consistent with this idea, results from laboratory experiments (Muramoto & Yamaguchi, 1997, 2003) show that, although Japanese make self-effacing attribution for their success and failure, they make group-serving attribution for their group's success and failure. The harmony norm also allows expressions of unrealistic positive perceptions of one's relationships. For example, Japanese perceive the quality of their relationships with the best friend, family members, and romantic partner to be more positive than that of the average other (Endo, Heine, & Lehman, 2000). Although East Asians do not directly communicate a positive self-view to others, they expect favorable evaluations of the self from their significant others. For example, although Japanese make internal attribution for failure and external attribution for success, when they experience success (failure), they expect their significant others (e.g., parents, siblings, close friends) to attribute the success (failure) to internal (external) factors (Muramoto, 2003).

In summary, like European Americans, East Asians also have the need to hold and express positive self-views. Nonetheless, they fashion the ways they express positive self-evaluations in accordance with the demands of certain prevalent cultural norms governing self-presentation (the dialectical self, modesty) and self-regulation (self-improvement, prevention focus, harmony). The more subtle and indirect ways in which East Asians self-enhance may have escaped researchers' attention, leading to the hasty conclusion that self-enhancement motivation is absent in East Asian contexts. Understanding the dynamics between self-expressive needs and normative expectations in East Asian contexts helps correct this hasty conclusion.

THE CONSEQUENCES OF SELF-ENHANCEMENT

Another argument for the presence of self-enhancement motivation among East Asians is that self-enhancement has important psychological benefits in East Asian cultures. Recent research has examined the relationship between self-enhancement and variables pertinent to individuals' psychological well-being in different cultural contexts.

The Well-Being Implications of Self-Enhancement across Cultures

The evidence just reviewed suggests that although the cultural requirements of modesty, self-improvement, dialectical self-presentation, prevention-focused self-regulation, and harmony lead East Asians to not display self-enhancive behaviors as often as European American do, they do self-enhance in the same ways that European Americans do – they evaluate the self more positively than they do others. Moreover, exhibition of such self-enhancive behaviors is associated with subjective well-being in East Asian contexts, as it is in European-American contexts.

For example, in a comparative study of individualist and collectivist cultures, Kurman (2003) measured self-enhancement in the academic domain by (a) assessing the difference between participants' perception of their ability and their actual ability, and (b) measuring the above-average effect (the participants' rating of personal traits relative to an average person in the pertinent reference group in the participants' culture). Next, she related these measures of self-enhancement to indices of psychological well-being (e.g., self-esteem, positive affectivity, negative affectivity, and emotional self-criticism). As expected, participants from collectivist cultures showed less self-enhancement than did those from individualist cultures. The associations between self-enhancement and various indices of psychological well-being were equally strong, however, in individualist and collectivist cultures. In other words, regardless of whether the participants came from individualist or collectivist cultures, those who self-enhanced more showed better psychological well-being.

In another study, Kim and Chiu (2010) compared academic self-enhancement of Hong Kong and American students. They measured self-enhancement with the discrepancy between participants' perceived performance and their actual performance. The results show that although Hong Kong participants (vs. American participants) self-enhanced less, in both samples, those who self-effaced more were more depressed. In conclusion, despite variations in the mean level of self-enhancive behaviors across cultures, such behaviors seem to serve the same psychological functions across cultures.

Well-Being Implications of Culture-Characteristic
Self-Enhancive Behaviors

Nevertheless, as evident from the results reviewed in the previous section, East Asians and European Americans differ in the ways in which they self-enhance. Interestingly, the characteristic methods of self-enhancement in a certain culture are particularly predictive of subjective well-being in that culture (see Chapter 9, this volume).

For example, as mentioned earlier, only East Asians self-enhance by exhibiting the group-serving bias or by overrating the quality of their relationship. In addition, only collectivists show self-enhancement on communal traits. These findings indicate that being viewed by others as having high social standing and good relationships is important to East Asians' self-image. Not surprisingly, East Asians' subjective well-being is linked to the perceived quality of their relationship (Kang, Shaver, Min, & Jin, 2003; Suh, 2002). For example, Suh (2002) showed that East Asians' subjective well-being is related to the social approval gained from their significant others. A recent study by Kim and Cohen (2010) also showed that East Asians' subjective well-being is related to how positively they believe their significant others would view their social relationships.

East Asians also display self-enhancive behaviors by showcasing their self-improvement motivation and prevention focus. Not surprisingly, research has related East Asians' subjective well-being to their self-improvement motivation and prevention focus. For example, Asakawa and Csikszentmihalyi (1998) reported that East Asians were happy when they pursued an important future goal, whereas European Americans were happy when they pursued an important current goal. There is also evidence that European Americans who use prevention-focused regulation to attain goals are less satisfied with their life, but this is not the case among East Asians (e.g., Asakawa & Csikszentmihalyi, 2000; Elliot, Chirkov, Kim, & Sheldon, 2001; Oishi & Diener, 2001). Whereas European Americans are happier when they pursue promotion goals, East Asians are happier and more satisfied with their life when they pursue prevention goals.

CONCLUSIONS

In this chapter, I contend that, like European Americans, East Asians have a need for self-enhancement and that they would express self-enhancive behaviors, cognitions, and affect when the prevalent cultural norms permit such expressions. I also contend that self-enhancement is associated with positive psychological well-being in both European and East Asian cultures. Indeed, self-enhancement may be one of the most fundamental human motivations. East Asian and European-American cultures do not differ in whether this motivation is present or not; they differ only in the ways in which it is expressed and the conditions under which it is expressed.

Thus, self-enhancement can be understood as a basic motive or abstract goal, and there can be many ways individuals can pursue this goal (Kruglanski et al., 2002). Nonetheless, the choice of the means to fulfill self-enhancement goals is not random but reflects a discriminative response to normative expectations and situation-specific features of the immediate context. East Asians pursue self-enhancement goals by using culturally approved means; these means might not overlap completely with the means that European Americans prefer. Likewise, the preferred means of self-enhancement in European American contexts may not always appeal to East Asians. Differences in strategic choices reflect cultural divergence in the prevalent cultural norms and values (also see Chapter 4, this volume). Naturally, the preferred self-enhancement means in a culture that emphasizes modesty, self-improvement, and harmony are markedly different from those in a culture that values self-assertiveness, directness, and individuality. In conclusion, understanding self-enhancive behaviors across cultures requires deep understanding of the cultural processes that underlie dynamic transactions of basic individual motivations and normative cultural influences.

REFERENCES

Alicke, M. D., Klotz, M. L., Breitenbecher, D. L., Yurak, T. J., & Vredenburg, D. S. (1995). Personal contact, individuation, and the better-than-average effect. *Journal of Personality and Social Psychology, 68*, 804–825.

Asakawa, K., & Csikszentmihalyi, M. (1998). The quality of experience of Asian American adolescents in academic activities: An exploration of educational achievement. *Journal of Research on Adolescence, 8*, 241–262.

Asakawa, K., & Csikszentmihalyi, M. (2000). Feelings of connectedness and internalization of values in Asian American adolescents. *Journal of Youth and Adolescence, 29*, 121–145.

Azuma, H., Kashiwagi, K., & Hess, R. (1981). *The influence of attitude and behavior upon the child's intellectual development.* Tokyo: University of Tokyo Press.

Bandura, A. (1977). *Social learning theory.* Englewood Cliffs, NJ: Prentice-Hall.

Baumeister, R. F., Hamilton, J. C., & Tice, D. M. (1985). Public versus private expectancy of success: Confidence booster or performance pressure. *Journal of Personality & Social Psychology, 48*, 1447–1457.

Baumeister, R. F., & Tice, D. M. (1985). Self-esteem and responses to success and failure: Subsequent performance and intrinsic motivation. *Journal of Personality, 53*, 450–467.

Bond, M. H., Leung, K., & Wan, K. C. (1982). How does cultural collectivism operate? The impact of task and maintenance contributions on reward distribution. *Journal of Cross-Cultural Psychology, 13*, 186–200.

Brown, J. D. (2003). The self-enhancement motive in collectivistic cultures. The rumors of my death have been greatly exaggerated. *Journal of Cross-Cultural Psychology, 34*, 603–605.

Bushman, B. J., & Baumeister, R. F. (1998). Threatened egotism, narcissism, self-esteem and direct and displaced aggression: Does self-love or self-hate lead to violence? *Journal of Personality and Social Psychology, 75,* 219–229.

Cai, H., Brown, J. D., Deng, C., & Oakes, M. A. (2007). Self-esteem and culture: Differences in cognitive self-evaluations or affective self-regard? *Asian Journal of Social Psychology, 10,* 162–170.

Chang, E. C., & Asakawa, K. (2003). Cultural variations on optimistic and pessimistic bias for self versus a sibling: Is there evidence for self-enhancement in the West and for self-criticism in the East when the referent group is specified? *Journal of Personality and Social Psychology, 84,* 569–581.

Chang, E. C., Asakawa, K., & Sanna, L. J. (2001). Cultural variations in optimistic and pessimistic bias: Do Easterners really expect the worst and Westerners really expect the best when predicting future life events? *Journal of Personality and Social Psychology, 81,* 476–491.

Chiu, C.-y., & Hong, Y.-y. (2006). *Social psychology of culture.* New York: Psychology Press.

Chiu, C.-y., Hong, Y.-y., & Dweck, C. S. (1997). Lay dispositionism and implicit theories of personality. *Journal of Personality and Social Psychology, 73,* 19–30.

Choi, I., & Choi, Y. (2002). Culture and self-concept flexibility. *Personality and Social Psychology Bulletin, 28,* 1508–1517.

College Board. (1976–1977). *Student descriptive questionnaire.* Princeton, NJ: Educational Testing Service.

Cross, P. (1977, Spring). Not can but will college teaching be improved? *New Directions for Higher Education, 17,* 1–15. Reported in D. G. Myers (1990), *Social Psychology* (3rd ed.). New York: McGraw-Hill.

Elliot, A. J., Chirkov, V. I., Kim, Y.-M., & Sheldon, K. M. (2001). A cross-cultural analysis of avoidance (relative to approach) personal goals. *Psychological Science, 12,* 505–510.

Endo, Y., Heine, S. J., & Lehman, D. R. (2000). Culture and positive illusions in relationships: How my relationships are better than yours. *Personality and Social Psychology Bulletin, 26,* 1571–1586.

Gibbons, F. X., & McCoy, S. B. (1991). Self-esteem, similarity, and reactions to active versus passive downward comparison. *Journal of Personality and Social Psychology, 60,* 414–424.

Greenberg, J., Soloman, S., Pyszczynski, T., Rosenblatt, A., Burling, J., Lyon, D., et al. (1992). Why do people need self-esteem? Converging evidence that self-esteem serves an anxiety-buffering function. *Journal of Personality and Social Psychology, 63,* 913–922.

Heine, S. J., & Hamamura, J. (2007). In search of East Asian self-enhancement. *Personality and Social Psychology Review, 11,* 1–24.

Heine, S. J., Kitayama, S., & Lehman, D. R. (2001). Cultural differences in self-evaluation: Japanese readily accept negative self-relevant information. *Journal of Cross-Cultural Psychology, 32,* 434–443.

Heine, S. J., Kitayama, S., Lehman, D. R., Takata, T., Ide, E., Leung, C., et al. (2001). Divergent consequences of success and failure in Japan and North America:

An investigation of self-improving motivations and malleable selves. *Journal of Personality and Social Psychology, 81*, 599–615.

Heine, S. J., & Lehman, D. R. (1995). Cultural variation in unrealistic optimism: Does the West feel more invulnerable than the East? *Journal of Personality and Social Psychology, 68*, 595–607.

Heine, S. J., Lehman, D. R., Markus, H. R., & Kitayama, S. (1999). Is there a universal need for positive self-regard? *Psychological Review, 106*, 766–794.

Kang, S., Shaver, P. R., Min, K., & Jin, H. (2003). Culture-specific patterns in the prediction of life satisfaction: Roles of emotion, relationship quality, and self-esteem. *Personality and Social Psychology Bulletin, 29*, 1596–1608.

Kim, Y.-H., & Chiu, C.-y. (2010). *Emotional costs of inaccurate self-assessments: Both self-effacement and self-enhancement can lead to dejection.* Unpublished manuscript.

Kim, Y.-H., Chiu, C.-y., Peng, S., Cai, H., & Tov, W. (2010). Explaining East-West differences in the likelihood of making favorable self-evaluations: The role of evaluation apprehension and directness of expression. *Journal of Cross-Cultural Psychology, 41*, 62–75.

Kim, Y.-H., & Cohen, D. (2010). Information, perspective, and judgments about the self in Face and Dignity cultures. *Personality and Social Psychology Bulletin, 36*, 537–550

Kim, Y.-H., Peng, S., & Chiu, C.-y. (2008). Explaining self-esteem differences between Chinese and North Americans: Dialectical self (vs. self-consistency) or lack of positive self-regard. *Self and Identity, 7*, 113–128.

Kitayama, S., Markus, H. R., Matsumoto, H., & Norasakkunkit, V. (1997). Individual and collective processes in the construction of the self: Self-enhancement in the United States and self-criticism in Japan. *Journal of Personality and Social Psychology, 72*, 1245–1267.

Kruglanski, A. W., Shah, J. Y., Fishbach, A., Friedman, R., Chun, W. Y., & Sleeth-Keppler, D. (2002). A theory of goal systems. In M. Zanna (Ed.), *Advances in experimental social psychology, Vol. 34* (pp. 331–378). San Diego, CA: Academic Press.

Kudo, E., & Numazaki, M. (2003). Explicit and direct self-serving bias in Japan: Reexamination of self-serving bias for success and failure. *Journal of Cross-Cultural Psychology, 34*, 511–521.

Kuiper, N. A., & MacDonald, M. R. (1982). Self and other perception in mild depressives. *Social Cognition, 1*, 233–239.

Kurman, J. (2001). Self-enhancement: Is it restricted to individualistic cultures? *Personality and Social Psychology Bulletin, 12*, 1705–1716.

Kurman, J. (2003). Why is self-enhancement low in certain collectivistic cultures? An investigation of two competing explanations. *Journal of Cross-Cultural Psychology, 34*, 489–510.

Kurman, J., & Sriram, N. (2002). Interrelationships among vertical and horizontal collectivism, modesty, and self-enhancement. *Journal of Cross-Cultural Psychology, 33*, 71–86.

Kwan, V. S. Y., Bond, M. H., & Singelis, T. M. (1997). Pancultural explanations for life satisfaction: Adding relationship harmony to self-esteem. *Journal of Personality and Social Psychology, 73*, 1038–1051.

Lee, A., Aaker, J., & Gardner, W. (2000). The pleasures and pains of distinct self-construals: The role of interdependence in regulatory focus. *Journal of Personality and Social Psychology, 78*, 1122–1134.

Markus, H. R., & Kitayama, S. (1991). Culture and the self: Implications for cognition, emotion, and motivation. *Psychological Review, 98*, 224–253.

Miller, M. J., Wiley, A. R., Fung, H., & Chung-Hui, L. (1997). Personal storytelling as a medium of socialization in Chinese and American families. *Child Development, 68*, 557–568.

Muramoto, Y. (2003). An indirect self-enhancement in relationship among Japanese. *Journal of Cross-Cultural Psychology, 34*, 552–566.

Muramoto, Y., & Yamaguchi, S. (1997). Another type of self-serving bias: Coexistence of self-effacing and group-serving tendencies in attribution in the Japanese culture. *Japanese Journal of Experimental Social Psychology, 37*, 65–75.

Muramoto, Y., & Yamaguchi, S. (2003). When "self-effacement" disappears: Narratives of personal and group successes depending on an ingroup relationship. *Japanese Journal of Psychology, 74*, 253–262.

Oishi, S., & Diener, E. (2001). Goals, culture, and subjective well-being. *Personality and Social Psychology Bulletin, 27*, 1674–1682.

Sedikides, C., Gaertner, L., & Toguchi, Y. (2003). Pancultural self-enhancement. *Journal of Personality and Social Psychology, 84*, 60–79.

Sedikides, C., Gaertner, L., & Vevea, J. L. (2005). Pancultural self-enhancement reloaded: A meta-analytic reply to Heine (2005). *Journal of Personality and Social Psychology, 89*, 539–551.

Spencer-Rodgers, J., Peng, K., Wang, L., & Hou, Y. (2004). Dialectical self-esteem and East-West differences in psychological well-being. *Personality and Social Psychology Bulletin, 30*, 1416–1432.

Steele, C. M. (1988). The psychology of self-affirmation: Sustaining the integrity of the self. In L. Berkowitz (Ed.), *Advances in experimental social psychology, Vol. 21* (pp. 261–302). New York: Academic Press.

Suh, E. M. (2002). Culture, identity consistency, and subjective well-being. *Journal of Personality and Social Psychology, 83*, 1378–1391.

Takata, T. (2003). Self-enhancement and self-criticism in Japanese culture: An experimental analysis. *Journal of Cross-Cultural Psychology, 34*, 542–551.

Taylor, S. E., & Brown, J. D. (1988). Illusion and well-being: A social psychological perspective on mental health. *Psychological Bulletin, 103*, 193–210.

Tice, D. M., & Baumeister, R. F. (1990). Self-esteem, self-handicapping, and self-presentation: The strategy of inadequate practice. *Journal of Personality, 58*, 443–464.

Weinstein, N. D. (1980) Unrealistic optimism about future life events. *Journal of Personality and Social Psychology, 39*, 806–820.

Weinstein, N. D. (1987). Unrealistic optimism about susceptibility to health problems: Conclusions from a community-wide sample. *Journal of Behavioral Medicine, 10*, 481–500.

Yoshida, T., Kojo, K., & Kaku, H. (1982). A study on the development of self-presentation in children. *Japanese Journal of Educational Psychology, 30,* 120–127.

Zuckerman, M. (1979). Attribution of success and failure revisited, or: The motivational bias is alive and well in attribution theory. *Journal of Personality, 47,* 245–287.

9

Cultural Processes Underlying Subjective Well-Being

YOUNG-HOON KIM AND WILLIAM TOV

The subjective well-being (SWB) of an individual refers to her or his own sense of wellness and consists of a variety of cognitive and emotional components. Cognitive SWB includes life satisfaction, which taps into individuals' own evaluation of their lives. Emotional SWB is commonly assessed by the frequency of pleasant emotions and infrequency of negative emotions. Although survey studies of SWB have been conducted since the mid-20th century (see Diener, 1984), extensive research on SWB – cross-cultural research in particular – did not begin to accumulate until the 1990s. In particular, overall levels of SWB as well as its correlates and possible psychological causes have been of great interest to recent cross-cultural researchers.

In this chapter, we highlight cross-cultural differences in SWB and provide a theoretical foundation for understanding the psychological processes related to those differences. We restrict our comparisons to those between European American and East Asian (Chinese, Korean, and Japanese) samples in part because research on these groups is extensive. In both groups, SWB may be influenced by common psychological factors (e.g., goal attainment, self-esteem). The nature of these factors and the degree to which they covary with SWB may differ across groups, however. For example, self-esteem is more strongly correlated with SWB in Western nations (around .60) than in Asian nations (around .40; Diener, Diener, & Diener, 1995). In other words, how positively individuals perceive themselves might be less predictive of life satisfaction in East Asian cultures. Our interpretation of these differences draws largely on the cultural psychology of self-construals (Markus & Kitayama, 1991), which assumes that individuals can define themselves either in reference to or in isolation from their social roles and that certain cultures may value one type of self-construal over another.

We will first elaborate on self-construal theory and how it applies to European American and East Asian cultural patterns. We will then discuss how these divergent patterns might explain two common findings in culture and well-being research: differences in (a) the correlates and causes and (b) the mean levels of SWB across cultures.

THEORETICAL BACKGROUND

It is a theme in social psychology that our cognition, motivation, and emotions are often influenced by others. The presence of other people is more essential and critical in East Asians' cognition and behavior than in those European Americans, however. The self is primarily a member of a social group (e.g., family), and being mindful of one's interrelation with others is a culturally valued way of being. Markus and Kitayama (1991) defined this influence of other people on East Asians' cognition, motivation, and emotion as an interdependent self-construal in which "one's behavior is determined, contingent on, and, to a large extent organized by what the actor perceives to be the thoughts, feelings, and actions of others in the relationship" (p. 227). This theory implies that East Asians' SWB (emotional and cognitive states) should be related to their perception of other people. These perceptions matter in two ways. First, they frequently guide behavior and feelings. In combination with other aspects of East Asian culture (e.g., valuing adjustment and self-criticism; Heine, Lehman, Markus, & Kitayama, 1999), attention to others may influence the desirability and frequency of various emotions and cognitions. Second, they include perceptions of what others *think* about the self. Triandis (1989) referred to such perceptions as the collective self, and maintained that such beliefs are distinguishable from what one privately believes about oneself, as well as what one believes about others (other-perceptions). If interpersonal roles are indeed central to East Asian self-definitions, then collective self-perceptions may be particularly important. Thus, we theorize that the SWB of East Asians is enhanced by collective self-perceptions and other-perceptions that imply that the self is in good social standing. In detail, East Asians are happy when (a) they perceive that other people approve of their lives, (b) they perceive that other people think they are good agents, (c) they perceive that they are in good relational harmony with other people, and (d) they perceive emotional support from other people. The first two beliefs are examples of collective self-perceptions, whereas the latter two beliefs are examples of other-perceptions.

In contrast, compared with East Asians, European American self-definitions are less influenced by the presence of other people. Instead, European Americans put more weight and importance on their own distinctive qualities, independent of other people. The self that is culturally valued is a unique, active agent responsible for one's own cognitive, emotional, and behavioral manifestation. Markus and Kitayama (1991) labeled this an *independent* self-construal in which "behavior is organized and made meaningful primarily by reference to one's own internal repertoire of thoughts, feelings, and action, rather than by reference to the thoughts, feelings, and actions of others" (p. 226). Thus, the SWB of European Americans may be more strongly associated with their own, private self-perceptions than with their collective self-perceptions or other-perceptions. Therefore, we postulate that European Americans are happy when they perceive themselves to be in good states. In detail, European Americans are happy when (a) they have positive self-regard, (b) they perceive self-consistency, and (c) they pursue self-oriented goals.

We propose that cultural differences in the predominant forms of self-construal affect well-being in two ways. First, whether the self is emphasized in reference to or separate from social roles influences the correlates and causes of SWB. Second, within the ethos of each culture, chronic attention to self versus others influences the frequency and desirability of certain emotions, with implications for overall mean levels of SWB. Thus, the *nature* of well-being is shaped not by self-construals alone, but *in combination with* other values and beliefs specific to each culture.

THE CORRELATES AND CAUSES OF SWB ACROSS CULTURES

There are many factors that play a role in individuals' SWB differentially and dynamically across cultures. We will flesh out the dynamics of these factors in terms of how they are related to private and collective self-perception as well as other-perceptions. Research on culture and well-being suggests that private self-perceptions may be central to the SWB of European Americans, whereas collective self-perceptions and other-perceptions may be particularly important for the SWB of East Asians. Simply put, European Americans are happy when they are *perceived by themselves* as good *independent* agents in their cultural contexts. This premise is based on the theoretical framework that the self of European Americans is constructed as an *independent* agent. In contrast, East Asians are happy when they are *perceived by other people* as good *interdependent* agents in their cultural contexts. This premise is based on the assumption that the self of East Asians is developed as an *interdependent* agent. In short, self-perceptions help validate and affirm self-construals. Moreover, self-construals influence the informational value of private and collective self-perceptions.

We do not mean to oversimplify these cultural differences. Both types of self-perceptions are related to SWB across cultures. We believe, however, that cultural variation in the correlates and causes of SWB is influenced by the relative importance of private and collective self-perceptions, as well as other-perceptions. First, how strongly other-perceptions and self-perceptions relate to SWB may differ in magnitude across cultures. Second, the motivation to maintain different self-perceptions might influence which goals are pursued and which are predictive of SWB. Third, striving to maintain positive collective self-perceptions might reduce the importance of self-consistency for well-being. We now will explore each of these possibilities.

Relation of Self-Perceptions and Other-Perceptions to SWB

Self-Perceptions and SWB
If European Americans rely more on independent self-construals, then their own thoughts and feelings should be referenced when judging their well-being. In contrast, if East Asians rely more on interdependent self-construals, then the thoughts and feelings of others should be referenced when judging their well-being. It follows that private self-perceptions such as self-esteem should be strong predictors of well-being for European Americans, whereas other types of perceptions should be important for East Asian well-being. Consistent with this interpretation, Park and Huebner (2005) found this pattern in a sample of U.S. and Korean adolescents.

This, however, does not mean that East Asians' SWB is not predicted from positive private self-perceptions at all. East Asians' SWB is also influenced by their positive private self-perception. For example, in data from Diener, Diener, and Diener (1995), the correlation between self-esteem and life satisfaction among Japanese participants was .44. Similarly and interestingly enough, Kim, Cai, Gilliand, Tov, Tam, Peng, Xia, and Lee (2010, Study 1) found that Asian-Americans' life satisfaction was predicted from the private positive perception on their past self as well as on their current self. In contrast, life satisfaction of European Americans was predicted from the private positive perception on their current self only. In another study, Kim, Cai, and colleagues (2010, Study 2) experimentally demonstrated that Chinese participants reported higher SWB after they described an interpersonal event that happened at least three months before and made them feel good about themselves than after they described a negative event in the past. This difference also was found after describing a current positive (vs. negative) interpersonal event although the effect was weaker. Among European Americans, this difference was found only after they had described the current posi-tive (vs. negative) interpersonal event, which made them feel good (vs. bad) about themselves. This finding might suggest that the present is a continuation of the past to Asians so that their current SWB is also affected by their perception of the past, whereas the present is a distinctive time frame from the past to European Americans so that their current SWB should not be influenced by how they think of the past. The important point here, beyond the discussion of this cross-cultural difference, is that positive self-perceptions predict SWB quite well across European Americans and East Asians.

In both European American and East Asian samples, other researchers observed that self-esteem correlated with various psychological well-being scales (positive affectivity, negative affectivity, and emotional self-criticism; Kurman, 2003) and other measures such as goal-setting, perceived opti-mism, challenge seeking, and intellectual persistency (Kim, Peng, & Chiu, 2008). Taken together, the extant research implies that SWB is predicted from positive private self-perceptions, but this trend is stronger among European Americans than among East Asians.

Other-Perceptions to SWB

For East Asians, the smaller association of self-esteem with SWB may be attributable to the importance of other-perceptions and collective self-perceptions. Three types of other-perceptions that may be important for East Asians' SWB are (a) perceived norms for life satisfaction, (b) rela-tionship harmony, and (c) perceived emotional support from others. The perceived normative or *ideal* level of life satisfaction in a culture might influence East Asians' judgments of their own life satisfaction. Suh, Diener, Oishi, and Triandis (1998) found that, in collectivist cultures (including China and South Korea), life satisfaction was predicted not only from one's emotions, but also from the perceived norm for life satisfaction. In contrast, in individualist cultures (e.g., the United States), life satisfaction was more strongly predicted from emotions than from perceived norms. The domi-nant influence of emotions in judgments of life satisfaction in individualist contexts is consistent with the notion that European Americans' indepen-dent self-construals lead them to prioritize their own thoughts and feelings when forming judgments.

Relationship harmony may be another correlate of SWB for East Asians. Distinguishing it from relationship satisfaction, Kwan, Bond, and Singelis (1997) defined relationship harmony as an evaluation of the balance and quality of one's relationships with others. Whereas relationship satisfaction concerns how one feels about a relationship, relationship harmony is an appraisal of the relationship *itself*. Kwan and colleagues (1997) found that, for European Americans, life satisfaction was more strongly associated with self-esteem than with relationship harmony. In contrast, for Hong Kong Chinese, self-esteem and relationship harmony were equally associated with life satisfaction. Kang, Shaver, Sue, Min, and Jing (2003) replicated these findings in Korea and mainland China and also observed that relationship quality was associated with greater self-esteem in these samples. Thus, other-perceptions might have indirect effects on SWB by supporting positive, private self-perceptions. We speculate that East Asians who perceive relationship harmony might also feel well-adjusted and competent in their social relationships, with added benefits for their mental health.

A construct related to relationship harmony is perceived emotional support from other people. Uchida, Kitayama, Mesquita, and Rayes (2001) found that, among participants from Japan and the Philippines, happiness was predicted by perceived emotional support from other people as well as self-esteem. In contrast, happiness was predicted only from self-esteem among Americans. A possible implication of perceived emotional support may be seen in a cross-cultural study of the influence of divorce on children's life satisfaction. Gohm, Oishi, Darlington, and Diener (1998) found that college students whose parents divorced reported higher life satisfaction than those whose parents were in high-conflict marriages. This pattern, however, was found only in samples from collectivist cultures. One conjecture is that children of divorced parents are more likely to receive emotional support from their family networks in collectivist than in individualist cultures.

Research on the implications of collective self-perceptions for SWB is a relatively recent development. Although past research has tended to emphasize private self-perceptions, we believe that important aspects of East Asians' well-being may have been overlooked in the process. Whereas people in European-American cultural contexts tend to describe themselves in terms of their personal abilities, uniqueness, traits, and characteristics, people in East Asian cultural contexts tend to describe themselves in terms of their diverse relationships with other people, their roles in various groups, and their social obligations (see Markus & Kitayama, 1991). Consistent with these findings, several studies have shown that people in East Asian cultures are more concerned with other people's judgments and approval than are people in European-American cultures (e.g., Suh, 2002) and that East Asians may be more likely than people from European-American cultures to take into consideration the other person's perspective when experiencing the self (Cohen & Gunz, 2002; Leung & Cohen, 2007), and they may be more sensitive to the social context (Haberstroh, Oyserman, Schwarz, Kuhen, & Ji, 2002).

Research suggests that SWB of East Asians might be related to how they perceive that other people perceive them. Hitherto, we have not addressed the issue of causality, and much of the preceding literature on SWB and other- and self-perception has been correlational in nature. An experimental study by Kim and Cohen (2008), however, may shed light on the relation between self-perceptions and SWB. To investigate the causal effect of East Asians' collective self-perceptions on their SWB, Kim and Cohen (2010) manipulated participants' private and collective self-perceptions of their social relationships and then had the participants complete a life satisfaction measure. Participants answered 14 questions about the quality of their social relationships (e.g., How many friends can you call up to borrow $50.00 in an emergency situation? How many friends can drop by your house without prior notice?). To test the causal effect, four different questionnaire forms were developed and given randomly to each participant. Each questionnaire form corresponded to one of four experimental conditions: high private self-perception condition, low private self-perception condition, high collective self-perception condition, and low collective self-perception condition. In the *high* private self-perception (PS) condition, responses were made using a low frequency scale ranging from 0 to more than 4 friends, leading most participants to infer that they possessed a very high quality of social relationships. In the *low* PS condition, responses were made using a high frequency scale ranging from fewer than 5 to more than 14 friends, leading most participants to infer that they did not possess a high quality of social relationships. In both collective self-perception (CS) conditions, participants were instructed to think of how significant others in their life might see them and then answer the questions as if those significant others were filling out the questionnaires (e.g., Significant others think that I have ( ) friends to call to borrow $50.00 in an emergency situation). The scale manipulation (low vs. high frequency) was the same. Finally, in all conditions, participants rated their own satisfaction with life.

The results indicated that Asian-American participants' life satisfaction was significantly higher in the high CS condition than in the low CS condition. In other words, Asian-American participants were happier when collective self-perceptions implied that they were in good rather than poor social relationships. No differences in life satisfaction were found, however, between the high and low PS conditions. Thus, in this study, Asian-American participants' SWB was more affected by collective self-perceptions than private self-perceptions of their relationships. The exact reverse pattern was found among European Americans: Life satisfaction was higher when participants believed that they were in good social relationships than when they thought that they were not in good social relationships. Their perception of other people's perception of them did not make any difference in their life satisfaction, however. Thus, European Americans' SWB was more affected by private self-perceptions than by collective self-perceptions of their relationships. In sum, this study suggests the indespensible importance of positive collective self-perceptions in the life satisfaction judgments of East Asians.

Goals and the Motivation to Maintain Positive Self-Perceptions

Previous studies of goal-systems theory (see Kruglanski et al., 2002) suggest that people experience positive emotions when they experience the attainment of their goals because people may feel right (or good) after achieving their own goals (Camacho, Higgins, & Luger, 2003; Cesario, Grant, & Higgins, 2004; Spiegel, Grant-Pillow, & Higgins, 2004). There are cross-cultural differences, however, in the type of goals that are associated with SWB. For instance, Oishi and Diener (2001) found that European-Americans' life satisfaction was predicted from attaining *independent* goals, which concern personal enjoyment. In contrast, East Asian and Asian-Americans' life satisfaction was related to attaining *interdependent* goals, which concern bringing well-being to their significant others. Again, this does not mean that European Americans (East Asians) are not happy when they achieve interdependent (independent) goals. For example, Sheldon and colleagues (2003) showed that both European Americans and East Asians were happy when they achieved goals they freely had chosen. In sum, it might be universal for individuals to feel good when they achieve their chosen goals, but, for East Asians, achieving interdependent goals may be more strongly associated with SWB than may be achieving independent goals. The reverse may be true for European Americans. These findings map onto the self-construals believed to be dominant within each cultural group.

The exact process by which goal attainment enhances SWB across cultures remains to be studied. We propose that self-construals acquire motivational force in part by influencing the desirability of different self-perceptions. The desirability of different self-perceptions in turn affects how ready one is to pursue independent or interdependent goals. For East Asians, the dominance of interdependent self-construals implies that positive collective self-perceptions are particularly desirable. If significant others think and feel positively toward one's self, then one is succeeding as an interdependent agent. Pursuing and attaining interdependent goals may help to foster and sustain positive collective self-perceptions and SWB. For European Americans, the dominance of independent self-construals implies that positive private self-perceptions are particularly desirable. If one can think and feel positively about one's *own* self, then one is succeeding as an independent agent. Thus, pursuing and attaining independent goals may help foster and sustain positive private self-perceptions and SWB.

The desire to maintain different self-perceptions may influence not only the type of goals that are pursued, but also the manner in which they are pursued in different cultures. European Americans may focus on approach and promotion (maximizing gains). Such goals are related mainly to personal achievement and becoming distinctive from other people, which helps substantiate positive private self-perceptions. In contrast, East Asians might aim at avoidance and prevention goals (minimizing losses). Such goals may involve fitting in and not distinguishing oneself from others, which helps maintain positive collective self-perceptions. Indeed, Elliot, Chirkov, Kim, and Sheldon (2001) found that Koreans listed more avoidance goals than did European Americans. Moreover, avoidance goals were negatively associated with SWB for European Americans, but were not associated with SWB for Koreans. Noting that their measures of SWB consisted of emotions and life satisfaction, Elliot and colleagues (2001) suggested that, for East Asians, avoidance goals might predict other aspects of well-being, such as relationship harmony. In addition, future research should assess not just the quantity but also the attainment of avoidance goals, along with self-perceptions. If maintaining self-perceptions does indeed motivate the manner of goal pursuit, then attaining avoidance goals should be associated with positive collective self-perceptions and greater SWB for East Asians.

The Importance of Self-Consistency to SWB

Self-consistency, as it has often been operationalized, primarily concerns the coherence of personal beliefs about the self (i.e., private self-perceptions). Across cultures, preference for one type of self-construal over another might influence the importance of perceiving a self that is consistent across situations and social roles. To construct *independent* self-construals in Western cultures, individuals should strive to be coherent and congruent across situations. This consistency motivation was shown to be stronger among individualists than collectivists (Cialdini, Wosinska, Barrett, Butner, & Gornik-Durose, 1999), perhaps because consistency in attitudes helps individualists maintain private self-perceptions that one is a coherent, context-independent entity. For example, North American undergraduates who rate themselves as extroverted do not rate themselves as introverted, and vice versa (Choi & Choi, 2002). Furthermore, North Americans tend to agree with positive self-statements and disagree with negative self-statements and to attribute many more positive than negative characteristics to the self (Spencer-Rodgers, Peng, Wang, & Hou, 2004). East Asians, however, are encouraged to adjust themselves to social situations as an *interdependent* self. Although adjustment may help East Asians preserve positive collective self-perceptions, it may also result in inconsistent self-ratings. For example, Koreans rate themselves more extroverted when asked how extroverted they are than when asked how introverted they are (Choi & Choi, 2002). Additionally, Chinese people tend to agree with both positive self-statements (e.g., "I feel that I have a number of good qualities") and negative self-statements (e.g., "I think I am not good at all") (Kim, Peng, & Chiu, 2008).

As a consequence, the positive relationship between self-consistency across situations and psychological outcomes observed in Western cultures (e.g., Swann, de la Ronde, & Hixon, 1994) may not generalize to East Asian cultures. Consistent with this prediction, Suh (2002) found that European Americans showed greater role consistency across situations than did Koreans and that consistency was a stronger predictor of life satisfaction for European Americans than for Koreans. In contrast, perceived social-appraisal (believing that others approve of one's life) was a much stronger predictor of life satisfaction for Koreans than for European Americans. Interestingly, Suh (2002) also found evidence that consistent individuals are rewarded differently in the two cultures. Such individuals were rated as more likable and socially skilled by European-American informants than by Korean informants. Although this work needs to be replicated with other samples, it suggests that the value that East Asians place on collective self-perceptions may simultaneously reduce the emphasis on self-consistency. Again, we are not arguing that East Asians do not value self-consistency motivation or that SWB among East Asians is not explained by self-consistency. Rather, we posit that self-consistency is particularly functional in supporting private self-perceptions and independent self-construals and that, as a consequence, SWB is more strongly predicted from self-consistency among people who follow the values of individualist societies.

SELF-CONSTRUALS AND THE MEANING OF MEAN LEVELS OF SWB

A common finding in culture and SWB research is that aggregate levels of SWB are lower in East Asian samples than in samples from North America, Latin America, and Western Europe (Diener, Diener, & Diener, 1995; Kang et al., 2003; Park & Huebner, 2005; Suh, 2002). Oftentimes life satisfaction is the measure of SWB employed. Similar differences have been reported, however, using measures of emotion such as affect balance. Higher scores on affect balance suggest that positive emotions are experienced more frequently than negative emotions. Oishi and Diener (2003) found that East Asians not only report lower life satisfaction than do people from other cultures, but they also tend to have lower affect balance scores.

A critical question is whether measures of SWB can be compared across cultures. If they cannot, then mean level differences may not be meaningful. A few researchers have closely investigated the psychometric properties of the Satisfaction With Life Scale (SWLS; Diener, Emmons, Larsen, & Griffin, 1985). Vitterso, Roysamb, and Diener (2002) conducted extensive confirmatory factor analyses on the SWLS and concluded that the concept of life satisfaction was fairly coherent across the 41 nations in their sample. More recently, Oishi (2006) applied item response theory to an analysis of the SWLS in Chinese and American respondents. He found that Chinese and Americans tended to respond differently to two items. Chinese who were satisfied with their lives were still less likely than Americans to endorse such items as "So far I have gotten the important things I want in life" and "If I could live my life over, I would change almost nothing." Even when these items were weighted less than unbiased items, however, Chinese participants still manifested lower mean levels of life satisfaction than did Americans. These findings suggest that comparisons can be made, but with caution (see Tov & Diener, 2007, for an extended discussion).

Although levels of SWB are lower among East Asians, it is important to note that the difference is relative rather than absolute. That is, *relative* to European Americans and other groups, East Asians report lower life satisfaction and affect balance. Their life satisfaction is still above the midpoint (i.e., slightly positive), however, and affect balance is still greater than zero (rarely negative). In the remainder of this section, we consider several theories that might account for the lower levels of SWB in East Asians. We believe that self-construals are still relevant to the discussion, but other elements of East Asian cultural ethos must also be considered. These elements include (a) the value of self-improvement, self-criticism, and modesty; (b) the valuation of low-arousal rather than high-arousal affective states; and (c) philosophical beliefs about moderation and dialecticism.

Self-Improvement, Self-Criticism, and Modesty

Cross-cultural differences in mean levels of SWB might be explained, in part, by East Asians' greater emphasis on self-discipline and self-improvement. Heine and colleagues (1999) argued that the self-improvement ethic in Japan is related to the importance of fulfilling social roles and maintaining harmony within the group. To know what to improve upon, one must develop a tendency to be self-critical – to be mindful of one's shortcomings. The importance of self-improvement among East Asians (Chiu, Hong, & Dweck, 1997; Heine et al., 1999; Miller, Wang, Sandel, & Cho, 2002; Oishi & Sullivan, 2005) might influence their willingness to express or report that they are satisfied with themselves and their lives. If individuals are already satisfied with themselves, what motivation is there to improve? Instead, a modest, self-critical self might be a more successful interdependent agent. The value of self-criticism might explain why Chinese respondents were reluctant to report that they have everything they want or would never change anything even when they were generally satisfied with the external conditions of their lives (Oishi, 2006). Another illustration of self-criticism might be East Asians' greater tendency to agree with negative traits compared to European Americans (Kim, Peng, & Chiu, 2008; Spencer-Rodgers et al., 2004).

The self-criticism hypothesis suggests two possible interpretations. The first is that East Asians are actually much happier, but report lower levels of SWB to appear modest. If this is so, then East Asians might tend to give neutral responses in their judgments of satisfaction. Diener, Suh, Smith, and Shao (1995), however, did not find support for this hypothesis in their sample of Chinese, Japanese, and Korean respondents. More research on self-presentation strategies are needed before firm conclusions can be drawn. The second interpretation is that self-criticism influences the actual experience of well-being. The formulation of self-criticism by Heine and colleagues (1999) suggests that East Asians may be especially likely to self-criticize when they experience success. Furthermore, when failure is experienced, East Asians may tend to infer that greater effort is required. Such a pattern of self-criticism would constrain the frequency of pleasant emotions without necessarily increasing unpleasant emotions. For this reason, self-criticism would result in lower affect balance scores and influence life satisfaction judgments to some extent (cf. Suh et al., 1998). Indeed, using experience sampling, Scollon, Diener, Oishi, and Biswas-Diener (2004) found that Asians in their samples reported less frequent experiences of pleasant emotions than did European Americans but did not differ in the frequency of unpleasant emotions. The emotion regulatory function of self-criticism is an interesting possibility but has not been well-researched.

Affect Valuation

The interdependent self-construal of East Asians might influence the desirability of certain emotions, with implications for the meaning of mean levels of emotional well-being. If East Asians tend to construe the self as interdependent with others, then their attention might be drawn more toward the social field than toward their own internal states (Nisbett, Peng, Choi, & Norenzayan, 2001). As a result, East Asians might prefer certain affective states over others. Namely, low-arousal positive emotions (e.g., serenity) might be preferable over high-arousal emotions (e.g., excitement) because the former facilitates attention toward others. Tsai, Knutson, and Fung (2006) suggested that discrepancies between the emotions that people *want* to feel (ideal affect) and the emotions that they *actually* feel (real affect) have implications for mental health. They found that for Hong Kong Chinese, discrepancy in low-arousal but not high-arousal positive affect was significantly associated with depression. The reverse was true for European Americans.

Another dimension of emotions that might be differentially valued by East Asians and European Americans is the extent to which the emotion involves a focus on the self versus others. The independent self-construal of European Americans implies that self-focused positive emotions such as pride might be valued concomitants of positive private self-perceptions. The interdependent self-construal of East Asians, in contrast, implies that other-focused emotions might be valued concomitants of positive collective self-perceptions or other-perceptions. Kitayama, Markus, and Kurokawa (2000) referred to emotions that were self-focused as *disengaged* and to those that were other-focused as *engaged*. They showed that the general happiness of Japanese participants was more strongly related to positive *engaged* emotions (e.g., friendly feelings) than to positive *disengaged* emotions. In contrast, the general happiness of European Americans was more strongly related to the latter than to the former.

Affect valuation might influence mean levels of emotional well-being by determining frequency and recall of emotions. For instance, if East Asians place less value on high-arousal positive emotions, they may be less likely to pursue situations to experience these states (see, e.g., Oishi & Diener, 2003). Alternatively, individuals may simply pay more attention to and remember emotional experiences that are valued. A possible implication of these findings is that the meaning of emotional well-being may differ across cultures. Although affect balance scores are lower among East Asians, the positive emotions that researchers have used may not have been the ones that East Asians value. For instance, Scollon and colleagues (2004) examined happiness, affection, pride, and joy. Two of the four emotions could be interpreted as high-arousal (joy) or self-focused (pride). If more low-arousal or other-focused emotions are included, then mean levels of emotional well-being in East Asians may not be lower than those in European Americans.

Philosophical Beliefs

The influence of specific philosophical beliefs has occasionally been evoked to explain the emotional experience of East Asians. For instance, Asian philosophies such as Buddhism and Taoism may encourage dialectical thinking. According to Peng and Nisbett (1999), East Asians may be prone to dialectical thinking entailing a more holistic perspective such that both sides of a contradiction are accepted as equally likely. In contrast, European Americans favor a more linear, analytical style of thought. For example, Kim, Peng, and Chiu (2008) showed that Chinese-American differences in self-esteem level were driven primarily by Chinese participants' greater tendency to agree with negatively worded self-esteem items. As a consequence, the negative correlation between the five positive and five negative items of the self-esteem scale was greater among European Americans than among East Asians. In other words, among East Asians, reporting negative attributes does not mean the absence of positive attributes, whereas this is true among European Americans.

Differences in reasoning may influence the value of and memory for emotional experiences. For instance, whereas European Americans consistently value pleasant emotions over unpleasant emotions, East Asians have been found to value both equally (Diener & Suh, 1999). Moreover, the reported frequencies of pleasant and unpleasant emotions are less negatively correlated among East Asians than among European Americans (Bagozzi, Wong, & Yi, 1999; Kitayama et al., 2000; Schimmack, Oishi, & Diener, 2002). If East Asians do indeed engage in more holistic thinking, then they may be more likely to remember negative as well as positive experiences. To date, however, few studies have specifically measured and examined holistic thinking and its influence on emotional experience.

Instead of holistic or dialectical thinking, other theorists have highlighted the ideal of moderation in East Asian philosophies (Markus & Kitayama, 1994). Rather than focusing on contradiction, the notion of moderation simply emphasizes balance. In practice, however, the ideal of moderation might be applied asymmetrically. That is, the frequency of pleasant emotions may be regulated downward, but the frequency of unpleasant emotions may not necessarily be regulated upward. In contrast, the cultural ethos of European Americans encourages pleasant emotions and positive self-perceptions. Numerous studies indicate that the European Americans who maintain unrealistically positive self-perceptions show higher levels of well-being (Taylor & Brown, 1988). These positive illusions may manifest themselves in recalled experiences of well-being. For example, a one-week daily diary study found that European Americans and East Asians did not differ in levels of daily satisfaction (Oishi, 2002). When participants judged their satisfaction over the past week, however, European Americans overestimated their level of satisfaction, whereas East Asians did not.

Both holistic thinking and moderation hypotheses predict lower affect balance scores in East Asians. If holism, however, leads East Asians to take a broader view in assessing their well-being, one might expect them to recall more negative experiences than would European Americans. Although this might lower life satisfaction, it might also increase reported frequencies of unpleasant emotions. East Asians do not consistently report more unpleasant emotions than do European Americans, however. Thus it seems that the evidence tentatively favors the moderation hypothesis that East Asians simply down-regulate pleasant emotions, which lowers their overall level of affect balance. More systematic studies are clearly needed.

CONCLUSION

It is a well-known saying that most people want to be happy. Consistently, research evidence suggests that happiness is one of the most important goals in individuals' lives. Recent cross-cultural studies claim, however, that culture plays a role in the correlates and causes as well as the levels of individuals' SWB dynamically. East Asians' emphasis on the *interdependent* self-construal that imposes importance to sensitivity to other people leads them to be happy when they think that other people perceive them as good *interdependent* agents. In contrast, European Americans are happy when they perceive themselves as good *independent* agents, independent of how other people perceive them.

In addition, the well-established lower levels of SWB among East Asians compared with European Americans may also be explained by cross-cultural differences in self-construal and related values and norms. In interdependent societies where individuals are socialized to focus on self-improvement, moderation, and modesty, evaluating their life in an unrealistically positive way is restricted. In contrast, remembering and reporting more pleasant emotions, relative to unpleasant emotions, and evaluating lives in positive ways are encouraged and promoted in independent societies.

REFERENCES

Bagozzi, R. P., Wong, N., & Yi, Y. (1999). The role of culture and gender in the relationship between positive and negative affect. *Cognition and Emotion, 13,* 641–672.

Camacho, C. J., Higgins, E. T., & Luger, L. (2003). Moral value transfer from regulatory fit: What feels right is right and what feels wrong is wrong. *Journal of Personality and Social Psychology, 84,* 498–510.

Cesario, J., Grant, H., & Higgins, E. T. (2004). Regulatory fit and persuasion: Transfer from "feeling right." *Journal of Personality and Social Psychology, 86,* 388–404.

Chiu, C-y., Hong, Y. Y., & Dweck, C. S. (1997). Lay dispositionism and implicit theories of personality. *Journal of Personality and Social Psychology, 73,* 19–30.

Choi, I., & Choi, Y. (2002). Culture and self-concept flexibility. *Personality and Social Psychology Bulletin, 28,* 1508–1517.

Cialdini, R. B., Wosinska, W., Barrett, D. W., Butner, J., & Gornik-Durose, M. (1999). Compliance with a request in two cultures: The differential influence of social proof and commitment/consistency on collectivists and individualists. *Personality and Social Psychology Bulletin, 25,* 1242–1253.

Cohen, D., & Gunz, A. (2002). As seen by the other: Perspective on the self in the memories and emotional perceptions of Easterners and Westerners. *Psychological Science, 13,* 55–59.

Diener, E. (1984). Subjective well-being. *Psychological Bulletin, 95,* 542–575.

Diener, E., Diener, M., & Diener, C. (1995). Factors predicting the subjective well-being of nations. *Journal of Personality and Social Psychology, 69,* 851–864.

Diener, E., Emmons, R. A., Larson, R. J., & Griffin, S. (1985). The satisfaction with life scale. *Journal of Personality Assessment, 49,* 71–75.

Diener, E., & Suh, E. M. (1999). National differences in subjective well-being. In D. Kahneman, E. Diener, & N. Schwarz (Eds.), *Well-being: The foundations of hedonic psychology* (pp. 434–450). New York: Russell Sage Foundation.

Diener, E., Suh, E. M., Smith, H., & Shao, L. (1995). National differences in reported subjective well-being: Why do they occur? *Social Indicators Research, 34,* 7–32.

Elliot, A. J., Chirkov, V. I., Kim, Y., & Sheldon, K. M. (2001). A cross-cultural analysis of avoidance (relative to approach) personal goals. *Psychological Science, 12,* 505–510.

Gohm, C. L., Oishi, S., Darlington, J., & Diener, E. (1998). Culture, parental conflict, parental marital status, and the subjective well-being of young adults. *Journal of Marriage and the Family, 60,* 319–334.

Haberstroh, S., Oyserman, D., Schwarz, N., Kuhen, U., & Ji, L-j. (2002). Is the interdependent self more sensitive to question context than the independent self? Self-construal and the observation of conversational norms. *Journal of Experimental and Social Psychology, 38,* 323–329.

Heine, S. J., Lehman, D. R., Markus, H. R., & Kitayama, S. (1999). Is there a universal need for positive self-regard? *Psychological Review, 106,* 766–794.

Kang, S.-M., Shaver, P. R., Sue, S., Min, K.-H., & Jing, H. (2003). Culture-specific patterns in the prediction of life satisfaction: Roles of emotion, relationship quality, and self-esteem. *Personality & Social Psychology Bulletin, 29,* 1596–1608.

Kim, Y-H., Cai, H., Gilliand, M., Tov, W., Tam, K-P., Peng, S., Xia, S., & Lee, H-M. (2010). *Let bygones be bygone or alive: A cross-cultural difference in the cause of subjective-well being between Americans and Asians.* Unpublished manuscript, the University of Illinois at Urbana-Champaign.

Kim, Y-H., & Cohen, D. (2010). Information, perspective, and judgments about the self in Face and Dignity cultures. *Personality and Social Psychology Bulletin, 36,* 537–550.

Kim, Y-H., Peng, S., & Chiu, C-y. (2008). Explaining self-esteem differences between Chinese and North Americans: Dialectical self (vs. self-consistency) or lack of positive self-regard. *Self and Identity, 7,* 113–128.

Kitayama, S., Markus, H. R., & Kurokawa, M. (2000). Culture, emotion, and well-being: Good feelings in Japan and the United States. *Cognition and Emotion, 14,* 93–124.

Kruglanski, A. W., Shah, J. Y., Fishbach, A., Friedman, R., Chun, W. Y., & Sleeth-Keppler, D. (2002). A theory of goal systems. In M. Zanna (Ed.), *Advances in experimental social psychology, Vol. 34* (pp. 331–378). San Diego, CA: Academic Press.

Kurman, J. (2003). Why is self-enhancement low in certain collectivist cultures? An investigation of two competing explanations. *Journal of Cross-Cultural Psychology, 34,* 496–510.

Kwan, V. S. Y., Bond, M. H., & Singelis, T. M. (1997). Pancultural explanations for life satisfaction: Adding relationship harmony to self-esteem. *Journal of Personality and Social Psychology, 73,* 1038–1051.

Leung, A. K-y., & Cohen, D. (2007). The soft embodiment of culture: Camera angles and motion through time and space. *Psychological Science, 18,* 824–830.

Markus, H. R., & Kitayama, S. (1991). Culture and the self: Implications for cognition, emotion, and motivation. *Psychological Review, 98,* 224–253.

Markus, H. R., & Kitayama, S. (1994). The cultural construction of self and emotion: Implications for social behavior. In S. Kitayama & H. R. Markus (Eds.), *Emotion and culture: Empirical studies of mutual influence* (pp. 89–130). Washington, DC: American Psychological Association.

Miller, P. J., Wang, S., Sandel, T., & Cho, G. E. (2002). Self-esteem as folk theory: A comparison of European American and Taiwanese mother's beliefs. *Parenting, Science and Practice, 2,* 209–239.

Nisbett, R., Peng, K., Choi, I., & Norenzayan, A. (2001). Culture and systems of thought: Holistic versus analytic cognition. *Psychological Review, 108,* 291–310.

Oishi, S. (2002). The experience and remembering of well-being: A cross-cultural analysis. *Personality and Social Psychology Bulletin, 28,* 1398–1406.

Oishi, S. (2006). The concept of life satisfaction across cultures: An IRT analysis. *Journal of Research in Personality, 40,* 411–423.

Oishi, S., & Diener, E. (2001). Goals, culture, and subjective well-being. *Personality and Social Psychology Bulletin, 27,* 1674–1682.

Oishi, S., & Diener, E. (2003). Culture and well-being: The cycle of action, evaluation, and decision. *Personality and Social Psychological Bulletin, 29,* 939–949.

Oishi, S., & Sullivan, H. W. (2005). The mediating role of parental expectations in culture and well-being. *Journal of Personality, 73,* 1267–1294.

Park, N., & Huebner, E. S. (2005). A cross-cultural study of the levels and correlates of life satisfaction among adolescents. *Journal of Cross-Cultural Psychology, 36*, 444–456.

Peng, K., & Nisbett, R. E. (1999). Culture, dialectics, and reasoning about contradiction. *American Psychologist, 54*, 741–754.

Schimmack, U., Oishi, S., & Diener, E. (2002). Cultural influences on the relation between pleasant emotions and unpleasant emotions: Asian dialectic philosophies or individualism-collectivism? *Cognition and Emotion, 16*, 705–719.

Scollon, C. N., Diener, E., Oishi, S., & Biswas-Diener, R. (2004). Emotions across cultures and methods. *Journal of Cross-Cultural Psychology, 35*, 304–326.

Sheldon, K. M., Elliot, A. J., Ryan, R. M., Chirkov, V., Kim, Y., Wu, C., et al. (2003). Self-concordance and subjective well-being in four cultures. *Journal of Cross-Cultural Psychology, 35*, 209–223.

Spencer-Rodgers, J., Peng, K., Wang, L., & Hou, Y. (2004). Dialectical self-esteem and East-West differences in psychological well-being. *Personality and Social Psychology Bulletin, 30*, 1416–1432.

Spiegel, S., Grant-Pillow, H., & Higgins, E. T. (2004). How regulatory fit enhances motivational strength during goal pursuit. *European Journal of Social Psychology, 4*, 39–54.

Suh, E., Diener, E., Oishi, S., & Triandis, H. C. (1998). The shifting basis of life satisfaction judgments across cultures: Emotions versus norms. *Journal of Personality and Social Psychology, 74*, 482–493.

Suh, E. M. (2002). Culture, identity consistency, and subjective well-being. *Journal of Personality and Social Psychology, 83*, 1378–1391.

Swann, W. B., Jr., de la Ronde, C., & Hixon, G. (1994). Authenticity and positivity strivings in marriage and courtship. *Journal of Personality and Social Psychology, 66*, 857–869.

Taylor, S. E., & Brown, J. D. (1988). Illusion and well-being: A social psychological perspective on mental health. *Psychological Bulletin, 103*, 193–210.

Tov, W., & Diener, E. (2007). Culture and subjective well-being. In S. Kitayama & D. Cohen (Eds.), *Handbook of cultural psychology* (pp. 691–713). New York: Guilford.

Triandis, H. (1989). The self and social behavior in differing cultural contexts. *Psychological Review, 96*, 506–520.

Tsai, J., Knutson, B., & Fung, H. H. (2006). Cultural variation in affect valuation. *Journal of Personality and Social Psychology, 90*, 288–307.

Uchida, Y., Kitayama, S., Mesquita, B., & Rayes, J. A. (2001). *Interpersonal sources of happiness: The relative significance in the three cultures.* Paper presented at 13th annual convention of the American Psychological Society, Toronto, Canada.

Vittersø, J., Røysamb, E., & Diener, E. (2002). The concept of life satisfaction across cultures: Exploring its diverse meaning and relation to economic wealth. In E. Gullone & R. A. Cummins (Eds.), *The universality of subjective wellbeing indicators* (pp. 81–103). Dordrecht, The Netherlands: Kluwer Academic Publishers.

10

Cultural Processes in Teams: The Development of Team Mental Models in Heterogeneous Work Teams

JING QIU, ZHI-XUE ZHANG,[1] AND LEIGH ANNE LIU

Nowadays, more and more organizations are dependent on work teams for developing innovative products, making important business decisions, and improving efficiency. Therefore, understanding how diversity in the composition of organizational work teams affects outcomes such as job satisfaction, creativity, and turnover will be of increasing importance. Research has advised that, unless corporations start managing diversity, they will find themselves at a competitive disadvantage.

Whereas American management literature, both popular and scholarly, is rife with advice that managers should increase workforce diversity to enhance work team effectiveness, empirical research has inconsistent findings on the impact of team diversity on performance. Several studies of team diversity have demonstrated that it has positive effects at the individual and small-group levels (Cox, Lobel, & McLeod, 1991; Watson, Kumar, & Michaelson, 1993), but others have concluded that such diverse teams perform less well than do homogeneous teams (Pelled, Eisenhardt, & Xin, 1999; Tsui, Egan, & O'Reilly, 1992). To explore the black box of diversity, researchers suggest taking a more dynamic perspective and examining the underlying mechanisms and team processes through which team diversity influences team functioning and performance.

An abundance of research has been conducted on the factors that contribute to high team performance. One variable that has recently received much theoretical attention concerns the influence of team members' mental models on team-related processes and behaviors (Cannon-Bowers, Salas, & Converse, 1993; Klimoski & Mohammed, 1994). A team mental model is "an organized understanding of relevant knowledge that is shared by team

[1] Preparation of this chapter was supported by a grant awarded to the second author by the National Natural Science Foundation of China (Project No: 70572019).

members" (Mohammed & Dumville, 2001, p. 89). The general thesis of the team mental model literature is that team effectiveness will improve if team members have an adequate shared understanding of the task, team, equipment, and situation (e.g., Mathieu, Heffner, Goodwin, Salas, & Cannon-Bowers, 2000). Team mental models are especially valuable in heterogeneous teams, because such teams are often plagued by poor communication patterns, excessive conflicts, and difficult coordination (Ancona & Caldwell, 1992; Jehn, Northcraft, & Neale, 1999). Developing shared understanding within heterogeneous teams will decrease conflicts among and coordinate behaviors of heterogeneous team members, which will contribute to effective team functioning.

The development of mental models within a heterogeneous team is similar to how culture evolves in a population. Culture as a shared knowledge system emerges as people in a human group frequently interact with each other and gradually come to share a set of elements around a common theme (see Chapter 3, this volume). Heterogeneous team members develop their team mental models in the same way, through repeated interactions, and finally will come to share many elements, meanings, practices, and mental events. In addition, the specific goals that team members need to achieve together facilitate and regulate their interaction and communication (Kozlowski & Ilgen, 2006), which will then expedite the emergence of shared knowledge systems among heterogeneous members. Therefore, a team mental model is a network of specific knowledge that is produced, distributed, and reproduced among a group of interdependent members. In this sense, a work team is a miniature of the society where team-specific knowledge is distributed and shared among the members in that team.

The purpose of this chapter is to establish a conceptual understanding of the evolution of team mental models in heterogeneous work teams and its importance for team performance. We will first introduce research on the team mental model. Then we will investigate how team mental models evolve in heterogeneous work teams. Finally we propose that, by developing team mental models over time, heterogeneous teams are more likely to be able to surmount the difficulties in team coordination and leverage on diversity.

TEAM MENTAL MODELS

Mental Models

The term *mental model* has been used as an explanatory mechanism in a variety of disciplines over the years (Wilson & Rutherford, 1989). Essentially, mental models are organized knowledge structures that allow individuals to interact with their environment. Specifically, mental models allow people to predict and explain the behaviors of the world around them, to recognize and remember relationships among components of the environment, and to construct expectations for what is likely to occur next (Rouse & Morris, 1986). Furthermore, mental models allow people to draw inferences, make predictions, understand phenomena, decide which actions to take, and experience events vicariously (Johnson-Laird, 1983). For the purpose of this chapter, we define a mental model, in keeping with Rouse and Morris (1986), as a "mechanism whereby humans generate descriptions of system purpose and form, explanations of system functioning and observed system states, and predictions of future system states" (p. 360). Hence, mental models serve three crucial purposes: They help people describe, explain, and predict events in their environment. Mental models specify relevant knowledge content as well as the relationships between knowledge components (Webber, Chen, Payne, Marsh, & Zaccaro, 2000). An individual's mental model reflects the individual's perception of reality (Brunswik, 1956). Accordingly, mental models vary in their accuracy and coherence (McKeithen, Reitman, Rueter, & Hirtle, 1981; Rentsch & Hall, 1994). Furthermore, mental model accuracy is predictive of individual performance (Kraiger, Salas, & Cannon-Bowers, 1995; Rowe & Cooke, 1995).

Team Mental Models

When the members of a team organize their knowledge of team tasks, equipment, roles, goals, and abilities in a similar way, they share a mental model, or more accurately, a team mental model. When team members share a team mental model, we can argue that they have arrived at an intersubjective consensus of various team-related operating mechanisms within the work team (see Chapter 3, this volume). The notion of a team mental model has been developed to help account for the fluid, implicit coordination frequently observed in effective teams and to advance the understanding of how teams function in complex, dynamic, and ambiguous situations (Cannon-Bowers et al., 1993). It refers to team members' shared, organized understanding and mental representation of knowledge about key elements of the team's relevant environment (Klimoski & Mohammed, 1994). Many factors instigate the need for shared understanding, ranging from a simple need to define the situation, reduce uncertainty, create common ground, complete a joint task, or ingratiate oneself to another, which recognize and necessitate interdependence among team members (Thompson & Fine, 1999).

Team mental models allow team members to interpret cues in a similar manner, anticipate one another's actions, make compatible decisions, and coordinate their behaviors (Cooke, Salas, Cannon-Bowers, & Stout, 2000; Klimoski & Mohammed, 1994; Mohammed & Dumville, 2001), especially when time and circumstances do not permit overt and lengthy communication and strategizing among team members. Under these circumstances, team members must rely on preexisting knowledge to predict the actions of their teammates and to respond in a coordinated way to urgent, high stakes and novel task demands (Marks, Zaccaro, & Mathieu, 2000; Mathieu, Heffner, Goodwin, Salas, & Cannon-Bowers, 2000).

Multiple Team Mental Models

Scholars have suggested that members of a team are likely to hold not one but multiple mental models (Klimoski & Mohammed, 1994). Cannon-Bowers, Salas, and Converse (1993) proposed that at least four domains may constitute the contents of team mental models: equipment, taskwork, team members, and teamwork. Equipment refers to the technology or equipment with which team members are interacting. Taskwork mental models describe and organize knowledge about how the task is accomplished in terms of procedures, task strategies, likely contingencies or problems, and environmental conditions. Team member models contain information that is specific to the member's teammates – their knowledge, skills, attitudes, preferences, strengths, weaknesses, tendencies, and so forth. Finally, teamwork mental models are concerned with how the team interacts and describe the roles and responsibilities of team members, interaction patterns, information flow and communication channels, role interdependencies, and information sources. Each mental model may be influential in predicting team performance.

The four types of models just described can be viewed as reflecting two major content domains: (a) task-related aspects (e.g., the technology/equipment and job/task models) and (b) team-related aspects (e.g., the team interaction and team models) (Mathieu et al., 2000). This division is also consistent with the idea that teams develop two tracks of behavior – a teamwork track and a taskwork track (McIntyre & Salas, 1995; Morgan, Glickman, Woodard, Blaiwes, & Salas, 1986). These researchers argue that, to be successful, team members not only need to perform task-related functions well but also must work well together as a team.

Two Dimensions of Team Mental Models

Researchers have highlighted at least two dimensions of shared mental models: convergence and accuracy. Convergence refers to the extent to which team members agree on the knowledge related to taskwork and teamwork. Convergent team mental models enhance team effectiveness by providing a common interpretation of the team's task and process, and are likely to enable team members to predict one another's behavior accurately.

Researchers have conducted several empirical studies to examine the effect of team mental model convergence on team performance. For example, Mathieu and colleagues (2000) assessed the convergence of team members' mental models and its effect on team processes and performance using two-person, undergraduate teams performing a personal computer (PC)-based flight/combat simulation. Results indicated that both teamwork mental model convergence and taskwork mental model convergence were significantly positively related to team process (e.g., coordination, cooperation, and communication), which were in turn significantly related to team performance. The direct relationship between team mental model similarity and performance was not significant, however. In a similar, but more recent laboratory-based study, Mathieu, Heffner, Goodwin, Cannon-Bowers, and Salas (2005) showed that taskwork mental model convergence, but not teamwork mental model convergence, was significantly related to both team processes and team performance. Rentsch and Klimoski (2001) conducted a study in a naturalistic work setting involving 315 individuals who comprised 41 teams. Team members' teamwork mental model convergence was assessed using multidimensional scaling to analyze paired comparison ratings. Their results indicated that team members' mental model convergence was significantly related to team effectiveness.

The convergence or sharedness of team mental models is only a part of the picture (Cooke et al., 2000; Rentsch & Hall, 1994). Just as the accuracy of an individual's mental models may influence the quality of the individual's decision making and task performance (Rowe & Cooke, 1995), the accuracy of a team's mental models may also influence the quality of the team's decision making and task performance. Team mental model accuracy is distinct from team mental model convergence; all team members could have similar knowledge about a team (high team mental model convergence), and they could all be wrong (low team mental model accuracy). Alternatively, all members could have dissimilar knowledge, yet, overall, the team could be highly accurate.

As Lim and Klein (2006) pointed out, if a team's taskwork mental model is to some extent inaccurate – if, for example, team members' understanding of task priorities is shared, but misguided – team performance is likely to suffer. For example, team members may work in a coordinated way to achieve ancillary, rather than primary, goals. Similarly, if team members' shared teamwork mental model is inaccurate, team members are likely to suffer fewer conflicts regarding team process issues, but they may nevertheless work inefficiently and ineffectively toward their goals (Marks et al., 2000).

For instance, some researchers specifically examined the accuracy of individuals' judgments of teammates' skills, expertise, strengths, and weaknesses, which is termed *transactive memory accuracy*. Transactive memory accuracy is similar to Henry's (1993, 1995) concept of group judgment accuracy, in which group members' estimates of trivia test scores of their group mates are compared to actual test scores. Libby, Trotman, and Zimmer (1987) and Littlepage and Silbiger (1992) found that this type of cognitive accuracy leads to better group performance on problem-solving tasks. In her empirical study on the effect of transactive memory in organizational teams, Austin (2004) also demonstrated that accuracy was positively related to team performance.

Both team mental model convergence and accuracy are critical to team processes and performance. In research by Mathieu and colleagues (2005), team mental model convergence failed to exhibit a significant linear relationship with team processes or performance, but it evidenced a multiplicative relationship with the quality of those models. Team processes and performance were better among teams evidencing mental model convergence and sharing higher-quality team mental models than among teams evidencing less convergence or having lower-quality team mental models.

THE EMBODIMENT OF CULTURAL PROCESSES IN HETEROGENEOUS WORK TEAMS: THE DEVELOPMENT OF TEAM MENTAL MODELS

Developing and creating team mental models among team members is important to team functioning. Simply put, they make coordination in a team easier and more efficient. In work teams, members with different mental models about how tasks should be completed have a hard time coordinating their activities. In fact, information-processing problems and conflict within teams can arise when individuals hold different mental models (Hinsz, Tindale, & Vollrath, 1997).

All of these problems and difficulties are observed quite often in heterogeneous work teams because of their diverse attitudes, working styles, and values. As research by Earley and Mosakowski on transnational work teams demonstrated, to function effectively, those teams have to create hybrid team cultures, consisting of an emergent and simplified set of rules and actions, work capability expectations, and member perceptions that individuals within a team develop, share, and enact after mutual interaction (e.g., Earley & Mosakowski, 2000). Therefore, examining how diversity would influence the development of team mental models contributes a lot to both diversity and team mental model research.

The primary mechanism through which team mental models are expected to become more similar among team members over time is interaction. As team members get together and interact, they gain experience both with the task and with each other and they accumulate information through observing others' behaviors, hearing others' explanations, or revising one's own models; thus, team mental models become more similar and accurate. In other words, the more that team members communicate and interact, the more likely they will form a common frame of reference and develop a shared team mental model among themselves (Klimoski & Mohammed, 1994). Empirical research has also demonstrated that team members develop more accurate and more similar models of who knows what within the group with increased time or exposure (Liang, Moreland, & Argote, 1995; Moreland, 1999). This is true not only at the team level, but at the larger organizational level. Interactions among organizational members lead to similar interpretations of organizational events (Schein, 1992; Schneiier & Reichers, 1983), help develop a strong understanding of one another's tactical expertise (Athans, 1982), and lead to more consensus and integrated team understandings (Forgas, 1981).

Research suggests, however, that the evolution of team mental models in heterogeneous work teams might be a complex process. Before going into details of that process, we will first discuss more on team diversity.

Types of Diversity

Diversity refers to differences between individuals on any attributes that may lead to the perception that another person is different from one's self (e.g., Jackson, 1992; Williams & O'Reilly, 1998). In principle, diversity could refer to an almost infinite number of dimensions, ranging from age to nationality, from cultural background to functional background, from task skills to relational skills, and from political preference to sexual preference (see Chapter 15, this volume). In practice, however, diversity research has mainly focused on gender, age, race/ethnicity, tenure, educational background, and functional background (Milliken & Martins, 1996; Williams & O'Reilly, 1998).

Researchers have generated numerous dimensions for classifying different types of diversity (Horwitz & Horwitz, 2007; Tsui et al., 1992). One common distinction is between diversity on observable or readily detectable attributes such as race or ethnic background, age, and gender and diversity with respect to less visible or underlying attributes such as education, technical abilities, functional background, tenure in the organization, socioeconomic background, personality characteristics, as well as values, attitudes, preferences, and beliefs (Cummings, Zhou, & Oldham, 1993; Harrison, Price, & Bell, 1998; Jackson, May, & Whitney, 1995; Tsui et al., 1992)

One reason for differentiating between observable and unobservable types of diversity is that, when differences between people are visible, they are particularly likely to evoke responses that are due directly to biases, prejudices, or stereotypes. Those unobservable differences can create major differences in how people approach certain issues and in how they deal with interpersonal transactions. We should note, however, that these two types of diversity are not mutually exclusive. Those detectable differences in backgrounds may incite some prejudices or stereotypes, but at the same time diversity may also be associated with differences on underlying attributes (e.g., communication styles and values).

Because work team diversity could be associated with a variety of psychological responses and interaction processes, its effects on team mental model development are also complex. Researchers have identified two main processes linking team diversity to the development of team mental models: the social categorization process and the informational integration process.

Social Categorization Process

Similarities and differences among members are likely to be used as a basis for categorizing self and others into groups, with ensuing categorizations distinguishing between one's own ingroup and one or more outgroups. People tend to like and trust ingroup members more than outgroup members and thus generally tend to favor ingroups over outgroups (Brewer, 1979; Tajfel & Turner, 1986). Consistent with research on similarity/attraction (Williams & O'Reilly, 1998), the presence of ingroup-outgroup distinction signifies that work team members are more positively inclined toward their team and the people within it if fellow team members are similar rather than dissimilar to the self. Moreover, categorization processes may produce subgroups within the work team and give rise to problematic intersubgroup relations. As a result, the more homogeneous the work team, the higher the member commitment (Riordan & Shore, 1997; Tsui et al., 1992) and team cohesion (O'Reilly, Caldwell, & Barnett, 1989), the fewer relational conflicts (Jehn et al., 1999; Pelled et al., 1999), and the lower membership turnover (Wagner, Pfeffer, & O'Reilly, 1984).

There is abundant empirical literature exploring the effects of background diversity, focusing on the experiences of individuals who are dissimilar from the majority in the team or from their supervisors. For instance, findings suggest that individuals who are different from their work units in racial or ethnic background tend to be less psychologically committed to their organizations, less inclined to stay with the organization, and more likely to be absent (Tsui et al., 1992). Greenhaus, Parasuraman, and Wormley (1990) also found that African Americans felt less accepted in their organizations, perceiving that they had less decision-making power and autonomy than White Americans had in the same organization. Furthermore, research on racial differences in performance rating by supervisors indicates that African Americans generally got lower ratings than White Americans, were more likely to have reached career plateaus, and were assessed as having less potential for promotion (Greenhaus et al., 1990; Lefkowitz, 1994; Mount, Hazucha, Holt, & Sytsma, 1995; Sackett & Dubois, 1991). In a study of workers in the Netherlands, Verkuyten, de Jong, and Masson (1993) found that individuals who were not Dutch felt less satisfied with their jobs than did their Dutch counterparts. The more time they spent with colleagues of similar ethnic backgrounds, the higher their level of satisfaction.

Field studies also show that differences in educational background are related to increased conflicts in work teams (Jehn, Northcraft, & Neale, 1999) and that differences in functional specialization are frequently related to coordination and integration difficulties (Olson, Walker, Ruekert, & Bonner, 2001). Chatman and Flynn (2001) found that greater demographic heterogeneity led to group norms emphasizing low cooperation at the beginning stage among student teams and offices from ten business units of a financial services firm. Even in teams demonstrating performance benefits from membership diversity, team members report the experience of frustration and dissatisfaction (Amason & Schweiger, 1994; Baron, 1990).

In sum, teams with different levels of diversity experience dissimilar categorization processes and team processes. Within homogeneous teams, members tend to communicate with one another more often and in a greater variety of ways. According to the social identity theory, homogeneity in teams may thus increase satisfaction and cooperation and decrease emotional conflicts (Tajfel & Turner, 1986; Williams & O'Reilly, 1998). Because homogeneous teams do not have significant barriers to social intercourse, positive ingroup social contacts and interactions are fostered (Blau, 1977). This formulation suggests that deleterious social identity and social categorization processes will not inhibit a work team with homogeneous members. With increased communication and interaction, team members gain experience, and thus their mental models are more likely to converge.

As team diversity increases, the effects of social categorization become more salient and more likely for ingroup/outgroup biases to emerge, which create barriers to social interaction (Blau, 1977; Tsui et al., 1992). These processes may lead individuals to seek solidarity with others in that group, to conform to group norms, and to discriminate against outgroups (Tajfel & Turner, 1986). To the extent that multiple subgroups exist in moderately heterogeneous teams, conflict is potentially maximized (Earley & Mosakowski, 2000; Lau & Murnighan, 1998), and intergroup interaction and communication may be blocked (Alexander, Nuchols, Bloom, & Lee, 1995; Blau, 1977). For example, Earley and Mosakowski (2000) found that moderately heterogeneous transnational teams exhibited communication problems. Therefore, communication difficulties associated with moderate levels of cultural diversity within those multicultural teams may bring about difficulties in developing a high level of team mental model convergence.

Although moderate levels of diversity may create barriers to effective interaction among team members, high levels of diversity could actually weaken these barriers (Blau, 1977), because team members will be more evenly diffused over different categories and ingroup/outgroup identities will be less salient (Alexander et al., 1995). In teams with high levels of diversity, casual social communication and interaction are more likely to involve members of different groups. Furthermore, the ingroup pressures that inhibit social interaction with outgroup members should be weakened (Blau, 1977). Outgroup discrimination is thus less likely to occur. In fact, few common bases for subgroup formation and ingroup/outgroup identity are likely to exist in those work teams with relatively high levels of diversity (Earley & Mosakowski, 2000; Richard, Barnett, Dwyer, & Chadwick, 2004).

In short, we expect that diversity in work teams will exhibit a U-shaped relationship with team mental model convergence. Relative to moderately diverse teams, homogeneous and highly heterogeneous teams will develop more convergent team mental models.

Informational Integration Process

Heterogeneous teams are more likely to possess a broader range of task-relevant knowledge, skills, and abilities that are distinct and nonredundant and to have different opinions and perspectives on the task at hand.

Differences in information and viewpoints may give rise to task conflict and dissent (Jehn et al., 1999; Pelled et al., 1999). Faced with the need to solve these conflicts and reconcile opposing views, team members may engage in more elaborate processing of task-relevant and team-related information. They exchange information and perspectives, process the information and perspectives at the individual level, provide feedback on the results of this individual-level processing to the group, and discuss and integrate its implication (Van Knippenberg, De Dreu, & Homan, 2004). Such thorough information processing and integration will help team members better identify the situation and problems, and have more accurate understanding of their task- and teamwork. Therefore, working as part of a heterogeneous work team may enhance the accuracy of team mental models. There will be a positive relationship between diversity and team mental model accuracy; homogeneous teams will exhibit lower levels of team mental model accuracy than moderately or highly diverse teams. In their study, McLeod and Lobel (1992) found that groups that were heterogeneous with respect to the ethnic backgrounds of their members produced higher quality ideas in a brainstorming task than more homogeneous groups did.

Summary

By taking into account the two processes – the social categorization process and the informational integration process associated with team diversity, we addressed the issue: How does a team's diversity level influence the development of team mental model, with respect to both its accuracy and convergence? Team diversity is likely to have a U-shaped relationship with the convergence of team mental models as members may be differently motivated to communicate with others who are perceived to belong to different social groups and it is likely to have positive impacts on the development of its accuracy.

In heterogeneous teams, both team mental model convergence and accuracy matter in team outcomes. Considering these two aspects of team mental model development helps resolve the inconsistency in previous research findings on the relationship between team diversity and team performance. For instance, this contention is corroborated by an interesting longitudinal laboratory study of decision making conducted by Watson and colleagues (1993) in the United States. They examined cultural diversity's impact on team performance by comparing homogeneous and heterogeneous task groups. Their findings suggest that a team's diversity had different impacts on team process and performance at different time points in the experiment.

Initially, homogeneous teams scored higher on both process and performance effectiveness. Over time, both teams showed improvement on process and performance, and the between-group differences converged. By the end of the experiment, the heterogeneous team scored higher on the two task measures. These results suggest that diversity in cultural background may have negative effects on the development of team mental model convergence early in a team's life, presumably because it takes some time for team members to get over their interpersonal differences on observable dimensions that tend to be associated with lower levels of initial attraction and social integration. After this stage, however, when a certain level of behavioral interaction (Hambrick, 1994) has been achieved, teams develop some convergent mental models and then will be able to benefit from the informational integration process within a diverse group.

CONCLUSION

A team mental model is a specific shared knowledge system that evolves within a work team. In this chapter, we examined how members with different backgrounds and characteristics could develop such a shared knowledge system within their team through repeated interactions.

The trend toward using teams to coordinate and manage work in organizations is increasing the amount of time that employees spend with people who may have different training, skills, functional background, and even values. Organizations need to learn how to manage more heterogeneous work teams than they have managed previously. Diversity is not an inherent characteristic of effective teams. Our chapter suggests that developing convergent and accurate team mental models might be an effective way to facilitate coordination and functioning in a heterogeneous work team and to enhance team performance.

REFERENCES

Alexander, J., Nuchols, B., Bloom, J., & Lee, S. (1995). Organizational demography and turnover: An examination of multiform and nonlinear heterogeneity. *Human Relations, 48,* 1455–1480.

Amason, A. C., & Schweiger, D. M. (1994). Resolving the paradox of conflict, strategic decision making and organizational performance. *International Journal of Conflict Management, 5,* 239–253.

Ancona, D. G., & Caldwell, D. F. (1992). Demography and design: Predictors of new product team performance. *Organization Science, 3,* 321–341.

Athans, M. (1982). The expert team of experts approach to command and control (C2) organizations. *IEEE Control Systems Magazine, September,* 30–38.

Austin, J. R. (2004). Transactive memory in organizational groups: The effects of content, consensus, specialization, and accuracy on group performance. *Journal of Applied Psychology, 88,* 866–878.

Baron, R. A. (1990). Countering the effects of destructive criticism: The relative efficacy of four interventions. *Journal of Applied Psychology, 75,* 235–245.

Blau, P. M. (1977). *Inequality and heterogeneity.* New York: Free Press.

Brewer, M. B. (1979). In-group bias in the minimal intergroup situation: A cognitive-motivational analysis. *Psychological Bulletin, 86,* 307–324.

Brunswik, E. (1956). *Perception and the representative design of psychological experiments.* Berkeley, CA: University of California Press.

Cannon-Bowers, J. A., Salas, E., & Converse, S. A. (1993). Shared mental models in expert team decision making. In N. J. Castellan, Jr. (Ed.), *Current issues in individual and group decision making* (pp. 221–246). Hillsdale, NJ: Lawrence Erlbaum Associates.

Chatman, J. A., & Flynn, F. J. (2001). The influence of demographic heterogeneity on the emergence and consequences of cooperative norms in work teams. *Academy of Management Journal, 44,* 956–974.

Cooke, N. J., Salas, E., Cannon-Bowers, J. A., & Stout, R. J. (2000). Measuring team knowledge. *Human Factors, 42,* 151–173.

Cox, T. H., Lobel, S. A., & McLeod, P. L. (1991). Effects of ethnic group cultural differences on cooperative versus competitive behavior on a group task. *Academy of Management Journal, 34,* 827–847.

Cummings, A., Zhou, J., & Oldham, G. R. (1993). *Demographic differences and employee work outcomes: Effects on multiple comparison groups.* Paper presented at the annual meeting of the Academy of Management, Atlanta, GA.

Earley, C., & Mosakowski, E. (2000). Creating hybrid team cultures: An empirical test of transnational team functioning. *Academy of Management Journal, 43,* 26–49.

Forgas, J. P. (1981). Social episodes and group milieu: A study in social cognition. *British Journal of Social Psychology, 20,* 77–87.

Greenhaus, J. H., Parasuraman, S., & Wormley, W. M. (1990). Effects of race on organizational experience, job performance evaluations, and career outcomes. *Academy of Management Journal, 33,* 64–86.

Hambrick, D. C. (1994). Top management groups: A conceptual integration and reconsideration of the "team" label. In B. M. Staw (Ed.), *Research in organizational behavior, Vol. 16* (pp. 171–213). Greenwich, CT: JAI Press.

Harrison, D. A., Price, K. H., & Bell, M. P. (1998). Beyond relational demography: Time and the effects of surface- and deep-level diversity on work group cohesion. *Academy of Management Journal, 41,* 96–107.

Henry, R. A. (1993). Group judgment accuracy: Reliability and validity of post discussion confidence judgments. *Organizational Behavior and Human Decision Processes, 56,* 11–27.

Henry, R. A. (1995). Improving group judgment accuracy: Information sharing and determining the best member. *Organizational Behavior and Human Decision Processes, 62,* 190–197.

Hinz, V. B., Tindale, R. S., & Vollrath, D. A. (1997). The emerging conceptualization of groups as information processors. *Psychological Bulletin, 121,* 43–64.

Horwitz, S. K., & Horwitz, I. B. (2007). The effects of team diversity on team outcomes: A meta-analytic review of team demography. *Journal of Management, 33,* 987–1015.

Jackson, S. (1992). Team composition in organizations. In S. Worchel, W. Wood, & J. Simpson (Eds.), *Group process and productivity* (pp. 138–176). London: Sage.

Jackson, S. E., May, K. E., & Whitney, K. (1995). Understanding the dynamics of diversity in decision-making teams. In R. A. Guzzo & E. Salas (Eds.), *Team decision-making effectiveness in organizations* (pp. 204–261). San Francisco: Jossey-Bass.

Jehn, K. A., Northcraft, G. B., & Neale, M. A. (1999). Why differences make a difference: A field study of diversity, conflict, and performance in workgroups. *Administrative Science Quarterly, 44,* 741–763.

Johnson-Laird, P. N. (1983). *Mental models.* Cambridge, MA: Harvard University Press.

Klimoski, R., & Mohammed, S. (1994). Team mental model: Construct or metaphor? *Journal of Management, 20,* 403–437.

Kraiger, K., Salas, E., & Cannon-Bowers, J. A. (1995). Measuring knowledge organization as a method for assessing learning during training. *Human Factors, 37,* 804–816.

Kozlowski, S. W. J., & Ilgen, D. R. (2006). Enhancing the effectiveness of work groups and teams. *Psychological Science in the Public Interest, 7,* 77–124.

Lau, D. C., & Murnighan, J. K. (1998). Demographic diversity and faultlines: The compositional dynamics of organizational groups. *Academy of Management Review, 23,* 325–340.

Lefkowitz, J. (1994). Race as a factor in job placement: Serendipitous findings of "ethnic drift." *Personnel Psychology, 47,* 495–513.

Liang, D. W., Moreland, R., & Argote, L. (1995). Group versus individual training and group performance: The mediating role of transactive memory. *Personality and Social Psychology Bulletin, 21,* 384–393.

Libby, R., Trotman, K. T., & Zimmer, I. (1987). Member variation, recognition of expertise, and group performance. *Journal of Applied Psychology, 72,* 81–87.

Lim, B. C., & Klein, K. J. (2006). Team mental models and team performance: A field study of the effects of team mental model similarity and accuracy. *Journal of Organizational Behavior, 27,* 403–418.

Littlepage, G. E., & Silbiger, H. (1992). Recognition of expertise in decision-making groups: Effects of group size and participation patterns. *Small Group Research, 23,* 344–355.

Marks, M. A., Zaccaro, S. J., & Mathieu, J. E. (2000). Performance implications of leader briefings and team-interaction training for team adaptation to novel environments. *Journal of Applied Psychology, 85,* 971–986.

Mathieu, J. E., Heffner, T. S., Goodwin, G. F., Cannon-Bowers, J. A., & Salas, E. (2005). Scaling the quality of teammates' mental models: Equifinality and normative comparisons. *Journal of Organizational Behavior, 26,* 37–56.

Mathieu, J. E., Heffner, T. S., Goodwin, G. F., Salas, E., & Cannon-Bowers, J. A. (2000). The influence of shared mental models on team process and performance. *Journal of Applied Psychology, 85,* 273–283.

McIntyre, R. M., & Salas, E. (1995). Measuring and managing for team performance: Emerging principles from complex environment. In R. Guzzo and E. Salas (Eds.), *Team effectiveness and decision making in organizations* (pp. 149–203). San Francisco: Jossey-Bass.

McKeithen, K. B., Reitman, J. S., Rueter, H. H., & Hirtle, S. C. (1981). Knowledge organization and skill differences in computer programmers. *Cognitive Psychology, 13*, 307–325.

McLeod, P. L., & Lobel, S. A. (1992). The effects of ethnic diversity on idea generation in small groups. *Academy of Management Best Paper Proceedings*, 227–231.

Milliken, F. J., & Martins, L. L. (1996). Searching for common threads: Understanding the multiple effects of diversity in organizational groups. *Academy of Management Review, 21*, 402–433.

Mohammed, S., & Dumville, B. C. (2001). Team mental models in a team knowledge framework: Expanding theory and measurement across disciplinary boundaries. *Journal of Organizational Behavior, 22*, 89–106.

Moreland, R. L. (1999). Transactive memory: Learning who knows what in work groups and organizations. In L. L. Thompson, J. M. Levine, & M. Messick (Eds.), *Shared cognition in organizations: The management of knowledge* (pp. 3–31). Mahwah, NJ: Lawrence Erlbaum Associates.

Morgan, B. B., Jr., Glickman, A. S., Woodard, E. A., Blaiwes, A. S., & Salas, E. (1986). *Measurement of team behaviors in a Navy environment* (Naval Training Systems Center [NTSC}Tech. Rep. No. 86–014). Orlando, FL: NTSC.

Mount, M. K., Hazucha, J. F., Holt, K. E., & Sytsma, M. (1995). Rater-ratee race effects in performance ratings of managers. *Academy of Management Best Papers Proceedings*, 141–145.

Olson, E. M., Walker, O. C., Ruekert, R. W., & Bonner, J. M. (2001). Patterns of cooperation during new product development among marketing, operations and R&D: Implications for project performance. *Journal of Product Innovation Management, 18*, 258–271.

O'Reilly, C. A., Caldwell, D. F., & Barnett, W. P. (1989). Work group demography, social integration, and turnover. *Administrative Science Quarterly, 34*, 21–37.

Pelled, L. H., Eisenhardt, K. M., & Xin, K. R. (1999). Exploring the black box: An analysis of work group diversity, conflict, and performance. *Administrative Science Quarterly, 44*, 1–28.

Rentsch, J. R., & Hall, R. J. (1994). Members of great teams think alike: A model of team effectiveness and schema similarity among team members. *Advances in Interdisciplinary Studies of Work Teams, 1*, 223–261.

Rentsch, J. R., & Klimoski, R. J. (2001). Why do "great minds" think alike? Antecedents of team member schema agreement. *Journal of Organizational Behavior, 22*, 107–120.

Richard, O. C., Barnett, T., Dwyer, S., & Chadwick, K. (2004). Cultural diversity in management, firm performance, and the moderating role of entrepreneurial orientation dimensions. *Academy of Management Journal, 47*, 255–266.

Riordan, C., & Shore, L. (1997). Demographic diversity and employee attitudes: Examination of relational demography within work units. *Journal of Applied Psychology, 82*, 342–358.

Rouse, W. B., & Morris, N. M. (1986). On looking into the black box: Prospects and limits in the search for mental models. *Psychological Bulletin, 100,* 349–363.

Rowe, A. L., & Cooke, N. J. (1995). Measuring mental models: Choosing the right tools for the job. *Human Resource Development Quarterly, 6,* 243–262.

Sackett, P. R., & DuBois, C. L. Z. (1991). Rater-ratee race effects on performance evaluation: Challenging meta-analytic conclusions. *Journal of Applied Psychology, 76,* 873–877.

Schein, E. H. (1992). *Organizational culture and leadership.* San Francisco: Jossey-Bass.

Schneider, B., & Reichers, A. E. (1983). On the etiology of climates. *Personnel Psychology, 36,* 19–39.

Tajfel, H., & Turner, J. C. (1986). The social identity theory of intergroup behavior. In S. Worchel & W. G. Austin (Eds.), *Psychology of intergroup relations* (pp. 33–47). Chicago: Nelson-Hall.

Thompson, L., & Fine, G. A. (1999). Socially shared cognition, affect, and behavior: A review and integration. *Personality and Social Psychology Review, 3,* 278–302.

Tsui, A. S., Egan, T. D., & O'Reilly, C. (1992). Being different: Relational demography and organizational attachment. *Administrative Science Quarterly, 37,* 549–579.

Van Knippenberg, D., De Dreu, C. K., & Homan, A. C. (2004). Work group diversity and group performance: An integrative model and research agenda. *Journal of Applied Psychology, 89,* 1008–1022.

Verkuyten, M., de Jong, W., & Masson, C. N. (1993). Job satisfaction among ethnic minorities in the Netherlands. *Applied Psychology: An International Review, 42,* 171–189.

Wagner, W., Pfeffer, J., & O'Reilly, C. (1984). Organizational demography and turnover in top management groups. *Administrative Science Quarterly, 29,* 74–92.

Watson, W. E., Kumar, K., & Michaelson, L. K. (1993). Cultural diversity's impact on interaction process and performance: Comparing homogeneous and diverse task groups. *Academy of Management Journal, 36,* 590–602.

Webber, S. S., Chen, G., Payne, S. C., Marsh, S. M., & Zaccaro, S. J. (2000). Enhancing team mental model measurement with performance appraisal practices. *Organizational Research Methods, 3,* 307–322.

Williams, K. Y., & O'Reilly, C. A. (1998). Demography and diversity in organizations: A review of 40 years of research. *Research in Organizational Behavior, 20,* 77–140.

Wilson, J. R., & Rutherford, A. (1989). Mental models: Theory and application in human factors. *Human Factors, 31,* 617–634.

11

Harmony, Illusory Relationship Costs, and Conflict Resolution in Chinese Contexts

ZHI-XUE ZHANG,[1] YAN ZHANG, AND MIN WANG

Management of interpersonal conflicts has attracted researchers' interest in the fields of psychology and management. Previous studies have documented drastic cultural differences in preferred conflict management styles, with Chinese people having a greater preference for conflict avoidance (e.g., Tjosvold & Sun, 2002) and Westerners having a greater preference for direct, confrontational strategies (Friedman, Chi, & Liu, 2006; Morris et al., 1998). The need to understand this cultural difference has become more pressing than ever given the rising economic power of China and the increasing prominence of Chinese companies as global business partners or competitors in international business.

In this chapter, we will provide a cultural explanation for Chinese people's tendency to avoid conflicts. This explanation pertains to the importance that Chinese culture accords to the values of maintaining harmonious interpersonal relationships. The concern with interpersonal harmony could lead Chinese people to erroneously overestimate the relationship costs of direct confrontation, believing that using a direct approach to conflict management would evoke strong negative reactions from and hurt the relationship with the other disputant. This belief would result in a preference for conflict avoidance, which ironically could increase tension in future interactions between the disputants.

The present chapter consists of five sections. We will start with a brief review of the concerns of Chinese people for interpersonal relationships and harmony, as well as the implications of these concerns on choices for conflict resolution strategy. In the second part, we report evidence from our

[1] The studies reported in this chapter were supported by two grants from the National Natural Science Foundation of China (No. 70872002) and the National Natural Science Funds for Distinguished Young Scholar (No. 70925002) to the first author.

studies for the link between these concerns and strategy choice in conflict management. Next, we will argue with support from our research findings that conflict avoidance can produce negative downstream consequences on subsequent social interactions between the disputants. In the fourth section of this chapter, we will show that the concern over relationship costs that motivates Chinese people's conflict avoidance has gone overboard. By having Chinese people go through a perspective-taking exercise, we were able to substantially reduce this excessive concern and increase the likelihood of adopting a direct approach to conflict resolution. In the final section, we will discuss theoretical contributions and practical implications of our results.

CONCERNS FOR HARMONY AND INTERPERSONAL RELATIONSHIPS

Many scholars have commented on the fundamental role that *guanxi* (or relationship with others) plays in Chinese people's social behaviors and judgments (Hwang, 1987; Jacobs, 1979). Some scholars have characterized Chinese culture as a relationship-oriented culture; this characterization highlights the heavy emphasis that Chinese culture places on interpersonal harmony, group solidarity, and fulfillment of social obligations (Ho, Chan, & Chiu, 1991; Yang, 1995). Accordingly, the social psychology of Chinese people must be understood in the context of relationships (Ho, Chen, & Zhang, 2001).

Aside from maintaining relationships, Chinese people are also expected to treat people in their relationships generously and charitably through helping, caring, and showing sympathy. Zhang and Yang (1998, 2001) related these normative expectations to the *renqing* norm in Chinese societies, which prescribes emitting appropriate human emotional responses to people in their relationships for the purpose of maintaining harmony. The renqing norm also prescribes fulfillment of obligations and duties in one's social relationships, reciprocation of favors, helping those who experience difficulties, and maintaining interpersonal harmony. Adherence to the renqing norm is a major dimension of social perception in Chinese culture. Zhang and Yang (2001) asked Chinese respondents to list traits or attributes that came to their minds when they thought of people who "have renqing." The results showed that the respondents associated "having renqing" with such positive traits as helpfulness, warmth, caring for others, flexibility, understanding, amicability, and so forth. Moreover, "lacking renqing" was connected to negative attributes such as indifference to others, selfishness, being calculative, being arrogant, and being eccentric. Given these results, it is not surprising that the respondents evaluated people who had renqing favorably and those who did not unfavorably. Most respondents also indicated a desire to interact with people who had renqing and to avoid those who did not.

The heavy emphasis on relationships and interpersonal harmony in Chinese culture gives rise to some culture-characteristic behavioral styles among Chinese people. For example, when allocating reward, aside from considering the team members' relative contributions to the task, Chinese individuals also consider relationships among the team members (e.g., Chiu, 1991a; Leung & Bond, 1984; Zhang & Yang, 1998). Some researchers have advanced the view that the concept of Chinese justice is tied to fulfilling role obligations and adhering to the norm of maintaining harmony in interpersonal transactions (Chiu, 1991b; Chiu & Hong, 1997; Zhang, 2006).

Latent conflicts often develop when individuals with divergent interests and priorities work together. A latent conflict may escalate to an explicit one and threaten to ruin the collaborations between the involved parties. How the disputants perceive, interpret, and react to the conflict could have important implications for its outcomes and attendant consequences. As mentioned, Westerners typically recognize the existence of a conflict and try to resolve it. In contrast, Chinese people are generally conflict-aversive; they seldom acknowledge the existence of a conflict or take direct actions to resolve it.

The dual-concern model of conflict resolution styles (Rahim, 1983; Thomas & Kenneth, 1976) distinguishes five conflict resolution styles based on interacting parties' concerns for one's own outcome and for the other party's outcome: competing (high self-concern, low other-concern), accommodating (high other-concern, low self-concern), avoiding (low on both self- and other-concerns), compromising (moderate on both kinds of concerns), and integrating (high on both kinds of concerns). Cross-cultural studies have revealed a greater preference among the Chinese (vs. Westerners) for avoiding (Morris et al., 1998; Ting-Toomey et al., 1991).

The origin of this cultural difference is not clear, however, and there is a dearth of conceptual and empirical works that examine this issue. A popular explanation relates Chinese people's greater preference for conflict avoidance to the higher levels of collectivism in Chinese culture. Individualism versus collectivism is an extensively researched dimension of cultures. Individualist cultures emphasize self-reliance, independence from others, and uniqueness. People in individualist cultures value personal goals, needs, and rights over those of the group. In contrast, people in collectivist cultures value the goals, responsibilities, and obligations of the group over those of the individual. In collectivist cultures, people are interdependent with their ingroup; they give priority to the goals of their ingroups, behave with reference to ingroup norms, and act in a communal way (Hofstede, 1980; Triandis, 1994).

A defining characteristic of people in collectivist cultures is their heightened concern with relationships. In conflict situations, people in collectivist cultures are primarily concerned with maintaining relationships with others, whereas people in individualist cultures are concerned with achieving justice (Ohbuchi, Fukushima, & Tedeschi, 1999). Numerous studies comparing the preferred conflict management styles in individualist and collectivist cultures have consistently shown that people from collectivist cultures prefer nonconfrontational strategies (Cai & Fink, 2002; Ting-Toomey et al., 1991). Ting-Toomey and her colleagues (1991) found that people in collectivist countries (e.g., China, Korea, and Japan) tend to devalue competing and value accommodating and avoiding conflict resolution styles. These investigators interpreted their findings in terms of the disputants' face maintenance concerns. Specifically, two kinds of face maintenance concerns in a conflict situation have been identified: self-face concerns and other-face concerns. Ting-Toomey and her colleagues argue that people in collectivist cultures have a greater concern for maintaining others' face in conflict situations than do people in individualist cultures. In collectivist cultures, assertiveness and confrontation are discouraged because these actions are likely to be interpreted as an intention to undermine harmony (Kozan, 1997). In contrast, individualist cultures champion the individual and are tolerant of aggressive pursuit of personal goals. Chua and Gudykunst (1987) found that students from low context cultures (which are typically individualist cultures) are more confrontational than are students from high context cultures (which are usually collectivist cultures) when resolving a conflict.

Consistent with the view that Chinese culture is more collectivistic than American culture, Chinese people favor conflict resolution procedures that do not threaten relationships but are instrumental in restoring harmony (e.g., informal bargaining and mediation), whereas Americans prefer going to court to settle disputes directly (Leung, 1987, 1997). Morris and his colleagues (1998) also showed that compared to each other, Chinese are more likely to adopt an avoidance strategy to deal with conflicts, and Americans are more likely to use a competitive or dominating strategy. Furthermore, the greater tendency of Chinese to avoid conflict can be explained by the greater emphasis on the values of tradition and conformity among the Chinese population. Friedman, Chi, and Liu (2006) also found that Chinese are more likely to avoid conflict than are Americans, and this difference can be attributed to (a) Chinese people's stronger expectation that direct confrontation will hurt the relationship with the other party involved in the conflict situation, and (b) Chinese people's greater concern for the other party. Results from the study by Friedman and colleagues also ruled out the possibility that Chinese people's preference for conflict avoidance results from expecting more attractive payoffs from maintaining good relationships with the disputant. That is, Chinese people's preference for conflict avoidance is not driven by instrumental concerns. Rather, it is motivated by adherence to the prevalent norms that prescribe maintenance of harmonious relationships.

RELATIONSHIP CONCERNS IN CONFLICT MANAGEMENT STRATEGY CHOICE: EMPIRICAL STUDIES

Although past studies have found a consistent Chinese–American difference in conflict avoidance, with a few exceptions, they have not linked this difference to specific elements of Chinese culture. Morris and colleagues (1998) empirically connected this difference to the values of tradition and conformity, but their study did not examine the mediation role of specific concerns in Chinese culture. Friedman and colleagues (2006) explained Chinese people's preference for conflict avoidance in terms of the specific belief that direct confrontation will hurt the relationship with the other party involved in the conflict and Chinese people's care for others. This study does not explain *how* this belief and social concern impact choices of conflict resolution strategy, however. The decision to adopt a certain conflict resolution strategy depends on interlocking psychological processes such as making sense of the conflict, assessing the possible outcomes of different resolution approaches, and comparing the most preferred style with alternatives.

We contend that the choice of conflict resolution style is a function of both prevalent interpersonal concerns and people's appraisal of the conflict situation. In this section, we present a series of studies that examined the Chinese tendency to avoid conflict. The results of these studies pinpoint the concerns regarding interpersonal harmony that are the most relevant to conflict resolution strategy choice in Chinese contexts and shed light on how these concerns influence people's appraisal of specific conflict situations.

The First Study

To study strategy choice in conflict situations, we created a vignette that depicts a realistic conflict situation in China. Pilot studies confirmed that many Chinese people found this vignette to be realistic – either they had heard of similar situations or thought that such a conflict could occur. As people's responses may be affected by the disputant's gender, we used a gender-neutral name for the disputant in the scenario. The vignette used in the study is as follows:

> One day you asked one of your friends to go shopping with you. In a shoe store, he/she found a pair of shoes he/she liked and decided to buy it. Unfortunately, he/she forgot to bring his/her credit card, and did not have enough cash – he/she needed 300 yuan[2] more. There was no ATM machine nearby, so he/she asked you to loan him/her 300 yuan. You did and he/she happily bought the shoes. He/she told you he/she would return the money to you very soon.
>
> A few weeks had passed, and he/she never mentioned when he/she was going to return the money, even though you had met him/her several times. It seemed that he/she had already forgotten the loan.

In the Chinese context, the scenario constitutes a conflict situation from the money lender's perspective: If the lender does not ask for the money back, he/she will lose 300 yuan; if the lender asks for the money back, he/she may worry that the request would evoke a negative reaction from the borrower or hurt the relationship with the borrower.

Each participant was asked to take the lender's role and to indicate whether he/she would (a) directly ask for the money back, (b) only indirectly remind the borrower to return the money, or (c) never ask the friend to return the money (i.e., no action would be taken). Among 47 managers (78.72% males) with a mean age of 35.43 years (standard deviation [SD] = 5.61) who responded to the scenario, 11 (23.4%) chose to ask for the money back, 15 (31.9%) chose to indirectly remind the borrower, and 21 (44.7%) would not ask for the money back.

To understand why the participants made their choices, we asked them to give reasons for their choices. The justifications provided by the participants are summarized in the next paragraph, with the frequency of each response listed in parentheses. Because some participants reported multiple reasons, the total frequency is greater than the number of participants.

For those who directly asked for the money back, the reasons they mentioned include: "This is my right" (8); "I am a direct person and would thus like to be direct" (2); "Being indirect in this situation may mislead the other party" (5); "If I were in the other party's role, I would not have negative

<hr />

[2] Yuan is the unit of Chinese currency; 1 U.S. dollar is equivalent to 7 yuan.

reactions to the lender who directly asks for the money back" (5); and "I will not feel comfortable if I am unassertive" (3).

Participants who preferred to indirectly remind the borrower to return the money gave the following reasons: "Being direct will hurt the other party's face" (9); "Being indirect allows me to test the other party's integrity" (5); "Being indirect and subtle will be beneficial for our relationship" (4); and "The other party will not mind if I indirectly remind him/her" (4).

Participants who would not take any action gave the following reasons: "Being direct will make the other party uncomfortable" (13); "The other party will consider me as penny-pinching" (9); and "Being direct will hurt the other party's face and damage our relationship" (10).

These results clearly show that concerns for the relationship and fear of evoking negative reactions were the primary reasons behind the choice of the indirect or no action strategies.

Follow-Up Studies

Strategy Choice
Choice of conflict resolution strategy might be affected by many factors, two of which are (a) the amount of money involved and (b) relationship close-ness. When the value of the loan is negligible, most people would not bother to ask for the money back. When the value of the loan increases, however, the lender would be more motivated to ask for the money back. Results from our pretests showed that, when the value of the loan amounted to 1/15 to 1/12 of their monthly income, participants would start to experience a conflict between relationship maintenance and recovering a monetary loss. Likewise, when the borrower has a close relationship with the lender, the lender would be more motivated to maintain the relationship than risk it by asking for the money back.

To control for these variables and to establish the robustness of our results, follow-up studies were carried out with a revised vignette. In the revised vignette, we fixed the lender's monthly income (e.g., 4,500 yuan). We also included a scale to measure the perceived size of the loan. The scale was a 4-point Likert scale ranging from 1 (very small) to 4 (very large). In addition, we described in the vignette that the relationship between the lender and the borrower was not very close, although they had moderately frequent interactions. Holding frequency of interaction constant in the vignette is important in Chinese settings because Zhang (2001) has demonstrated that Chinese participants treat their colleagues in the same organization quite differently according to frequency of interactions.

We presented this modified scenario to different samples. The results were similar to those obtained in the first study. For example, in a sample of 101 part-time Master of Business Administration (MBA) students, 73 (72.3%) participants indicated that they either would not ask for the money back or would try other ways to ask for the money back, and only 28 (27.7%) participants chose to directly ask for the money back.

Perceptions of the Assertive Borrower
People in Western culture prefer to act assertively in conflict situations because they anticipate positive evaluations by others of their assertive action. Indeed, previous studies conducted in Western cultural contexts consistently showed that, compared to unassertive individuals, assertive individuals are considered as more fair, nonrevengeful, appropriate, educated, intelligent, and superior. They are also viewed as more skilled, effective, and capable in handling conflicts, although assertive actors are also rated less favorably on likeability attributes such as being inoffensive, friendly, agreeable, pleasant, considerate, flexible, open minded, sympathetic, good natured, kind, likeable, thoughtful, warm, and attractive (Kelly et al., 1982) and are regarded as unsympathetic, aggressive, dominant, impolite, and hostile (Hull & Schroeder, 1979; Woolfolk & Dever, 1979).

In contrast, in the Chinese context, people would avoid assertive actions because they anticipate negative evaluations from others of such actions. Recall that Chinese people tend to associate not having "renqing" with being unsympathetic, impolite, hostile, and dominant, and evaluate those lacking "renqing" negatively (Zhang & Yang, 2001). Thus, the tendency to avoid confrontation with the borrower in the present study could result from anticipated negative evaluations of assertive behaviors.

To provide a direct test of this idea, following the strategy choice, participants were asked to respond to six items that assessed the anticipated relationship costs of direct confrontation with the borrower. The open-ended results from the first study showed that those participants who chose to ask for the money back indirectly or not to make a request at all expected that their relationship with the borrower would deteriorate if they directly asked the borrower to return the money. Based on these responses, we created six items to measure the perceived relationship costs of directly asking the borrower to return the money. The six items are: "By doing this, I will offend my colleague"; "My colleague will think I am penny-pinching"; "My colleague will think I am not friendly to him/her"; "My colleague will think that I am not humane enough"; "Our relationship will deteriorate"; and "We will interact less frequently afterwards." Participants were asked to respond to these items on a 7-point scale (1 = strongly disagree; 7 = strongly agree). Based on the data from various samples, the scale's alpha was greater than .90. We labeled the construct measured with this scale Perceived Relationship Costs.

We also developed a scale to measure Concern for Relationship based on Swap and Rubin's (1983) interpersonal orientation scale and other related measures. Specifically, we included eight items that assess individuals' adherence to the reciprocity norm in social interactions, their investment in maintaining a positive relationship with others, their concern about how others evaluate them, and their sensitivity to others' attitudes and emotions. The items are: "When I receive a gift, I find myself thinking about its value"; "It's important for me to work with people with whom I get along well, even if that means I get less done"; "The more other people reveal about themselves, the more inclined I feel to reveal things about myself"; "When someone does me a favor I usually feel compelled to return it"; "I care about other people's impression of me"; "I am greatly influenced by the moods of the people I am with"; "What others think about my actions is of great importance to me"; and "I am interested in what other people are really like." In a validation study, we asked MBA students and undergraduate students in a university in China to rate these items on a 5-point Likert scale (1 = strongly disagree, 5 = strongly agree). Results from exploratory and confirmatory factor analyses of the data collected from the two samples indicated that all eight items loaded on one factor, with item-total correlations for all items greater than .30. We refer to this factor as Concern for Relationship.

Concern for Relationship captures Chinese people's emphasis on interpersonal relationship, harmony, and the interacting parties' feelings (Ho et al., 1991; Yang, 1995; Zhang & Yang, 2001). Using data gathered from 195 MBA students, we found that the scale (a) had an alpha of .75, (b) was positively related to Singelis's (1994) interdependent self-construal ($r = .47$, $p < .001$), (c) was not related to independent self-construal ($r = .06$, not significant [ns]), (d) was positively related to negative affectivity ($r = .20$, $p < .01$; Agho, Price, & Mueller, 1992), and (e) was not significantly related to positive affectivity ($r = -.14$, ns). These results provide support for the scale's convergent and discriminant validity. We predict that the emphasis on interpersonal harmony would reinforce the expectation that confronting a conflict will incur relationship costs, which in turn would motivate people to avoid (vs. approach) the conflict.

Regression analyses were performed to examine the relationship between Concern for Relationship (independent variable) and Perceived

Relationship Costs, with the perceived value of the loan as a control variable. Results showed that Concern for Relationship was positively related to Perceived Relationship Costs ($\beta = .34$, $N = 101$, $p = .06$); participants who had a greater concern for relationships expected direct confrontation to have higher relationship costs. The perceived value of the loan was negatively related to Perceived Relationship Costs ($\beta = -.65$, $p < .05$). In other words, the higher the perceived value of the loan, the less costly direct confrontation is perceived to be.

We also found a positive correlation between Perceived Relationship Costs and choice of conflict resolution strategy (1 = directly asking, 2 = indirectly reminding, 3 = no action) ($r = .40$, $N = 89$, $p < .001$). Participants who anticipated higher relationship costs of direct confrontation tended to avoid confronting the borrower.

Summary

In summary, our results demonstrated that concern for relationships and perceived relationship costs of direct confrontation are two important factors that contribute to Chinese people's aversion to direct confrontation. Our findings support the argument of Friedman and colleagues (2006) that Chinese people's tendency to avoid conflict results from the expectation that a direct confrontation will hurt their relationships with others. Moreover, our study showed that emphases on relationship and concern for interpersonal harmony are positively related to the anticipated relationship costs of directly confronting the disputant. Such anticipation in turn predicts the tendency to avoid confrontation. In other words, Chinese people's aversion to confrontation is partly driven by anticipated negative consequences of acting assertively.[3]

DOWNSTREAM RELATIONSHIP CONSEQUENCES OF CONFLICT AVOIDANCE

If Chinese people's aversion to direct confrontation is motivated by the desire to avoid negative interpersonal consequences, is this strategy effective? We do not think so. A conflict does not simply disappear as long as the disputants are required to work together or to be interdependent. When future interactions between the disputants are expected, the only productive

---

[3] Even in the West, if assertiveness elicits negative reactions from others, individuals may not act assertively even after receiving assertiveness training (Kazdin, 1974; McFall & Lillesand, 1971).

way of managing the future relationship is to face and resolve the conflict (Zhang, 2005).

Results from one of our studies support this idea. In this study, participants responded to two scenarios consecutively. In the first scenario, participants were asked to take the role of the Research and Development (R&D) department manager in the S company, which is a branch of a multinational company producing high-end computer accessories. The manager of the production department joined the S company recently. The rest of the scenario is as follows:

> You and the production department manager have met many times, but are not quite familiar with each other. The two of you have maintained a typical work relationship without many personal contacts. On a weekend, you and the production manager attend a business gathering. After the gathering, the production manager invites you to go shopping in the newly opened mall nearby. You agree, as you are free over the weekend.

At this point the participants were randomly assigned to the experimental or control condition. In the experimental condition, the participants went on to read the second part of the story, which was identical to the shoes purchase scenario in the first study, with the exception that the amount of money borrowed was increased to 600 yuan. We considered this modification necessary because participants of this study were mostly senior company managers and thus had higher monthly incomes. Participants were asked to imagine themselves in the described situation and indicate whether they would (a) directly ask for the money back, (b) indirectly remind the colleague to return the money, or (c) take no action. After participants made a choice, they were asked to respond to the second scenario.

In the control condition, the shoes purchase story was omitted, and the participants proceeded directly to the second scenario after reading the first part of the first scenario.

In the second scenario, participants learned that, soon after the shopping incident described in the first scenario, S company reorganized its structure to meet the market competition. The company decided to reorganize its functional departments structure into a matrix organization. Top managers were required to form different task forces to carry out some challenging tasks. Each task force consisted of one vice president and two department managers. Each manager could choose another manager at will to form the task force.

Participants were asked to take the role of the R&D manager and to decide whether they would choose the production manager as the teammate. Each

Table 11.1. *Downstream relationship consequences of conflict avoidance*

Choice of the manager as the teammate?	Money borrowing occurred before and conflict not resolved			No money borrowing before
	Direct	Indirect	No action	
Priority	2(20%)	7(18.9%)	10(15.4%)	17(23.9%)
No	2(20%)	8(21.6%)	18(27.7%)	12(16.9%)
No preference	6(60%)	22(59.5%)	37(56.9%)	42(59.2%)

participant was asked to choose one of the following response options: (a) the production manager is my priority, (b) I would not choose the production manager, or (c) I have no preference.

The study adopted a between-subjects design, and the dependent variable was participant's choice of teammate. The only difference between the experimental and the control conditions is that, in the control condition, the two managers did not take part in the money-borrowing incident.

We predicted that, if the lender avoided the conflict and took no action, he/she would be *less* likely to choose the borrower as the teammate because, with the conflict evoked by the loan lingering on, the relationship between the two parties had been adversely affected. The lender might want to avoid being taken advantage of by the borrower in future interactions and hence be reluctant to collaborate with the borrower.

Table 11.1 displays participants' choice in the two conditions. Of the 112 participants in the experimental condition, only 10 (8.9%) preferred a direct approach, 37 (33%) preferred sending indirect signals to the borrower, and 65 (58%) would not take any action. Table 11.1 also shows the participants' teammate choices in the two experimental conditions. Compared to the control condition in which the conflict did not occur, participants who took no action in the conflict were less likely to choose the borrower as their teammate (15.4% vs. 23.9%), and more likely to avoid the borrower (27.7% vs. 16.9%).

Thus, although Chinese people seek to avoid conflicts, the effects of an unresolved conflict would linger on and undermine future collegiality between the disputants. Our results suggest that avoidance may facilitate a fight-or-flight strategy in conflict situations, which could damage personal and work relationships between the disputants. If that is the case, what could be done to help Chinese people manage conflicts constructively? We now turn to this important and interesting question.

ILLUSORY RELATIONSHIP COSTS

Overestimation of Relationship Costs

Concern for relationships motivates Chinese people to take an indirect approach to conflict resolution for the purpose of avoiding anticipated negative reactions from the other disputant. Is Chinese people's anticipation of negative reactions to direct confrontation realistic? Do Chinese people really react negatively to direct confrontation? Our studies showed that Chinese people have typically overestimated the relationship costs of direct confrontation; more often than not, Chinese people react to direct confrontation favorably rather than negatively.

We have carried out studies that involved different samples and used different scenarios to verify whether Chinese people would react negatively to direct confrontation in conflict situations. In these studies, we randomly divided the sample into two groups, and each group read a different version of the loan scenario. The two versions described the same two persons, the same situation, and the same amount of money being borrowed. The only difference was that the participants played the role of the lender in the first version and the role of the borrower in the second version.

We also used a different version of the six-item Perceived Relationship Costs scale in the two experimental conditions. For example, in the participant as lender condition, one item was "What you did would offend your friend/colleague"; in the participant as borrower condition, this item was changed to "What my friend/colleague did would offend me."

Compared to the participants in the borrower condition, participants in the lender condition anticipated a much higher level of relationship costs if a direct strategy was adopted. This difference was highly significant ($p < .001$) for all of the six Perceived Relationship Costs items, and the result was replicated in all samples. Table 11.2 shows the results of one sample of 87 managers (79.8% males) with an average age of 34.97 years ($SD = 6.02$). Results from other samples were the same despite variations in the amount of money borrowed (e.g., 300 yuan, 400 yuan, 600 yuan, or 750 yuan) and in the degree of relationship closeness (e.g., friends, classmates, or colleagues) across different samples. In other words, to Chinese people, when somebody borrows money from them and forgets to return the money, they generally believe that confronting the borrower will evoke negative reactions from the borrower and hurt the relationship with him/her. When they borrow money from others and forget to return the money, however, Chinese people actually appreciate direct confrontation from the lender. This result shows

Table 11.2. *Mean and SD values (in parentheses) of ratings on the Perceived Relationship Costs items in the two perspective conditions*

Item	Lender perspective condition ($N = 40$)	Borrower perspective condition ($N = 47$)	t-value ($df = 85$)
What he/she (I) did would offend me (him/her)	3.07 (1.54)	1.74 (1.51)	4.06
I (He/she) would think that he/she is (I am) stingy	3.93 (1.83)	2.28 (1.74)	4.30
I (He/she) would think that he/she is (I am) unfriendly	3.54 (1.65)	1.83 (1.24)	5.48
I (He/she) would think that he/she is (I am) not empathetic	3.35 (1.58)	2.04 (1.36)	4.21
The relationship between us will deteriorate	2.93 (1.31)	1.65 (1.11)	4.88
We will interact less frequently afterwards	3.13 (1.42)	1.66 (1.27)	5.08
Average perceived relationship costs	3.33 (1.19)	1.87 (1.06)	6.04

Note: All mean differences were significant at the .001 level.

that Chinese people may have excessive concern over negative relationship consequences of direct confrontation. Nonetheless, such excessive concern has discouraged Chinese people from engaging in constructive resolutions of interpersonal conflicts through taking a direct approach.

In summary, our results suggest that people tend to overestimate the negative relationship consequences of taking a direct approach to conflict resolution. This overestimation reflects a cognitive bias or an illusion commonly held by Chinese people. This illusion discourages the use of direct communication between individuals. It is beyond this chapter's scope to discuss the sources of this bias. Inspired by Harvey's (1974) insights into the Abilene Paradox, we label this phenomenon "illusory relationship costs."

The Abilene Paradox

The Abilene Paradox describes the fact that people frequently take actions with unintended opposite consequences and therefore defeat the very purpose of what they want to achieve. Harvey (1974) identified this phenomenon from an interesting life experience. On a Sunday afternoon in

Coleman, Texas, it was extremely hot, and the wind was fiercely blowing the topsoil toward the house. Four adults were enjoying Dominoes and drinking cold lemonade at home, with a fan going on the back porch. The father-in-law suddenly broke the peaceful gathering by proposing to go to Abilene for dinner. One man among the four did not like the idea – Abilene is 53 miles away, there was a dust storm and heat, and the car was not air-conditioned. Before he clarified and articulated his thoughts, his wife and subsequently his mother-in-law acclaimed the proposal. The man did not want to discourage their enthusiasm and so followed them into the car. They suffered the brutal heat and the West Texas dust, and just ended up with mediocre food in Abilene. This 106-mile trip took four hours, and all of them were exhausted when they returned home to Coleman. After a while, the mother-in-law began to blame the other three for being overly enthusiastic about the terrible trip because she wanted to stay at home all along. The man said that he did not want to go but only did so to satisfy the rest. The wife said the two men wanted to go and she just wanted to be sociable and to keep them happy. The father explained with anger that he thought all the others became bored, so he proposed the dinner trip. Actually, he preferred to play games and eat at home.

The irony in the Abilene Paradox results from people's misperceptions of each other's desires and their failure to accurately communicate their beliefs with each other (Harvey, 1974). Chinese people's tendency to avoid conflict may also arise from this mechanism of falling into one's misperception: People do not directly communicate with each other but just conjecture how others will respond. With interpersonal harmony as the priority goal in their culture, Chinese people often assume, inaccurately, that others will be easily offended if they do not behave properly. This perceptual illusion of others' reactions leads to conflict avoidance.

Given that anticipated negativity of others' responses to direct confrontation could be an illusion, it might be possible to reduce and even eliminate it. In a series of studies, we sought to accomplish this goal by asking participants to engage in a perspective-taking exercise. Because perceptions from perspectives of the lender and the borrower are markedly different, we believe that asking participants to play the role of the borrower could attenuate or eliminate the negativity illusion. After this perspective-taking exercise, participants indicated what they would do if somebody borrowed money from them and did not return it.

In one study, we assigned managers in one of the two experimental groups. Managers in the first group responded to the loan scenario by indicating what they would do if a colleague did not return the borrowed money. Managers in the other group read the same scenario, but, before indicating what they would do, they were asked to spend 3 minutes on a perspective-taking exercise. The instructions of the exercise were as follows: "Imagine in the situation, it is you who borrowed the money from the colleague, and the colleague directly asked you to return the money. Please write down your feelings or responses."

The results are revealing. In the first (control) condition, among the 39 managers, only 8 (20.5%) decided to directly ask for the money back, 17 (43.6%) would never ask for the money back, and 14 (35.9%) would try other ways to get the money back. In the second (perspective-taking) condition, of the 34 managers in this condition, 14 (41.2%) decided to directly ask for the money back, 12 (35.3%) would never ask for the money back, and 8 (23.5%) would try other ways to get the money back. In other words, after the perspective-taking exercise, more managers would directly ask for their money back, and fewer managers would not ask for the money back or use indirect ways.

THEORETICAL CONTRIBUTIONS AND PRACTICAL IMPLICATIONS

Theoretical Contributions

Our research extends the existing knowledge on Chinese conflict resolution styles. Previous research has shown that, relative to their Western counterparts, Chinese people have a greater tendency to avoid and not to confront conflicts. Few studies, however, have examined the specific symbolic elements in Chinese culture that explain such cultural difference. Culture is an elusive concept. Unless specific symbolic elements of Chinese culture are identified to be responsible for the observed cultural difference, attributing a cultural difference to culture risks making a tautological argument. In our research, we advance this literature by pinpointing concern for relationships as the specific cultural concern that is responsible for Chinese people's greater tendency to avoid conflict.

In addition, past research has not yet revealed the mechanism through which Chinese culture influences people's conflict resolution strategy choice. Our research fills this gap and suggests that Chinese people's concern for relationships makes them anticipate negative relationship consequences of direct confrontation, which in turn leads to conflict avoidance. We suggest that excessive concern with the relationship costs of confrontation may discourage Chinese people from acknowledging the presence of a conflict, openly exploring the conflict in discussion, and taking constructive actions to resolve it. Thus, our research links a major cultural concern (concern for relationships) to appraisal of conflict situations (anticipated relationship costs in the situation) and people's conflict resolution strategy choice (avoid or confront the conflict). This model is particularly useful for deepening the understanding of the processes and mechanisms that mediate Chinese people's tendency to avoid conflict. As shown in our research, after we have established the empirical support for this link, we are well-positioned to design interventions to reduce overestimation of relationship costs of direct confrontation and to lead Chinese people to manage conflicts more openly and directly.

Finally, our research has implications regarding the relationship between culture and human behavior. Chiu and Hong (2006) defined culture as a network of knowledge that is produced, distributed, and reproduced among a collection of interconnected people. Taking this definition of culture, Chiu and Chen (2004) advanced the view that people, as carriers of culture, can either create a culture guiding their social practices or disidentify and change a culture. According to this view, people do not passively receive cultural influences. Rather, they also create a culture to efficiently solve complex social problems that require smooth coordination of social actions (Chiu & Chen, 2004; Chiu & Hong, 2006; Cohen, 2001; Fiske, 2000).

Our research provides an instructive illustration of this knowledge perspective to culture (Chiu & Hong, 2006). Chinese culture privileges interpersonal harmony. People are led by this shared cultural concern to expect high relationship costs of direct confrontation. Although the perceived relationship costs of direct confrontation are exaggerated, most people in Chinese culture take it for granted that others will react negatively when confronted directly. Despite the illusory nature of such perceptions and the fact that the lender will lose a considerable amount of money for not confronting the borrower, most Chinese people submit themselves to the influence of these perceptions and do not ask for the money back. This example underscores the influence of culture as an intersubjective reality, even when the intersubjective reality is divorced from the objective reality (see Chapter 3, this volume). These cultural processes create a double irony: Because most Chinese people take it for granted that the intersubjective assumption regarding the relationship costs is valid, they adhere to the culturally prescribed practice of conflict avoidance, only to find out later that they have lost money without actually addressing the conflict or improving the relationship.

Our results also show that culture does not rigidly determine people's behaviors. When given the opportunity to critically reflect on the negative implications of a well-established cultural practice, as when the participants in our studies were given the perspective-taking exercise, many Chinese people are able to adopt an alternative conflict management strategy that is more adaptive than the culturally prescribed one. This finding suggests that even a dominant cultural practice could be changed when people are guided to reflect critically on the limitations of the prevailing cultural practice as a device for coordinating social actions among people.

All these research findings suggest that culture is malleable. Indeed, there are reports on radical changes in Chinese people's social values (see McEwen, Fang, Zhang, & Burkholder, 2006). In particular, younger people in China have stronger desires than the older generation to express their individuality, give priority to their personal rights, and follow their wishes (Zhang, 2007). The emerging values may become a new intersubjective reality in China – one that may have authority over behaviors, particularly among Chinese people who accept this new reality.

Signs of such cultural changes are evident in young Chinese college students' responses to our loan scenario. When we compared the loan scenario responses of undergraduates at Peking University with those of middle-aged managers, after controlling for the perceived value of the loan, we found a significant difference between the two samples in both the likelihood of adopting the direct approach and perceived relationship costs: Compared to middle-aged managers, college students are more likely to take a direct approach to conflict resolution and anticipate smaller relationship costs of the direct approach. It has also been demonstrated that, in Hong Kong, where people have been exposed to Western cultural values for many years, engineers and managers now tend to use a confrontational style to manage conflicts (Cheung & Chuah, 2000). These emerging cultural norms regarding interpersonal relationships among the younger generations and in the more Westernized regions of China may increase the variability of conflict resolution styles within China.

Practical Implications

Our research findings have implications for conflict management and resolution in both ordinary social life and organizational settings. When people who are interdependent have different needs, preferences, and interests, conflicts are likely to emerge. Although, on the surface, avoiding conflicts seems useful for maintaining a harmonious relationship between the disputants, it just suppresses the conflicts. An unresolved conflict may disrupt future interactions and lead to accumulation of more conflicts and escalation of hidden ones. As a result, the relationship could be adversely affected.

Put differently, the intention to avoid conflict for the purpose of maintaining interpersonal harmony could backfire and disrupt interpersonal harmony (Zhang, 2005). As a general rule to manage conflicts, people should recognize the conflict and work together constructively to find mutually acceptable solutions. Obsession with avoiding negative interpersonal consequences of taking a direct approach to conflict resolution can also create an unnecessary psychological burden that prevents people from managing conflicts effectively.

In organizations, conflict management and resolution is particularly important because conflict could hurt organizational performance and employees' job satisfaction (Tjosvold, 1985). Avoiding conflict is counterproductive, and often leads to poor and self-defeating decisions. In organizational settings, the desire to avoid conflict will be particularly strong because of the presence of hierarchical relationships, pressure to conform to peers, and the presence of organizational politics. Zhang (2005) has described a case in which the human resources committee of a company in China recruited an unqualified employee whose application package was delivered to the committee from the Chief Executive Officer (CEO). Although all five committee members were confident that the person was not qualified for the job, they did not express their opinions. All of them assumed that the CEO seriously recommended this person and they expected that other committee members also shared this view. Thus they all agreed to offer this candidate the job. They blamed each other for the decision later when the CEO announced that he was surprised at the hiring decision.

When an organization's members are unwilling to express what they think and believe, they will develop inaccurate perceptions of each other's opinions. If the organizational climate or culture discourages members from expressing conflicting opinions out of the fear of being viewed by others as being uncooperative or unsupportive to the superiors, the survival of the organization is at risk. To enhance an organization's members' understanding of each other and to improve the quality of organizational decision making, it is crucial to encourage the members to engage in open discussions and to constructively express their views on controversial issues.

REFERENCES

Agho, A. O., Price J. L., & Mueller, C. W. (1992). Discriminant validity of measures of job satisfaction, positive affectivity and negative affectivity. *Journal of Occupational and Organizational Psychology, 65*, 185–196.

Cai, D. A., & Fink, E. L. (2002). Conflict style differences between individualists and collectivists. *Communication Monographs, 69*, 67–87.

Cheung, C. C., & Chuah, K. B. (2000). Intergroup conflict management framework for Hong Kong's manufacturing industry. *Engineering Management Journal, 12,* 26–33.

Chiu, C-y. (1991a). Hierarchical social relations and justice judgment among Hong Kong Chinese college students. *Journal of Social Psychology, 131,* 885–887.

Chiu, C-y. (1991b). Righteousness: The notion of justice in Chinese societies. In C. F. Yang & H. S. R. Kao (Eds.), *Chinese people and Chinese mind: The cultural tradition* (pp. 261–285). Taipei, Taiwan: Yuan-Liu Publishing Co. (in Chinese).

Chiu, C-y., & Chen, J. (2004). Symbols and interactions: Application of the CCC model to culture, language, and social identity. In S. H. Ng, C. Candlin, & C. Chiu (Eds.), *Language matters*. Hong Kong: City University of Hong Kong Press.

Chiu, C-y., & Hong, Y. (1997). Justice from a Chinese perspective. In H. S. R. Kao & D. Sinha (Eds.), *Asian perspectives on psychology* (pp. 164–184). New Delhi, India: Sage Publications.

Chiu, C-y., & Hong, Y. (2006). *Social Psychology of Culture*. New York: Psychology Press.

Chua, E. G., & Gudykunst, W. B. (1987). Conflict resolution styles in low- and high-context cultures. *Communications Research Reports, 4,* 32–37.

Cohen, D. (2001). Cultural variation: Considerations and implications. *Psychological Bulletin, 127,* 451–471.

Fiske, A. P. (2000). Complementarity theory: Why human social capacities evolved to require cultural complements? *Personality and Social Psychology Review, 4,* 76–94.

Friedman, R., Chi, S. C., & Liu. L. A. (2006). An expectancy model of Chinese-American differences in conflict-avoiding. *Journal of International Business Studies, 37,* 76–91.

Harvey, J. B. (1974). The Abilene Paradox: The management of agreement. *Organizational Dynamics, Summer,* 63–80.

Ho, D. Y. F., Chan, S. J., & Chiu, C-y. (1991). Relational orientation: An inquiry on the methodology of Chinese social psychology. In K. S. Yang & K. K. Hwang (Eds.), *Chinese psychology and behavior* (pp. 49–66). Taipei, Taiwan: Kuei-Kuan Publishing Co. (in Chinese).

Ho, D. Y. F., Chen, S. F. F., & Zhang, Z. X. (2001). Metarelational analysis: An answer to "What is Asian about Asian social psychology?" *Journal of Psychology in Chinese Societies, 2,* 7–26.

Hofstede, G. (1980). *Culture's consequences*. Beverly Hills, CA: Sage.

Hull, D. B., & Schroeder, H. E. (1979). Some interpersonal effects of assertion, nonassertion and aggression. *Behavioral Therapy, 10,* 20–28.

Hwang, K. K. (1987). Face and favor: The Chinese power game. *American Journal of Sociology, 92,* 944–974.

Jacobs, B. J. (1979). A preliminary model of particularistic ties in Chinese political alliance: "Renqing" and "guanxi" in a rural Taiwanese Township. *China Quarterly, 78,* 237–273.

Kazdin, A. E. (1974). Effects of covert modeling and model reinforcement on assertive behavior. *Journal of Abnormal Psychology, 83,* 240–252.

Kelly, J. A., St. Lawrence, J. S., Bradlyn, A. S., Himadi, W. G., Graves, K. A., & Keane, T. M. (1982). Interpersonal reactions to assertive and unassertive styles when handling social conflict situations. *Journal of Behavior Therapy and Experimental Psychiatry, 13,* 33–40.

Kozan, M. K. (1997). Culture and conflict management: A theoretical framework. *International Journal of Conflict Management, 8,* 338–360.

Leung, K. (1987). Some determinants of reaction to procedural models for conflict resolution: A cross-national study. *Journal of Personality and Social Psychology, 53,* 898–908.

Leung, K. (1997). Negotiation and reward allocations across cultures. In P. E. Christopher & M. Erez (Eds.), *New perspectives on international industrial organizational psychology* (pp. 640–675). San Francisco: New Lexington.

Leung, K., & Bond, M. H. (1984). The impact of cultural collectivism on reward allocation. *Journal of Personality and Social Psychology, 47,* 793–804.

McEwen, W., Fang, X., Zhang, C., & Burkholder, R. (2006). Inside the mind of the Chinese consumer. *Harvard Business Review, March,* 1–7.

McFall, R. M., & Lillesand, D. (1971). Behavior rehearsal with modeling and coaching in assertive training. *Journal of Abnormal Psychology, 77,* 313–323.

Morris, M. W., Willians, K. Y., Leung, K., Larrick, R., Mendoza, M. T., Bhatnagar, D., et al. (1998). Conflict management style: Accounting for cross-national differences. *Journal of International Business Studies, 29,* 729–748.

Ohbuchi, K-I., Fukushima, O., & Tedeschi, J. T. (1999). Cultural values in conflict management: Goal orientation, goal attainment, and tactics decision. *Journal of Cross-Cultural Psychology, 30,* 51–71.

Rahim, M. A. (1983). A measure of styles of handling interpersonal conflict. *Academy of Management Journal, 26,* 368–376.

Singelis, T. M. (1994). The measurement of independent and interdependent self-construals. *Personality and Social Psychology Bulletin, 20,* 580–591.

Swap, W. C., & Rubin, J. Z. (1983). Measurement of interpersonal orientation. *Journal of Personality and Social Psychology, 44,* 208–219.

Thomas, R. L., & Kenneth, T. W. (1976). Support for a two-dimensional model of conflict behavior. *Organizational Behavior and Human Performance, 16,* 142–155.

Ting-Toomey, S., Gao, G., Trubisky, P., Yang, Z., Kim, H. S., Lin, S. L., et al. (1991). Culture, face maintenance, and styles of handling interpersonal conflict: A study of five cultures. *International Journal of Conflict Management, 2,* 275–292.

Tjosvold, D. (1985). Implications of controversy research for management. *Journal of Management, 11,* 21–37.

Tjosvold, D., & Sun, H. (2002). Understanding conflict avoidance: Relationship, motivation, actions, and consequences. *International Journal of Conflict Management, 13,* 142–164.

Triandis, H. C. (1994). *Culture and social behavior.* New York: McGraw-Hill.

Woolfolk, R. L., & Dever, S. (1979). Perceptions of assertion: An empirical analysis. *Behavioral Therapy, 10,* 404–411.

Yang, K. S. (1995). Chinese social orientation: An integrative analysis. In T. Y. Lin, W. S. Tseng, & E. K. Yeh (Eds.), *Chinese societies and mental health* (pp. 19–39). Hong Kong: Oxford University Press.

Zhang, Z. X. (2001). The effects of frequency of social interaction and relationship closeness on reward allocation. *Journal of Psychology, 135,* 154–164.

Zhang, Z. X. (2005). Renqing and conflict: Doing harms with a good intention. *PKU Business Review, May*, 133–137 (in Chinese).

Zhang, Z. X. (2006). Chinese conceptions of justice and reward allocation. In U. Kim, K. S. Yang, & K. K. Hwang (Eds.), *Indigenous and cultural psychology: Understanding people in context* (pp. 403–420). New York: Springer.

Zhang, Z. X. (2007). The barrier to organizational harmony: Mismatch between managers and employees in mindset. *PKU Business Review, January*, 24–29 (in Chinese).

Zhang, Z., & Yang, C. F. (1998). Beyond distributive justice: The reasonableness norm in Chinese reward allocation. *Asian Journal of Social Psychology*, *1*, 253–269.

Zhang, Z. X., & Yang, C. F. (2001). An investigation of the concept of renqing. In C. F. Yang (Ed.), *Interpersonal relationship, trust, and affect* (pp. 223–246). Taipei: Yuan Liu (in Chinese).

PART FIVE

TRANSCULTURAL PROCESSES

12

Bicultural Identity Negotiation

SUN NO, CHING WAN, MELODY MANCHI CHAO,
JENNIFER L. ROSNER, AND YING-YI HONG

Increased intercultural contacts within and across national boundaries have raised pressing questions for individuals and societies such as: How do individuals make sense of themselves as multicultural beings? How can societies cultivate the benefits of increased heterogeneity within its populace (e.g., creativity and productivity) and simultaneously resolve possible intergroup tensions? How can social policies be formulated to foster an overarching inclusive identity for all members from different ethnic and cultural backgrounds? Consider the fact that the 2005 riots in France (along with a shorter-lived repeat in 2007), and the terrorist attacks in Britain during the summers of 2005 and 2007, can be partially attributed to ethnic minority youths' perceived exclusion from the mainstream society (Sciolino, 2007; Smith, 2005). There is no doubt that high rates of unemployment due to racial and religious discrimination, along with perceptions of police insensitivity, combined to fuel weeks of violence and car burnings across France. The anger and frustration felt by French-born and France-identified youth and by young adults of Arab and African ancestry regarding belonging and acceptance had long preceded these events, however. A *Time Europe Magazine* special report on the cause of the riots provided insight into the tensions behind identity and exclusion: "The young men behind the violence 'are rioting, not because they hate the Republic,' says Dounia Bouzar, an anthropologist who has worked extensively with [public housing project] delinquents, 'but because they want to be included in it'" (Geary & Graff, 2005).

Incidents such as the French riots underscore the pressing need to understand identity negotiations within multicultural settings. Although there have been attempts to examine these processes from a psychological standpoint, these issues have yet to be adequately addressed, and the available research is widely scattered within topics such as immigration, mixed-race peoples, ethnic identity, and intercultural communication. In this chapter, we propose a framework for examining bicultural identity negotiation processes, which we consider to be a subset of multicultural identity negotiation. Our objective in introducing this framework is to stimulate further research on this timely topic in the current era of hyperconnectivity within and across national boundaries. Through our model, we also aim to direct attention to the view of bicultural identities as continuously unfolding coconstructions linked to personal resources, situation-embedded goals, and even specific interaction partners.

Importantly, in discussing the psychological trials and tribulations of individuals who must incorporate multiple social identities into their self-concept, the existing literature predominantly focuses on the *bi*cultural experience and the negotiation of *two* cultural identities. Although this literature is useful such that it applies to many individuals who find themselves "caught between two worlds," we should not allow the terminology to limit our study to *only* bicultural persons. Indeed, although we use the terms "bicultural" and "dual identities" throughout the chapter, the "bicultural" framework presented can most definitely be applied to tricultural persons (e.g., those who must manage their ethnic heritage identity, their new national identity, and their religious identity; see Rosner & Gardner, 2006) and even to multicultural persons.

Beyond the presentation of our framework, the chapter is organized into three main areas of concern with respect to processes surrounding bicultural identity negotiation. The first section deals with the precursors (past and ongoing) to bicultural identity construction: personal characteristics, social structure, and bicultural identity negotiation strategies that continuously update the current construction of the individual's identity via situational salience of either the ethnic or mainstream identity or both. In the second section, we address possible identity negotiation outcomes, which can range from bicultural competence (acting appropriately and effectively in differing cultural environments) to identity ambivalence (the anxious feelings and/or distancing associated with incompletely connected cultural identities). The last section includes a discussion of the changing dynamic of bicultural identity negotiation across the life span and across generations. Implications for social policy are also highlighted.

A FRAMEWORK FOR UNDERSTANDING BICULTURAL IDENTITY NEGOTIATION

Figure 12.1 depicts our general model of bicultural identity negotiation processes. Negotiation necessarily implies goals as well as a certain flexibility

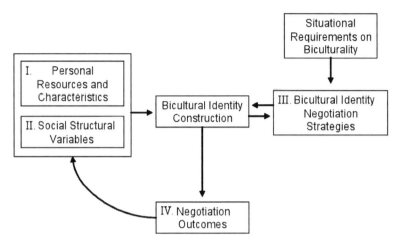

Figure 12.1. Bicultural identity negotiation processes.

of options that can be chosen to meet those goals. Individuals negotiating bicultural identities may choose to emphasize aspects of the self that meet desired goals, whether through explicit, thoughtful decision making (i.e., enrolling in heritage language or history courses) or through implicit, automatic shifts in behavior (i.e., displaying appropriate behaviors in alignment with the cultural context at an all-White university).

The process of negotiating identities is undeniably impacted by the particulars of the situation, such as relevant goals or situational constraints (Ellemers, Spears, & Doosje, 2002), yet there exists a great deal of choice and variation available to individuals (DiMaggio, 1997). The wide range of negotiation strategies available to individuals is a direct result of the variety of personal characteristics (such as beliefs, goals, socialization history), social structural variables (such as social norms and conventions, background context of stereotyping, prejudice, and discrimination), and the specific situations in which individuals find themselves (Deaux, 2000). We argue that personal characteristics, social structural variables, and the particular circumstances of the situation dynamically interact to direct the form that negotiation takes. Thus, bicultural identity negotiation processes vary according to the specific situation, the larger societal context, and the personal resources the individual has at hand. Such a wide range of key variables attests to the fluid nature of bicultural identity negotiation.

For instance, a person living in the United States who is categorized as belonging to a minority culture is requested to educate others about his/her minority heritage culture. Although this person may consider his/her ethnic heritage culture important, he/she may also lack relevant cultural knowledge about this heritage culture. Thus, he/she would negotiate a bicultural identity that emphasizes belonging to the minority cultural group, and he/she would feel positively about the experience if he/she perceived the situation to be a validating one where all those involved affirmed his/her identity as a member of the minority culture. In a different situation, particularly one where the minority culture is viewed unfavorably, this same individual may choose to emphasize his/her mainstream American identity and downplay his/her heritage culture. The following sections of the chapter detail what we mean by social structural variables, personal characteristics, and the situational requirements of the situation, as well as negotiation strategies and outcomes. Before discussing our framework in more depth, however, it is necessary to address the assumptions of our model.

Assumption 1: Cultural self and cultural knowledge are distinct (see Chapter 3, this volume). Identity negotiation strategies depend on cultural knowledge or identification with the cultural group. Our framework purposefully does not specify the placement of the bicultural self (an internally coherent collection of cultural identities) because we see the bicultural self as being either an antecedent or a consequence (or at times both) of engaging in bicultural identity negotiation processes.

Assumption 2: Aside from individual goals to assert, modify, or challenge particular identities, there exist shared goals with interaction partners to arrive at a similar understanding of the situation. We explore this assumption more fully in the subsection "Strategies of Bicultural Identity Negotiation," which deals with communicative goals.

Assumption 3: Individuals negotiate bicultural identities with background motives of maintaining or enhancing self-esteem, continuity, efficacy, and meaning as well as achieving an optimal balance between belongingness and distinctiveness (Brewer, 1991; Vignoles, Regalia, Manzi, Golledge, & Scabini, 2006).

Assumption 4: Negotiation proceeds within a particular cultural context; therefore, negotiation acts are interpreted within the meanings afforded by that particular setting, the situational norms, and the cultural valuation of specific behaviors.

PRECURSORS TO BICULTURAL IDENTITY CONSTRUCTION

As research on bicultural identity construction is scattered across a variety of topic headings, the use of the term *bicultural* is often left vague and undefined. From our perspective, there are multiple ways of being bicultural.

The attributes that are typically used to characterize biculturality by researchers, such as being first- or second-generation immigrants, may not be the only modes of being bicultural. Instead, we posit that individuals are open to define themselves with as many knowledge traditions as deemed necessary to satisfy immediate needs and lifelong goals. Thus, bicultural identities are constructed by immigrants; children of immigrants; biracial individuals; transracial or international adoptees; ethnic, racial, and linguistic minorities; and individuals navigating across socioeconomic class or age categories. In our framework, bicultural identity construction is fueled by the combination of personal characteristics, social structural variables, and ongoing bicultural identity negotiation strategies. By personal characteristics we mean elements such as physical appearance, beliefs (e.g., beliefs concerning the nature of race), and socialization history. By social structural variables we mean background context of stereotyping, prejudice, and discrimination; identity validation versus identity denial; and norms and social conventions. In this section, bicultural identity negotiation processes refer to the variety of methods that bicultural individuals may either habitually or intermittently employ that continuously "update" the current state of bicultural identity construction.

Personal Characteristics

Physical Appearance
Outward features are important in the construction of bicultural identities, as ascribed identities are partially determined by how one looks. In contrast to individuals whose appearance is less like the dominant group, White Americans of various European ethnicities are likely to participate in symbolic ethnicity when it is convenient for them, such as during family celebrations and other leisure time activities (Waters, 1990). Therefore, White Americans, and individuals whose phenotypes more closely match that of White Americans, are less likely to develop a bicultural or multicultural orientation. Conversely, for individuals whose phenotype sets them apart from White Americans, there may be greater pressure both internally and externally (via discrimination and exclusion) to identify as bicultural and display more interest in the ethnic heritage community, despite being multiple generations removed from initial migration (AhnAllen, Suyemoto, & Carter, 2006). Indeed, Vazquez, Garcia-Vazquez, Bauman, and Sierra (1997) have shown that biculturally oriented, darker skinned Latino Americans from a majority fifth-generation sample from the American Southwest were more likely to express interest in the Latino community than were

their counterparts who were lighter skinned. As such, appearances tend to constrain identity options for individuals who look less typical of mainstream members of the society and spur the development of bicultural or ethnic and racial identities (Brunsma & Rockquemore, 2001).

Racial Essentialism

For individuals who are phenotypically distinguishable from mainstream members of a society, race may be a salient feature of interactions with others. Race itself may take on different meanings, as some believe that race is biologically rooted, reflects abilities and traits, and is unchangeable, whereas others believe that race is socially constructed, arbitrary, and fluid across time and contexts (No et al., 2008). Belief in racial essentialism may impede the development of bicultural identities for racial minority individuals, in that what is perceived to be natural is that which is ethnic (Tsang, Irving, Alaggia, Chau, & Benjamin, 2003). For instance, Chao, Chen, Roisman, and Hong (2007) showed that Chinese-American bicultural persons who endorsed racial essentialism had more difficulty in cognitively shifting across American and Chinese cultures and responded with more emotional reactivity when describing experiences with both cultures. These results are thought to relate to perceiving more discreteness and less permeability in cultural boundaries. Belief in racial essentialism may also interact with other variables, such as generational status, to impact bicultural orientations (Hong & No, 2005).

Belongingness Motives

Identity construction is influenced by the fulfillment of multiple motives (Vignoles et al., 2006). Among these motives is the fundamental human need for belonging (Baumeister & Leary, 1995). As identification with a group fulfills the need to belong, people should be more likely to identify with groups that can provide them with a sense of belonging. There is evidence suggesting that bicultural identification is related to a lower level of loneliness among bicultural individuals (Suarez, Fowers, Garwood, & Szapocznik, 1997) and that ethnic identification is related to a sense of self-affirmation and belonging (Yuh, 2005). Also, feelings of exclusion from a cultural group predict lower identification with that group (AhnAllen et al., 2006). Thus, how bicultural individuals negotiate the existence of their two cultural identities could depend on their perceived inclusion in the relevant cultural groups. When there is perceived acceptance by a valued cultural group, the person is more likely to identify with that group. It is also possible that bicultural individuals with a stronger need for belonging would seek to identify more strongly with the two cultural groups to which they belong.

Socialization History

How bicultural individuals negotiate two cultural identities is also affected by the individuals' experiences in environments within and outside of the family. Family environment plays an important role in the socialization of bicultural identity. Children's participation in ethnic cultural behaviors and social networks is influenced by the cultural behaviors and social networks of their parents (Killian & Hegtvedt, 2003). Also, when an ethnic minority family provides a strong ethnic socialization environment, adolescents in that family are more likely to develop a stronger and more mature identification with their ethnic ingroup (McHale et al., 2006; Umaña-Taylor, Bhanot, & Shin, 2006). In studies of adoption, the adopted ethnic minority children's cultural identity is influenced by the adopted parents' ethnicity, attitudes, and perceptions (Andujo, 1988; McRoy, Zurcher, Landerdale, & Anderson, 1982, 1984).

Outside of the family, the neighborhood climate affects the family's socialization process and the possibilities of bicultural identity development. On the one hand, a negative social climate toward minorities directs parents' socialization efforts toward the prejudice and discrimination faced by the group (Caughy, Nettles, O'Campo, & Lohrfink, 2006). On the other hand, a multicultural neighborhood promotes ethnic identification (Garcia & Lega, 1979; Verkuyten, 2004). In a larger societal context, the possibilities for bicultural identity negotiation are affected by the dominant group's view on intercultural contact. In societies where pluralism is promoted, bicultural individuals would have more freedom to develop their two cultural identities and integrate them into one.

Social Structure

Stereotypes, Prejudice, and Discrimination

Stereotypes, prejudice, and discrimination are category-based biases toward members of social groups. These biases are rooted in the assumption that members of a social group are homogenous with little within-group variation and, hence, can be treated interchangeably (Fiske, 2004). Briefly defined, stereotypes are cognitive representations of a particular social group. *Prejudice* refers to the affective components of the category-based responses toward the social group. Discrimination entails biased (and often harmful) actions and behaviors that are directed toward the social group (Fiske, 1998, 2004). Although these three components are closely related, they are not identical concepts. For example, one can endorse the stereotypes of a certain group, but not feel or act positively or negatively toward members of the group. One can also feel negatively toward a group without linking that feeling to specific stereotypical representations. In general, however, these cognitive, affective, and behavioral biases go together. Specifically, prejudice correlates more highly with discriminative behaviors than do stereotypes (Dovidio, Brigham, Johnson, & Gaertner, 1996).

Stereotypes, prejudice, and discrimination do not only set up the environment in which bicultural individuals negotiate their cultural identities – they also help individuals organize and make sense of the world in which they live, and color the lens through which bicultural individuals look at the world, others, and the self.

The stereotypes, prejudice, and discrimination associated with certain ethnocultural groups can be positive (e.g., Asian Americans as a hardworking and high-achieving model minority) or negative (e.g., Arab Americans as suspicious terrorists). Although these biases were not formed without any (historical or political) basis, treating any single individual member of a group as representative of the group and as highly interchangeable with other members of that group is prone to error and could lead to negative social and psychological consequences, even if the biases are positive (Deaux, 2006). For example, in an ethnically diverse American school setting, teachers might show preferential treatment toward Asian students over other ethnic minority students (e.g., Latinos, African Americans) based on the model minority belief. As a result of this differential treatment, the interethnic group boundary will become salient, resulting in discriminatory treatment not only from the teachers, but also among students from different ethnic groups (Rosenbloom & Way, 2004). In this context, ingroup–outgroup boundaries become salient. Subsequently, polarization of attitudes and escalation of group conflicts are not uncommon consequences. Furthermore, on an individual level, when group boundaries are made chronically salient and when one's ethnicity becomes perceptually distinctive in the environment, the individual's ethnic identity becomes a central part of the self (McGuire, McGuire, Child, & Fujioka, 1978; Turner, Hogg, Oakes, Reicher, & Wetherell, 1987), and might lead the person to adopt different identity negotiation strategies.

Stereotype Threat

Category-based biases not only influence individuals through intergroup perceptions and interethnic relationships, they can also have direct and profound effects on an individual's behavior – from test performance (Aronson et al., 1999; Spencer, Steele, & Quinn, 1999; Steele & Aronson, 1995) to athletic performance (Stone, Lynch, Sjomeling, & Darley, 1999). Claude Steele and colleagues (Aronson et al., 1999; Steele & Aronson, 1995) coined the term *stereotype threat* to describe this phenomenon. Stereotype threat is a "threat in the air." When the stereotypes of a group become personally relevant for members of that group in a specific situation, the individuals might become anxious about being judged in terms of these group stereotypes. Consequently, the threat of this lurking unearned judgment leads to a reduction in performance in domains with which an individual personally identifies. For example, an African-American student in an elite school might show a decrement in test performance when the potential for him to be judged as academically inferior is made salient. This perceived threat would have implications for the individual's personal as well as social identity.

Identity Threat and Identity Denial
Stereotypes can also propagate discriminative behaviors toward minority groups, with or without an individual's conscious awareness, and can threaten one's social identity. For example, the stereotype of Asian Americans as model minorities might appear positive, and at first glance might seem to glorify Asian Americans' success over other ethnic minority groups. Nonetheless, the label of "minority" inevitably implies that Asian Americans are considered "less American" than other Americans, as demonstrated across a series of studies (Cheryan & Monin, 2005; Devos & Banaji, 2005). A question as simple as, "Where are you *really* from?" and an apparently friendly remark such as, "Your English is really good!" from a fellow American student sends signals to individuals that their identity as American is not recognized by other group members. In response to this instance of denial, individuals should strategize to reaffirm their social identity (Cheryan & Monin, 2005).

Race-Based Rejection Sensitivity
Stereotypes, prejudice, and discrimination exert their influence on an individual to the extent that the individual is aware of the stereotypes regarding his or her own group and is sensitive to the potential negative consequences (Mendoza-Denton, Downey, Purdie, Davis, & Pietrzak, 2002; Pinel, 1999). Research has shown that African-American students who are sensitive to race-based rejection experienced greater discomfort around their professors and demonstrated a lower feeling of belongingness toward the college. They also reported more distrust toward the institution's administration (Mendoza-Denton et al., 2002). Although these particular studies were conducted within the university setting, when the findings were applied to the larger social institutional context, they suggested that rejection sensitivity might lead individuals to distrust the social institution constructed by the

dominant groups and to decrease their sense of belongingness. These feelings of distrust and detachment often lead to marginalization or separation.

STRATEGIES OF BICULTURAL IDENTITY NEGOTIATION

Cultural identity for bicultural individuals is a complex construct as they experience two cultural identities at the same time. Each cultural identity is associated with a set of shared cultural knowledge and norms, behavioral expectations, social relationships, and emotional ties. When two cultural identities coexist, the associations of the identities might be overlapping and compatible, or separate and conflicting. Bicultural individuals often find themselves trying to reconcile the presence of the two cultural identities, and individuals vary in how they negotiate the existence of the two cultural identities. In this section, we discuss the strategies that bicultural individuals might adopt when engaging in bicultural identity negotiation. The three strategies are alternation, integration, and synergy (Hong, Wan, No, & Chiu, 2007). The focus of this discussion is on the possible ways that people might handle two cultural identities at the same time. In doing so, we are aware that some individuals with extensive experience in two cultures identify with only one culture [e.g., Berry's (2001) assimilation and separation strategies] or do not identify at all with either culture [e.g., Berry's (2001) marginalization strategy]. Our interest, however, is in the complexity that is a result of dealing with two cultural identities within the same person. To this end, Berry's model may not be useful as it is more relevant for static, end-result strategies than for dynamic processes involving situation-to-situation negotiation between personal goals and social interaction demands. To fill this void, we elaborate on the aforementioned three modes of bicultural identity negotiation and explain that each represents a different level of overlap between a bicultural individual's heritage and mainstream identities. These modes are not mutually exclusive, however. A bicultural individual most likely engages in all three at different points in time depending on the situation. These modes complement each other in describing the complex experience of the life of a bicultural individual.

Alternation

With alternation, the bicultural individual switches back and forth between two cultural identities without seeing much overlap between the two cultures (LaFromboise, Coleman, & Gerton, 1993; Phinney & Devich-Navarro, 1997). Bicultural individuals are able to, and often do, switch between two modes of behavior depending on situational demands. They adopt the language, problem-solving strategy, social behavior, response style, and self-description that are characteristic of one of the two cultures so as to create a context-dependent cultural identity(e.g., Gardner, Gabriel, & Dean, 2004; LaFromboise & Rowe, 1983; Ross, Xun, & Wilson, 2002, Verkuyten & Pouliasi, 2002). For example, immigrants often find themselves speaking the language and participating in rituals of their heritage culture while at home and speaking the language and adopting the practices of the host culture while at school or work. Behavioral alternation is possible because bicultural individuals possess knowledge about the two cultures and can switch between the two cultural frames depending on the situational salience of the two cultures (Hong, Morris, Chiu, & Benet-Martínez, 2000). After being activated, a cultural frame would guide a person's behavior whenever applicable (Hong, Benet-Martínez, Chiu, & Morris, 2003).

Cultural frame switching is only part of cultural identity switching. Alternation, when applied to cultural identity, has the bicultural individual keep the two cultural identities separate. Instead of a hyphenated identity, the person often compartmentalizes the two cultural identities and sees the self as exclusively of one culture or the other depending on the situation (Roccas & Brewer, 2002). Alternation of cultural identities is also situational in that bicultural individuals would feel one identity strongly in one situation and the other more strongly in another situation. For example, Chinese-American adolescents feel more Chinese on days when they engage in behaviors that remind them of their ethnic culture, such as speaking Chinese or eating Chinese food (Yip & Fuligni, 2002). In another study, Greek- and Italian-Australian adolescents report feeling strong Greek/Italian identity when they are with their family and participating in social activities with others from their ethnic ingroup, and feeling strong Australian identification when they are with their Australian friends (Rosenthal & Hrynevich, 1985). Alternation occurs when the two cultures are seen as different from each other and are difficult to combine as one. They do not necessarily entail perceived conflict between the two cultural identities. Nonetheless, the bicultural individual would be sensitive to the differences between the two cultures and feel the need to choose one of the two in particular situations.

Integration

When bicultural individuals see similarity and overlap between their two cultures, they can integrate the two identities into their bicultural self. The resulting identity is a hyphenated one in which the two cultural identities are blended and combined so that the person is equally both (Birman, 1998; Phinney & Devich-Navarro, 1997). Integration has received much attention in the literature on intercultural contact. In his framework of intercultural contact, Berry (2001) identified the two major concerns that individuals have during intercultural contact as maintaining (a) the heritage culture and (b) a good relationship with the host culture. Different levels of fulfillment of these two concerns give rise to four acculturative styles. Integration occurs when a person maintains the heritage culture and a good relationship with the host culture, identifying with both cultures at the same time. Integration as conceptualized in Berry's model has arguably received the most attention in the literature. His conceptualization, however, is very much silent on the blending of two cultures into a cohesive one, which is an important element of an integrated bicultural identity. On a more relevant note, Benet-Martínez and colleagues developed the construct of bicultural identity integration (Benet-Martínez & Haritatos, 2005; Benet-Martínez, Leu, Lee, & Morris, 2002), which tackles directly the issue of compatibility and cohesion of bicultural identities. Bicultural individuals who score high on the bicultural identity integration measure developed by Benet-Martinez and Haritatos (2005) see the two cultural identities as similar and compatible, whereas those who score low see the two identities as different and conflicting. Interestingly, the level of bicultural identity integration is not related to adoption of Berry's integration strategy (Benet-Martínez & Haritatos, 2005). The finding that bicultural identity integration and integration strategy is unrelated is not surprising, as Berry's framework does not directly deal with the cohesion of two identities.

Integration is similar to alternation in that elements of both cultures are present in the individual and that situational cues can trigger elements of one of the two cultures. Integration and alternation differ, however, in how the cultural elements and the corresponding cultural identities are organized within the individual. With alternation, the two identities are kept separate without much overlapping whereas, with integration, the two identities are mixed into one unitary bicultural identity. A Chinese-American bicultural person who alternates would refer to the self as Chinese in some contexts and American in some other contexts. In contrast, the same bicultural person when integrating would refer to the self as Chinese American.

Synergy

Synergy takes the blending of two cultures to a new level. In addition to blending the elements of the two cultures into one, a new culture that is distinct from the two origin cultures is formed as a result. This is akin to the idea of fusion (LaFromboise et al., 1993; Phinney & Devich-Navarro, 1997) and hybridity (Anthias, 2001) in the literature, as cultural elements are combined and synthesized to produce new forms. The process can best be exemplified in the process of Creolization. Creolization in language happens when groups speaking different languages have extended contact and develop a common language that has its basis in the different languages spoken by the original groups but is distinct from both as an end product. Creolization also refers to the formation of a new culture with inputs from the contacting groups' various cultures of origin. A new common identity is often formed surrounding the Creole language and culture. Examples can be found on islands in the Caribbean and Indian Ocean (e.g., Medea, 2002) and in Louisiana in the United States (Dubois & Melançon, 2000).

Much research has been done on the linguistic characteristics of Creoles. Not much empirical study in psychology has been conducted, however, to examine the formation of a bicultural identity based on synergy. Along this vein, we have started a line of research that examines cultural hybridization for Korean Americans and Chinese Americans (No, Wan, & Chiu, 2005). With continuous contact with mainstream American culture and the specific cultural experience of ethnic minorities, it is possible that the Korean or Chinese culture that early immigrants brought to the United States has been transformed beyond a mere addition of American cultural elements. This transformation might create a Korean or Chinese American culture that is more than the summation of the culture from Korea or China and the culture of the United States. If this is the case, then individuals who identify themselves as Korean American or Chinese American would endorse a knowledge tradition that is unique to Korean or Chinese American culture.

What are the situational antecedents that would lead bicultural individuals to use the alternation, integration, or synergy mode of identity negotiation? Most research on bicultural identity negotiation has focused on the acculturative strategies that bicultural individuals adopt in general across situations. The question of how two cultural identities may be negotiated in specific situations has not been explored in the literature, however. Next, we provide some preliminary insights into this very issue.

AN EXAMPLE OF WHAT WE MEAN BY "SITUATION": COMMUNICATIVE GOALS AND IDENTITY NEGOTIATION

Social interaction is an important channel for cultural knowledge exchange and negotiation. Communication requires the building of a shared reality and the use of such shared reality as common ground for fluent interaction between interlocutors (Clark & Brennan, 1991; Higgins, 1992). Information is successfully exchanged and relationships positively maintained if interlocutors accommodate each other's linguistic and nonlinguistic characteristics (Gallois, Ogay, & Giles, 2005). When people communicate with fellow members of their cultural group, the shared cultural knowledge that all parties understand and the shared norms by which the parties abide would be expended as the basis for successful communication. Arguably, bicultural individuals' social interaction platforms are often culturally more diverse and complex than those experienced by individuals whose cultural experience is predominantly reserved to one culture. Bicultural individuals often face situations that differ in the dominance of one of the two cultures or they may experience cultural salience of both cultures at the same time. For example, a second-generation Chinese American teenager might face a predominantly American cultural environment while at school, but a predominantly Chinese environment while at home with parents and relatives. When the Chinese American student socializes with fellow second-generation Chinese American teenagers, the cultural setting might become a mix of both Chinese and American cultures, instead of having one of the two cultures as dominant. These varied cultural platforms create different situational demands for particular identity negotiation strategies.

If successful communication requires interlocutors to accommodate to one another, then one might expect bicultural individuals to assimilate their identity negotiation strategy to the cultural perspective dominant within the particular social situation. Along this line, Tadmor and Tetlock (2006) have proposed a model that captures such assimilation in the exploration of the influence of accountability on the development of bicultural identity. According to the model, acculturating individuals experience accountability pressures as their daily social interactions require them to adhere to certain cultural knowledge that the interaction audience holds. In doing so, the chosen identity negotiation strategy would depend on the cultural membership of that audience. On the one hand, when the bicultural individual is accountable to an audience holding only one of the two cultural perspectives, the individual would likely adopt the one culture that is shared with the audience, instead of integrating the two cultures into one. On the other hand, when the individual is accountable to a mixed audience holding at least two different cultural perspectives, the demands of the mixed audience requires the person to somehow integrate the two cultural perspectives into one, which would likely result in integration or synergy. Thus, if a bicultural individual is often exposed to monocultural audiences, then alternation might be more frequently observed. If the individual is often exposed to audiences who also hold an integrated or synergistic bicultural perspective, however, the individual might follow suit in his or her identity negotiation.

The propositions just discussed assume an assimilation motive in which the individual's communication style accommodates the cultural perspective of the audience for successful communication and social approval. People do not always hold assimilation motives during communication, however; rather, communication can be used to accentuate the difference in social identities between interlocutors (Gallois et al., 2005). It is possible for bicultural individuals to actively choose to contrast themselves from the cultural perspective of the audience. Specifically, when faced with an audience from predominantly one cultural perspective, the individual might want to assert the existence of the other culture, the possibility of integrating the two cultures, or even create a new culture beyond the combination of the two. Similarly, when faced with an audience that presents a mix of the cultures, a desire to separate the self from the audience might result in the individual choosing between one of the two cultures instead of integrating the two.

In short, the choice of the three identity negotiation strategies – alternation, integration, and synergy – could be a function of the situational demands on communicators and the assimilation-versus-contrast social motives that the communicators hold. Extant research is lacking in this area. Further research that treats bicultural identity negotiation as a dynamic process that could change depending on situational demands and the individual's current motivations would be needed to test these ideas.

POSSIBLE OUTCOMES OF BICULTURAL IDENTITY NEGOTIATION STRATEGIES

A broad range of outcomes is possible through engagement in bicultural identity negotiation strategies. On the more positive end of the spectrum, intensive experiences with two cultures may lead to bicultural competence or the flexible display of culturally appropriate behaviors. On the negative end, individuals may experience identity ambivalence, identity conflict, marginalization, and alienation. Here we focus on outcomes to the individual, rather than to society, and the last section of the chapter includes a discussion of the society-level ramifications and social policy implications of biculturalism.

Bicultural Competence

Through repeated practice in negotiation interactions across diverse settings, individuals may acquire effective language, social, and behavioral skills to adjust to different cultural contexts (LaFromboise et al., 1993). Individuals may also integrate their different identity components (Amiot, de la Sablonnière, Terry, & Smith, 2007). According to Haritatos and Benet-Martínez (2002), being biculturally competent is much the same as having a biculturally integrated identity, such that individuals see both of their cultural identities as well-matched and non-antagonistic, and have little difficulty in integrating both cultures into everyday thought and behavior. Thus, individuals may become more adaptive and flexible as they engage in bicultural identity negotiation strategies, particularly alternation strategies (Bacallao & Smokowski, 2005) and integration strategies. For example, acting as language and cultural brokers for parents and other family members may allow for greater facility in dual languages as well as for becoming more informed of subtle and nuanced knowledge of both cultures (Trickett & Jones, 2007).

Identity Ambivalence

Identity ambivalence may result from others' fluctuating responses to strategies employed by individuals negotiating bicultural identities. Depending on the salient identity features of a context (Turner, 1982), individuals may be approached with intimacy and familiarity in one context and responded to with fear and distance by the same person in another context (Zaharna, 1989). These inconsistencies in how others relate to the self may lead to further ambivalence, as one develops simultaneous approach–avoidance orientation toward one's dual cultural identities ("We got the best of both worlds, we got the worst of both worlds; nevertheless, we are stigmatized, rejected, and told that we don't belong to either world" in Vivero & Jenkins, 1999). In a similar vein, identity ambivalence may result from intragroup conflicts among newly arrived and established cultural groups that settle within the same geographical area. For the newly arrived immigrants, perceived exclusion by the more established group disrupts the "natural" sense of affiliation experienced when around similar others (Castillo, Conoley, Brossart, & Quiros, 2007).

Identity Confusion and Conflict

Identification with multiple cultural groups engenders psychological conflict when values and practices of heritage and mainstream cultural groups are perceived to be too distant or in opposition (Benet-Martínez et al., 2002). Confusion and conflict may also result from others' overt lack of affirmation of one's claim to a bicultural identity (Bryant & LaFromboise, 2005). As with identity ambivalence, identity conflict may arise from experiences of exclusion or rejection by desired cultural groups. Identity conflict may be a more salient experience for younger individuals because of adolescence being a crucial time period for identity exploration and for persons who have not yet achieved an integrated bicultural identity (Shi & Lu, 2007). Biracial individuals may experience identity conflict when they realize that others' perceptions of them do not match their own internal sense of self (Buchanan & Acevedo, 2004).

Cultural Inauthenticity

In repeatedly engaging and participating in multiple cultural systems, individuals may acquire the knowledge and skills necessary to develop repertoires of behaviors, thoughts, and feelings appropriate to each cultural context (Hong, Morris, Chiu, & Benet-Martínez, 2000; LaFromboise et al., 1993). Attainment of cultural knowledge, however, does not preclude the subjective experience of impostorism or inauthenticity, a concept that LaFromboise, Coleman, and Gerton (1993) recognized in their widely cited review article on biculturalism: "Words... such as 'apple,' 'banana,' or 'oreo' reflect the negative stereotype often applied to people who have intimate relationships with two or more cultures" (p. 395). Owing to these commonly held images regarding individuals who reside in the juncture of two or more cultures, competence in one cultural system may be perceived as (cultural) betrayal by an alternative cultural group; bicultural or multicultural persons may not always feel authentic or true when dealing simultaneously with several cultural groups. Their divided loyalties, whether real or imagined, may become internalized to characterize the self as being an inauthentic member of one or multiple cultural groups.

Marginalization and Alienation

In an early analysis of migration and identity, Park (1928) approached the internal conflict and ambivalence arising from identification with multiple cultural groups through the notion of the *marginal man*, a person who feels simultaneous detachment and involvement with multiple cultural groups. The *deficit model* of biculturalism, as Park's (1928) notion of the marginal man has come to be referenced in the literature, has largely been disproved (Padilla, 2006). There is ample qualitative and quantitative evidence, however, that individuals do experience moments of "cultural homelessness" (Vivero & Jenkins, 1999) or profound alienation and social invalidation.

Research in social psychology and related disciplines has provided a strong foundational literature in the area of bicultural identity construction and negotiation, but we now turn to less developed perspectives and lingering questions. Here we focus on how bicultural identity negotiation processes may be examined through developmental perspectives and cross-generational shifts in preferred negotiation strategy. We also explore the policy implications of increasing populations of bicultural and multicultural groups within societies.

Developmental Perspectives

Locating bicultural identity construction within a developmental perspective, we might expect individuals to be prompted to rethink, reevaluate, and recreate their bicultural identity as a result of a number of important developmental transition periods, such as growing into young adulthood, choosing a life partner, and having children. For example, individuals may settle into a predictable pattern of negotiating their bicultural identity in young adulthood but have questions of identity negotiation come to the fore once more when they become a parent and must decide what, if any, cultural heritage they will pass on. Although not all models of racial/ethnic identity development specify a strictly linear progression, bicultural identities may be constructed and understood differently according to the person's particular stage in life. Amiot and colleagues (2007) recently proposed a model of identity development based on neo-Piagetian ideas: Individuals are thought to continuously integrate multiple identities as new cognitive resources emerge across the life span. They posit that, at particular key moments of change in a person's life, certain inhibiting (e.g., threat and uncertainty or status and power) and facilitating (e.g., coping and adaptation) factors may hinder or enhance integration of multiple identities and hence affect motivation and commitment to identities.

Our own framework of bicultural identity negotiation places heavy emphasis on the dynamic interactions of multiple factors in the negotiation and construction of bicultural identities, such as the gender of the individual (Dion & Dion, 2004), birthplace and generational status (if immigrants or sojourners, the cultural and demographic features of the region of settlement; Padilla, 2006), whether of mixed ethnicity or race (Oikawa & Yoshida, 2007) or transracial or international adoptee (Freidlander et al., 2000; Ward, 2006), the relative status of cultural groups within a society as well as the particular socioeconomic status of the individual or family, and the extent of transmission of cultural knowledge and language from the immediate family (Nauck, 2001). Particularly for immigrant groups that are distinguishable by phenotype as being different from the majority group, bicultural identity may initially be constructed on physical differences (Willgerodt, Miller, & McElmurry, 2002). As individuals grow older, experience with discrimination may increase motivation to learn about the ethnic heritage culture (Pahl & Way, 2006).

Despite the different factors implicated in the construction of bicultural identities, the literature is most fully developed with respect to how immigrants and ethnic/racial minorities negotiate bicultural identities over the life course. In one such example, Mahalingam's (2006) developmentally informed model of idealized cultural identities asserts that internalized representations of the ideal cultural being (e.g., woman, student, son) are employed by individuals to meet negotiation goals. As such, our model incorporates findings from the ethnic/racial identity literature in our attempt to elaborate how individuals falling within rough age groups (childhood, adolescence, early adulthood, and late adulthood) negotiate bicultural identities. It is important to note that throughout these periods of development there is substantial variability, which is dependent on the specific context in which individuals find themselves (i.e., at home vs. at school; Bacallao & Smokowski, 2005), and that we only highlight main themes from each age group.

Children who construct dual cultural identities are socialized into two distinct modes of being. Regardless of whether these bicultural children receive cultural knowledge from parents or from teachers and peers, they are taught two languages and aspects of two cultures ranging from the general (values and beliefs) to the particular (holidays and practices surrounding holidays, what being polite means and how to be polite; Vivero & Jenkins, 1999). During childhood, immigrant children may be required to act as translators and cultural brokers (Weisskirch, 2007). Through repeated experiences of mediating between parents and the dominant culture, these children may develop bicultural knowledge and a bicultural identity. In addition, immigrant children may be exposed to prejudice and discrimination for the first time through participation in the public school system.

Parents of second- and later generation immigrant children may also enroll their children in weekend language schools in an effort to have their children retain fluency in the ethnic language (Lu, 2001).

In adolescence, access to dual cultures may lead to greater conflict among bicultural youth in comparison to monocultural youth, as this period is characterized by attempts to resolve the question of "Who am I?" and a greater concern for appearance and interpersonal relationships with peers (Phinney, 1989). Adolescents may receive conflicting messages regarding their identification from parents, other family members, teachers, peers, and the media. Parents and grandparents may exert continued pressure on adolescents to further develop their ethnic language skills, and adolescents may admit to benefits in being fluent in a second language (Shi & Lu, 2007). Adolescents may make use of their knowledge of ethnic heritage language to develop a wider social network, or they may ignore their ethnic culture by disassociating from more recently arrived immigrants (Pyke & Dang, 2003).

Later on, as second-generation individuals leave the home and enter higher education, bicultural identities are reconstructed as these individuals take formal courses in their heritage language and history or attempt to blend in with the majority group (Ethier & Deaux, 1994). Young adults may develop a greater appreciation for their dual cultural orientations with the recognition that fluency in their ethnic language helps them connect with grandparents and extended family and gives them an advantage in their careers (Shi & Lu, 2007). As second-generation individuals transition into careers, choosing partners, and having children, bicultural identities may become more overtly recognized by individuals as being a matter of picking and choosing what is comfortable for them in the current situation (Willgerodt et al., 2002).

In older adulthood, immigrants may again have to transit to a life without (adult) children in the same household. As many immigrant parents rely on their children for language and cultural brokering, along with economic assistance as children grow into employable ages, older immigrants may face the challenge of developing bicultural skills and self-reliance at ages when their nonimmigrant peers are enjoying comfortable retirements (Wong, Yoo, & Stewart, 2006).

The developmental trajectory of bicultural identity negotiation across childhood, adolescence, young adulthood, and older adulthood can be placed within the wider context of intergenerational development of cultural identities. As individuals negotiate bicultural identities in their own lifetimes, their choices may be transferred to their children's generation, which in turn may also affect how their grandchildren negotiate cultural identities. Additionally, choices in negotiation strategies may be due to the juxtaposition of two or more distinct immigrant generations residing in the same location (Buriel, 1993). Rosner and Gardner (2006) explored this potential for a macro-level, cross-generational shift in bicultural identity by examining recent Russian-Jewish immigrants to the United States and third- and later generation American Jews of Eastern European descent. Their results showed that recent Russian-Jewish immigrants who deemed their Jewish identity as central to their self-concept saw less distance between their American and Russian identities. These individuals also used their Jewish identity as a bridge to bring their Russian and American identities together and to develop a more cohesive *tri*cultural identity. In contrast, for established American Jews, a moderate (and marginal) negative relationship was found between Jewish identity centrality and perceived distance between the two national identities, suggesting that, over time, the Jewish identity may either prohibit enhanced assimilation into the American culture or, more favorably, serve to make the American Jew positively distinct from the mainstream American identity.

In total, the findings just mentioned support the claim that differences across the life span and across generations may yield differential reliance on particular negotiation strategies. The first round of results exploring cross-generational comparisons suggests that choice of bicultural identity negotiation strategy may be dependent on current motives to either ease the assimilation process or stand out as distinct from the mainstream. Future research employing developmental perspectives, rather than focusing exclusively on momentary choices, is essential for determining what type of negotiation strategy is employed as well as the reasons for those choices.

Implications for Social Policies

As we saw earlier, several beneficial and detrimental outcomes of bicultural identity negotiation are possible for any given individual. The pressing concern for societies more generally is to identify potential outcomes of biculturalism that are beneficial to all members and then to direct and implement necessary policies to ensure those outcomes. As we have witnessed increases in the worldwide flow of transmigrations, intermarriage across ethnic and religious lines, and cultural hybridization, there have also been associated increases in the voicing of fears that increased biculturalism and multiculturalism may destroy loyalty to the nation and have detrimental effects on the unity of the country. In multicultural countries, it is becoming commonplace to hear disparaging remarks about immigrant *cultural practices* that are perceived as too bizarre in comparison to the dominant group (Ben-Eliezer, 2004). This new brand of modern racism targets cultural elements of difference and argues that they are irreconcilable with the mainstream as to be un-American (or un-Israeli, etc.). These often embittered sentiments highlight the crucial need for society-wide policies to contain and reduce negative consequences of intergroup contact and increase respect and tolerance toward difference.

As such, research suggests that individuals' racial attitudes are malleable, depending on the social contexts in which they are situated (Wolsko, Park, Judd, & Wittenbrink, 2000). In addition, the promotion of multicultural ideology not only helps reduce racial bias (Richeson & Nussbaum, 2004), but it also fosters trust toward the community (Purdie, Steele, Davies, & Crosby, 2001; cited in Steele, Spencer, & Aronson, 2002). Therefore, advocating multicultural policies that encourage different ethnic groups to maintain their own identity while respecting other groups can help reduce intergroup conflict and foster a harmonious society, which in turn provides the context in which individuals negotiate their bicultural identities.

The promotion of biculturalism itself has been argued to allow members of society to more effectively cope with the existence of discrimination, as biculturality encourages flexibility, creativity, and adaptability (Padilla, 2006). Perhaps what is needed are educational interventions directed at *all* children and adolescents, not merely immigrants or ethnic minorities, to promote multiple social identity exploration and experimentation (Quintana, 2007). We may also encourage superordinate categorization with the nation, with the caveat that all subgroup identities are actively valued and kept distinct (Amiot et al., 2007). Such a nationwide policy of embracing biculturalism may minimize both explicit and implicit bias against minority groups, as has been documented with New Zealand Māori and Pākehā (Sibley & Liu, 2007).

Concluding Remarks

In this chapter, we have proposed a framework to understand how bicultural individuals construct and negotiate their cultural identities. Specifically, we examine the roles that individual characteristics (such as belief about race and the motivation to belong) and social structural factors (such as discrimination and rejection) play in the identity negotiation process. We recognize that individuals are active participants of this dynamic process; at the same time, social forces help shape individuals' bicultural experiences.

In sum, the bicultural identity negotiation process is complex. We introduced a framework for understanding how bicultural identities are constructed, coconstructed, negotiated, and renegotiated in ongoing interactions with socially relevant others. We recognize that our framework is rather preliminary in that it does not draw out all causal pathways. Part of the reason for this incompleteness is the highly individualized and situation-dependent nature of bicultural identity negotiation processes; another part is the lack of systematic research into which personal, social, and situational variables produce which bicultural identity strategies and outcomes. Our hope is that this framework will inspire further research into bicultural identity negotiation processes, such that soon there will be a pressing need to modify and refine the framework. Individuals' personal characteristics and sociocultural contexts interplay in shaping bicultural experiences. The model introduced in this chapter represents an initial attempt to integrate research from different areas to better understand this dynamic cultural process.

REFERENCES

AhnAllen, J. M., Suyemoto, K. L., & Carter, A. S. (2006). Relationship between physical appearance, sense of belonging and exclusion, and racial/ethnic self-identification among multiracial Japanese European Americans. *Cultural Diversity & Ethnic Minority Psychology, 12*, 673–686.

Amiot, C. E., de la Sablonnière, R., Terry, D. J., & Smith, J. R. (2007). Integration of social identities in the self: Toward a cognitive-developmental model. *Personality and Social Psychology Review, 11*, 364–388.

Andujo, E. (1988). Ethnic identity of transethnically adopted Hispanic adolescents. *Social Work, 33*, 531–535.

Anthias, F. (2001). New hybridities, old concepts: The limits of "culture." *Ethnic & Racial Studies, 24*, 619–641.

Aronson, J., Lustina, M. J., Good, C., Keough, K., Steele, C. M., & Brown, J. (1999). When white men can't do math: Necessary and sufficient factors in stereotype threat. *Journal of Experimental Social Psychology, 35*, 29–46.

Bacallao, M. L., & Smokowski, P. R. (2005). "Entre dos mundos" (between two worlds): Bicultural skills training with Latino immigrant families. *Journal of Primary Prevention, 26*, 485–509.

Baumeister, R. F., & Leary, M. R. (1995). The need to belong: Desire for interpersonal attachments as a fundamental human motivation. *Psychological Bulletin, 117*, 497–529.

Ben-Eliezer, U. (2004). Becoming a black Jew: Cultural racism and anti-racism in contemporary Israel. *Social Identities: Journal for the Study of Race, Nation and Culture. Special Focus on Racism in Israeli Society, 10*, 245–266.

Benet-Martínez, V., & Haritatos, J. (2005). Bicultural Identity Integration (BII): Components and psychosocial antecedents. *Journal of Personality, 73*, 1015–1050.

Benet-Martínez, V., Leu, J., Lee, F., & Morris, M. W. (2002). Negotiating biculturalism: Cultural frame switching in biculturals with oppositional versus compatible cultural identities. *Journal of Cross-Cultural Psychology, 33,* 492–516.

Berry, J. W. (2001). A psychology of immigration. *Journal of Social Issues, 57,* 615–631.

Birman, D. (1998). Biculturalism and perceived competence of Latino immigrant adolescents. *American Journal of Community Psychology, 26,* 335–354.

Brewer, M. B. (1991). The social self: On being the same and different at the same time. *Personality and Social Psychology Bulletin, 17,* 475–482.

Brunsma, D. L., & Rockquemore, K. A. (2001). The new color complex: Appearances and biracial identity. *Identity: An International Journal of Theory and Research, 3,* 225–246.

Bryant, A. J., & LaFromboise, T. D. (2005). The racial identity and cultural orientation of Lumbee American Indian high school students. *Cultural Diversity & Ethnic Minority Psychology, 11,* 82–89.

Buchanan, N. T., & Acevedo, C. A. (2004). When face and soul collide: Therapeutic concerns with racially ambiguous and nonvisible minority women. *Women & Therapy, 27,* 119–131.

Buriel, R. (1993). Acculturation, respect for cultural differences, and biculturalism among three generations of Mexican American and Euro American school children. *Journal of Genetic Psychology, 154,* 531–543.

Castillo, L. G., Conoley, C. W., Brossart, D. F., & Quiros, A. E. (2007). Construction and validation of the intragroup marginalization inventory. *Cultural Diversity and Ethnic Minority Psychology, 13,* 232–240.

Caughy, M. O., Nettles, S. M., O'Campo, P. J., & Lohrfink, K. F. (2006). Neighborhood matters: Racial socialization of African American children. *Child Development, 77,* 1220–1236.

Chao, M. M., Chen, J., Roisman, G. I., & Hong, Y. (2007). Essentializing race: Implications for bicultural individuals' cognition and physiological reactivity. *Psychological Science, 18,* 341–348.

Cheryan, S., & Monin, B. (2005). "Where are you really from?": Asian Americans and identity denial. *Journal of Personality and Social Psychology, 89,* 717–730.

Clark, H. H., & Brennan, S. E. (1991). Grounding in communication. In L. B. Resnick & J. M. Levine (Eds.), *Perspectives on socially shared cognition* (pp. 127–149).Washington, DC: American Psychological Association.

Deaux, K. (2000). Surveying the landscape of immigration: Social psychological perspectives. *Journal of Community and Applied Social Psychology. Special Issue: Social Changes in Globalised Societies and the Redefinition of Identities: Social Psychological Perspectives, 10,* 421–431.

Deaux, K. (2006). *To be an immigrant.* New York: Russell Sage Foundation.

Devos, T., & Banaji, M. R. (2005). American = white? *Journal of Personality and Social Psychology, 88,* 447–466.

DiMaggio, P. (1997). Culture and cognition. *Annual Review of Sociology, 23,* 263–287.

Dion, K. K., & Dion, K. L. (2004). Gender, immigrant generation, and ethnocultural identity. *Sex Roles, 50,* 347–355.

Dovidio, J. F., Brigham, J. C., Johnson, B. T., & Gaertner, S. L. (1996). Stereotyping, prejudice, and discrimination: Another look. In C. N. Macrae, C. Stangor, & Y. M. Hewstone (Eds.), *Stereotypes and stereotyping*. New York: Guilford.

Dubois, S., & Melançon, M. (2000). Creole is, Creole ain't: Diachronic and synchronic attitudes toward Creole identity in southern Louisiana. *Language in Society, 29,* 237–258.

Ellemers, N., Spears, R., & Doosje, B. (2002). Self and social identity. *Annual Review of Psychology, 53,* 161–186.

Ethier, K. A., & Deaux, K. (1994). Negotiating social identity when contexts change: Maintaining identification and responding to threat. *Journal of Personality and Social Psychology, 67,* 243–251.

Fiske, S. T. (1998). Stereotyping, prejudice, and discrimination. In D. T. Gilbert, S. T. Fiske, & G. Lindzey (Eds.), *Handbook of social psychology, Vol. 2* (4th ed., pp. 357–411). New York: McGraw Hill.

Fiske, S. T. (2004). *Social beings: A core motives approach to social psychology* (1st ed.). Hoboken, NJ: John Wiley & Sons, Inc.

Freidlander, M. L., Larney, L. C., Skau, M., Hotaling, M., Cutting, M. L., & Schwam, M. (2000). Bicultural identification: Experiences of internationally adopted children and their parents. *Journal of Counseling Psychology, 47,* 187–198.

Gallois, C., Ogay, T., & Giles, H. (2005). Communication accommodation theory. In W. B. Gudykunst (Ed.), *Theorizing about intercultural communication* (pp. 121–148). Thousand Oaks, CA: Sage.

Garcia, M., & Lega, L. I. (1979). Development of a Cuban ethnic identity questionnaire. *Hispanic Journal of Behavioral Sciences, 1,* 247–261.

Gardner, W. L., Gabriel, S., & Dean, K. K. (2004). The individual as "melting pot": The flexibility of bicultural self-construals. *Current Psychology of Cognition, 22,* 181–201.

Geary, J., & Graff, J. (2005, November 13). Restless youth: Can France bring order to the streets and hope to the restive minorities of the banlieues? *Time Europe Magazine.* Retrieved on March 17, 2008 from http://www.time.com/time/europe/html/051121/story.html.

Haritatos, J., & Benet-Martínez, V. (2002). Bicultural identities: The interface of cultural, personality, and socio-cognitive processes. *Journal of Research in Personality, 36,* 598–606.

Higgins, E. T. (1992). Achieving "shared reality" in the communication game: A social action that creates meaning. *Journal of Language and Social Psychology, 11,* 107–131.

Hong, Y., Benet-Martínez, V., Chiu, C.-y., & Morris, M. W. (2003). Boundaries of cultural influence: Construct activation as a mechanism for cultural differences in social perception. *Journal of Cross-Cultural Psychology, 34,* 453–464.

Hong, Y., Morris, M. W., Chiu, C.-y., & Benet-Martínez, V. (2000). Multicultural minds: A dynamic constructivist approach to culture and cognition. *American Psychologist, 55,* 709–720.

Hong, Y., & No, S. (2005). Bicultural individuals' representation of cultures and the self: Comparing first and later generation Asian Americans. In P. K. Oles & H. J. M. Hermans (Eds.), *The dialogical self: Theory and research* (pp. 61–70). Wydawnictwo KUL: Lublin.

Hong, Y., Wan, C., No, S., & Chiu, C.-y. (2007). Multicultural identities. In S. Kitayama & D. Cohen (Eds.), *Handbook of cultural psychology* (pp. 323–345). New York: Guilford Press.

Killian, C., & Hegtvedt, K. A. (2003). The role of parents in the maintenance of second generation Vietnamese cultural behaviors. *Sociological Spectrum, 23,* 213–245.

LaFromboise, T., Coleman, H. L., & Gerton, J. (1993). Psychological impact of biculturalism: Evidence and theory. *Psychological Bulletin, 114,* 395–412.

LaFromboise, T. D., & Rowe, W. (1983). Skills training for bicultural competence: Rationale and application. *Journal of Counseling Psychology, 30,* 589–595.

Lu, X. (2001). Bicultural identity development and Chinese community formation: An ethnographic study of Chinese schools in Chicago. *Howard Journal of Communications, 12,* 203–220.

Mahalingam, R. (2006). Cultural psychology: An introduction. In R. Mahalingam (Ed.), *Cultural psychology of immigrants* (pp. 1–12). Mahwah, NJ: Lawrence Erlbaum Associates.

McGuire, W. J., McGuire, C. V., Child, P., & Fujioka, T. (1978). Salience of ethnicity in the spontaneous self-concept as a function of one's ethnic distinctiveness in the social environment. *Journal of Personality and Social Psychology, 36,* 511–520.

McHale, S. M., Crouter, A. C., Kim, J., Burton, L. M., Davis, K. D., Dotterer, A. M., et al. (2006). Mothers' and fathers' racial socialization in African American families: Implications for youth. *Child Development, 77,* 1387–1402.

McRoy, R. G., Zurcher, L. A., Landerdale, M. L., & Anderson, R. E. (1982). Self-esteem and racial identity in transracial and inracial adoptees. *Social Work, 27,* 522–526.

McRoy, R. G., Zurcher, L. A., Lauderdale, M. L., & Anderson, R. E. (1984). The identity of transracial adoptees. *Social Casework, 65,* 34–39.

Medea, L. (2002). Creolisation and globalization in a neo-colonial context: The case of reunion. *Social Identities, 8,* 125–141.

Mendoza-Denton, R., Downey, G., Purdie, V., Davis, A., & Pietrzak, J. (2002). Sensitivity to status-based rejection: Implications for African American students' college experience. *Journal of Personality and Social Psychology, 83,* 896–918.

Nauck, B. (2001). Intercultural contact and intergenerational transmission in immigrant families. *Journal of Cross-Cultural Psychology, 32,* 159–173.

No, S., Hong, Y., Liao, H., Lee, K., Wood, D., & Chao, M. M. (2008). Lay theory of race affects and moderates Asian Americans' responses toward American culture. *Journal of Personality and Social Psychology, 95,* 991–1004.

No, S., Wan, C., & Chiu, C.-y. (2005). Cultural hybridization among Chinese and Korean ethnics residing in the United States. Unpublished data.

Oikawa, S., & Yoshida, T. (2007). An identity based on being different: A focus on biethnic individuals in Japan. *International Journal of Intercultural Relations, 31,* 633–653.

Padilla, A. M. (2006). Bicultural social development. *Hispanic Journal of Behavioral Sciences, 28,* 467–497.

Pahl, K., & Way, N. (2006). Longitudinal trajectories of ethnic identity among urban Black and Latino adolescents. *Child Development, 77,* 1403–1415.

Park, R. E. (1928). Human migration and the marginal man. *The American Journal of Sociology, 33,* 881–893.

Phinney, J. S. (1989). Stages of ethnic identity development in minority group adolescents. *Journal of Early Adolescence, 9,* 34–49.

Phinney, J. S., & Devich-Navarro, M. (1997). Variations in bicultural identification among African American and Mexican American adolescents. *Journal of Research on Adolescence, 7,* 3–32.

Pinel, E. C. (1999). Stigma consciousness: The psychological legacy of social stereotypes. *Journal of Personality and Social Psychology, 76,* 114–128.

Purdie, V. J., Steele, C. M., Davies, P. G., & Crosby, J. R. (2001, August). *The business of diversity: Minority trust within organizational cultures.* Presented at the annual meeting of the American Psychological Association, San Francisco, CA.

Pyke, K., & Dang, T. (2003). "FOB" and "whitewashed": Identity and internalized racism among second generation Asian Americans. *Qualitative Sociology, 26,* 147–172.

Quintana, S. M. (2007). Racial and ethnic identity: Developmental perspectives and research. *Journal of Counseling Psychology. Special Issue: Racial and Ethnic Identity Theory, Measurement, and Research in Counseling Psychology: Present Status and Future Directions, 54,* 259–270.

Richeson, J. A., & Nussbaum, R. J. (2004). The impact of multiculturalism versus color-blindness on racial bias. *Journal of Experimental Social Psychology, 40,* 417–423.

Roccas, S., & Brewer, M. B. (2002). Social identity complexity. *Personality and Social Psychology Review, 6,* 88–106.

Rosenbloom, S. R., & Way, N. (2004). Experiences of discrimination among African American, Asian American, and Latino adolescents in an urban high school. *Youth and Society, 35,* 420–451.

Rosenthal, D. A., & Hrynevich, C. (1985). Ethnicity and ethnic identity: A comparative study of Greek-, Italian-, and Anglo-Australian adolescents. *International Journal of Psychology, 20,* 723–742.

Rosner, J. L., & Gardner, W. L. (2006). Bridge or barrier? Judaism's role in the acculturation process of Russian Jews in the United States. Unpublished data.

Ross, M., Xun, W. Q. E., & Wilson, A. E. (2002). Language and the bicultural self. *Personality and Social Psychology Bulletin, 28,* 1040–1050.

Sciolino, E. (2007, November 28). In French suburbs, same rage, but new tactics. *New York Times.* Retrieved on March 17, 2008 from http://www.nytimes.com/2007/11/28/world/europe/28france.html?_r=1 &scp=3&sq=france+riot+2005 &st=nyt&oref=slogin.

Shi, X., & Lu, X. (2007). Bilingual and bicultural development of Chinese American adolescents and young adults: A comparative study. *Howard Journal of Communications, 18,* 313–333.

Sibley, C. G., & Liu, J. H. (2007). New Zealand = bicultural? Implicit and explicit associations between ethnicity and nationhood in the New Zealand context. *European Journal of Social Psychology, 37,* 1222–1243.

Smith, C. S. (2005, November 11). What makes someone French? *New York Times.* Retrieved on March 17, 2008 from http://www.nytimes.com/2005/11/11/international/europe/11france.html?fta=y.

Spencer, S. J., Steele, C. M., & Quinn, D. M. (1999). Stereotype threat and women's math performance. *Journal of Experimental Social Psychology, 35,* 4–28.

Steele, C. M., & Aronson, J. (1995). Stereotype threat and the intellectual test performance of African Americans. *Journal of Personality and Social Psychology, 69,* 797–811.

Steele, C. M., Spencer, S. J., & Aronson, J. (2002). Contending with group image: The psychology of stereotype and social identity threat. In M. P. Zanna (Ed.), *Advances in experimental social psychology, Vol. 34* (pp. 379–440). San Diego, CA: Academic Press, Inc.

Stone, J., Lynch, C. I., Sjomeling, M., & Darley, J. M. (1999). Stereotype threat effects on black and white athletic performance. *Journal of Personality and Social Psychology, 77,* 1213–1227.

Suarez, S. A., Fowers, B. J., Garwood, C. S., & Szapocznik, J. (1997). Biculturalism, differentness, loneliness, and alienation in Hispanic college students. *Hispanic Journal of Behavioral Sciences, 19,* 489–505.

Tadmor, C. T., & Tetlock, P. E. (2006). Biculturalism: A model of the effects of second-culture exposure on acculturation and integrative complexity. *Journal of Cross-Cultural Psychology, 37,* 173–190.

Trickett, E. J., & Jones, C. J. (2007). Adolescent culture brokering and family functioning: A study of families from Vietnam. *Cultural Diversity and Ethnic Minority Psychology, 13,* 143–150.

Tsang, A. K. T., Irving, H., Alaggia, R., Chau, S. B. Y., & Benjamin, M. (2003). Negotiating ethnic identity in Canada: The case of the "satellite children." *Youth & Society, 34,* 359–384.

Turner, J. C. (1982). Towards a cognitive redefinition of the social group. In H. Tajfel (Ed.), *Social identity and intergroup relations.* Cambridge: Cambridge University Press.

Turner, J. C., Hogg, M. A., Oakes, P. J., Reicher, S. D., & Wetherell, M. S. (1987). *Rediscovering the social group: A self-categorization theory.* Cambridge, MA: Basil Blackwell.

Umaña-Taylor, A. J., Bhanot, R., & Shin, N. (2006). Ethnic identity formation during adolescence: The critical role of families. *Journal of Family Issues, 27,* 390–414.

Vazquez, L. A., Garcia-Vazquez, E., Bauman, S. A., & Sierra, A. S. (1997). Skin color, acculturation, and community interest among Mexican American students: A research note. *Hispanic Journal of Behavioral Sciences, 19,* 377–386.

Verkuyten, M. (2004). *Ethnic identity and social context.* New York: Psychology Press.

Verkuyten, M., & Pouliasi, K. (2002). Biculturalism among older children: Cultural frame switching, attributions, self-identification, and attitudes. *Journal of Cross-Cultural Psychology, 33,* 492–516.

Vignoles, V. L., Regalia, C., Manzi, C., Golledge, J., & Scabini, E. (2006). Beyond self-esteem: Influence of multiple motives on identity construction. *Journal of Personality and Social Psychology, 90,* 308–333.

Vivero, V. N., & Jenkins, S. R. (1999). Existential hazards of the multicultural individual: Defining and understanding "cultural homelessness." *Cultural Diversity & Ethnic Minority Psychology, 5,* 6–26.

Ward, C. (2006). Acculturation, identity and adaptation in dual heritage adolescents. *International Journal of Intercultural Relations, 30,* 243–259.

Waters, M. C. (1990). *Ethnic options: Choosing identities in America.* Berkeley: University of California Press.

Weisskirch, R. S. (2007). Feelings about language brokering and family relations among Mexican American early adolescents. *Journal of Early Adolescence, 27,* 545–561.

Willgerodt, M. A., Miller, A. M., & McElmurry, B. J. (2002). Becoming bicultural: Chinese American women and their development. *Health Care for Women International, 23,* 467–480.

Wolsko, C., Park, B., Judd, C. M., & Wittenbrink, B. (2000). Framing interethnic ideology: Effects of multicultural and color-blind perspective on judgments of groups and individuals. *Journal of Personality and Social Psychology, 78,* 635–654.

Wong, S. T., Yoo, G. J., & Stewart, A. L. (2006). The changing meaning of family support among older Chinese and Korean immigrants. *Journals of Gerontology: Series B: Psychological Sciences and Social Sciences, 61,* S4–S9.

Yip, T., & Fuligni, A. J. (2002). Daily variation in ethnic identity, ethnic behaviors, and psychological well-being among American adolescents of Chinese descent. *Child Development, 73,* 1557–1572.

Yuh, J. (2005). Ethnic identity and its relation to self-esteem and ego identity among college students in a multiethnic region. *Journal of Applied Social Psychology, 35,* 1111–1131.

Zaharna, R. S. (1989). Self-shock: The double-binding challenge of identity. *International Journal of Intercultural Relations, 13,* 501–525.

13

Multicultural Experiences and Intercultural Communication

ANGELA K.-Y. LEUNG AND CHI-YUE CHIU[1]

As mentioned in Part II of this volume, culture consists of shared knowledge in the forms of societal norms, lay beliefs, values, practices, and routines. Through participating in culture and engaging in communication with other cultural members, people grasp the shared reality in their culture and use it as behavioral guides both when they communicate with people in their culture and when they interact with people from a different culture. Not surprisingly, the role of communication in cultural processes has been extensively discussed in the research literature. In contrast, how cultural *processes* affect communication has been relatively unexplored, although there is ample research on cultural differences in communication processes.

The goal of this chapter is to fill this gap by focusing on *how* multicultural experiences may impact intercultural communication. Drawing on the cultural competence model proposed by Chiu and Hong (2006), we contend that effective intercultural communication requires nuanced understanding of cultural differences and discriminative application of cultural knowledge to guide interactions in different cultural contexts. We further contend that multicultural experiences confer opportunities for intercultural learning. Thus, individuals with rich, multicultural experiences are expected to possess nuanced knowledge of cultural differences and be able to use such knowledge discriminatively to guide interactions in changing cultural contexts. In this chapter, we will discuss these contentions and review the pertinent supporting evidence. Finally, we will discuss how cultural identification and need for cognitive closure may moderate the effects of multicultural experiences on intercultural learning and discriminative

---

[1] Preparation of this chapter was supported by a grant awarded to the second author from the Ministry of Education, Singapore.

242

application of cultural knowledge. To provide the context for these discussions, in the next section, we will briefly review the role of communication and intercultural communication in cultural processes.

THE ROLE OF COMMUNICATION IN CULTURAL PROCESSES

As discussed in Chapter 3, sharedness is an important aspect of culture; culture is made up of a set of meanings or mental representations that are shared (or at least perceived to be shared) among a group of interconnected individuals in a society (D'Andrade, 1987; Kashima, 2002; Wan et al., 2007). In a metaphorical illustration, Dan Sperber (1996) compared the evolution of culture to the occurrence of an epidemic. An epidemic occurs when there is a widespread occurrence of an infectious disease in a community at a certain time. Likewise, when a knowledge representation is spread like a contagious virus to many human carriers in the community, the knowledge representation becomes a part of the culture.

Communication is a major channel through which cultural knowledge representations spread to others and become consensual knowledge in the culture. As Sperber (1996) put it, "those representations which are repeatedly communicated and minimally transformed in the process will end up belonging to the culture" (p. 88). The dynamic social impact theory offers an elaborate explanation of the role of communication in the evolution of culture-like spatial clusters of opinion (Latané, 1996; Latané & Bourgeois, 1996). According to this theory, through communication and social influence, opinions that were scattered spatially at the beginning will self-organize into culture-like spatial clusters of opinions. When people engage in social interactions, they tend to communicate with those who are physically close to them, such as those in the same neighborhood. Through this communicative process, people living in the same neighborhood will share similar opinions, which are different from those in other neighborhoods. Furthermore, within the same neighborhood, previously unrelated opinions will be assimilated into a stable conglomerate set of opinions that define the neighborhood.

When a conglomerate set of opinions is formed in a human group, the communication process will help stabilize it (Chiu, Leung, & Kwan, 2007). Kashima, Woolcock, and Kashima (2000) have proposed a connectionist model to account for the reproduction of conventional ideas in a society. According to this model, each cultural member is a unit in a network of connections. Serial communications take place when individuals receive information and communicate it to other individuals in the network. As reproductions are subject to memory decay and influence from preexisting schemata, some information may be transmitted but some may be distorted or lost in the process. In several experiments using a story reproduction paradigm, the researchers showed that stereotypical or conventionalized information has a higher chance than does nonstereotypical information to be retained and transmitted from one individual to another in a sequence of communication trials (Kashima, 2000; Lyons & Kashima, 2001, 2003). The connectionist model illustrates how cultural stability can be maintained through serial reproduction of communicative messages, which tend to incorporate conventionalized and widely distributed information and eliminate counterstereotypical information.

Against this theoretical context, intercultural communication plays a critical role in enriching and even transforming a culture. At a relatively superficial level, intercultural communication results in the importation of novel ideas from foreign cultures and hence provides the raw ideological materials to stimulate cultural change. Given that nonconventional ideas are unlikely to survive the serial communication test, however, most imported ideas from foreign cultures would not be retained in the culture.

At a deeper level, as we argue later in this chapter, successful communication requires sensitivity to distribution of ideas in the addressee's culture and customization of communicative messages and communication styles to the knowledge, preferences, beliefs, and values of the addressee's culture. Accordingly, individuals who are motivated to have successful intercultural communication will want to acquire nuanced understanding of the knowledge in the addressee's culture and be prepared to accommodate their communicative messages and communication style to the preferred mode and style of communication in the addressee's culture (see Chapter 12, this volume). From this perspective, intercultural communication could jump-start an intercultural learning process and create an incentive for reproducing otherwise novel and unconventional ideas and communicative styles from a foreign culture in serial communications. Such reproductions would occur primarily in intercultural contexts, at least in the individuals' early encounters with the foreign culture. Subsequently, as discussed in Chapter 12, the ideas that are often communicated in intercultural interactions may be incorporated into the communicators' multicultural identity. For this reason, aside from the practical benefits of improving intercultural understanding and quality of intercultural interactions, intercultural communication is a theoretically important phenomenon for understanding basic cultural processes.

MAJOR OBSTACLES IN INTERCULTURAL COMMUNICATION

Although successful intercultural interactions typically require effective intercultural communication, there are many cultural and psychological obstacles to effective intercultural communication. Some of these obstacles pertain to stable qualities of the individuals involved in intercultural communication. Others pertain to cultural differences in communication styles.

Person-Level Obstacles

For instance, people often feel anxious and distressed when interacting with people from a markedly different culture. People may experience feelings of ambivalence and culture shock during intercultural encounters (Hong, Wan, No, & Chiu, 2007). Thus, participation in intercultural communication requires some psychological preparation. Some people are less willing than others to get prepared to interact with people from other cultures (Chen & Isa, 2003). Kim (1997) used the term *preparedness* to refer to an individual difference in the potential to be adaptive to intercultural encounters. Compared to prepared individuals, individuals who are ill prepared to enter into an intercultural interaction experience more intense anxiety and psychological distress in intercultural encounters. They are also less willing to engage in cultural learning and less prepared to broaden their awareness of and reflect on the characteristics of diverse cultures.

Close-mindedness is another personal obstacle to effective intercultural communication. Individuals who are open to experience are those who are appreciative of new experiences and are receptive to a variety of perspectives and thoughts (Costa & McCrae, 1992; McCrae & Costa, 1997). People who are open to experience have a predisposition to learn from new cultural experiences and engage in intercultural interactions. In contrast, people with low levels of openness may find encountering foreign cultures to be overwhelming, shocking, and even threatening (Leung & Chiu, 2008). Thus, individuals who are not open to new experiences may appraise and experience intercultural encounters negatively. These individuals are not well prepared to enter intercultural communication.

Cultural Differences in Communication Styles

Even among individuals who are open and prepared to enter intercultural communication, communicating effectively with individuals from a different culture – particularly a culture with markedly different communication norms and styles – is difficult, because these individuals may not have sufficient knowledge of the dominant communication norms and styles in the interaction partners' culture.

Research on intercultural communication has revealed many cross-cultural differences in communication norms and styles. As an illustration, power distance is a major factor affecting interpersonal communication style (Cody & McLaughlin, 1985; Wish & Kaplan, 1977). For example, individuals who are assigned the role of a supervisor tend to use more confrontational conflict management techniques, whereas those who are assigned the role of a subordinate tend to use less controlling strategies (Putnam & Wilson, 1982). Cultures differ in the extent to which their members are sensitive to power or status distinctions in the communication context. Brew and Cairns (2004) showed that, compared to Westerners, East Asians are more responsive to the status distinction of the disputants when handling conflicts; they use a more indirect style when dealing with a superior than with a subordinate. Another study (Lee & Rogan, 1991) also found that Koreans become more confrontational in communication when they register an increase in their power and status relative to their communication partner, whereas Americans maintain the same communication style despite the change in their relative power or status.

Given the prevalence of cultural differences in communication norms and styles, a key predictor to effective intercultural communication is the extent to which communicators have at their disposal accurate knowledge regarding the communication norms and styles in their communication partner's culture. From this perspective, multicultural experiences, which confer opportunities to acquire such knowledge, should facilitate effective intercultural communication.

A COMMUNICATION MODEL OF INTERCULTURAL COMPETENCE

As an extension of their social competence model, Chiu and Hong (2006) have proposed a model of cultural competence. Whereas social competence refers to people's sensitivity to subtle cues about the psychological meanings of changing situations, as well as discriminative use of appropriate behavioral strategies in certain situations (Cheng, Chiu, Hong, & Cheung, 2001), cultural competence refers to people's sensitivity to the distribution of knowledge in a cultural group and their flexibility in switching the cultural lens and applying context-appropriate cultural knowledge to accomplish valued goals in intercultural interactions.

Applying this model to intercultural communication, we posit that effective intercultural communication occurs when the communication partners (a) have nuanced understanding of the dominant preferences and norms in their own and their communication partner's culture, and (b) can flexibly and discriminatively apply such knowledge in intercultural communication in a culturally sensitive manner. Because shared knowledge of one's own and foreign culture(s) can be acquired through extensive experiences in the culture, through multicultural experiences individuals can acquire the pertinent cultural knowledge. Furthermore, multicultural experiences also confer opportunities for practicing discriminative use of cultural knowledge in intercultural communication. Thus, multicultural experiences should contribute to effective intercultural communication. We will review evidence for each of these propositions in this section.

Knowledge Estimation and Communication

A key assumption in the proposed model is that having refined knowledge of the shared preferences and norms in a certain culture is critical to effective communication with members in that culture. Consistent with this assumption, research has shown that, when communicating with others in the community, people retrieve from memory knowledge that is assumed to be shared in the community (Keysar, Barr, Balin, & Brauner, 2000). They would assess what information is mutually known and formulate a message based on the estimated common ground.

Indeed, people seem to possess remarkably accurate knowledge regarding what people in their community know and what they do not know. In one experiment, Fussell and Krauss (1992) had American college students view pictures of U.S. public figures (e.g., Woody Allen, George Bush). For each target, they rated how identifiable the target was, named the target if they could, and estimated the proportion of undergraduates from their university who could name the target. Participants were remarkably accurate in estimating the distribution of knowledge of the public figures among students at their own university. In follow-up studies, the same result was obtained when students were asked to estimate their peers' knowledge of other everyday objects (e.g., kitchen utensils, tools). In another study that used the same methodology (Lau, Chiu, & Hong, 2001), Hong Kong participants were asked to estimate other Hong Kong residents' knowledge of specific landmarks in Hong Kong, Macau, and New York City. To create an objective measure of the proportion of people who actually knew the landmarks, the participants were also asked to identify the landmarks. Again, the participants in this study were remarkably accurate in estimating the distribution of knowledge of the landmarks in their community.

Furthermore, people used their social knowledge to guide message generation. In the Fussell and Krauss (1992) study, participants were also asked to describe the public figures to an ingroup addressee so that the addressee could identify who the public figures were from the descriptions. Results showed that participants generated shorter or more succinct messages when they described public figures who were believed to be widely known in their culture than when they described public figures who were expected to be unfamiliar in the culture.

When people describe to an addressee the picture of a landmark that is assumed to be widely known in the community, they tend to generate concise descriptions. In fact, oftentimes, the speakers will mention the name of the landmark only (e.g., "This is the Statue of Liberty."). In the study by Lau and colleagues (2001), the Hong Kong Chinese participants were also asked to describe the landmarks to an ingroup addressee so that the addressee could identify from the descriptions what the landmarks were. Again, participants customized their messages according to their estimation of the addressee's knowledge of landmarks: They generated shorter descriptions for presumably well-known landmarks than for presumably unfamiliar ones. Furthermore, Isaacs and Clark (1987) found that, when American participants described New York City landmarks to an ingroup addressee, the participants were more likely to mention the name of the landmarks when these landmarks were famous (e.g., the Statue of Liberty) than when they were not (e.g., the General Grant Memorial). Consistent with this result, Lau and colleagues (2001) also reported that, when describing landmarks, the Hong Kong Chinese participants were more likely to mention the names of the landmarks when the landmarks were believed to be famous (vs. not famous) among Hong Kong people.

It should also be pointed out that, in the study by Lau and colleagues (2001), although descriptions of the well-known landmarks were relatively short, they were as communicative as the detailed descriptions of the unfamiliar landmarks. When a separate group of undergraduates from the same campus were asked to identify the landmarks described in each message, accuracy of decoding was equally high for the relatively short descriptions of the well-known landmarks and the relatively detailed descriptions of the unfamiliar ones.

Taken collectively, the evidence indicates that people have refined knowledge about the distribution of knowledge in their own culture and are able to use this knowledge to formulate communicative message for their addressee. They take knowledge of the addressee into account in message formulation and generate messages that contain sufficient information for effective communication of the intended referential meanings.

If individuals can acquire social knowledge through cultural immersion, individuals with extensive experiences in multiple cultures may possess nuanced knowledge of what people in different cultures know and do not know. These individuals may also be able to use knowledge about the pertinent culture to customize their message for addressees of different cultural backgrounds. From this perspective, multicultural experiences should be accompanied by relatively effective intercultural communications. We now turn to the theories and research evidence pertinent to these possibilities.

Multicultural Experiences and Intercultural Communication

Related Theories

Broadly speaking, intercultural communication happens when individuals from two cultures speak to or interact with each other. Through immersion in multiple cultures, multicultural individuals may acquire refined knowledge regarding what people in different cultures know, believe in, prefer, and value. If they customize the contents and styles of their communications based on their nuanced understanding of cultural differences in knowledge, beliefs, preferences, and values, they would be effective when communicating to people of different cultural backgrounds. Consistent with this idea, Wiseman (2002) contends that knowledge of and attitude toward other cultures are key contributors to effective intercultural communication. As Wiseman (2002) pointed out, "a knowledgeable communicator needs information about the people, the communicator rules, the context, and the normative expectations governing the interaction with the member of another culture" (p. 211).

Our idea is consistent with current theorizations of the effect of intercultural interactions. For instance, Chen and Isa (2003) contend that frequent interactions with people from a foreign culture confer opportunities for experiential cultural learning, which in turn should foster nuanced understanding of cultural differences. In her network approach to the study of intercultural communication, Kim (1986) suggested that people who have a culturally heterogeneous personal network tend to have high levels of intercultural communication adaptability, which is reflected in (a) the ability to acquire knowledge and discern meanings, (b) the tendencies to display appropriate emotions and to willingly accommodate to culturally appropriate practices, and (c) the ability to act flexibly and resourcefully in intercultural encounters. Multicultural individuals are likely to have culturally heterogeneous social networks (Leung, Maddux, Galinsky, & Chiu, 2008), and hence should have many opportunities to engage in experiential cultural learning. Accordingly, these individuals should have developed a more nuanced understanding of cultural differences and should be effective in intercultural communication.

Also consistent with our view are the results from a cluster analysis study of the personal qualities of effective intercultural communicators carried out by Arasaratnam and Doerfel (2005). That investigation revealed several qualities that are necessary for developing intercultural communication competence, two of which are knowledge and motivation. Specifically, competent intercultural communicators are other-centered and observant: They are sensitive and open to others and have good communication skills. More importantly, they have strong interest in and are well aware of cultural matters. Their prior cross-cultural experiences and non-ethnocentric global outlook also make it easier for them to learn the norms and practices in other cultures. In general, the qualities that favor the development of intercultural communication competence appear to be the same qualities characterizing multicultural individuals (Leung & Chiu, 2008).

Research Evidence

As discussed in Part II of this volume, cultures differ in the relative prevalence of domain-specific lay theories, preferences, and norms. For example, research has found clear cross-cultural differences in the relative popularity of different self-regulatory preferences (Lalwani, Shrum, & Chiu, 2009), conflict management style (Fu, Chiu, Morris, & Young, 2007), and negotiation strategies (Fu et al., 2007). In the next section, we will review research evidence that links multicultural experiences to nuanced understanding of cultural differences and addressee-centered customization of communicative strategies in intercultural interactions.

KNOWLEDGE ESTIMATION. In one study (Zou et al., 2009), the researchers asked American undergraduate students to indicate how they themselves would respond to the Regulatory Focus Questionnaire (Higgins et al., 2001), which is a measure of two self-regulatory preferences. One of these preferences is promotion focus, or the tendency to be motivated by aspirations toward ideals; this motivational focus develops from a personal history of reaching personal ideals. The other preference is prevention focus, or the tendency to be motivated by fulfillment of duties or obligations; this motivational focus develops from a personal history of successfully avoiding social disapproval. Based on the responses of this group of participants, the researchers obtained the actual relative preferences of American undergraduates for promotion and prevention focus. In this study, American undergraduates had a slightly stronger preference for promotion focus over prevention focus.

Next, the researchers had undergraduate students from the United States, Hong Kong, and Beijing estimate how an average American college student would respond to the Regulatory Focus Questionnaire. Studies conducted at about the same time showed that, compared to Beijing Chinese undergraduates, Hong Kong Chinese undergraduates had more experience with American culture (Sui, Zhu, & Chiu, 2007). By comparing the estimated responses from the three groups against the actual responses from the American students, the investigators assessed how experiences with American culture are linked to accuracy in estimating American students' responses.

Not surprisingly, American students made highly accurate estimations of their peers' relative preference for promotion and prevention focus. Hong Kong Chinese students' estimations were not as accurate as those of American students, but were significantly more accurate than those of Beijing Chinese students, who tended to overestimate (by three times) American students' relative preference for promotion (vs. prevention).

In another study that used the same methodology (Leung, Chiu, & Hong, 2003), the investigators in the first part of the study compared bicultural Chinese Americans' and monocultural European Americans' estimations of how an average Chinese and an average European American would respond to the Regulatory Focus Questionnaire (Higgins et al., 2001). American students had a greater preference for promotion focus than did the Chinese students. More importantly, Chinese Americans were accurate in estimating the American–Chinese difference in promotion focus, whereas European Americans erroneously believed that Chinese had a greater preference for promotion focus than did Americans. Taken together, the results suggest that extent of exposure to American culture is associated with accuracy in estimating American students' motivational preferences.

PERSUASIVE COMMUNICATION. Aside from having a more nuanced understanding of cultural differences, bicultural individuals are also more facile than are monocultural individuals at customizing their communications based on the cultural identity of their addressee. In the second part of the study by Leung and colleagues (2003), participants were asked to imagine that they worked for an international insurance company. Their task was to generate three arguments to persuade either a Chinese or an American client to sign up for an insurance plan. The client's cultural identity was embedded in a subtle manner in the client's personal profile presented to the participants. Results showed that Chinese Americans used more promotion-focused arguments to persuade the American client than they did the Chinese client, which was consistent with their estimation of a greater preference for promotion focus among Americans (vs. Chinese). In contrast, European Americans generated predominantly promotion-focused arguments for both the American and Chinese clients. This finding indicates that bicultural individuals are able to customize the contents of their persuasive communications based on the addressee's cultural identity.

DIRECTNESS IN COMMUNICATION. As another example of bicultural individuals' behavioral flexibility in communication, consider the Protestant Relational Ideology. This ideology prescribes direct communication and proscribes relational concerns and emotional detachment in work (vs. nonwork) settings (Sanchez-Burks, 2002; Sanchez-Burks, Nisbett, & Ybarra, 2000). This ideology evolved from the beliefs and social practices of the Calvinist Protestants who were active in 17th- and 18th-century America (Weber, 1947), and is more widespread in Western cultures than in East Asian cultures. In a series of studies (Sanchez-Burks et al., 2003), through assessing the occurrence of errors in decoding indirect messages presented in work or nonwork situations (Study 1) and by gathering self-report ratings on the extent of indirectness expressed toward coworkers and nonwork acquaintances (Study 2), the investigators showed that only Americans attended less to indirectness cues in work settings than in nonwork settings. In their last study, Thai-American bicultural managers were experimentally induced to switch their cultural frames by filling out either a Thai or an English version of the same survey. When assigned to complete the Thai version, participants, whose East Asian cultural knowledge was activated, displayed indirect communication style in both work and nonwork settings. When assigned to complete the English version, participants, whose Western cultural knowledge was activated, displayed less indirectness in work settings than in nonwork settings.

These findings revealed intricate differences between East Asians and Westerners in the preferred level of indirectness in communication. Nonetheless, Thai-American managers, as a result of their bicultural experiences, have nuanced knowledge of these cultural differences. Moreover, they can flexibly switch their communication pattern in response to the cultural and situational demands of the communication context.

CONFLICT RESOLUTION. Evidence for bicultural individuals' behavioral flexibility has also been reported outside the domain of intercultural communication. For example, Hong Kong Chinese, who are conversant in both Chinese and American cultures, preferred distribution of reward based on contribution more (an allocation favored by Americans) when they were primed with American culture (incidentally exposed to icons of American culture) than when they were primed with Chinese culture (incidentally exposed to icons of Chinese culture), and they preferred equal distribution to team members (an allocation favored by Chinese) when they were primed with Chinese (vs. American) culture (Fu et al., 2007). Hong Kong Chinese primed with Chinese (vs. American) culture also made more cooperative choices when they played the Prisoner's Dilemma game with ingroup members (Wong & Hong, 2005).

One well-documented cross-cultural difference in conflict management is the greater preference for direct confrontation with the disputant parties in Western culture and the greater preference for indirect or avoidance tactics in Eastern culture. That is, Westerners prefer using assertive or question-and-answer communication style to interrogate their disputant. In contrast, Easterners prefer using indirect tactics to avoid public acknowledgement of the dispute and thus save face for the parties involved (Brown & Levinson, 1987; Ting-Toomey & Kurogi, 1998; Triandis, 1994; see also Chapter 11, this volume). Consistent with the idea that bicultural experience is associated with behavioral flexibility, Chan and Goto (2003) reported that Hong Kong Chinese are more likely to use inaction to resolve conflict (a relationship preserving strategy) when they deal with a Hong Kong Chinese disputant than when they deal with an American disputant, indicating that the strategy choice of bicultural Hong Kong Chinese depends on the negotiation partner's cultural identity.

Bicultural individuals' behavioral flexibility has also been observed among non-Asian bicultural individuals. For instance, whereas East Asian monocultural individuals indiscriminately prefer indirect conflict management styles more when negotiating with a superior than with a subordinate, bicultural Australian expatriates in East Asia are sensitive to the cultural identity of the disputant: They use more indirect styles when negotiating with an Asian than with a Westerner (Brew & Cairns, 2004).

These results show that bicultural experiences are associated with having nuanced understanding of cultural differences and flexibility in responding to specific demands for culturally appropriate behaviors in intercultural contexts. Across studies, bicultural individuals tend to flexibly tune their communicative messages to the preferred self-regulatory style of their client and to the preferred conflict resolution style of their disputant, taking into account the cultural identity of the interaction partner.

At this point, readers may wonder whether bicultural individuals' nuanced understanding of cultural differences and behavioral accommodation would lead to effective intercultural communication or interaction. Recent research evidence indicates that they would. First, research has consistently shown that, in intercultural communication, people like those who accommodate their communication style to the style of one's cultural group more than they like those who do not (Giles & Powesland, 1975). For example, in cross-cultural negotiation, Party A comes from a culture that favors indirect exchange of offers and counteroffers and Party B comes from a culture that favors direct negotiation strategy. A would like B more if B would accommodate his or her negotiation strategy to the indirect negotiation strategy favored by A than if B would not. There is also evidence that, among new immigrants, those who have acquired more nuanced knowledge of the values in the host culture report more harmonious relationships with people in the host culture as well as more efficacious goal pursuits (Li & Hong, 2001).

BOUNDARIES OF THE BENEFITS OF MULTICULTURAL EXPERIENCES

As discussed in Part III of this volume, culture serves self-identity and epistemic functions. Thus, when identity or epistemic needs are salient in the immediate context, rather than critically reflect on their cultural experiences and learn about a new culture, individuals in an intercultural encounter will feel an increased need to adhere to their own culture. Thus, although multicultural experience can lead to accrual of useful knowledge of cultural differences, which is a valuable cognitive asset in intercultural communication, these benefits would emerge only when the following conditions are met: (a) the intercultural boundary is not salient or is perceived to be malleable; and (b) the communicators are not pressured by their epistemic need to stick to their own cultural traditions.

Cultural Identification and Intercultural Boundary

Intercultural communication inevitably involves communication between people from different cultural groups. Thus, intercultural communication can be understood as a special form of intergroup communication. As such, factors that affect intergroup relations (e.g., social identity, power or status differential, perceived threat) should also affect the quality of intercultural communication.

According to the social identity theory, people seek self-enhancement through associating the self with a positive group. For self-enhancement purpose, people also tend to focus on the perceived positive distinctiveness of the group with which they identify. As a consequence, they favor the ingroup over outgroup (Tajfel, 1982; Tajfel & Turner, 1986) and exaggerate the positive qualities that uniquely define the ingroup and the negative qualities that distinguish the outgroup from the ingroup.

Individuals' social identity need and its attendant ingroup-favoring perceptual biases become particularly salient in the presence of identity threats (Roccas & Schwartz, 1993; van Knippenberg & Ellemers, 2003). In one study, it was found that, when group identity was threatened, participants defended their threatened identity by evaluating more favorably the creativity of ingroup products and allocating more resources to ingroup members (Jetten, Spears, & Manstead, 1997). Such identity-driven biases would discourage individuals from engaging in critical reflections of their own culture or in intercultural learning. Indeed, research has consistently shown that cultural identity salience discourages accommodation to the speech characteristics of the outgroup culture in intercultural communication (Tong, Hong, Lee, & Chiu, 1999; see also Chapter 12 for an extensive discussion on how salience of cultural identity concerns could create intercultural tensions).

The negative effects of cultural identification on intercultural learning are particularly pronounced when people perceive the intergroup boundary to be discrete and impermeable. When the intergroup boundary is perceived to be impermeable, establishment of common ground through intergroup communication would seem difficult, if not impossible. A group may be viewed as an entity with impermeable boundaries because it is seen to possess some defining essence or perceived to be an agentic unit (Brewer, Hong, & Li, 2004). Members of an *essentialized* group are believed to share inherently unalterable psychological attributes, and essence is often attributed to the group because its members possess the same physical characteristics (e.g., skin color, facial features). In contrast, members in an *agentic* group are perceived to pursue common goals, and agency is attributed to the group when its members display concerted group behaviors (e.g., display similar actions or behaviors; Ip, Chiu, & Wan, 2006).

A recent study (Yokota & Yuki, 2007) has examined the attendant intergroup emotions of these two different kinds of entitativity perceptions – perceptions of a collection of individuals as an entity with relatively discrete boundaries. This study found that encountering an essentialized outgroup (i.e., a group with shared physical attributes) might evoke fear of contamination – the fear that the outgroup will threaten the health and/or moral purity of the ingroup. Such fear would in turn evoke feelings of disgust and the tendency to avoid outgroup members to minimize the chance of contacting the physical and/or moral contaminants. In contrast, encountering an agentic outgroup (i.e., a group sharing similar behaviors) is likely to evoke the perception of an obstacle threat – the fear that the outgroup would pose a threat to the ingroup's safety. A perceived obstacle threat would in turn evoke anger as well as aggression toward the outgroup.

Given these findings, we expect that perceived threats from an outgroup culture and the negative emotions that accompany such perceptions would adversely affect intergroup communication. Consistent with this expectation, research on intercultural interaction shows that experiencing an outgroup as a threat to the purity and integrity of one's own culture could evoke nationalistic, exclusionary reactions toward the outgroup culture (Chiu & Cheng, 2007).

Need for Cognitive Closure

Time pressure evokes the need for cognitive closure or the need for firm answers; it reinforces reliance on established cultural norms that offer firm answers to otherwise ambiguous problems (Chiu, Morris, Hong, & Menon, 2000; Fu et al., 2007). Time pressure also evokes a sense of time urgency, which pushes people to pursue the dominant group goal in the immediate context when managing intercultural interactions.

Brew and Cairns (2004) studied the management of organizational conflicts among a group of Western expatriates and Asian host nationals in urgent (vs. nonurgent) situations. These investigators posit that the prevailing economic mentality at fast-paced corporate workplaces is efficiency, which is epitomized in the popular saying of "Time is money." Efficiency as the dominant organizational goal requires employees to resolve conflicts directly; otherwise more time would have to be spent if one seeks to negotiate diplomatically and to exert efforts in safeguarding each other's face. Thus, when required to solve organizational conflicts in urgent (vs. nonurgent) situations, Western expatriates and Asian host nationals reacted similarly by being frank and undiplomatic. When a potential conflict had not yet surfaced, however, time urgency actually heightened both groups' preference for avoidance strategies.

When the context of the conflict changes from corporate culture to national culture, time pressure should push individuals to adhere to the dominant norms in the national culture. Consistent with this expectation, Fu and colleagues (2007) found that Americans and East Asians showed conflict-settling preferences, information-seeking behaviors in disputes, and fairness judgment in reward allocation that are characteristic of their own culture only when the need for cognitive closure was high. Taken together, when the needs for social identification and firm answers are salient, individuals encountering a new culture tend to follow the dominant conventional norms in their own culture and are unlikely to engage in intercultural learning. As a consequence, they will forego opportunities to acquire nuanced knowledge of cross-cultural differences and practice behavioral flexibility.

Nevertheless, after individuals have acquired refined knowledge about a foreign culture, the effect of the need for cognitive closure would reverse because, relative to knowledge of one's own culture, knowledge of a foreign culture would now offer more valid behavioral guides in intercultural encounters. For example, when a Chinese businessperson has acquired refined knowledge of the behavioral norms in American culture, he or she would perceive knowledge of American culture to be more valid and useful behavioral guides than knowledge of Chinese culture when interacting with her American business partners. In this circumstance, if a higher need for cognitive closure fosters reliance on valid cultural knowledge, that higher need should increase both (a) adherence to the cultural norms in one's own culture in interactions with members of the ingroup culture and (b) adherence to the cultural norms in the foreign culture in interactions with members of this foreign culture.

Results from a recent study (Chao, Zhang, & Chiu, 2010) confirmed this prediction. The participants in this study were Master of Business Administration (MBA) students in China who had a fair amount of exposure to business practices in the United States. When queried about the cultural norms for allocating rewards in China and the United States, these participants correctly recognized the greater preference for the contribution rule in the United States and the greater preference for the equality rule in China. Among these participants, those with a higher need for cognitive closure favored the contribution rule more when making reward allocation in the United States and the equality rule more when making reward allocation in China. Furthermore, the extent of cultural identification did not weaken this result. On the contrary, Chinese cultural identification increased the perceived differences between American and Chinese cultures and rendered the perceived cultural differences in allocation rule preferences more discrete and real. As a consequence, the extent of cultural identification magnified the need for cognitive closure effect. Participants with a high need for cognitive closure favored the equality rule more in the Chinese context and the contribution rule more in the American context, particularly when they strongly identified with Chinese culture. In summary, although cultural identification and the need for cognitive closure tend to discourage inter-cultural learning, paradoxically, after individuals have acquired sufficient knowledge of a foreign culture through their multicultural experiences, cultural identification and the need for cognitive closure could reinforce discriminative application of cultural knowledge in intercultural encoun-ters (see Chapter 5, this volume).

Conclusions

In conclusion, although the role of communication in cultural processes has been extensively discussed and researched, only a few studies have examined the role of multicultural experiences in intercultural communi-cation. In this chapter, we filled this gap by suggesting a set of propositions regarding the relationship between multicultural experiences and intercul-tural communication. Specifically, we contend that exposure to multicul-tural experiences is positively related to effective intercultural communica-tion because multicultural experiences afford opportunities for acquiring nuanced understanding of cross-cultural differences and for practicing dis-criminative application of cultural knowledge in intercultural interactions. Although the evidence reviewed in this chapter is still preliminary, it is con-sistent with this proposition. Also interestingly, we further posit that, on the one hand, the positive relationship between multicultural experiences and intercultural learning may be broken when cultural identification and the need for cognitive closure are heightened; on the other hand, after indi-viduals have acquired sufficient nuanced knowledge of cultural differences, cultural identification and the need for cognitive closure could instead reinforce the tendency to apply cultural knowledge discriminatively when managing social situations in different cultural contexts.

REFERENCES

Arasaratnam, L. A., & Doerfel, M. L. (2005). Intercultural communication compe-tence: Identifying key components from multicultural perspectives. *International Journal of Intercultural Relations, 29*, 137–163.
Brew, F. P., & Cairns, D. R. (2004). Do culture or situational constraints determine choice of direct or indirect styles in intercultural workplace conflicts? *Interna-tional Journal of Intercultural Relations, 28*, 331–352.
Brewer, M. B., Hong, Y., & Li, Q. (2004). Dynamic entitativity: Perceiving groups as actors. In V. Yzerbyt, C. M. Judd, & O. Corneille (Eds.), *The psychology of*

group perception: Perceived variability, entitativity, and essentialism (pp.25–38). New York: Psychology Press.

Brown, P., & Levinson, S. (1987). *Politeness: Some universals in language usage.* Cambridge: Cambridge University Press.

Chan, D. K.-S., & Goto, S. G. (2003). Conflict resolutions in the culturally diverse workplace: Some data from Hong Kong employees. *Applied Psychology: An International Review, 52,* 441–460.

Chao, M. M., Zhang, Z.-X., & Chiu, C.-y. (2010). Adherence to perceived norms across cultural boundaries: The role of need for cognitive closure and ingroup identification. *Group Processes and Intergroup Relations, 13,* 69–89.

Chen, L., & Isa, M. (2003). Intercultural communication and cultural learning: The experience of Japanese visiting students in the U.S. *Howard Journal of Communications, 14,* 75–96.

Cheng, C., Chiu, C., Hong, Y., & Cheung, J. S. (2001). Discriminative facility and its role in the perceived quality of interactional experiences. *Journal of Personality, 69,* 765–786.

Chiu, C.-y., & Cheng, S. Y-y. (2007). Toward a social psychology of culture and globalization: Some social cognitive consequences of activating two cultures simultaneously. *Social and Personality Psychology Compass, 1,* 84–100.

Chiu, C.-y., & Hong, Y. (2006). *Social psychology of culture.* New York: Psychology Press.

Chiu, C.-y., Leung, A. K.-y., & Kwan, L. (2007). Language, cognition, and culture: Beyond the Whorfian hypothesis. In S. Kitayama & D. Cohen (Eds.), *Handbook of cultural psychology* (pp. 668–688). New York: Guilford.

Chiu, C.-y., Morris, M., Hong, Y., & Menon, T. (2000). Motivated cultural cognition: The impact of implicit cultural theories on dispositional attribution varies as a function of need for closure. *Journal of Personality and Social Psychology, 78,* 247–259.

Cody, M. J., & McLaughlin, M. L. (1985). The situation as a construct in interpersonal communication research. In M. L. Knapp & G. R. Miller (Eds.), *Handbook of interpersonal communication* (pp. 263–312). Beverly Hills, CA: Sage.

Costa, R. T., & McCrae, R. R. (1992). *Revised NEO Personality Inventory (NEO PI-R) and NEO Five-factor Inventory (NEO-FFI) professional manual.* Odessa, FL: Psychological Assessment Resources.

D'Andrade, R. (1987). A folk model of the mind. In D. Holland & N. Quinn (Eds.), *Cultural models in language and thought* (pp. 112–148). Cambridge, UK: Cambridge University Press.

Fu, H-y., Chiu, C.-y., Morris, M. W., & Young, M. (2007). Spontaneous inferences from cultural cues: Varying responses of cultural insiders and outsiders. *Journal of Cross-Cultural Psychology, 38,* 58–75.

Fussell, S. R., & Krauss, R. M. (1992). Coordination of knowledge in communication: Effects of speakers' assumptions about others' knowledge. *Journal of Personality and Social Psychology, 62,* 378–391.

Giles, H., & Powesland, P. F. (1975). *Speech style and social evaluation.* London: Academic Press.

Higgins, E. T., Friedman, R. S., Harlow, R. E., Idson, L. C., Ayduk, O. N., & Taylor, A. (2001). Achievement orientations from subjective histories of success: Promotion pride versus prevention pride. *European Journal of Social Psychology, 31*, 3–23.

Hong, Y.-y., Wan, C., No, S., & Chiu, C.-y. (2007). Multicultural identities. In S. Kitayama & D. Cohen (Eds.), *Handbook of cultural psychology*. New York: Guilford.

Ip, G. W.-m., Chiu, C.-y., & Wan, C. (2006). Birds of a feather and birds flocking together: Physical versus behavioral cues may lead to trait- versus goal-based group perception. *Journal of Personality and Social Psychology, 90*, 368–381.

Isaacs, E. A., & Clark, H. H. (1987). References in conversations between experts and novices. *Journal of Experimental Psychology: General, 116*, 26–37.

Jetten, J., Spears, R., & Manstead, A. S. R. (1997). Distinctiveness threat and prototypicality: Combined effects on intergroup discrimination and collective self-esteem. *European Journal of Social Psychology, 27*, 635–657.

Kashima, Y. (2000). Maintaining cultural stereotypes in the serial reproduction of narratives. *Personality and Social Psychology Bulletin, 26*, 594–604.

Kashima, Y. (2002). Culture and social cognition: Towards a social psychology of cultural dynamics. In D. Matsumoto (Ed.), *Handbook of culture and psychology* (pp. 325–360). New York: Oxford University Press.

Kashima, Y., Woolcock, J., & Kashima, E. (2000). Group impressions as dynamic configurations: The tensor product model of group impression formation and change. *Psychological Review, 107*, 914–942.

Keysar, B., Barr, D. J., Balin, J. A., & Brauner, J. S. (2000). Taking perspective in conversation: The role of mutual knowledge in comprehension. *Psychological Sciences, 11*, 32–38.

Kim, Y. Y. (1986). Understanding the social context of intergroup communication: A personal network theory. In W. Gudykunst (Ed.), *Intergroup communication* (pp. 86–95). London: Edward Arnold.

Kim, Y. Y. (1997). Adapting to a new culture. In L. A. Samovar & R. E. Porter (Eds.), *Intercultural communication: A reader* (pp. 404–416). Belmont, CA: Wadsworth.

Lalwani, A. K., Shrum, L. J., & Chiu, C.-y. (2009). Motivated response style: The role of cultural values, regulatory focus, and self-consciousness in socially desirable responding. *Journal of Personality and Social Psychology, 96*, 870–882.

Latané, B. (1996). Dynamic social impact: The creation of culture by communication. *Journal of Communication, 46*, 13–25.

Latané, B., & Bourgeois, M. J. (1996). Experimental evidence for dynamic social impact: The emergence of subcultures in electronic groups. *Journal of Communication, 46*, 35–47.

Lau, I. Y.-M., Chiu, C.-y., & Hong, Y. (2001). I know what you know: Assumptions about others' knowledge and their effects on message construction. *Social Cognition, 19*, 587–600.

Lee, H.-O., & Rogan, R. G. (1991). A cross-cultural comparison of organizational conflict management behaviors. *International Journal of Conflict Management, 2*, 181–199.

Leung, A. K.-y., & Chiu, C.-y. (2008). Interactive effects of multicultural experiences and openness to experience on creativity. *Creativity Research Journal, 20*, 376–382.

Leung, A. K.-y., Chiu, C.-y., & Hong, Y. (2003). *Bicultural individuals accommodate their interaction strategies to the projected distributions of promotion- and prevention-focused regulatory foci in interaction partner's cultural group.* Poster presented at the Annual Meeting of the Society for Personality and Social Psychology (SPSP), Austin, TX.

Leung, A. K.-y., Maddux, W. W., Galinsky, A. D., & Chiu, C.-y. (2008). Multicultural experience enhances creativity: The when and how. *American Psychologist, 63,* 169–181.

Li, Q., & Hong, Y. (2001). Intergroup perceptual accuracy predicts real-life intergroup interactions. *Group Processes and Intergroup Relations, 4,* 341–354.

Lyons, A., & Kashima, Y. (2001). The reproduction of culture: Communication processes tend to maintain cultural stereotypes. *Social Cognition, 19,* 372–394.

Lyons, A., & Kashima, Y. (2003). How are stereotypes maintained through communication? The influence of stereotype sharedness. *Personality and Social Psychology Bulletin, 85,* 989–1005.

McCrae, R. R., & Costa, P. T. (1997). Conceptions and correlates of openness to experience. In R. Hogan, J., Johnson, & S. Briggs (Eds.), *Handbook of personality psychology* (pp. 825–847). San Diego, CA: Academic Press.

Putnam, L. L., & Wilson, C. E. (1982). Communication strategies in organizational conflicts: Reliability and validity of a measurement scale. In M. Burgoon (Ed.), *Communication yearbook* (Vol. 6, pp. 629–652). Beverly Hills, CA: Sage Publications.

Roccas, S., & Schwartz, S. H. (1993). Effects of intergroup similarity on intergroup relations. *European Journal of Social Psychology, 23,* 581–595.

Sanchez-Burks, J. (2002). Protestant relational ideology and (in)attention to relational cues in work settings. *Journal of Personality and Social Psychology, 83,* 919–929.

Sanchez-Burks, J., Lee, F., Choi, I., Nisbett, R., Zhao, S., & Jasook, K. (2003). Conversing across cultures: East-West communication styles in work and non-work contexts. *Journal of Personality and Social Psychology, 85,* 363–372.

Sanchez-Burks, J., Nisbett, R., & Ybarra, O. (2000). Cultural styles, relational schemas and prejudice against outgroups. *Journal of Personality and Social Psychology, 79,* 174–189.

Sperber, D. (1996). *Explaining culture: A naturalistic approach.* Oxford, UK: Blackwell.

Sui, J., Zhu, Y., & Chiu, C.-y. (2007). Bicultural mind, self-construal, and recognition memory: Cultural priming effects on self- and mother-reference effect. *Journal of Experimental Social Psychology, 43,* 818–824.

Tajfel, H. (1982). *Social identity and intergroup relations.* Cambridge, UK: Cambridge University Press.

Tajfel, H., & Turner, J. C. (1986). The social identity theory of inter-group behavior. In S. Worchel & L. W. Austin (Eds.), *Psychology of intergroup relations.* Chicago: Nelson-Hall.

Ting-Toomey, S., & Kurogi, A. (1998). Facework competence in intercultural conflict: An updated face-negotiation theory. *International Journal of Intercultural Relations, 22,* 187–226.

Tong, Y., Hong, Y., Lee, S., & Chiu, C. (1999). Language as a carrier of social identity. *International Journal of Intercultural Relations, 23*, 281–296.

Triandis, H. C. (1994). *Culture and social behavior.* New York: McGraw-Hill.

van Knippenberg, D., & Ellemers, N. (2003). Social identity and group performance: Identification as the key to group-oriented efforts. In S. A. Haslam, D. van Knippenberg, M. J. Platow, & N. Ellemers (Eds.), *Social identity at work: Developing theory for organizational practice* (pp. 29–42). New York and Hove, UK: Psychology Press.

Wan, C., Chiu, C.-y., Tam, K.-p., Lee, S.-l., Lau, I. Y.-m., & Peng, S-q. (2007). Perceived cultural importance and actual self-importance of values in cultural identification. *Journal of Personality and Social Psychology, 92*, 337–354.

Weber, M. (1947). *Max Weber: The theory of social and economic organization* (A. M. Henderson & T. Parsons, Trans.). New York: The Free Press.

Wiseman, R. L. (2002). Intercultural communication competence. In W. B. Gudykunst & B. Mody, (Eds.), *International and intercultural communication* (2nd ed.; pp. 207–224). Thousand Oaks, CA: Sage.

Wish, M., & Kaplan S. J. (1977). Toward an implicit theory of communication. *Sociometry, 40*, 234–246.

Wong, R. Y.-M., & Hong, Y.-y. (2005). Dynamic influences of culture on cooperation in the Prisoner's Dilemma. *Psychological Science, 16*, 429–434.

Yokota, K., & Yuki, M. (2007, February). *Different facets of perceived entitativity lead to different types of intergroup threats and emotions.* Paper presented at the 8th Annual meeting of Society of Personality and Social Psychology, Memphis, TN.

Zou, X., Tam, K. P., Morris, M. W., Lee, S.-l., Lau, I. Y.-m., & Chiu, C.-y. (2009). Culture as common sense: Perceived consensus versus personal beliefs as mechanisms of cultural influence. *Journal of Personality and Social Psychology, 97*, 579–597.

14

Multicultural Experience Fosters Creative Conceptual Expansion

ANGELA K.-Y. LEUNG, JING CHEN, AND CHI-YUE CHIU[1]

Before you read on, take two minutes to draw a picture of an innovative kind of chocolate. Don't think too hard. Just draw it quickly.

This task was presented to the many designers, artists, and students from all over the world who took part in the Belgian chocolate initiative project organized by the Addict Creative Lab. When the famous Belgian chocolate company Isis Luxury approached this ethnically and functionally diverse group to brainstorm product branding and packaging strategies to enhance the product's marketability, Giovanna Massini, the Addict Creative Lab researcher who led the chocolate project, advised his lab members: "Chocolate in Belgium is an icon, like pasta in Italy. But why do we feel obliged by tradition? We must disturb the traditional shapes. We must create new combinations, new ingredients."

What did these designers do to revolutionize chocolate and challenge the traditional way we view this confection? Here are some novel ideas from the group: (a) chocolate molded picture frames to allow viewers to erase their beautiful details with their warm, playful hands; (b) daisy shaped chocolate with petals for plucking and the words "M'ama . . . non m'ama" ("She loves me, she loves me not") imprinted; and (c) engraved silver or gold rings surrounding chocolate centers; as the designer put it, "You can eat the chocolate out of the ring, or you can give the ring and the chocolate with it . . . It's a ritual."

This Belgian chocolate initiative was reported in an article on *Business-Week Online* titled "Thinking Outside the Chocolate Box" (Vadino, 2006). To some people, the ability to think outside the box seems sudden, intuitive, and without logic; creativity may leap into consciousness magically at times,

---

[1] Preparation of this chapter was supported by a grant awarded to the third author by the Research Grants Council, the Hong Kong Special Administrative Region.

or the illumination may never come. Creativity, however, is not as mysterious as it appears to be. As the Belgian chocolate example illustrates, creative ideas often emerge when individuals synthesize ideas from the knowledge traditions in different cultures or combine seemingly nonoverlapping ideas.

A wealth of empirical evidence has identified components of personality, affect, cognition, and motivation that facilitate or hinder creativity (see Amabile, 1996; Csikszentmihalyi, 1996; Sawyer, 2006; Simonton, 2000, 2003). To bring a fresh perspective into the existing literature on culture and creativity, the present chapter discusses how people's experience with multiple cultures can help break their routinized mindset and inspire them to take off their biased cultural "lens" when looking at the world. In this sense, multicultural experiences can be valuable intellectual resources for facilitating creative thinking. We argue that multicultural individuals are more adept at creative productions and more inclined to engage in creative processes, perhaps because these individuals have more experiences than do others with creative conceptual expansion – a key process that supports creativity according to the creative cognition approach (see the next section on Creative Cognition Approach).

Not everyone can capture the creative benefits of multicultural experiences, however. Individuals who do not have an open and accepting attitude toward foreign cultures may feel overwhelmed by unfamiliar cultural encounters. Likewise, not all multicultural encounters would bring creative benefits. When the situation puts people under time pressure or heightens existential concerns, the need for cultural conformity and hence the inclination to cling to familiar ideas in one's own culture will become salient, which in turn would hamper creative performance. Accordingly, it is useful to identify when people can benefit from their multicultural experiences and when they cannot. In this chapter, we will systematically examine the potential creative benefits of multicultural experiences and the boundaries of such benefits.

THE CREATIVE COGNITION APPROACH

In earlier definitions, creativity is usually defined as something new (Thurstone, 1952), as something nonconforming (Crutchfield, 1962), or as something that is surprising to people during the time of discovery (Barlett, 1958). Stein (1953) added to these definitions the appropriateness dimension of creativity – creativity is "a novel work that is accepted as tenable or useful or satisfying by a group at some point in time" (p. 311).

Although definitions vary, creativity typically refers to the ability to produce products that are novel, high in quality, appropriate, and useful.

Other researchers have performed systematic analysis on the creativity-supporting processes that promote people's creative performance. The creative cognition approach is a scientific approach to studying creativity through examining the cognitive mechanisms that produce creative ideas (Finke, Ward, & Smith, 1992; Ward, Smith, & Vaid, 1997). According to this approach, every person has the potential to become creative as long as they *know* how to use the ordinary cognitive processes to produce extraordinary outcomes. In this view, the interplay of two kinds of cognitive processes is implicated in creative thinking – generative processes and exploratory processes (Finke et al., 1992). The generative processes involve *active memory retrieval or searching* of relevant information to generate candidate ideas with differing creative potentials. The explorative processes involve *careful scrutiny* of these candidate ideas to determine which ones should receive further processing (e.g., modification, elaboration, and transformation).

Conceptual expansion is a strategy that makes use of the generative and explorative processes to support creative activities (Ward, Patterson, Sifonis, Dodds, & Saunders, 2002; Ward et al., 1997). Creative conceptual expansion takes place when attributes of seemingly irrelevant concepts are added to an existing concept to extend its conceptual boundary (Ward et al., 1997). In psychology, researchers may create new instances of an old construct by adding to it ideas from another theory. For instance, in psychoanalytical theory, transference refers to unconscious redirection of feelings from one person to another. Chen and Andersen (1999) shed new light on this construct by reinterpreting it from a social–cognitive perspective, positing that transference occurs when positive or negative evaluation of a new person is assimilated into an activated representation of a significant other. The expansion of an idea with the use of previously separate ideas is crucial to creative performance.

Outcomes of conceptual expansion are associated with different degrees of novelty. If the concepts employed to expand an existing idea are typically or frequently associated with that idea, conceptual expansion will be less creative. On the contrary, higher creativity occurs when the two concepts involved in conceptual expansion are not normally seen as overlapping (Wan & Chiu, 2002). Recruiting seemingly nonoverlapping concepts in the conceptual expansion process is by no means easy, however. Past research has documented that people's creative imagination is highly likely to be structured by existing conceptual frameworks or commonly encountered exemplars. For instance, when developing novel coins, participants tend to include attributes of known coins in their designs (Rubin & Kontis, 1983). These stable cognitive structures are hard to break even if people were instructed to use their wildest imagination to come up with creative ideas. For example, although participants were given such explicit instructions to be creative in drawing novel creatures on Mars, their drawings were characterized by highly accessible Earth animal characteristics (e.g., eyes, legs). Thus, the alien creatures still remarkably resemble existing animals on planet Earth (Ward, 1994; Ward & Sifionis, 1997). In another study, Ward and colleagues (2002) found that two-thirds of participants reported relying on specific Earth examples to guide their creation of novel instances of animals, fruit, and tools. In other words, prior knowledge restricts creative thinking and makes it difficult for people to think outside the box.

CULTURE AND CREATIVITY

Being immersed in one's own culture is a double-edged sword. On the one hand, as noted in Part III of this volume, culture serves important psychological functions. Culture as a network of shared knowledge representations consists of learned conventions that help individuals in a society coordinate their social behaviors, define their self-identities, manage their existential terror, and provide firm answers to important questions that people encounter in life (Chapters 5–7, this volume). On the other hand, people who are deeply immersed in their culture have also acquired the learned routines or conventional knowledge in that culture, which, as noted in the previous section, may limit creative conceptual expansion (Rubin & Kontis, 1983; Ward, 1994; Ward et al., 2002). Apparently, a major constraint on creative conceptual expansion is the influence of highly accessible exemplars commonly found in everyday life. To the extent that culture consists of a set of preexisting, routinized, and chronically accessible ideas, it may limit the generation of creative thoughts (Leung, Maddux, Galinsky, & Chiu, 2008).

Multicultural Experiences Enhance Creativity

Like the experience of being immersed in one's own culture, the experience of being exposed to multiple cultures can also be a double-edged sword. When individuals encounter a foreign environment, they may experience culture shock. They may feel anxious, uneasy, and disoriented when things they are used to and have taken for granted (the language, food, movies, and music of the home culture) suddenly become out of reach. Although culture shock has its dark side, after the initial, difficult adaptation stages have passed, encountering a foreign culture can also provide an opportunity for acquiring new perspectives on problem solving.

As a result, whereas culture may limit creativity, multicultural experiences may foster creative expansion of ideas. For example, consider two ideas: A and B. Idea A has high categorical accessibility in Culture I and low categorical accessibility in Culture II, and the reverse is true for Idea B. An individual who has extensive experiences in both cultures may be able to retrieve both ideas from memory spontaneously. The simultaneous memory retrieval of different ideas can inspire people to reappraise a situation, question entrenched assumptions, and reduce mental rigidity. Moreover, by cognitively placing two different ideas in juxtaposition, people may be able to integrate the two ideas into a novel idea. Indeed, many instances of creative conceptual expansion in daily life result from integrating indigenous cultural exemplars from diverse cultures. For example, McDonald's in Taiwan serves a rice burger – beef or chicken sandwiched between buns made of rice. Whereas hamburger is a more common food item in Western cultures, rice is a more common staple food in Asian cultures. The two, however, can be creatively synthesized into rice burgers through creative conceptual expansion.

Theoretically, multicultural experiences can contribute to creative expansion in at least four ways. First, people learn new ideas and concepts from multicultural experiences. These ideas can be the inputs for creative expansion processes. The more new ideas people have, the more likely they are to come up with novel combinations (Weisberg, 1999). Through multicultural experiences, people are also exposed to a broad range of novel behavioral and cognitive scripts, which can increase cognitive complexity (Tadmor & Tetlock, 2006).

Second, each culture's established conceptions present to its own people structured and often routinized responses to the environment; these cognitive structures may be destabilized as people acquire alternative conceptions through their experiences in other cultures. Intuitively, it stands to reason that exposure to a different cultural environment can train individuals to rethink and question their long-held assumptions, give individuals access to ideas that are unconventional in their own culture, and break individuals' mental set. Third, having acquired and successfully applied novel ideas from a foreign culture, people with rich multicultural experiences may be prepared to recruit and seek out ideas from other diverse sources and use them as inputs in the creative processes. Finally, foreign cultures may contain values and beliefs different from or even in conflict with those in one's own culture. Incongruent concepts invite exploration into their interrelations, the outcome of which may extend and enrich the concepts in question (Ward, 2001). Thus, multicultural experiences can positively impact creativity by offering people the opportunities to spontaneously recruit seemingly discrepant ideas from unfamiliar cultures, cognitively place them in juxtaposition, and through creative insights integrate these ideas in novel ways. Higher creativity is more likely when the two concepts involved in conceptual expansion are not normally seen as overlapping – these seemingly non-overlapping concepts can sometimes be associated with two distinct cultural sources.

In short, multicultural experience may foster creativity by (a) offering access to novel ideas and concepts in other cultures, (b) destabilizing routinized knowledge structures and increasing the cognitive accessibility of relatively inaccessible knowledge, (c) increasing the psychological readiness to recruit ideas from unfamiliar sources and places, and (d) fostering synthesis of seemingly incompatible ideas from diverse cultures.

RESEARCH EVIDENCE FOR THE CREATIVE BENEFITS OF MULTICULTURAL EXPERIENCES

Indirect Evidence

Earlier research has provided some indirect evidence for the positive link between multicultural experiences and creativity. For example, research has consistently shown that bilingual persons outperform monolingual persons on creativity tests (e.g., Carringer, 1974; Lambert, Tucker, & d'Anglejan, 1973; Okoh, 1980). Evidence from other studies that examined the effect of culture on children's overall creativity also shows that bicultural children such as children from Hong Kong (Rudowicz, Lok, & Kitto, 1995) or those of Chinese-American descent (Huntsinger, Schoeneman, & Ching, 1994) outperform monolingual white American children on various creativity assessments. To the extent that bilingual competence is a proxy for multicultural experiences, this finding suggests that exposure to more than one culture is conducive to creativity. Specifically, bilingualism may enable people to understand and appreciate diverse, linguistically encoded cultural ideas.

There is also evidence that creativity is facilitated in groups that allow and even encourage the expression of dissenting views (Nemeth & Wachter, 1983) and in groups that contain members from diverse cultural backgrounds (Guimerà, Uzzi, Spiro, & Amaral, 2005; Levine & Moreland, 2004).

The different views emanating from these groups can stimulate a reappraisal of the situation and widen people's perspectives (Nemeth & Kwan, 1987). Consideration of multiple alternatives coming from different knowledge traditions is conducive to generating novel points of view.

At the societal level, it has been documented that creative activity increases in places where people have been increasingly exposed to outside influences, whether through immigration, traveling or studying abroad, or learning from foreign teachers (Simonton, 1997). Living in diverse sociocultural environments that have a large number of politically fragmented states can also facilitate creativity (Simonton, 1975; Sorokin, 1969). As Simonton (2000) put it, "Nationalistic rebellion encourages cultural heterogeneity rather than homogeneity. Rather than everyone having to speak the same language, read the same books, follow the same laws, and so on, individuals are left with more options. These suggest that cultural diversity may facilitate creativity" (p. 155).

All these findings indicate that exposure to multicultural experiences lays the foundation for breaking mental set and boosting creative performance. The evidence for the creative benefits of multicultural experiences just reviewed is indirect and suggestive, however. Fortunately, more direct evidence for the positive link between multicultural experiences and creative conceptual expansion has recently started to emerge.

Direct Evidence

Causal Effects of Multicultural Experiences on Creative Productions
We have conducted the first controlled experiment to provide *direct* evidence for the causal effects of multicultural experiences on creative performance. These results have helped eliminate the alternative explanation in the previously reviewed correlational studies that creative people voluntarily seek out multicultural experiences. These results also rule out the possibility that the link between multicultural experiences and creativity is due to a third variable (e.g., bilingual competence and openness to experience increases both multicultural experiences and creativity).

The participants in this experiment were American college students of European descent. We manipulated participants' exposure to a foreign culture and assessed its *causal* impact on immediate and delayed creative performance (Leung & Chiu, in press). The experimental manipulation of foreign cultural exposure was administered in the first experimental session through showing respondents a 45-minute multimedia (with pictures, music, videos) PowerPoint presentation that depicted different aspects of one or two cultures. The slideshow materials covered a wide range of cultural facets including architecture, scenery, landscape, home decorations, furniture, apparel, cuisine, life, entertainment, recreation, music, movies, arts, and literature. Participants were randomly assigned to one of the five conditions: (a) American culture only, in which participants viewed a presentation of American culture; (b) Chinese culture only, in which participants viewed a presentation of Chinese culture only; (c) dual cultures, in which participants viewed a presentation of American and Chinese cultures back to back; or (d) fusion culture, in which participants viewed a presentation of a hybrid culture created by fusing American and Chinese cultures (e.g., McDonald's rice burger; *Reflection*, a Vanessa Mae music video); and (e) control condition, in which participants did not see a presentation. Subsequent to viewing the slideshow, participants in the four experimental conditions completed the first creativity task. Participants in the control condition did not see the presentation and proceeded directly to completing the creativity task. The study also included a second session that took place five to seven days later, in which a different creativity test was administered. The second creativity test allowed us to examine the durability of the creative effects of multicultural experiences.

Two features of this experiment are noteworthy. First, aside from manipulating whether participants were exposed to a foreign culture, the cultural exposure manipulation also manipulated *how* participants were exposed to a foreign culture (whether they were exposed to a foreign culture only in the Chinese slideshow condition or to a foreign culture and their own culture together in the joint and fusion slideshow conditions). This experimental setup could verify whether perceptual and cognitive juxtaposition of local and foreign cultures (vs. mere exposure to a foreign culture) is critical for promoting creative synthesis of ideas from diverse cultural sources.

Second, the two creativity tasks we used in this experiment did not require knowledge of American or Chinese culture. Thus, our results could not be explained simply by acquisition of knowledge about American or Chinese culture during the slideshow presentation. We assessed creative performance in the first session with a fairy tale rewriting task. Participants read a summary of the Cinderella tale and developed a new version of it for children in Turkey, a relatively unfamiliar culture to most European-American students. The participants were encouraged to use their wildest imagination to rewrite the story to make it creative, original, and coherent. Along with the summary of the original story, participants were also given some quick facts about Turkey's geographical location, climate, religion, economy, and industries and a narrative of Turkish people's everyday life.

To avoid practice effects, a different creativity test was used in the second session that took place five to seven days later. In the second session, participants in the experimental conditions first provided some personal thoughts regarding the presentation materials that they saw in the previous session. Next, among other filler tasks, they were asked to construct two creative analogies of "time" (e.g., "Time is like a newspaper") and to describe the connections between time and the analogy.

Results indicated that the participants who watched a presentation of only American or only Chinese culture did not have better creative performance than the control participants. Those who watched the dual cultures or fusion culture presentation, however, had better creative performance than the control participants in both the first and second experimental sessions, which were at least five days apart.

Two implications of the results should be highlighted. First, as noted, the two creativity tasks did not require knowledge of American or Chinese culture (writing a fairy tale for Turkish children and constructing analogies of time). Nonetheless, the cognitive benefits of experiencing Chinese culture were obtained in participants' creative products on these tasks. This result suggests that the creative effects of multicultural exposure may come from the development or practice of higher-order cognitive skills, such as the tendencies to sample ideas from divergent sources, compare and contrast the sampled ideas to explore their interrelations, and attempt creative integration of seemingly unconnected ideas (Wan & Chiu, 2002; Ward, 2001).

Second, the creative benefits of multicultural exposure were found only when American and Chinese cultures were presented simultaneously (i.e., in the joint or fusion conditions). This finding suggests that experiencing a single culture, even if it is a foreign culture (e.g., Chinese culture to European Americans), is not sufficient to facilitate creativity. The result supports the creative cognition perspective and underscores the importance of placing divergent cultural ideas in cognitive juxtaposition for generating creative insights.

Linking Multicultural Experiences to Engagement in Creative Processes
The study of creativity can be approached from a product perspective as well as from the process perspective. Whereas the product perspective focuses on creative outcomes or performance, the process perspective attends to the creativity-supporting processes. As creativity is manifest in both creative performance and engagement in creative processes, the product and process perspectives complement each other.

Our investigation, being inspired by the creative cognition approach, also aims to explicate *how* multicultural experiences may bring creative benefits, thus tapping into the creativity-supporting processes. To achieve this research goal, in one study we had European-American participants perform an idea sampling task that required them to develop a preliminary idea on happiness into a creative and original theory (Leung & Chiu, in press). At the beginning of the task, participants had the opportunity to consult ideas from American and other (Chinese and Turkish) cultures. Our major dependent measure was the preference to sample ideas from foreign cultures (vs. American culture). We predicted that extensiveness of multicultural experiences would be positively related to the tendency to sample ideas from other cultures.

To elaborate, participants were first presented with the following idea, allegedly taken from a psychology student's honor thesis: *People who have more friends are happier.* Their task was to write a short essay to expand the idea. They were encouraged to formulate their own creative ideas about happiness by seeking inspirations from the writings of esteemed scholars. In so doing, they could consult up to 7 (of 15) sayings about happiness, each written by an American, Turkish, or Chinese scholar. Brief background information of 15 scholars (5 American, 5 Turkish, and 5 Chinese) was presented. A sample scholar description is: "An American [Chinese or Turkish] researcher who has made several discoveries about human motivation." To ensure that participants' choices were not influenced by the specific contents of the background descriptions, in a pilot study, participants read the descriptions without the scholar nationality information and rated how likely they would consult each scholar's saying to better understand the nature of happiness. The scholar descriptions included in the current study did not differ on this measure in the pilot test. Furthermore, we counterbalanced the pairing of the scholar description and the scholar cultural identity: The scholar descriptions were divided into three sets of five descriptions, and each set was paired with American, Chinese, and Turkish scholars. Participants were randomly assigned to read one counterbalanced version of the descriptions.

After participants had indicated their choices, they received a set of sayings from the experimenter. The number of sayings in the set equaled the number of sayings requested by the participant. Unbeknownst to the participants, they received a set of sayings randomly selected from a pool of 15 sayings. These sayings were matched on ratings of familiarity, usefulness, originality, stimulation, persuasiveness, and creativity collected in a pilot study. A sample saying is "The secret of happiness is to make others believe they are the cause of it." Participants then wrote a short essay to expand the given preliminary idea on happiness with their chosen sayings.

Upon completing the idea sampling task, participants filled out a Multi-cultural Experience Survey that measured different aspects of multicultural exposures: (a) whether they spoke a foreign language, (b) the percentage of their lifetime they had lived outside their home State, (c) whether their father and mother were born outside the United States, (d) a self-report 10-point scale item on the extent of their exposure to a culture other than mainstream American culture, (e) the kind of cuisine served by their most favorite restaurants, (f) the ethnicity of their five favorite musicians, and (g) the ethnicity of their five closest friends. The survey appears to have high convergent and discriminant validity (see Leung & Chiu, 2008). Par-ticipants also filled out a creativity subscale of the Personal Value Scales (Scott, 1965) that measured their everyday creative behaviors. A sample item is "Developing new and different ways of doing things."

Recall that participants had a choice of consulting up to seven happiness sayings written by American, Turkish, or Chinese scholars in the idea sam-pling task. We found that participants with more extensive multicultural experiences tended to sample more ideas from foreign cultures (i.e., Turkish and Chinese sayings) in the task. In addition, the multicultural individuals had higher creativity score measured by the creativity subscale. This study showed that extensiveness of multicultural experiences is associated with the tendency to sample ideas from diverse cultures.

In another study, we examined another creativity-supporting process – the generation of normatively inaccessible ideas (Leung & Chiu, in press). To prepare for the study, we asked American college students to list five gifts that came to their mind if they were to offer a gift to an acquaintance, thus allowing us to establish the gift-giving norm in the sample. For all distinct gifts, we computed the dominance score by counting the number of participants who listed them (Ward et al., 2002). The higher the score, the more common the gifts are. We then recruited another group of participants from the same student population as the gift-giving norm study to take part in the main study. The main study involved the same gift-listing task and the Multicultural Experience Survey. Following Ward and colleagues (2002), we computed an average dominance/rank score of the five gift ideas generated; this score took into account how common the gifts were in the sample (i.e., the dominance score gathered from the gift-giving norm study) as well as how accessible the gifts were to the participants (i.e., how early they wrote down a certain gift on their list of five). In other words, a gift with a high dominance/rank ratio is one that many participants readily generated.

We found that participants with greater exposure to foreign cultures had a lower dominance/rank score. This study supported our prediction that multicultural experience is associated with a tendency to generate ideas that are unconventional in their own culture.

To summarize the research findings reviewed thus far, multicultural experiences predict both creative outcomes and creative processes. It is positively related to performance in fairy tale writing and generation of creative analogies. It also predicts the tendency to recruit ideas from foreign cultures for creative idea expansion and to access unconventional knowledge from memory.

BOUNDARIES OF THE CREATIVE BENEFITS

Although there is clear evidence for the creative benefits of multicultural experiences, as mentioned at the beginning of this chapter, not everybody benefits from multicultural experiences, and the creative benefits are not actualized in all situations. Creativity researchers have emphasized the important role of individual differences and situational constraints on the development of creativity (Rhodes, 1987). These researchers posit that creativity should be understood as resulting from the interplay of personal and situational variables. The person perspective focuses on identifying individual-level variables that distinguish creative and less creative individuals, such as personality traits, affect, and motivation (see Amabile, 1996; Barron & Harrington, 1981; Csikszentmihalyi, 1996; Sawyer, 2006). The situation perspective seeks to explicate the facilitative and inhibitory effects of the environmental context (e.g., resources, time constraint, role models, situational norms and expectations) on creativity (Rhodes, 1987). According to Murray (1938), the influence of situational variables on creativity may come from objective aspects of the environment or individuals' subjective interpretations of it. Although the person and situation perspectives have been developed to guide the study of creativity, the same framework can be applied to understand the relationship between multicultural experiences and creativity.

The Person Perspective

Our research showed that multicultural experiences could enhance creativity, possibly because multicultural individuals are more inclined to engage in the creativity-supporting cognitive processes – sampling of ideas from diverse cultures and spontaneous generation of normatively inaccessible knowledge. Although these findings lend support to the idea that exposure to multicultural experiences can expand an individual's creative horizon, nevertheless, encountering a different culture can also be cognitively and emotionally demanding, particularly for some people.

One person variable that predicts the likelihood of benefiting from multicultural experiences is the personality trait of openness to experience. Openness to experience has been singled out as the personality dimension most closely linked to creative behaviors (Costa & McCrae, 1992; Feist, 1998; McCrae & Costa, 1997). Individuals with high openness to experience are those who are appreciative of novel ideas and new experiences, receptive to a variety of perspectives and thoughts, and unafraid of recruiting unconventional ways to deal with problems at hand; they are also artistic, inventive, and curious (Costa & McCrae, 1992; McCrae & Costa, 1997). Therefore, to individuals with a high level of openness, multicultural exposure may enhance their receptiveness to new ideas (Leung & Chiu, 2008). With a receptive mind-set, these individuals are more prepared to retrieve from memory unconventional ideas and use them in creative activities. Accordingly, we predict that openness to experience would facilitate multicultural learning. When people who are open to experiences are exposed to new cultural experiences, they tend to learn from these experiences and become creative.

On the contrary, to some people, exposure to multicultural experiences may evoke feelings of ambivalence and even culture shock (Hong, Wan, No, & Chiu, 2007; Chapter 12, this volume). We submit that individuals who are not open to new experience may appraise and experience multicultural encounters negatively. To manage these negative appraisals and feelings, these individuals may develop a mind-set that resists novel ideas and fall back on the conventionalized ideas in their own culture. Some recent research findings are consistent with this idea. For example, when open-minded Chinese undergraduates were exposed to symbols of American culture (vs. culture-unrelated pictures), they spontaneously adopted American practices in managing conflict. When close-minded Chinese undergraduates were shown the same symbols (vs. culture-unrelated pictures), they resisted American cultural practices and held on strongly to Chinese conflict management strategies (Fu, Morris, Lee, Chao, Chiu, & Hong, 2007; see also Chiu, Morris, Hong, & Menon, 2000).

Accordingly, we contend that multicultural experiences would have beneficial effects on creativity only among persons who are open to experience (Leung & Chiu, 2008). We predict that, among participants who are low on openness, having more multicultural experiences would be negatively associated with creativity. These individuals may find unfamiliar ideas from other cultures to be overwhelming, shocking, and even threatening. To manage these negative reactions, they may cling to the prevailing conventional ideas in their own culture and develop a mind-set that resists new ideas. As a result, they are likely to retrieve conventional or normatively accessible exemplars for use in creativity tasks.

In one study (Leung & Chiu, 2008), we examined the role of openness to experience in the relationship between multicultural experiences and creativity. Creativity was assessed as engagement in the creative process in one task and in creative production in another. Specifically, we used an exemplar generation task to assess the creative process of retrieving unconventional or normatively inaccessible exemplars in a certain conceptual domain, and an Unusual Uses Test (Guilford, 1959) to assess the creative outcome of coming up with unconventional uses of a common object – a performance measure of divergent thinking.

In the exemplar generation task, participants wrote down the first 20 occupations that came to mind. All distinct occupation exemplars were identified after eliminating close synonyms (e.g., taxi driver and cab driver) and those that reflected minor inflection variations (e.g., policeman and policemen) (Barsalou, 1985; Battig & Montague, 1969). An output precedence score was compiled for each distinct occupation exemplar. To obtain this score, we computed the reverse ordinal position of each occupation on all participants' lists. For example, for a given participant, if the occupation "lawyer" was on the second position among the 20 occupations listed, then "lawyer" received a score of 19 (i.e., 21 – 2). By taking the sum of the reverse ordinal positions of a certain exemplar ("lawyer") from all participants who had listed this exemplar, the output precedence score of this exemplar was obtained. Thus, an exemplar's output precedence score indicates how frequently the exemplar is listed as well as how quickly it comes to the mind of an average participant. That is, this score serves as a measure of normative accessibility (Barsalou, 1985). An exemplar with a high (low) output precedence score is one that is normatively accessible (inaccessible). The three most accessible occupations are doctor, lawyer, and teacher, and the three least accessible ones are dialect coach, optician, and knife maker.

In the Unusual Uses Test (Guilford, 1959), participants listed as many uses for garbage bags as possible without limiting themselves to any kinds of garbage bag or to any uses they had seen or heard about before. We were interested in two creativity indicators from this test. First, fluency or the ability to produce a larger number of unusual uses was measured by the total number of responses that participants generated in the test after eliminating repetitive responses. Second, flexibility or the ability to generate different kinds of unusual uses was measured by the total number of categories of unusual uses generated (e.g., containers, waterproof materials, arts, weapons, and furniture).

Participants' degree of multicultural experiences and openness to experience were assessed by the Multicultural Experience Survey and the Openness Scale in the NEO-Five Factor Inventory (NEO-FFI; Costa & McCrae, 1992). We first confirmed that multicultural experiences and openness represent two different constructs. Although individuals who are open to experience may voluntarily seek out more multicultural experiences than would persons who are less open, some aspects of multicultural experiences assessed in the Multicultural Experience Survey are experiences beyond personal control (e.g., parents' country of birth, the availability of foreign cultures in one's living environment). As expected, we found a low and nonsignificant positive correlation between the extent of multicultural experiences and openness to experience.

As predicted, the degree of multicultural experiences was positively linked to the tendency to generate normatively inaccessible exemplars as well as their creative performance on the Unusual Uses Test only among individuals who were open to experience. Among participants who were not open, having more multicultural experiences was associated with lower levels of creativity. In the face of overwhelming encounters with foreign cultures, less open individuals may not be psychologically prepared for accepting new ideas. Indeed, this argument is also supported by another recent study, which reported higher creative tendencies among individuals who are more able to adapt to a foreign culture while living abroad (Maddux & Galinsky, 2009). Therefore, people are more likely to benefit from multicultural experiences with a receptive mind-set and readiness to adapt.

The Situation Perspective

Multicultural experiences afford opportunities to think outside the box; these experiences can be valuable, creativity-enhancing cognitive resources. Not all multicultural individuals will benefit to the same degree from their multicultural experiences, however. For instance, being open to experience is important for actualizing the creative benefits of multicultural experiences. Furthermore, the situation perspective on the study of multicultural experiences and creativity holds that individuals may not benefit to the same degree from their multicultural experiences in *all* situations.

In some situations, people feel pressured to adhere to the conventional norms of their own culture. In these situations, individuals (independent of their amount of multicultural experiences) would tend to resist ideas from foreign cultures. Two kinds of environments that have been found to motivate cultural conformity are (a) high time pressure environment (which increases the need for firm answers), and (b) mortality salient environment (which puts people under existential terror).

High Time Pressure Environment
Feeling time urgency in situations can increase people's need for cognitive closure (NFCC) or the need for firm answers (Heaton & Kruglanski, 1991; Kruglanski & Webster, 1996). Cultural conventions provide definite answers with high consensual validity. Individuals with high NFCC prefer firm answers and dislike ambiguities. Thus, these individuals are particularly motivated to follow cultural conventions (Fu et al., 2007). Specifically, high (vs. low) NFCC individuals are more likely to display culture-characteristic social perceptual styles (Chiu et al., 2000) and to readily retrieve from memory conventional exemplars of a conceptual category (e.g., high NFCC European Americans tend to retrieve apple vs. durian as an exemplar of fruit; Ip, Chen, & Chiu, 2006). High (vs. low) NFCC immigrants or sojourners adhere more strongly to their heritage culture and are more unsettled in the host culture, particularly when they move to the host culture with their conationals (Kosic, Kruglanski, Pierro, & Mannetti, 2004; Kashima & Loh, 2006). Finally, high (vs. low) NFCC American-Chinese bicultural individuals are less susceptible to situational cueing of culture-characteristic judgments – unlike their low NFCC counterparts, they do not make characteristically Chinese (American) judgments when primed with Chinese (American) cultural cues (Fu et al., 2007).

In one study, we assessed how likely people working under high or low time pressure situations would be willing to recruit ideas with foreign cultural origins in an idea sampling task (Study 4, Leung & Chiu, in press). The task, which measured the tendency to sample American versus foreign sayings to creatively expand a preliminary idea regarding the nature of happiness, was identical to the one described earlier. European-American participants either worked on the task at their own pace (low time pressure condition), or were regularly reminded by the experimenter to finish the task on time (high time pressure condition). When participants were not under time pressure, those with extensive multicultural experiences were more motivated to recruit sayings from relatively unfamiliar Turkish and

Chinese cultures (vs. American culture). This association between degree of multicultural experiences and sampling of foreign sayings was reversed, however, when participants were placed under time pressure. For these participants, the more multicultural exposure they had, the less likely they were to recruit foreign ideas. A possible reason for this result is that individuals under time pressure desire firm answers rather than exploring foreign ideas that would engage divergent thinking. Individuals with rich multicultural experiences would expect ideas from foreign cultures to be particularly engaging. Thus, these individuals would be particularly motivated to avoid foreign ideas when they are under time pressure.

Mortality Salient Environment

In addition to a high time pressure situation, being exposed to a mortality salient situation may also limit multicultural individuals' receptiveness to foreign ideas. According to the Terror Management Theory (TMT; Greenberg, Solomon, & Pyszczynski, 1997; Greenberg, Pyszczynski, Solomon, Rosenblatt, Veeded, & Kirkland, 1990), when individuals are reminded of their eventual finitude, they experience existential terror (see Chapter 6, this volume). To cope with it, they increase their adherence to cultural conventions and through this strategy obtain a sense of symbolic immortality – the body may perish after death but the culture to which one belongs will continue to propagate (Solomon, Greenberg, Schimel, Arndt, & Pyszczynski, 2004). TMT researchers have garnered considerable evidence for this hypothesis. As shown in many studies, increasing the salience of mortality in a situation can result in stronger cultural identification (Kashima, Halloran, Yuki, & Kashima, 2004), more favorable responses to people who support their cultural worldview and less favorable responses to people who threaten it (e.g., Christians respond more positively to a fellow Christian than to a Jew Greenberg et al., 1990; American students respond more favorably to an exchange student who praises America than to a student who criticizes America Greenberg, Pyszczynski, Solomon, Simon, & Breus, 1994), and greater affective aversion toward creative activities (Arndt, Greenberg, Solomon, Pyszczynski, & Schimel, 1999).

In our study, we tested the moderation effect of mortality salience on the positive association between multicultural experiences and receptiveness to ideas from foreign cultures (Study 5, Leung & Chiu, in press). Participants took part in the same idea sampling task described earlier in this chapter. Before working on the task, however, half of the participants received the standard mortality salience manipulation used in the TMT research

(Rosenblatt, Greenberg, Solomon, & Pyszczynski, 1989); they were asked to vividly visualize what would happen to their body as they died and after they died. The remaining participants were assigned to the control condition and were asked to describe the experience of dental pain. After completing the idea sampling task, participants completed the Multicultural Experience Survey. As past studies (Greenberg et al., 1997) showed that the mortality salience effect is particularly pronounced on perceived desirability of symbolic elements from outgroup cultures, participants also rated each sample saying on four attributes: persuasiveness, helpfulness, stimulation, and creativity on an 11-point scale.

Although the degree of multicultural experiences did not predict the likelihood of participants sampling foreign sayings, it was related to their evaluations of foreign versus American sayings. Specifically, in the mortality nonsalient condition, participants with richer multicultural experiences evaluated the American sayings significantly less positively and the foreign sayings significantly more positively. In the mortality salient condition, however, the amount of multicultural experience was not related to the relative evaluation of ideas from foreign (vs. American) cultures.

In summary, although multicultural experiences can increase creativity, there are limits to their creative benefits. When multicultural individuals are not open to new experiences, or when the situation evokes an NFCC or existential terror, the potential creative benefits of multicultural experiences are limited.

IMPLICATIONS FOR MANAGEMENT AND EDUCATION

Our research on multicultural experiences and creativity has important ramifications for both organizational innovation and student learning. As a result of the inherent cultural heterogeneity in multinational corporations, understanding intercultural dynamics has become increasingly critical in the management of these corporations (Jenn, Northcraft, & Neale, 1999; Williams & O'Reilly, 1998). When employees from different cultural backgrounds work as a team or in the same department, they will interact with each other frequently. This interaction provides to the employees one form of multicultural experience that can potentially increase their facility in generating novel ideas and creative problem solving. The same is true for employees who are sent to work or receive training in overseas offices.

Accordingly, human resources managers or specialists should recognize the positive aspects of the growing diversity of the workforce and put that diversity to good use to benefit both organizations and employees. Indeed, an increasing number of organizations have created a Chief Diversity Officer (CDO) position to address the pressing need to effectively manage workforce diversity in multicultural organizations (Johansson, 2005). With a deeper understanding of the psychology of multicultural experiences and creativity, diversity specialists can implement policies to motivate employees to integrate native and foreign cultural knowledge to boost cognitive and behavioral flexibility in response to the changing demands of intercultural business contexts. The finding that multicultural experiences can facilitate creativity can also be incorporated into the design of both cultural competence and creativity training programs for a wide range of purposes. Similarly, possible boundaries of the cognitive benefits of multicultural experiences should be recognized and considered in the formulation of human resources policies and strategies. Concrete recommendations on human resources management will be discussed in the next chapter (see Chapter 15, this volume).

The results reviewed in this chapter also have significant implications on education. Maehr and Yamaguchi (2001) once commented on cultural diversity and education, suggesting that educators should first recognize the positive features of cultural diversity. They also posit that the ultimate challenge is to transform school contexts that value diversity. To our knowledge, few studies have systematically explicated the potential beneficial role of multicultural experience in student learning (e.g., acquiring new perspectives and creative abilities). We hope that our research findings can convince educators and practitioners of the benefits of cultural diversity in the cognitive development of both majority and minority students and hence give educators and practitioners the confidence and motivation to promote learning in a multicultural education setting.

CONCLUDING REMARKS

In this chapter, we discussed how multicultural experiences can be a valuable cognitive resource in creative thinking. Specifically, multicultural experiences may promote creativity through preparing individuals to sample ideas from diverse cultural sources and providing them ready access to unconventional and normatively inaccessible knowledge. Nonetheless, we have also identified a personal factor (openness to experience) and some situational factors (time pressure and mortality salience) that could limit the creative benefits of multicultural experiences. Future research would likely identify other boundaries of the creative benefits of multicultural experiences. Thus, multicultural experiences do not always lead to creativity; sometimes, they may even hamper creativity. To maximize the potential creative benefits of multicultural experiences, it is important to place the right person in the right situation.

REFERENCES

Amabile, T. M. (1996). *Creativity in context.* Boulder, CO: Westview Press.
Arndt, J., Greenberg, J., Solomon, S., Pyszczynski, T., & Schimel, J. (1999). Creativity and terror management: Evidence that creative activity increases guilt and social projection following mortality salience. *Journal of Personality and Social Psychology, 77,* 19–32.
Barron, F., & Harrington, D. M. (1981). Creativity, intelligence, and personality. *Annual Review of Psychology, 32,* 439–476.
Barsalou, L. W. (1985). Ideals, central tendency, and frequency of instantiation as determinants of graded structure in categories. *Journal of Experimental Psychology: Learning, Memory, and Cognition, 11,* 629–654.
Bartlett, F. C. (1958). *Thinking: An experimental and social study.* New York: Basic Books.
Battig, W. F., & Montague, W. E. (1969). Category norms for verbal items in 56 categories: A replication and extension of the Connecticut category norms. *Journal of Experimental Psychology Monographs, 80* (3, Pt 2).
Carringer, D. C. (1974). Creative thinking abilities of Mexican youth: The relationship of bilingualism. *Journal of Cross-Cultural Psychology, 5,* 492–504.
Chen, S., & Andersen, S. M. (1999). Relationships from the past in the present: Significant-other representations and transference in interpersonal life. In M. P. Zanna (Ed.), *Advances in experimental social psychology, Vol. 31* (pp. 123–190). San Diego, CA: Academic Press.
Chiu, C-y., Morris, M., Hong, Y., & Menon, T. (2000). Motivated cultural cognition: The impact of implicit cultural theories on dispositional attribution varies as a function of need for closure. *Journal of Personality and Social Psychology, 78,* 247–259.
Costa, R. T., & McCrae, R. R. (1992). *Revised NEO Personality Inventory (NEO PI-R) and NEO Five-factor Inventory (NEO-FFI) professional manual.* Odessa, FL: Psychological Assessment Resources.
Crutchfield, R. S. (1962). Conformity and creative thinking. In H. Gruber, G. Terrell, & M. Wertheimer (Eds.), *Contemporary approaches to creative thinking.* New York: Atherton.
Csikszentmihalyi, M. (1996). *Creativity: Flow and the psychology of discovery and invention.* New York: HarperCollins.
Feist, G. J. (1998). A meta-analysis of the impact of personality on scientific and artistic creativity. *Personality and Social Psychological Review, 2,* 290–309.
Finke, R. A., Ward, T. B., & Smith, S. M. (1992). *Creative cognition: Theory, research, and applications.* Cambridge, MA: MIT Press.
Fu, H., Morris, M. W., Lee, S., Chao, M., Chiu, C.-y., & Hong, Y. (2007). Epistemic motives and cultural conformity: Need for closure, culture, and context as determinants of conflict judgments. *Journal of Personality and Social Psychology, 9,* 191–207.

Greenberg, J., Pyszczynski, T., Solomon, S., Rosenblatt, A., Veeded, M., & Kirkland, S. (1990). Evidence for terror management theory II: The effects of mortality salience on reactions to those who threaten or bolster the cultural world view. *Journal of Personality and Social Psychology, 58*, 308–318.

Greenberg, J., Pyszczynski, T., Solomon, S., Simon, L., & Breus, M. (1994). Role of consciousness and accessibility of death-related thoughts in mortality salience effects. *Journal of Personality and Social Psychology, 67*, 627–637.

Greenberg, J., Solomon, S., & Pyszczynski, T. (1997). Terror management theory of self-esteem and cultural worldviews: Empirical assessments and conceptual refinements. In M. P. Zanna (Ed.), *Advances in experimental social psychology, Vol. 29* (pp. 61–139). New York: Academic Press.

Guilford, J. P. (1959). Traits of creativity. In H. H. Anderson (Ed.), *Creativity and its cultivation* (pp. 142–161). New York: Harper.

Guimerà, R., Uzzi, B., Spiro, J., & Amaral, L. A. N. (2005). Team assembly mechanisms determine collaboration network structure and team performance, *Science, 308*, 697–702.

Heaton, A. W., & Kruglanski, A. W. (1991). Person perception by introverts and extroverts under time pressure: Need for closure effects. *Personality and Social Psychology Bulletin, 17*, 161–165.

Huntsinger, C. S., Schoeneman, J., & Ching, W.-D. (1994). *A cross-cultural study of young children's performance on drawing and handwriting tasks.* Paper presented at the conference of the Midwestern Psychological Association, Chicago, IL.

Hong, Y.-y., Wan, C., No, S., & Chiu, C-y. (2007). Multicultural identities. In S. Kitayama & D. Cohen (Eds.), *Handbook of cultural psychology.* New York: Guilford.

Ip, G. W.-m., Chen, J., & Chiu, C.-y. (2006). The relationship of promotion focus, need for cognitive closure, and categorical accessibility in American and Hong Kong Chinese university students. *Journal of Creative Behavior, 40*, 201–215.

Jenn, K. A., Northcraft, G. B., & Neale, M. A. (1999). Why differences make a difference: A field study of diversity, conflict and performance in workgroups. *Administrative Science Quarterly, December*, 741–763.

Johansson, F. (2005). Masters of the multicultural. *Harvard Business Review, 83*, 8.

Kashima, E. S., Halloran, M., Yuki, M., & Kashima, Y. (2004). The effects of personal and collective mortality salience on individualism: Comparing Australians and Japanese with higher and lower self-esteem. *Journal of Experimental Social Psychology, 40*, 384–392.

Kashima, E. S., & Loh, E. (2006). International students' acculturation: Effects of international, conational, and local ties and need for closure. *International Journal of Intercultural Relations, 30*, 471–485.

Kosic, A., Kruglanski, A. W., Pierro, A., & Mannetti, L. (2004). The social cognitions of immigrants' acculturation: Effects of the need for closure and reference group at entry. *Journal of Personality and Social Psychology, 86*, 796–813.

Krugslanki, A. E., & Webster, D. M. (1996). Motivated closing of the mind: "Seizing" and "freezing." *Psychological Review, 103*, 263–283.

Lambert, W. E., Tucker, G. R., & d'Anglejan, A. (1973). Cognitive and attitudinal consequences of bilingual schooling: The St. Lambert project through grade five. *Journal of Educational Psychology, 65*, 141–159.

Leung, A. K.-y., & Chiu, C.-y. (2008). Interactive effects of multicultural experiences and openness to experience on creativity. *Creativity Research Journal, 20,* 376–382.

Leung, A. K.-y., & Chiu, C.-y. (in press). Multicultural experiences, idea receptiveness, and creativity. *Journal of Cross-Cultural Psychology.*

Leung, A. K.-y., Maddux, W. W., Galinsky, A. D., & Chiu, C.-y. (2008). Multicultural experience enhances creativity: The when and how? *American Psychologist, 63,* 169–181.

Levine, J. M., & Moreland, R. L. (2004). Collaborations: The social context of theory development. *Personality and Social Psychology Review, 8,* 164–172.

Maddux, W. W., & Galinsky, A. D. (2009). Cultural borders and mental barriers: The relationship between living abroad and creativity. *Journal of Personality and Social Psychology, 96,* 1047–1061.

Maehr, M. L., & Yamaguchi, R. (2001). Cultural diversity, student motivation and achievement. In F. Salili & C.-y. Chiu (Eds.), *Student motivation: The culture and context of learning* (pp. 123–148). New York: Plenum.

McCrae, R. R., & Costa, P. T. (1997). Conceptions and correlates of openness to experience. In R. Hogan, J. Johnson, & S. Briggs (Eds.), *Handbook of personality psychology* (pp. 825–847). San Diego, CA: Academic Press.

Murray, H. (1938). *Explorations in personality.* New York: Oxford University Press.

Nemeth, C., & Kwan, J. (1987). Minority influence, divergent thinking and detection of correct solutions. *Journal of Applied Social Psychology, 17,* 788–799.

Nemeth, C., & Wachter, J. (1983). Creative problem solving as a result of majority vs. minority influence. *European Journal of Social Psychology, 13,* 45–55.

Okoh, N. (1980). Bilingualism and divergent thinking among Nigerian and Welsh school children. *Journal of Social Psychology, 110,* 163–170.

Rhodes, M. (1987). An analysis of creativity. In S. G. Isaksen (Ed.), *Frontiers of creativity research: Beyond the basics* (pp. 216–222). Buffalo, NY: Bearly.

Rosenblatt, A., Greenberg, J., Solomon, S., & Pyszczynski, T. (1989). Evidence for terror management theory I: The effects of mortality salience on reactions to those who violate or uphold cultural values. *Journal of Personality & Social Psychology, 57,* 681–690.

Rubin, D. C., & Kontis, T. C. (1983). A schema for common cents. *Memory and Cognition, 11,* 335–341.

Rudowicz, E., Lok, D., & Kitto, J. (1995). Use of the Torrance Tests of Creative Thinking in an exploratory study of creativity in Hong Kong primary school children: A cross-cultural comparison. *International Journal of Psychology, 30,* 417–430.

Sawyer, K. (2006). *Explaining creativity: The science of human motivation.* New York: Oxford University Press.

Scott, W. A. (1965). *Values and organizations: A study of fraternities and sororities.* Chicago: Rand McNally.

Simonton, D. K. (1975). Sociocultural context of individual creativity: A transhistorical time-series analysis. *Journal of Personality and Social Psychology, 32,* 1119–1133.

Simonton, D. K. (1997). Foreign influence and national achievement: The impact of open milieus on Japanese civilization. *Journal of Personality and Social Psychology*, *72*, 86–94.

Simonton, D. K. (2000). Creativity: Cognitive, personal, developmental, and social aspects. *American Psychologist*, *55*, 151–158.

Simonton, D. K. (2003). Scientific creativity as constrained stochastic behavior: The integration of product, person, and process perspectives. *Psychological Bulletin*, *129*, 475–494.

Solomon, S., Greenberg, J., Schimel, J., Arndt, J., & Pyszczynski, T. (2004). Human awareness of mortality and the evolution of culture. In M. Schaller & C. S. Crandall (Eds.), *The psychological foundations of culture* (pp. 15–40). Mahwah, NJ: Lawrence Erlbaum Associates.

Sorokin, M. I. (1969). *Society, culture, and personality*. New York: Cooper Square.

Stein, M. I. (1953). Creativity and culture. *Journal of Psychology*, *36*, 311–322.

Tadmor, C. T., & Tetlock, P. E. (2006). Biculturalism: A model of the effects of second-culture exposure on integrative complexity. *Journal of Cross-Cultural Psychology 37*, 173–190.

Thurstone, L. L. (1952). Creative talent. In L. L. Thurstone (Ed.), *Applications of psychology* (pp. 18–37). New York: Harper and Row.

Wan, W., & Chiu, C.-y. (2002). Effects of novel conceptual combination on creativity. *Journal of Creative Behavior*, *36*, 227–241.

Ward, T. B. (1994). Structured imagination: The role of conceptual structure in exemplar generation. *Cognitive Psychology*, *27*, 1–40.

Ward, T. B. (2001). Creative cognition, conceptual combination, and the creative writing of Stephen R. Donaldson. *American Psychologist*, *56*, 350–354.

Ward, T. B., Patterson, M. J., Sifonis, C. M., Dodds, R. A., & Saunders, K. N. (2002). The role of graded category structure in imaginative thought. *Memory and Cognition*, *30*, 199–216.

Ward, T. B., Smith, S. M., & Vaid, J. (1997). Conceptual structures and processes in creative thought. In T. B. Ward, S. M. Smith, & J. Vaid (Eds.), *Creative thought: An investigation of conceptual structures and processes*. Washington, DC: American Psychological Association Books.

Weisberg, R. W. (1999). Creativity and knowledge: A challenge to theories. In R. J. Sternberg (Ed.), *Handbook of creativity* (pp. 226–250). Cambridge, England: Cambridge University Press.

Williams, K., & O'Reilly, C. (1998). The complexity of diversity: A review of forty years of research. In B. Staw & R. Sutton (Eds.), *Research in organizational behavior, Vol. 21* (pp. 77–140). Greenwich, CT: JAI Press.

Vadino, D. (2006). *Thinking outside the chocolate box: A conceptual Belgian project challenges the way we view chocolate*. Retrieved December 6, 2006, from http://www.businessweek.com/innovate/content/dec2006/id20061206_931012.htm?campaign_id=rss_daily.

15

Workforce Diversity and Creativity: A Multilevel Analysis

JIAN HAN,[1] SIQING PENG, CHI-YUE CHIU,[2]
AND ANGELA K.-Y. LEUNG

The previous chapter examined the relationship between multicultural experience and creativity. In this chapter, we will extend this analysis by exploring several related topics in organizational management, particularly regarding workforce diversity management and creativity.

Workforce diversity management has become a major concern in industrialized societies and global business (Harrison & Klein, 2007; Prasad, Pringle, & Konrad, 2006). As a consequence of the recent large-scale population movements across the world (Appadurai, 1990) and the resulting increase in the heterogeneity of the workforce in many countries, Western countries such as the United States, United Kingdom, Canada, and Australia have introduced legislation that draws attention to issues arising from the increased amount of workforce diversity (e.g., Title VII of the Civil Rights Act; various pieces of antidiscrimination legislation; affirmative action in the United States and Australia; employment equity in Canada and the United Kingdom; Prasad, Mils, Elmes, & Prasad, 1997; Yakura, 1996). In addition, with the rapid change in the demographic and skill compositions of the workforce in the global labor market, business practitioners and management researchers realize that workforce diversity presents both a major management challenge and a new opportunity for organizational growth. As a consequence, effective management of diversity is pushed up the management agenda (Thomas & Ely, 1996). Many companies are interested in how corporate diversity initiatives can be used to improve organizational performance. These organizations see the prospect of leveraging differences

[1] Preparation of this chapter was supported by a National Science Foundation of China grant awarded to the first author (Grant No. 70602007).
[2] Preparation of this chapter was supported by a grant awarded to the third author by the Ministry of Education, Singapore.

for the benefit of the organization – collaboration of different cultures, ideas, and perspectives is now considered an organizational asset that can bring creativity and innovation (Jayne & Dipboye, 2004).

The increasingly dynamic, globalized, and competitive business environment also contributes to the pressing need to harness creativity from a diverse workforce for business success. Given the increased diversity of the organizational stakeholders, customers, and market segments, having a workforce made up of an optimal combination of employees with different demographic backgrounds, knowledge, perspectives, and skills that can inspire creative synergies will make a substantial contribution to organizational excellence (Wentling & Palma-Rivas, 2000).

The prospect of harnessing creativity from workforce diversity for business success has sparked a search in both academia and the business community for theoretical models that would explicate what types of diversity would, under what conditions, foster individual and work team creativity (West & Anderson, 1996). In this chapter, we integrate literature from multiple disciplines such as sociology, cognitive psychology, social psychology, and human resource management to provide a theoretical understanding of how workforce diversity can enhance individual and group creativity and how organizational practices can help promote creativity through workforce diversity.

A MULTILEVEL MODEL OF WORKFORCE DIVERSITY

The theoretical model that guides our analysis distinguishes between the effects of workforce diversity on creativity at the individual, team, and organizational levels. At the individual level, employees in a diverse workforce have many opportunities to be exposed to novel ideas. Creative synthesis of these ideas with existing ideas will enhance creativity (Finke, Ward, & Smith, 1992; Ward, Paterson, Sifonis, Dodds, & Saunders, 2002). Employees who can readily adapt to an intellectually diverse work environment (e.g., those who have rich multicultural experiences and are open to experiences) are particularly likely to benefit from this process (see Chapter 14, also see Leung, Maddux, Galinksky, & Chiu, 2008).

At the team and organizational levels, the likelihood of engaging in creative activities as part of a diverse work team depends on the employees' motivation to be connected to the group and to express unique ideas during teamwork. This engagement motivation is strengthened when the employees feel that they can verify their self-assessment through others in the organization; that is, when others' assessment of the self matches the individuals' self-assessment (Swann, 1983). Workforce diversity, however, often draws attention to the employees' background differences and the attendant status implications (Berger, Cohen, & Zelditch, 1972; Wagner & Berger, 1993). When employees feel that they are evaluated primarily on the basis of their background characteristics rather than on their individual ideas, their need for self-verification will be frustrated and the motivation to contribute to the group's creative performance will decrease. Organizational management practices (e.g., staffing policies) that highlight status distinctions based on employees' background characteristics within a work team tend to aggravate their negative impact on creativity.

The organization of this chapter is structured as follows. First, we will define workforce diversity (the antecedent) and creativity (the outcome variable) in our model. Second, we will explain how workforce diversity can increase or decrease creativity at the individual and work team levels. Next, we will expand on the previous discussion regarding the relationship between workforce diversity and creativity by explaining the factors that would moderate the diversity–creativity nexus at both the individual and team levels. Despite the early enthusiasm for the creativity benefits of workforce diversity, contemporary assessments of the research evidence found that the performance advantage of diversity is often found under narrow conditions (Mannix & Neale, 2005, for reviews see Jackson, Joshi, & Erhardt, 2003; Milliken & Martins, 1996; Williams & O'Reilly, 1998). Although the effect of diversity on team performance is not consistent, we believe that systematic relationships between diversity and creativity can be discerned when the pertinent mediating processes and moderating factors are identified. Our model suggests that workforce diversity can lead to positive or negative creativity outcomes depending on the level of analysis and the presence or absence of some moderators within each level of analysis. In this chapter, we discuss the moderating roles of individual adaptability to diversity and the organization's diversity management capability in harnessing creative benefits from workforce diversity. Thus, our model has the potential of reconciling the conflicting results in past research and offering an integrative theoretical framework for further advancing our knowledge of the diversity–creativity link in future research and for guiding organizational practices. These discussions will then lead to the conclusion that the link between workforce diversity and creativity is an outcome of a comprehensive diversity management system that requires individual, team, and organizational level initiatives.

Definitions and Categories of Workforce Diversity

Diversity is a unit level, compositional construct (Harrison & Klein, 2007). It is a characteristic of groups (Tilly, 1998). To say that a group is diverse implies some recognition of qualitative or categorical distinctions among group members and hence of internal divisions within the group. The group may not consciously address these distinctions. Nevertheless, these distinctions often have important influences on group processes (DiTomaso, Post, & Parks-Yancy, 2007).

Broadly defined, diversity refers to variations among people based on any attribute (e.g., sex, age, nationality, ethnicity, socioeconomic status, religion, unionization) that people can use to differentiate themselves from others (Jackson, 1992; Williams & O'Reilly, 1998). Some scholars have argued for more specific definitions of diversity. For example, in a recent review of the definitions and measures of workforce diversity, Harrison and Sin commented that diversity has often been studied in "an indeterminate manner" because "the substantive meaning or constitutive definition of diversity often is not clearly specified" (2006, p. 192). To address this issue, they proposed to define diversity as "the collective amount of difference among members within a social unit" (Harrison & Sin, 2006, p. 196). They also encouraged researchers to restrict the realm of workforce diversity to demographics, skills, abilities, cognitive styles, perpetual orientations, personality dimensions, values, attitudes, and beliefs, because these attributes are most relevant to group functioning (Harrison, Price, & Bell, 1998; Pelled, 1996). The same investigators also emphasized the importance of matching the measurement of diversity to the way that diversity is conceptualized in research (Harrison & Klein, 2007).

The analysis in this chapter is restricted to demographic diversity and knowledge and skill diversity in work teams because of their likely importance to creativity (our focal performance outcome) and potential relevance to status demarcation (a key variable in our model) in work teams and organizations (see Chapter 10, this volume).

The term *demographic diversity* refers to the degree to which a unit (e.g., a work group or organization) is heterogeneous with respect to demographic attributes such as age, gender, race, ethnicity, marital status, and so on (Pelled, Eisenhardt, & Xin, 1999). *Knowledge and skill diversity* refers to diversity in education or occupational background and work experiences in specific areas such as finance, marketing, or operations. With the professionalization of employee groups through education and training, many organizations now need to hire employees with diverse professional backgrounds (DiMaggio & Powell, 1991), knowledge, and skill base. For instance, a financial service firm may need to hire accountants, lawyers, tax specialists, stockbrokers, and venture capitalists. This development has greatly elevated the level of knowledge and skill diversity in organizations.

Facets of Creativity

In our model, creativity is a multilevel, multifaceted construct. It consists of the *process* and *product* facets of creativity measured at both individual and team levels. According to the system theory of creativity (Horn & Salvendy, 2006; Rhodes, 1961; Richards, 1999), creativity consists of four major components: *person* (a person's creative nature, such as active imagination, flexibility, or curiosity), *process* (the combination and demonstration of specific cognitive processes that are associated with producing creative thoughts or products, e.g., divergent thinking or problem recognition), *product* (the characteristics of the outcome of creative process, e.g., originality, usefulness, or understandability), and *press* (the circumstances in which a person or product exists that influence creativity, e.g., supervisory encouragement, workload pressure, freedom of choice, resource availability, or organizational impediments). Among these four components, process and product are often used as measures of creativity in creativity research (Leung & Chiu, in press). According to the multilevel approaches to creativity (Drazin, Glynn, & Kazanjian, 1999), creativity at the group level cannot be decomposed to creativity at the individual level. Thus, we include creative engagement (process) and output (product) at both individual and work team levels as the four indicators of creativity: (a) individual creativity output, (b) individual creative engagement, (c) work team creativity output, and (d) work team creative activities.

Following Mayer (1999), we define *individual creativity output* as the creation of new and useful products, including ideas as well as concrete objects. This definition is consistent with the definitions of creativity output in most creativity studies that emphasize the original and valuable attributes of creativity output. Such a general definition also provides some flexibility for future empirical work in different contexts, which may measure creativity as a global ability (an ability that can be used in a range of settings) or domain-specific abilities (abilities required in different settings).

Individual creativity engagement refers to the engagement of an individual in a creative act. In the workplace, individual employees may choose to engage in a set of cognitive, emotive, and behavioral processes to produce novel and useful ideas in the workplace (Kahn, 1990). They may engage in the processes of sensing problems, making guesses, formulating hypotheses, and communicating ideas for the purpose of creating novel products (Torrance, 1988). The choice to engage in these creative processes is personal, and the level of creative engagement varies from employee to employee (Ford, 1996; Kahn, 1990). Individual creativity engagement also refers to an employee's personal devotion to the creative processes (Kahn, 1990). In addition to individual characteristics such as curiosity, organizational culture and team climate may also influence the level of individual creativity engagement.

Work team creativity output refers to the outcome of creativity at the team level, which has a large role to play in organizational competitiveness. Thus, explicating the diversity and work team creativity connection is of particular importance to organizational policies and human resource management (Kurtzberg & Amabile, 2001). A highly valued creative output of a work team is its fluency in generating new ideas (Brown, Tumeo, Larey, & Paulus, 1998) and producing creative products. It is important to point out that work team creativity is not simply the sum of all team members' creative outputs, although the creativity level of the individual team members also contributes to work team creativity. Aside from individual creativity, for example, social processes may also influence work team creative outputs.

Finally, *work team creative activities* refer to team members' social interactions that can facilitate creative outputs such as idea sharing, brainstorming, and idea incubation (Paulus, 2000). Participation in team creative activities involves both cognitive and social involvement; in a work team that aims to produce creative products, team members interact in both intellectual and social domains.

THE DIVERSITY–CREATIVITY LINK

Creativity as a Social Cognitive Process

One oversimplified assumption about the diversity–creativity relationship is that groups with heterogeneous (rather than homogeneous) members would have better performance, particularly in complex tasks, because such tasks require creativity, cognitive complexity, and perspective switching

(Hoffman, 1959; Hoffman & Maier, 1961). Work team diversity, however, does not always lead to favorable creative outcomes because creativity in a work team is the result of many interacting cognitive and social factors. Likewise, team creative activities involve both cognitive and social activities that exert mutual influences on each other to affect creativity in a diverse work setting (Akgün, Lynn, & Byrne, 2003; Akgün, Lynn, & Yilmaz, 2006). For example, members of a demographically diverse work team bring to the workplace rich social and cultural experiences, different lifestyles, and thinking habits and expectations associated with different demographic categories, creating both opportunities and resources to enhance the cognitive process of generating novel ideas (e.g., Hoffman & Maier, 1961; McLeod & Lobel, 1992; Watson, Kumar, & Michaelsen, 1993). It should be noted that workers are likely to engage in the creative manipulations and use of the rich pool of intellectual resources that a diverse work team brings to the work setting only when the workers value and respect differences in the team. Meanwhile, conflicts within a diverse work team can attenuate the beneficial effects of workforce diversity. As Milliken and Martins (1996) pointed out, diversity in observable attributes has consistently been found to have negative effects on affective outcomes (e.g., identification with the group, job satisfaction) at both the individual and group levels of analysis.

Thus, in our conceptualization, both cognitive and social activities are implicated in team level creativity (Allard-Poesi, 1998; Gioia & Sims, 1986). This idea is consistent with the system theory of creativity, which maintains that creativity results from the interactions among the individual, the field (society or judges of creativity), and the domain (culture or environment in which creativity exists) (Csikszentmihalyi, 1988, 1999). Whereas the cognitive activities refer to the processes of acquiring, forming, storing, manipulating, discarding, and implementing information, the social activities refer to the social interactions that take place during a creative pursuit. Thus, we need to consider the creativity implications of both cognitive and social processes.

The Relationship between Diversity and Individual Creativity Output

Demographic diversity and knowledge and skill diversity foster individual creativity by bringing dissimilar ideas and perspectives to individual employees. Creative ideas are formed when employees exposed to dissimilar ideas of their colleagues attempt to integrate them into novel ideas. It has been shown that people can generate creative ideas by conceptually combining previously separate ideas, concepts, or other forms of knowledge (Rothenberg, 1979; Thagard, 1984; Wan & Chiu, 2002; Ward, 2001). Combining seemingly incompatible concepts is a crucial component in several cognitive models of creative functioning (Davidson, 1995; Mumford, Mobley, Uhlman, Reiter-Palmon, & Doares, 1991; Sternberg, 1988). Moreover, there is considerable evidence that mentally combining incompatible concepts often leads to novel ideas for useful products or marketing plans (e.g., Ward, Finke, & Smith, 1995).

To summarize, a workforce high in demographic and knowledge and skill diversities is made up of individuals with different experiences, perspectives, thinking styles, and expertise. These diversities provide individuals with rich intellectual materials and resources for generating creative ideas.

The Relationship between Diversity and Team Creativity Output

At the work team level, demographic and knowledge and skill diversities are expected to lead to favorable creative outcomes. First, it brings to the work team a rich pool of intellectual resources, composed of complementary ideas, knowledge, and skills that can be creatively integrated and synthesized to generate novel, creative solutions to current problems (e.g., Jehn, Northcraft, & Neale, 1999; Ward, 2004; Watson et al., 1993). Second, the multiple perspectives that employees with diverse knowledge and information backgrounds bring to the organization invite the organization to clarify, organize, and integrate new approaches for accomplishing its organizational goals (Thomas & Ely, 1996). Third, demographic diversity within a work group may foster a more robust critical evaluation of an idea before it is accepted. Critical evaluation of initial ideas may in turn reduce risk aversion, increase problem-solving efficiency, and improve decision-making quality in the group (Latimer, 1998). Finally, work units characterized by high levels of diversity are likely to have access to broader networks of contacts, which would enable the work units to acquire otherwise inaccessible but useful information. With this information, the work units can calibrate their decisions, increase their work commitment, and enhance their responsiveness to environmental turbulence (Donnellon, 1993; Tushman, 1997). Indeed, there is some empirical evidence that diversity in group composition contributes to work team creativity (e.g., Andrews, 1979; King & Anderson, 1995; Woodman, Sawyer, & Griffin, 1993). To summarize, the level of employees' demographic and knowledge and skill diversities will increase team creativity output, through the mediating effect of combining dissimilar ideas.

MODERATORS OF THE DIVERSITY–CREATIVITY LINK

The Moderating Role of an Individual's Adaptability to Diversity

Individuals are most creative when they are motivated by intrinsic engagement, challenge, and task satisfaction and when they are goal-oriented and possess the relevant self-regulatory competencies (Amabile, 1988; Amabile, Hill, Hennessey, & Tighe, 1994; Glynn & Webster, 1993; Kanfer, 1990). In addition, individuals with certain chronic tendencies are more likely to become creative in a nurturing environment (Oldham & Cummings, 1996). Thus, although an organization can through its organizational policy, structure, resources, climate, and technology create a nurturing environment to encourage creative performance (see Woodman et al., 1993 for a review), some individuals are more likely than others to benefit from such an environment. We refer to this individual difference as an *individual's adaptability to diversity*.

An individual's adaptability to diversity is made up of two component qualities. The first quality is the individual's multicultural experience. Based on the expectancy violation theory (Bettencourt, Dill, Greathouse, Charlton, & Mulholland, 1997; Biernat, Vescio, & Billings, 1999), people generally do not expect to be different from others with whom they have to work. Thus, finding oneself in a diverse workforce will violate this expectancy. As a result, instead of trying to learn from people who are different from the self, employees may retreat to their comfort zone and hold on to their habitual way of solving problems.

People who have more experience with working with diverse groups perform better in a diverse work team (Guimerà, Uzzi, Spiro, & Amaral, 2005; Kravitz, 2005). Similarly, people who have been exposed to diverse cultures may be more prepared to work with and learn from colleagues with diverse backgrounds. For example, employees with more multicultural experience may be able to adapt better to workforce diversity. Leung and colleagues (2008) have studied the association between multicultural experiences and creativity. In their studies, multicultural experience was measured by the amount of time a person has lived abroad and the extent of his or her interations with foreign cultures (Leung & Chiu, 2008; Maddux & Galinsky, 2009). Multicultural experience can also be activated by making a multicultural mind-set more accessible in an experiment (Leung & Chiu, in press). Using multiple methods, these investigators have found consistent positive effects of multicultural experiences on creativity engagement.

It should be noted that *culture* refers to an intellectual tradition produced and reproduced by a group of interconnected individuals (Chiu & Hong,

2005). That is, the concept of culture is not restricted to national culture; it also applies to the intellectual tradition in a certain demographic category, professional category, or organization. For example, an individual with rich multicultural experiences can be a person who has work experience in several geographical regions in a country, several unrelated or different professions, or several organizations with markedly different organizational cultures (Klafehn, Banerjee, & Chiu, 2008).

Multicultural experiences may contribute to creativity in several ways (Leung et al., 2008; Leung & Chiu, 2008; Leung & Chiu, in press). First, people learn new ideas and concepts from multicultural experiences: The more new ideas people have, the more likely they are to come up with novel combinations. Second, multicultural experiences may destabilize routine knowledge structures and increase the cognitive accessibility of relatively inaccessible knowledge. Third, multicultural experiences can increase the psychological readiness to recruit ideas from unfamiliar sources and places, and hence foster synthesis of seemingly incompatible ideas from diverse cultures.

Another component quality of an individual's adaptability to diversity is open-mindedness. Although multicultural experiences may enhance creativity, individuals need to be open-minded to benefit from their multicultural experiences (Klafehn et al., 2008; Leung & Chiu, 2008). Individuals become closed-minded when they have a strong desire for a firm answer and hence do not want to consider alternatives. Research has shown that individuals with a stronger desire for firm answers are less creative in general (Huang, Chi, & Lawler, 2005; Ip, Chen, & Chiu, 2006; King, Walker, & Broyles, 1996; Rietzschel, De Dreu, & Nijstad, 2007; Scratchley & Hakstian, 2001), benefit less from multicultural experiences (Leung & Chiu, 2008; Leung & Chiu, in press), and have poorer performance in diverse work teams (Van Der Zee, Atsma, & Brodbeck, 2004). We argue, on the basis of these research findings, that an employee's adaptability to workforce diversity is an important individual competence in the workplace. Employees with higher adaptability to workforce diversity will be more likely to assimilate demographic, knowledge, and skill diversities and transfer into individual- and team-level creative outputs.

The Status Implication of Workforce Diversity

When employee background characteristics are linked to the employees' status in a work team, group diversity may lower team creativity (Ely & Thomas, 2001; see Williams & O'Reilly, 1998, for a review) and increase interpersonal tension in the team (e.g., Jehn et al., 1999; Pelled et al., 1999).

Following Weber (1968), we define *status* as the relationship of deference or honor between and among groups. For historical and sociocultural reasons, some groups of individuals are perceived to be less competent than other groups (e.g., Eagly & Wood, 1982) and are systematically discriminated against and oppressed at work (Hays-Thomas, 2004; Linnehan & Konrad, 1999).

According to the status characteristics theory (Berger, 1977; Foschi, 1989; Wagner & Berger, 1993), a status characteristic is any characteristic around which expectations and beliefs about actions or performance come to be organized (Wagner & Berger, 1997). In a work setting of high demographic diversity and knowledge and skill diversities, there are two distinct forms of status characteristic: *diffuse status characteristics* and *specific status characteristics*. Diffuse status characteristics describe attributes that are relatively permanent, such as demographic factors (e.g., race, gender, or geographic origin). These characteristics acquire status value as people within a society come to agree that membership in one demographic group is somehow "better" than membership in another (Ridgeway, 1991; Ridgeway & Erickson, 2000). These characteristics in turn become associated with cultural beliefs that members of the more valued group are also more competent. For example, research suggests that it is perceived as more desirable to be a man than a woman (e.g., Broverman, Vogel, Broverman, Clarkson, & Rosenkrantz, 1972; Eagly & Wood, 1982), and men are widely judged to be generally more competent than women (Eagly, 1987; Wood & Karten, 1986). Another example would be when a group of young corporate professionals in Beijing enjoying dinner at an upscale restaurant overhear tourists from Gansu (an underdeveloped province in the Western region of China), notice their strong accents and less-than-fashionable clothing, and comment about the "hicks from the west coming to the big city." Such attitudes also find their way into the workplace when, for example, some employees raised and educated in the coastal cities of China disregard or undervalue the ideas or suggestions of a colleague who comes from the Western inland (Gundling & Zanchettin, 2007).

Whereas diffuse status characteristics attribute status to an individual as a function of group membership, *specific status characteristics* describe characteristics of people relevant to their abilities on specific tasks and activities. Indicators of task experience or task-relevant training and education are the most likely candidates of such specific cues. For instance, in the United Kingdom, a degree from a top-ranked university will give a person much better access to positions or professions that are well paid or have good prospect to be promoted to a higher rank. Similarly, elite graduates or employees with overseas degrees in Korean enterprises may feel entitled to more decision power in the organization than their colleagues who graduated from less prestigious local universities.

Although demographic and knowledge and skill diversities are present in most organizations and in most societies, organizations and societies differ in how strongly their employees' background characteristics are linked to different statuses. For instance, in some Scandinavian countries, the progressive laws protecting women's rights in the workplace have made gender discrimination less of a concern than in other countries such as Malaysia, where relatively blatant gender discrimination is practiced (Prasad et al., 2006).

Status characteristics may impact team creativity by depriving employees of the opportunity to seek self-verification through others. According to the self-verification theory (Swann, 1983, 1996; Swann, Kwan, Polzer, & Milton, 2003), people actively seek to externalize their self-view rather than deemphasize it; they are motivated to obtain verification of one's self-assessment through others. The need for self-verification is met when others' assessment of the self is congruent with the way the individuals assess themselves (cf. Lecky, 1945). There is evidence that individuals who receive self-verification in a relationship will find it to be intimate and feel satisfied with and committed to the relationship (Swann, Rentfrow, & Guinn, 2002).

Self-verification theorists (Swann et al., 2003) have offered several explanations for the benefits of self-verification in group functioning. First, self-verification makes team members feel more connected to the group and more motivated to immerse themselves in group activities. Second, self-verification makes team members feel that it is safe to express their ideas and behave authentically. Open expression of ideas and behaviors in turn exposes the team to a wide range of potentially useful ideas, which can be combined to generate creative ideas and new insights. Finally, trying to obtain self-verification from other group members is an effortful process that consumes cognitive resources (e.g., Swann, Hixon, Stein-Seroussi, & Gilbert, 1990). Thus, persons who have enjoyed self-verifying evaluations from other group members will be able to focus their effort on improving group outcomes. Based on these arguments, we suggest that the level of employees' self-verification will increase individual creativity engagement and team creative activity.

On the contrary, employees in a work team using status cues to form performance expectations for one another can affect the dynamics of group interaction. For instance, low expectations for members of a particular group may lead to discriminatory treatments – members of this group may be given less time to speak, are more likely to be interrupted, and may be given fewer opportunities to take on challenging tasks (Ridgeway, 2001). As a result, attaching different statuses to the employees' background characteristics may have profound adverse effects on team creative activities. When employees are categorized into groups with highly visible status distinctions, individuals in the low-status group would feel that they occupy a marginal status in the company; they may tend not to voice their ideas and to simply go along with the ideas of the high-status group. As a result, team level creativity suffers.

On the contrary, if there is no obvious status distinction within the group, employees can more freely seek verification of their self-view from others. In this circumstance, individual employees would feel safe to express their own ideas in the group. This, in turn, will increase team creative activities and, subsequently, creativity output. Therefore, the absence of a "superior status" and "privileged class" within the work team is a facilitative condition for harnessing creativity from diversity.

Strategic Staffing and Creativity

Many organizations use staffing strategies to create unequal terms of employment for different employees who have different strategic importance to the organization. Based on the human capital theory, transaction cost economics, and the resource-based view of the firm, strategic human resource management researchers have proposed the building of different employment relationship with "core" and "noncore" employees. For instance, Lepak and Snell (1999) have recommended using two dimensions – value (or strategic importance) and uniqueness of employee skills – as the primary building blocks of a human resources architecture. The grand plan of this human resources architecture is for the organization to cultivate different employment relationships with different groups of employees depending on their strategic importance and skill uniqueness in the organization. For instance, the company may develop a long-term relationship with employees who have valuable and unique human capital, invest in the employees' development, and allow employees greater participation in decision making. In contrast, employees rated as low in strategic value and uniqueness of human capital will be treated as temporary employees. They will be given transactional employment contracts with little job security, provided with only job-based compensation, and given fewer career development opportunities and limited employee benefits. Oftentimes, the distinction between employees with different terms of employment is highly visible in the organization.

Although such strategic staffing practices may generate better financial performance, they have several drawbacks when creativity is the focal outcome. Differentiated staffing practice creates unequal groups in the organization and increases employees' attention to the status distinction between the groups, adding to any preexisting diffused and specific status characteristics. The salience of status distinction increases tension and conflicts between high- and low-status members and groups and leads to self-censorship among low-status group members. Thus, we expect the use of differentiated staffing practices to have a negative impact on creativity.

Firms' Diversity Management Capability

The adverse effects of status distinction depicted in previous sections can be mitigated through effective diversity management, which involves careful identification of specific human resource management strategies, the target level of intervention (e.g., individual, group, organizational, or external stakeholder) (Kossek, Lobel, & Brown, 2006; Kossek, Markel, & McHugh, 2003), and systematic research on the joint effects of the variables that contribute to the positive outcomes of diversity (Richard, Kochan, & McMillan-Capehart, 2002). In this connection, Cox and Blake (1991) have suggested that effective organizational interventions can help heterogeneous organizations that value diversity to improve their quality of group decision making, creativity and innovation, organizational flexibility, the ability to attract and retain the best talent, and marketing capability. Likewise, Ford and Fisher (1996) have advocated training programs that aim to promote favorable attitudes toward diversity and reduce subtle forms of discrimination and unproductive exclusion. In support of these ideas, research has found a positive link between adopting diversity practices and increased productivity and market performance. For instance, Richard and Johnson (1999) found that the adoption of formal diversity practices reduces turnover.

In this chapter, we introduce the concept of *diversity management capability* as an organization-level moderator of the relationship between diversity and creativity. An organization's diversity management capability refers to the company's ability to systematically plan, educate, coordinate, and develop a diverse workforce, to coordinate their team work, to enhance trust among employees, and to promote workplace commitment. We propose that diversity management capability includes three bundles of practices: diversity assimilating, commitment building, and status neutralizing.

Diversity Assimilating Practices

Diversity assimilating practices include those that emphasize the inclusion of a diverse workforce for the purpose of fostering a positive attitude toward diversity among employees. Examples of these practices include flexible benefits that address a broad range of employees' work and family needs; expansion of recruiting efforts to specifically targeted audiences through periodicals, job fairs, and selected professional affiliation groups; and the provision of training and resources for diverse teams. Overall, research shows that these formalized human resource practices increase workforce diversity (Goodman, Fields, & Blum, 2003; Konrad & Linnehan, 1995; Leck & Saunders, 1992; Reskin & McBrier, 2000).

In addition to increasing diversity representation, diversity assimilating practices enable the company to incorporate employees' perspectives when formulating organizational goals, prioritizing the company's primary tasks, and defining and redefining its markets, products, strategies, missions, business practices, and even cultures (Thomas & Ely, 1996). A diversity mindset is emphasized in all aspects of human resource management, including recruitment, selection, and assignment of employees to work teams; the use of job analysis and job design; and generation of horizontal "fit" among all human resource areas (Wright & McMahan, 1992). For example, when making personnel decisions and job assignments, aside from attending to employees' skills and competencies, the manager also considers the employees' tasks and work context preferences in relation to their demographic and knowledge and information backgrounds. Through these diversity assimilating practices, diversity managers seek to create and maintain work teams with appropriate levels and types of diversity, which will generate and maintain the source of creativity.

Commitment Building Practices

Commitment building practices include those that work toward a common goal and achieve group cohesion. One objection to diversity is that it damages cohesiveness as heterogeneous groups have more conflicts, higher turnover, a lower level of social integration, and more problems with communication than do their homogeneous counterparts (Knight et al., 1999; O'Reilly, Caldwell, & Barnett, 1989; Williams & O'Reilly, 1998).

Identification with common goals can help alleviate conflicts and animosity within a group. Thus, to manage diversity, the firm needs to cultivate employees' commitment to approach a common purpose and a set of shared performance goals, for which all employees would hold themselves accountable, and to which all can contribute with complementary skill sets (Katzenbach & Smith, 1993).

Several key factors that would increase creativity and foster a collaborative organizational climate have been identified (Isaksen & Lauer, 2002). These factors are trust, team spirit, unified commitment, principled leadership, an elevating goal, a results-driven structure, standards of excellence, participatory decision making, external support and recognition, and an aptitude to adjust rules and behaviors to accommodate new emergent values. There is also considerable evidence from strategic human resource management research that most of these components are achievable through a "high-commitment work system" (e.g., Macduffie, 1995). A high-commitment system consists of a coherent package of practices covering most human resource management domains: socialization, training and development, job security, internal promotion, team-based reward systems, communication, and employee involvement programs. There is evidence that high-commitment human resource management practices can lead to creative outcomes. For example, in a study of 136 high-technology firms, Collins and Smith (2006) found that the use of high-commitment human resource management practices is conducive to the development of a trusting and collaborative organizational culture, which in turn has a positive impact on the distribution and integration of new products and services. It should be emphasized that the success of the high-commitment human resource system requires a synergic combination of recruitment and selection, performance management, training, and rewarding. Thus, any single practice by itself is not sufficient for creating a favorable environment for creativity (Laursen & Mahnke, 2001; Mendelson & Pillai, 1999).

Status Neutralizing Practices
This bundle of diversity management practices consists of interventions that aim to neutralize unequal statuses associated with the employees' background characteristics (DiTomaso et al., 2007). Research within social identity theory has suggested ways to change ingroup favoritism and outgroup biases on the basis of employee background characteristics. For instance, several strategies can be applied to neutralize the status difference attached to different categorizations including (a) making a superordinate identity (e.g., the organization) salient; this strategy reduces the motivation to engage in exclusionary behaviors against the subordinate outgroups (Gaertner, Mann, Dovidio, Murrell, & Pomare, 1990); (b) crossing one low-status identity (e.g., gender: woman) with another higher status identity (e.g., professional

identity: account manager); this strategy increases identity complexity and attenuates undue impact of an inferior categorical identity (e.g., Brewer & Brown, 1998); (c) strengthening the personal identity of each group member; this practice encourages employees to interact on a personal basis rather than as members of a certain group (Fiske, 2005); (d) restructuring the grouping of the employees in such a way that employees of different statuses are represented in the same groups (DiTomaso et al., 2007; Hewstone, Martin, Hammer-Hewstone, Crisp, & Voci, 2001); and (e) establishing relationship ties among employees as an alternative to status-based categorical memberships as a way to foster social commitment and mutual obligations in interdependent work teams (Brickson & Brewer, 2001).

Another practice of neutralizing status is to maintain a high level of justice in resource distribution. If resource allocation is disassociated from status value, or if privileged access to resources based on membership in selected groups is not permitted, the perception of status advantage of some groups will disappear (Jasso, 2001).

Other status neutralizing practices include increasing the permeability of boundaries between existing high- and low-status groups. Permeable boundaries allow low-status group members to move into high-status groups (Tajfel & Turner, 1986), and the prospect of joining high-status groups may motivate low-status group members to cooperate with high-status group members in team creative activities. For example, the rotation of project leadership roles in work teams permits low-status group members to move into high-status groups; such a belief in upward mobility may promote intergroup harmony. To conclude, we suggest that a company's diversity management capability, including diversity assimilating, commitment building, and status neutralizing practices, will mitigate the negative effects of status distinction on team creative activities in an organization with high levels of demographic and knowledge and skill diversities.

DISCUSSION AND CONCLUDING REMARKS

The major reasons cited by human resource executives for increasing diversity in the workplace include not only better utilization of talents and understanding of the marketplace but also enhanced creativity and problem-solving ability (Robinson & Dechant, 1997). The opportunity to synergize knowledge and promote efficiency and creative ideas does not happen automatically, however. Chapter 10 discusses the development of team mental models as a factor that moderates the relationship between diversity and performance. This chapter identifies several gaps that separate diversity and creativity. To close the gap, organizations need to build a creative environment, characterized by a common goal and the absence of a privileged employee class.

In this chapter, we discussed the status implications of diversity and proposed that individual members' self-verification process mediates the relationship between diversity and individual creativity engagement and team creative activities – the absence of a privileged employee class creates a positive prospect for self-verification in teams, thereby encouraging members to feel safe to express their true beliefs and ideas that are different from those of others. As suggested by Mannix and Neale, "If a team cannot create an environment that is tolerant of divergent perspectives and that reflects cooperative goal interdependence, then the individuals who carry the burden of unique perspectives may be unwilling to pay the social and psychological costs necessary to share their viewpoints" (2005; p. 46).

Two other factors can also strengthen the link between diversity and creativity. These factors are individual members' adaptability to diversity and an organization's diversity management capabilities. We believe that these two moderators can enhance a diverse work team's creative performance. In addition, both factors are malleable; they can be managed in an organization through appropriate human resource management strategies.

Many companies believe that, given the diversity of the employees, there may not be one best set of practices for motivating all of the employees within that company. Therefore, it is strategically savvy to make clear adaptations to the employment contracts for different employees according to their unique values, skills, and contributions to the company's performance (Lepak & Snell, 1999). When it comes to creativity as a performance measure, however, we argue that this strategy of creating unequal employment conditions for different employees signals clear status distinction among employees within the same work team or company. Such staffing strategy may compromise the prospect of employees' self-verification and hence result inadvertently in the suppression of voices from the low-status group. In short, increasing staffing differentiation may accentuate the negative effects of employee diversity in teamwork. If a company cannot avoid creating some degree of staffing differentiation in a work team, it would be prudent for the company to also invest in strengthening its diversity management capability to neutralize the negative impact of such staffing strategy to creativity.

In conclusion, to deepen our understanding of the relationship between workforce diversity and creativity, researchers and practitioners should work together to explore the complex relationships between different kinds of employee diversity and creativity at the individual, team, and organizational levels. We have proposed a conceptual framework to guide this exploration and hope to see more empirical studies that address these relationships, particularly those that would consider factors at different levels or with cross-level interactions between workplace diversity and creative performance. Because most diversity and creativity studies were carried out in laboratory settings or used top management teams, we are particularly eager to see more field studies that examine the relationship between diversity and creativity among rank-and-file employees.

REFERENCES

Akgün, A. E., Lynn, G. S., & Byrne, J. (2003). Organizational learning: A socio-cognitive framework. *Human Relations, 56*, 839–868.

Akgün, A. E., Lynn, G. S., & Yilmaz, C. (2006). Learning process in new product development teams and effects on product success: A socio-cognitive perspective. *Industrial Marketing Management, 35*, 210–224.

Allard-Poesi, F. (1998). Representations and influence processes in groups: Toward a socio-cognitive perspective on cognition in organization. *Scandinavian Journal of Management, 14*, 395–420.

Amabile, T. M. (1988). A model of creativity and innovation in organizations. In B. Staw & L. L. Cummings (Eds.), *Research in organizational behavior, Vol. 10* (pp. 123–167). Greenwich, CT: JAI Press.

Amabile, T. M., Hill, K. G., Hennessey, B. A., & Tighe, E. M. (1994). The work preference inventory: Assessing intrinsic and extrinsic motivational orientations. *Journal of Personality and Social Psychology, 66*, 950–967.

Andrews, F. W. (1979). *Scientific productivity.* Cambridge, UK: Cambridge University Press.

Appadurai, A. (1990). Disjuncture and difference in the global economy. *Public Culture, 2*, 15–24.

Berger, J. (1977). *Status characteristics and social interaction: An expectation-status approach.* New York: Elsevier.

Berger, J., Cohen, B. P., & Zelditch, M. (1972). Status characteristics and social interaction. *American Sociological Review, 37*, 241–255.

Bettencourt, B. A., Dill, K. E., Greathouse, S. A., Charlton, K., & Mulholland, A. (1997). Evaluations of ingroup and outgroup members: The role of category-based expectancy violation. *Journal of Experimental Social Psychology, 33*, 244–275.

Biernat, M., Vescio, T. K., & Billings, L. S. (1999). Black sheep and expectancy violation: Integrating two models of social judgment. *European Journal of Social Psychology, 29*, 523–542.

Brewer, M. B., & Brown, R. J. (1998). Intergroup relations. In D. T. Gilbert, S. T. Fiske, & G. Lindzey (Eds.), *Handbook of social psychology* (pp. 554–594). New York: McGraw-Hill.

Brickson, S. L., & Brewer, M. B. (2001). Identity orientation and intergroup relations in organizations. In M. A. Hogg & D. J. Terry (Eds.), *Social identity processes in organizational contexts* (pp. 49–66). Philadelphia: Psychology Press.

Broverman, I. K., Vogel, S. R., Broverman, D. M., Clarkson F. E., & Rosenkrantz, P. S. (1972). Sex-role stereotypes: A current appraisal. *Journal of Social Issues, 28,* 59–78.

Brown, V., Tumeo, M., Larey, T. S., & Paulus, P. B. (1998). Modeling cognitive interactions during group brainstorming. *Small Group Research, 29,* 495–526.

Chiu, C-y., & Hong, Y. (2005). Cultural competence: Dynamic processes. In A. Elliot & C. S. Dweck (Eds.), *Handbook of motivation and competence* (pp. 489–505). New York: Guilford.

Collins, C. J., & Smith, K. G. (2006). Knowledge exchange and combination: The role of human resource practices in the performance of high technology firms. *Academy of Management Journal, 49,* 544–560.

Cox, T. H., & Blake, S. (1991). Managing cultural diversity: Implications for organizational competitiveness. *Academy of Management Executive, 5,* 45–56.

Csikszentmihalyi, M. (1988). Society, culture, and person: A systems view of creativity. In R. J. Sternberg (Ed.), *The nature of creativity* (pp. 325–339). New York: Cambridge University Press.

Csikszentmihalyi, M. (1999). Implications of a systems perspective for the study of creativity. In R. J. Sternberg (Ed.), *Handbook of creativity* (pp. 35–61). Cambridge, UK: Cambridge University Press.

Davidson, J. E. (1995). The suddenness of insight. In R. J. Sternberg & J. E. Davidson (Eds.), *The nature of insight* (pp. 125–155). Cambridge, MA: MIT Press.

DiMaggio, P., & Powell, W. (Eds.) (1991). *The new institutionalism in organizational analysis.* Chicago: University of Chicago Press.

DiTomaso, N., Post, C., & Parks-Yancy, R. (2007). Workforce diversity and inequality: Power, status, and numbers. *Annual Review of Sociology, 33,* 473–501.

Donnellon, A. (1993). Cross-functional teams in product development: Accommodating the structure to the process. *Journal of Product Innovation Management, 10,* 377–392.

Drazin, R., Glynn, M. A., & Kazanjian, R. K. (1999). Multilevel theorizing about creativity in organizations: A sensemaking perspective. *Academy of Management Review, 24,* 286–308.

Eagly, A. H. (1987). *Sex differences in social behavior: A social role interpretation.* Hillsdale, NJ: Lawrence Erlbaum Associates.

Eagly, A. H., & Wood, W. (1982). Inferred sex differences in status as a determinant of gender stereotypes about social influence. *Journal of Personality and Social Psychology, 43,* 915–928.

Ely, R. J., & Thomas, D. A. (2001). Cultural diversity at work: The effects of diversity perspectives on work group processes and outcomes. *Administrative Science Quarterly, 46,* 229–273.

Finke, R. A., Ward, T. B., & Smith, S. M. (1992). *Creative Cognition: Theory, Research, and Applications.* Bardford, MA: The MIT Press.

Fiske, S. T. (2005). Social cognition and the normality of prejudice. In J. Dovidio, P. Glick, & L. Rudman (Eds.), *On the nature of prejudice: Fifty years after Allport.* New York: Academic Press.

Ford, C. M. (1996). A theory of individual creativity in multiple social domains. *Academy of Management Review, 21*, 1112–1134.

Ford, J., & Fisher, S. (1996). The role of training in a changing workplace and workforce: New perspectives and approaches. In E. Kossek & S. Lobel (Eds.), *Managing diversity: Human resource strategies for transforming the workplace* (pp. 164–193). Oxford: Blackwell.

Foschi, M. (1989). Status characteristics, standards, and attributions. In J. Berger, M. Zelditch, Jr., & B. Anderson (Eds.), *Sociological theories in progress: New formulations* (pp. 58–72). Newbury Park, CA: Sage.

Gaertner, S. L., Mann, J. A., Dovidio, J. F., Murrell, A. J., & Pomare, M. (1990). How does cooperation reduce intergroup bias? *Journal of Personality and Social Psychology, 59*, 692–704.

Gioia, D. A., & Sims, H. P. (1986). *The thinking organization: Dynamics of organizational social cognition.* San Francisco: Jossey-Bass.

Glynn, M. A., & Webster, J. (1993). Refining the nomological net of the Adult Playfulness Scale: Personality, motivational and attitudinal correlates for highly intelligent adults. *Psychological Reports, 72*, 1023–1026.

Goodman, J., Fields, D., & Blum, T. (2003). Cracks in the glass ceiling: In what kind of organizations do women make it to the top? *Group & Organization Management, 28*, 475–501.

Guimerà, R., Uzzi, B., Spiro, J., & Amaral, L. A. N. (2005). Team assembly mechanisms determine collaboration network structure and team performance. *Science, 308*, 697–702.

Gundling, E., & Zanchettin, A. (2007). *Global diversity: Winning customers and engaging employees within world markets.* Boston: Nicholas Brealey Publishing.

Harrison, D. A., & Klein, K. J. (2007). What's the difference? Diversity constructs as separation, variety, or disparity in organizations. *Academy of Management Review, 32*, 1199–1228.

Harrison, D. A., Price, K. H., & Bell, M. P. (1998). Beyond relationship demography: Time and the effects of surface- and deep-level diversity on work group cohesion. *Academy of Management Journal, 41*, 96–107.

Harrison, D. A., & Sin, H. S. (2006). What is diversity and how should it be measured? In A. M. Konrad, P. Prasad, & J. K. Pringle (Eds.), *Handbook of workplace diversity* (pp. 191–216). Newbury Park, CA: Sage.

Hays-Thomas, R. (2004). Why now? The contemporary focus on managing diversity. In M. S. Stockdale & F. J. Crosby (Eds.), *The psychology and management of workplace diversity.* Malden, MA: Blackwell Publishers.

Hewstone, M., Martin, R., Hammer-Hewstone, C., Crisp, R. J., & Voci, A. (2001). Minority-majority relations in organizations: Challenges and opportunities. In M. A. Hogg & D. J. Terry (Eds.), *Social identity processes in organizational contexts* (pp. 67–86). Philadelphia, PA: Psychology Press.

Hoffman, L. R. (1959). Homogeneity of member personality and its effect on group problem-solving. *Journal of Abnormal and Social Psychology, 58*, 27–32.

Hoffman, L. R., & Maier, N. R. F. (1961). Quality and the acceptance of problem solving solutions by members of heterogeneous and homogeneous groups. *Journal of Abnormal and Social Psychology, 62*, 401–407.

Horn, D., & Salvendy, G. (2006). Consumer-based assessment of product creativity: A review and reappraisal. *Human Factors and Ergonomics in Manufacturing, 16,* 155–175.

Huang, T-j., Chi, S-c., & Lawler, J. (2005). The relationship between expatriates' personality traits and their adjustment to international assignments. *Journal of Human Resource Management, 16,* 1656–1670.

Ip, G. W-m., Chen, J., & Chiu, C-y. (2006). The relationship of promotion focus, need for cognitive closure, and categorical accessibility in American and Hong Kong Chinese university students. *Journal of Creative Behavior, 40,* 201–215.

Isaksen, S. G., & Lauer, K. J. (2002). The climate for creativity and change in teams. *Creativity and Innovation Management, 11,* 74–86.

Jackson, S. (1992). Team composition in organizations. In S. Worchel, W. Wood, & J. Simpson (Eds.), *Group process and productivity* (pp. 138–173). Newbury Park, CA: Sage.

Jackson, S., Joshi, A., & Erhardt, N. (2003). Recent research on team and organizational diversity: WWOT analysis and implications. *Journal of Management, 29,* 801–830.

Jasso, G. (2001). Studying status: An integrated framework. *American Sociological Review, 66,* 96–124.

Jayne, M. E. A., & Dipboye, R. L. (2004). Leveraging diversity to improve business performance: Research findings and recommendations for organizations. *Human Resource Management, 43,* 409–424.

Jehn, K. A., Northcraft, G. B., & Neale, M. A. (1999). Why some differences make a difference: A field study of diversity, conflict, and performance in workgroups. *Administrative Science Quarterly, 44,* 741–763.

Kahn, W. A. (1990). Psychological conditions of personal engagement and disengagement at work. *Academy of Management Journal, 33,* 692–724.

Kanfer, R. (1990). Motivation theory and industrial/organization psychology. In M. D. Dunnette (Ed.), *Handbook of industrial and organizational psychology, Vol. 1* (pp. 75–170). Palo Alto, CA: Consulting Psychologists Press.

Katzenbach, J. R., & Smith, D. K. (1993). The discipline of teams. *Harvard Business Review, 71,* 111–120.

King, L. A., Walker, L. M., & Broyles, S. J. (1996). Creativity and the five-factor model. *Journal of Research in Personality, 30,* 189–203.

King, N., & Anderson, N. (1995). *Innovation and change in organizations.* London: Routledge.

Klafehn, J., Banerjee, P., & Chiu, C-y. (2008). Navigating cultures: A model of metacognitive intercultural intelligence. In S. Ang & L. Van Dyne (Eds.), *Handbook of cultural intelligence.* Armonk, NY: M. E. Sharpe.

Knight, D., Pearce, C. L., Smith, K. G., Olian, J. D., Sims, H. P., Smith, K. A., et al. (1999). Top management team diversity, group process, and strategic consensus. *Strategic Management Journal, 20,* 445–465.

Konrad, A., & Linnehan, F. (1995). Formalized human resource management structures: Coordinating equal opportunity or concealing organizational practices. *Academy of Management Journal, 38,* 787–820.

Kossek, E., Markel, K., & McHugh, P. (2003). Increasing diversity as an HRM change strategy. *Journal of Organizational Change Management, 16,* 328–352.

Kossek, E. E., Lobel, S. A., & Brown, J. (2006). Human resource strategies to manage workforce diversity: Examining "the business case." In A. M. Konrad, P. Prasad, & J. K. Pringle (Eds.), *Handbook of workplace diversity* (pp. 53–74). Newbury Park, CA: Sage.

Kravitz, D. A. (2005). Diversity in teams: A two-edged sword requires careful handling. *Psychological Science in the Public Interest, 6,* i–ii.

Kurtzberg, R. R., & Amabile, T. M. (2001). From Guilford to creative synergy: Opening the black box of team level creativity. *Creativity Research Journal, 13,* 285–294.

Latimer, R. L. (1998). The case for diversity in global business, and the impact of diversity on team performance. *Competitiveness Review, 8,* 3–17.

Laursen, K., & Mahnke, V. (2001). Knowledge strategies, innovative capacity and complementarity in human resource practices. *Journal of Management and Governance, 1,* 1–27.

Leck, J., & Saunders, D. (1992). Hiring women: The effect of Canada's employment equity act. *Canadian Public Policy, 18,* 203–221.

Lecky, P. (1945). *Self-consistency: A theory of personality.* New York: Island Press.

Lepak, D. P., & Snell, S. A. (1999). The human resource architecture: Toward a theory of human capital allocation and development. *Academy of Management Review, 24,* 31–48.

Leung, A. K-y., & Chiu, C-y. (2008). Interactive effects of multicultural experiences and openness to experience on creativity. *Creativity Research Journal, 20,* 376–382.

Leung, A. K-y. & Chiu, C-y. (in press). Multicultural experience, idea receptiveness, and creativity. *Journal of Cross-Cultural Psychology.*

Leung, A. K-y., Maddux, W. W., Galinsky, A. D., & Chiu, C-y. (2008). Multicultural experience enhances creativity: The when and how. *American Psychologist, 63,* 169–181.

Linnehan, F., & Konrad, A. M. (1999). Diluting diversity: Implications for intergroup inequality in organizations. *Journal of Management Inquiry, 8,* 399–414.

MacDuffie, J. P. (1995). Human resource bundles and manufacturing performance: Organizational logic and flexible production systems in the world auto industry. *Industrial and Labor Relations Review, 48,* 197–221.

Maddux, W.W., & Galinsky, A. D. (2009). Cultural borders and mental barriers: The relationship between living abroad and creativity. *Journal of Personality and Social Psychology, 96,* 1047–1061.

Mannix, E., & Neale, M. A. (2005). What differences make a difference? The promise and reality of diverse teams in organizations. *Psychological Science in the Public Interest, 6,* 31–55.

Mayer, R. E. (1999). Fifty years of creativity research. In R. J. Sternberg (Ed.), *Handbook of creativity* (pp. 449–460). Cambridge, UK: Cambridge University Press.

McLeod, P. L., & Lobel, S. A. (1992). The effects of ethnic diversity on idea generation in small groups. *Academy of Management Proceedings,* 227–231.

Mendelson, H., & Pillai, R. R. (1999). Information age organizations, dynamics, and performance. *Journal of Economic Behavior and Organization, 38*, 253–281.

Milliken, F., & Martins, L. (1996). Searching for common threads: Understanding the multiple effects of diversity in organizational groups. *Academy of Management Review, 21*, 102–433.

Mumford, M. D., Mobley, M. I., Uhlman, C. E., Reiter-Palmon, R., & Doares, L. M. (1991). Process analytic models of creative capacities. *Creativity Research Journal, 4*, 91–122.

Oldham, G. R., & Cummings, A. (1996). Employee creativity: Personal and contextual factors at work. *Academy of Management Journal, 39*, 607–643.

O'Reilly, C. A., Caldwell, D. F., & Barnett, P. (1989). Work group demography, social integration, and turnover. *Administrative Science Quarterly, 34*, 21–37.

Paulus, P. B. (2000). Groups, teams, and creativity: The creative potential of idea-generating groups. *Applied Psychology: An International Review, 49*, 237–262.

Pelled, L. H. (1996). Demographic diversity, conflict, and work group outcomes: An intervening process theory. *Organization Science, 6*, 207–229.

Pelled, L. H., Eisenhardt, K. M., & Xin, K. R. (1999). Exploring the black box: An analysis of work group diversity, conflict, and performance. *Administrative Science Quarterly, 44*, 1–28.

Prasad, P., Mils, J. A., Elmes, M., & Prasad, A. 1997. *Managing the organizational melting pot: Dilemmas of workplace diversity.* Thousand Oaks, CA: Sage.

Prasad, P., Pringle, J. K., & Konrad, A. M. (2006). Examining the contours of workplace diversity: Concepts, contexts and challenges. In A. M. Konrad, P. Prasad, & J. K. Pringle (Eds.), *Handbook of workplace diversity* (pp. 1–22). Newbury Park, CA: Sage.

Reskin, B., & McBrier, D. (2000). Why not ascription? Organizations' employment of male and female managers. *American Sociological Review, 65*, 210–233.

Rhodes, M. (1961). An analysis of creativity. *Phi Delta Kappan, 42*, 305–310.

Richard, O., & Johnson, N. 1999. Making the connection between formal human resource diversity practices and organizational effectiveness: Behind management fashion. *Performance Improvement Quarterly, 12*, 77–96.

Richard, O., Kochan, T., & McMillan-Capehart, A. (2002). The impact of visible diversity on organizational effectiveness: Disclosing the contents in Pandora's black box. *Journal of Business and Management, 8*, 1–26.

Richards, R. (1999). Four Ps of creativity. In M. Runco & S. R. Pritzker (Eds.), *Encyclopedia of creativity* (pp. 733–742). Boston: Academic Press.

Ridgeway, C. (1991). The social construction of status value: Gender and other nominal characteristics. *Social Forces, 70*, 367–386.

Ridgeway, C. L. (2001). Gender, status, and leadership. *Journal of Social Issues, 57*, 637–655.

Ridgeway, C. L., & Erickson, K. G. (2000). Creating and spreading status beliefs. *American Journal of Sociology, 106*, 579–615.

Rietzschel, E. F., De Dreu, C. K. W., & Nijstad, B. A. (2007). Personal need for structure and creative performance: The moderating influence of fear of invalidity. *Personality and Social Psychology Bulletin, 33*, 855–866.

Robinson, G., & Dechant, K. (1997). Building a business case for diversity. *Academy of Management Executive, 11*, 21–31.

Rothenberg, A. (1979). *The emerging goddess.* Chicago: University of Chicago Press.

Scratchley, L. S., & Hakstian. A. R. (2001). The measurement and prediction of managerial creativity. *Creativity Research Journal, 13*, 367–384.

Sternberg, R. J. (1988). A three-facet model of creativity. In R. J. Sternberg (Ed.), *The nature of creativity: Contemporary psychological perspectives* (pp. 125–147). Cambridge, UK: Cambridge University Press.

Swann, W., Kwan, V., Polzer, J., & Milton, L. (2003). Fostering group identification and creativity in diverse groups: The role of individuation and self-verification. *Personality and Social Psychology Bulletin, 29*, 1396–1406.

Swann, W. B., Jr. (1983). Self-verification: Bringing social reality into harmony with the self. In J. Suls & A. G. Greenwald (Eds.), *Social psychology perspectives on the self, Vol. 2* (pp. 33–66). Hillsdale, NJ: Lawrence Erlbaum Associates.

Swann, W. B., Jr. (1996). *Self-traps: The elusive quest for higher self-esteem.* New York: Freeman.

Swann, W. B., Jr., Hixon, J. G., Stein-Seroussi, A., & Gilbert, D. (1990). The fleeting gleam of praise: Behavioral reactions to self-relevant feedback. *Journal of Personality and Social Psychology, 59*, 17–26.

Swann, W. B., Jr., Rentfrow, P. J., & Guinn, J. S. (2002). Self-verification: The search for coherence. In C. R. Snyder & S. J. Lopez (Eds.), *Handbook of positive psychology* (pp. 366–381). New York: Oxford University Press.

Tajfel, H., & Turner, J. C. (1986). The social identity theory of inter-group behavior. In S. Worchel & L. W. Austin (Eds.), *Psychology of intergroup relations.* Chicago: Nelson-Hall.

Thagard, P. (1984). Conceptual combination and scientific discovery. In P. Asquity & P. Kitcher (Eds.), *Proceedings of the Biennial Meeting of the Philosophy of Science Association, Vol. 1* (pp. 3–12). East Lansing, MI: Philosophy of Science Association.

Thomas, D. A., & Ely, R. J. (1996). Making differences matter: A new paradigm for managing diversity. *Harvard Business Review, 74*, 79–90.

Tilly, C. (1998). *Durable inequality.* Berkeley: University of California Press.

Torrance, E. P. (1988). The nature of creativity as manifest in its testing. In R. J. Sternberg (Ed.), *The nature of creativity: Contemporary psychological views* (pp. 43–75). Cambridge, UK: Cambridge University Press.

Tushman, M. L. (1997). Special boundary roles in the innovation process. *Administrative Science Quarterly, 22*, 587–605.

Van Der Zee, K., Atsma, N., & Brodbeck, F. (2004). The influence of social identity and personality on outcomes of cultural diversity in teams. *Journal of Cross-Cultural Psychology, 35*, 283–303.

Wagner, D. G., & Berger, J. (1993). Status characteristics theory: The growth of a program. In J. Berger & M. Zelditch, Jr. (Eds.), *Theoretical research programs: Studies in the growth of theory* (pp. 23–63). Stanford: Stanford University Press.

Wagner, D. G., & Berger, J. (1997). Gender and interpersonal task behavior: Status expectation accounts. *Sociological Perspectives, 40*, 1–32.

Wan, W., & Chiu, C-y. (2002). Effects of novel conceptual combination on creativity. *Journal of Creative Behavior, 36*, 227–241.

Ward, T. B. (2001). Creative cognition, conceptual combination and the creative writing of Stephen R. Donaldson. *American Psychologist, 56*, 350–354.

Ward, T. B. (2004). Cognition, creativity, and entrepreneurship. *Journal of Business Venturing, 19*, 173–188.

Ward, T. B., Finke, R. A., & Smith S. M. (1995). *Creativity and the mind: Discovering the genius within.* New York: Plenum.

Ward, T. B., Patterson, M. J., Sifonis, C. M., Dodds, R. A., & Saunders, K. N. (2002). The role of graded category structure in imaginative thought. *Memory and Cognition, 30*, 199–216.

Watson, W. E., Kumar, K., & Michaelsen, L. K. (1993). Cultural diversity's impact on interaction process and performance: Comparing homogeneous and diverse task groups. *Academy of Management Journal, 36*, 590–602.

Weber, M. (1968). *Economy and society.* New York: Bedminster Press.

Wentling, R. M., & Palma-Rivas, N. (2000). Current status of diversity initiatives in selected multinational corporations. *Human Resource Development Quarterly, 11*, 35–60.

West, M. A., & Anderson, N. R. (1996). Innovation in top management teams. *Journal of Applied Psychology, 81*, 680–693.

Williams, K. Y., & O'Reilly, C. A. (1998). Demography and diversity in organizations: A review of 40 years of research. In B. Staw & R. Sutton (Eds.), *Research in organizational behavior, Vol. 20* (pp. 77–140). Greenwich, CT: JAI Press.

Wood, W., & Karten, S. J. (1986). Gender differences in interaction style as a product of perceived gender differences in competence. *Journal of Personality and Social Psychology, 50*, 341–347.

Woodman, R. W., Sawyer, J. E., & Griffin, R. W. (1993). Toward a theory of organizational creativity. *Academy of Management Review, 18*, 293–321.

Wright, P. M., & McMahan, G. C. (1992). Theoretical perspectives for strategic human resource management. *Journal of Management, 18*, 295–320.

Yakura, E. (1996). EEO law and managing diversity. In E. Kossek & S. Lobel (Eds.), *Managing diversity: Human resource strategies for transforming the workplace.* Cambridge, MA: Blackwell.

INDEX